D1519184

THE SECRETS OF A VATICAN CARDINAL

The Secrets of a
Vatican Cardinal

Celso Costantini's Wartime Diaries, 1938–1947

Edited by

BRUNO FABIO PIGHIN

Translated by Laurence B. Mussio

McGill-Queen's University Press
Montreal & Kingston • London • Ithaca

English edition
© McGill-Queen's University Press 2014

A translation of the Italian edition published as "Diario inedito del Cardinale
Celso Costantini. *Ai margini della Guerra (1938–1947)*"
© Marcianum Press S.r.l., Venezia – Italia 2010

ISBN 978-0-7735-4299-0 (CLOTH)
ISBN 978-0-7735-9005-2 (ePDF)
ISBN 978-0-7735-9006-9 (ePUB)

Legal deposit first quarter 2014
Bibliothèque nationale du Québec

Printed in Canada on acid-free paper that is 100% ancient forest free
(100% post-consumer recycled), processed chlorine free

The translation of this book has been funded by SEPS – Segretariato Europeo
per le pubblicazioni scientifiche (Via Val d'Aposa 7 – 40123 Bologna, Italy,
www.seps.it, seps@seps.it). This book has been published with the support
of donations received from the Rev. Vitaliano Papais and Ms. Chow Kit Man.

McGill-Queen's University Press acknowledges the support of the Canada
Council for the Arts for our publishing program. We also acknowledge
the financial support of the Government of Canada through the Canada Book
Fund for our publishing activities.

Library and Archives Canada Cataloguing in Publication

Costantini, Celso, 1876–1958
    [Ai margini della guerra. English]
    The secrets of a Vatican Cardinal: Celso Costantini's wartime diaries,
1938–1947/edited by Bruno Fabio Pighin; translated by Laurence B. Mussio.

    Translation of: Diario inedito del cardinale Celso Costantini: ai margini
della guerra (1938–1947).
    Includes bibliographical references and index.
    Issued in print and electronic formats.
    ISBN 978-0-7735-4299-0 (bound). – ISBN 978-0-7735-9005-2 (ePDF). –
ISBN 978-0-7735-9006-9 (ePUB)

    1. Costantini, Celso, 1876–1958 – Diaries. 2. Catholic Church – Italy –
History – 20th century – Sources. 3. World War, 1939–1945 – Personal
narratives, Italian. 4. Italy – History – 1922–1945 – Sources. 5. World War,
1939–1945 – Religious aspects – Catholic Church – Sources. 6. Cardinals –
Italy – Diaries. I. Mussio, Laurence B., translator II. Pighin, Bruno Fabio, editor
III. Title. III. Title: Ai margini della guerra. English.

BX4705.C7788A4 2013   282.092   C2013-907139-3

This book was typeset by Interscript in 10.5/13.5 Sabon.

Contents

Preface

I began this translation of the Costantini diary in 2010, the same year it was published in Italian by Marcianum Press of Venice under the title *Diario Inedito del Cardinale Celso Costantini. Ai Margini della Guerra (1938–1947)*. This work attracted national attention in Italy from leaders of both church and state. The book was launched in Rome on 28 May 2010 at a gathering in the Chamber of Deputies that mixed political and religious *prominenti*. The next day the editor of the book and the man who rescued the diary from archival obscurity, Professor Bruno Fabio Pighin, was invited to the Quirinale Palace to discuss the volume with Giorgio Napolitano, the octogenarian President of the Italian Republic.

Napolitano's interest was more than intellectual. As a partisan during the Second World War and an active supporter of the Italian Communist Party thereafter, he had experienced many of the issues and questions that Costantini's extraordinary diary confronts: war and the collapse of Fascism, the fall of the monarchy, and the establishment of the modern Italian republic. In recognition of Pighin's scholarly achievement, Napolitano presented him with the Presidential Medal.

The next day (30 May), in his Sunday Angelus remarks, Pope Benedict XVI described the diary as having "great historical interest." The Pope remarked that Costantini had been "very close to Pope Pius XII," writing his diary when he was Secretary of the Congregation of the *Propaganda Fide*. The Pope told the crowd gathered at St Peter's that the diary "bears witness to the immense work carried out by the Holy See in those dramatic years to promote peace and to help all those in need."[1]

---

[1] The text of Pope Benedict XVI's remarks in the original Italian can be found at the Vatican's website at www.vatican.va.

That two men of such different backgrounds – one secular, republican, *partigiano*, and a lifelong Communist; the other, a Catholic cleric, theologian, and successor of St Peter – should have found such merit in the same work highlights its authenticity and historical importance. It was indeed the favourable reception of the diary at both the Quirinale and the Vatican that inspired me to translate the diary into English. It was obvious to me that Cardinal Costantini's *Diario* deserved the broadest possible readership, and it was with this in mind that I undertook the present work. My purpose is to make a riveting document accessible to a wider readership of European and Church historians and scholars. I was in Italy at the time of the publication of the diary, and I started the project while there. In the manner of displaced peoples of war, *Secrets of a Vatican Cardinal* was thus conceived in Rome, born in Venice, adopted in Montreal, and grew to maturity in Toronto.

Diaries, memoirs, and first-hand accounts can be of varying interest and salience to historians. There are many factors that determine the authority of such evidence. Scholars must take into account the occupation of the diarist, his character and connections, his intended purpose and prospective audience, and a variety of other factors. In my own work as a historian, I have used diaries extensively and done many oral history interviews. Experience has shown me that having access to an authentic, authoritative, well-informed, and balanced first-hand account of events can make an enormous difference in the writing of history. In Canada, for example, the diaries of Prime Minister William Lyon Mackenzie King are an indispensable resource for the study of the country's political history from the late nineteenth century to the mid-twentieth century. In the United States the diaries of President Harry Truman have likewise shaped understanding of the past, as have diaries kept in the United Kingdom by close wartime advisers of Prime Minister Winston Churchill. Bystanders to great events (this is how Costantini defined himself) can also leave revealing accounts, the value of such diaries lying in an author's knowledge, experience, proximity to decision makers, and understanding of character and motivation. For the historian, the key questions about any diary are simple: What does it tell us that is new? How does it add to historical understanding?

The readers of Cardinal Costantini's diary can answer these questions for themselves. My own view is that his record of events meets the most exacting standards of historical relevance. First of all, his is the *only* available diary from the period in question by a senior Vatican figure.

Moreover, Costantini had a considerable talent for writing elegant but incisive prose. His proximity to the centre of power in both the Vatican and the Italian state gave him a unique perspective on events for which scholars of his time have reason to be grateful. Costantini's candid views about the state of Italian politics and the future of the Catholic Church are especially rich and reveal much about hopes and fears in the Rome of the 1940s. Given his frankness, it is little wonder that Costantini worried that his diary might fall into the hands of the Italian Fascists or the German occupiers of Rome after 1943. His day-to-day record of events adds new evidence to the continuing debate about the wartime role of Pope Pius XII, with whom he was closely associated. But his diary reaches far beyond the leadership of the Church and considerations of high politics and military strategy. In the attention he gives to the trials and tragedies of ordinary people, the hard fate of the Jews of Rome, and the daily privations of life under occupation, Costantini has left a record that is at once moving and instructive.

What makes this diary so extraordinary? One answer is to be found in Costantini's vantage point. For the duration of the war and during its aftermath, he lived at the Palazzo di Propaganda Fide (Palace of the Propagation of the Faith) on the south side of Rome's Piazza di Spagna. In other words, he was at the centre of the action as it unfolded. Second, Costantini's network of relationships embraced an astonishing spectrum of people and roles: within the Church; in Italy's political, social, arts, and economic elites; and among common, everyday folk. In other words, the diary metaphorically captures within its cast of characters the motto of Rome itself: SPQR – *senatus populusque romanus* – the Senate and the people of Rome. Of course, by virtue of his position at the *Propaganda Fide*, his network extended beyond Rome to the wider world.

But Costantini's networks in Italian civil society and within the Catholic Church are only part of the story. Thanks to his insight and his deep knowledge of people, circumstances, and context, his diary is a considered, elegant, balanced, and fair-minded account. He is at varying times witness, commentator, observer of, and occasional participant in the political and human dramas that unfolded around him. His position and connections and his intuitive, remarkable understanding of a rapidly evolving national and international context provide us with an extraordinary first-hand account of how the Second World War unfolded. In sum, the Costantini diary provides a valuable perspective on everything from the prosecution of the war to the serial political, military, and strategic blunders of Mussolini, the decline and fall of the House of Savoy, and the actions of Pius XII in the face of Nazi tyranny. His account of Italy's post-war political arrangements, leading to the referendum of 2 June 1946 and the choice of the republican option, is equally insightful. The latter section of the diary is all the more compelling because Costantini sheltered Italy's first post-war republican head of state, Alcide De Gasperi, during the darkest days of the Nazi occupation of Rome in 1944. Their conversations about the present and future of Italy must have been both frequent and fascinating.

My translation of the diary was facilitated by Costantini's direct, clear, and accessible prose. The conversion from the Italian was, therefore, relatively straightforward. Throughout, I have sought to be faithful to Costantini's meaning and nuance. He was a masterful writer and an incisive analyst, and I have attempted to the best of my ability to convey this in another language. Of course, any translation of this sort is an exercise in cross-cultural interpretation. For a historical diary, moreover, the temporal dimension must also be taken into account. Six and a half decades separate us from the last entries in the diary, and, by definition, I have had to establish context for the reader; more than a few passing references required research and confirmation. Fortunately for me, Bruno Pighin was always available to answer my questions. I could not have asked for a more helpful collaborator.

I am also most grateful for the interest that many other colleagues and friends have shown in my translation project. Publication has been made possible through the generosity of the Rev. Father Vitaliano Papais and Ms Chow Kit Man. My work has also been supported by benefactors who wish to remain anonymous but whose interest in promoting European, Italian, and Church scholarship is gratifying. Through their encouragement and commitment, the donors to this book have sought to ensure that an important historical document would be readily available to English-language readers.

I am also thankful for the support I received from McGill-Queen's University Press. In particular, I thank Philip Cercone, executive director, for his many actions to ensure that a complex international collaboration would have a successful outcome. His advice and friendship have been invaluable over the years on the many projects that have brought us together. I also thank Professor John Zucchi of McGill University for his inspiring advocacy about the importance of this translation. *Grazie molte*, John. In the same spirit, I thank the Marcianum Press of Venice for its cooperation and help, and my McGill-Queen's editor Carlotta Lemieux for her contribution in bringing my manuscript to the high standard set by McGill-Queen's. Thank you also to all at MQUP who helped all the way to publication. I would also like to acknowledge Professor Peter Neary, a friend of over thirty years, for his excellent editorial advice and encouragement. Above all, I thank my wife Flavia who took a special interest in the diary translation and provided the right encouragement at the right time to ensure that everything remained on track. Together, through our travels and this translation, we have come to know both the Rome of Costantini and the magnificent lands of the Italian northeast (from which he came) far more intimately than we could once have dared hope. In both travels and translations, I could not have asked for a more faithful companion. *Grazie, amore!*

Laurence B. Mussio
Toronto, 2 June 2013

Introduction

On 17 May 1958 Cardinal Celso Costantini, aware that his life on earth was coming to an end, wrote to one of his four executors, Don Antonio Ornella, and placed his trust specifically in him to keep his memory[1] alive. For this purpose he brought to his attention one of his unpublished works: "In my manuscripts there is a volume, *Ai margini della guerra*, which may be published only after my death and after the death of the Holy Father Pius XII."[2]

In truth, some years earlier, the Friulian cardinal had already expressed his intention to publish the aforementioned work. With this goal in mind, he had turned to the Pope's pro-secretary of state, H.E. Monsignor Giovanni Battista Montini, and on 6 January 1954 had written to him asking if he could submit the manuscript for his appraisal. He did this in order to obtain authorization for the publishing project: "If they will allow me to publish it," he stated, "I reserve the right to make some clarifications and revisions; and I will be happy to effect any corrections that may be suggested to me."[3]

---

[1] In the letter sent from Rome on 17 May 1958 to Don Antonio Ornella, a professor at the Diocesan Seminary in Pordenone, Cardinal Celso Costantini stated, "I have appointed you executor along with Augusto Costantini and Giacomo Tasca and a prelate from Rome." The letter quoted above can be found in Archivio Storico Diocesano di Concordia-Pordenone (ASDCP), Fondo Celso Costantini (translated in this volume as the Celso Costantini Collection).

[2] Ibid.

[3] Copy of the letter from Cardinal Celso Costantini written from Rome on 6 January 1954 and sent to H.E. Mons. Giovanni Battista Montini, pro-secretary of state to Pius XII; it can be found in ASDCP, Celso Costantini Collection.

In the same letter he touched on the spirit with which the book was written and the times in which it was composed: "a work that I prepared during the last war and that I recently reorganized. It was created as an act of ministry in service of the Holy Church."⁴ The second of the two phases he mentions, the one pertaining to the reorganization of the notes written during the global conflict, made it necessary for him to include names that were for the most part omitted or identified with initials in the original manuscript, and to bring together all of the instalments that were produced and intentionally scattered throughout many locations. The material was in fact extremely "stinging" at the time, especially before 25 July 1943, as he revealed in his diary on that day: "Writing these notes, I was always terrified that this notebook might fall into the hands of the Fascists. I have conducted no smear campaign or propaganda against them; to the contrary, I always offered words of moderation and calm. But we were reduced to the following: that one was afraid even to think or write something that went against the idol who was served by a clique of cowards and corrupt men."

In order to avoid the danger he feared – that it would bring obvious negative consequences for him and for those mentioned – Costantini adopted various precautions. As he revealed, "I had been warned not to write the names of people in full. I had hidden many documents and my pieces of writing inside the Propaganda's archive, scattering the material in large old registers of past accounts or between the pages of books in storage."⁵

The cardinal expected to receive immediate permission from the secretary of state of the Holy See in response to his request to publish the book. This was also, he maintained, so that the opinions chronologically ordered in his diary would not implicate the authority of the Church: "Naturally, I take full personal responsibility for the judgments that are

---

⁴ Ibid.

⁵ Please see the diary entry of 6 June, which discusses the liberation of Rome from German occupation and from Fascist rule. The recovery of the scattered pages, or at least most of them, took place on 23 August 1944 with the assistance of Father Wang and Don Mazza – as can be read in this book in the entry for August 1944. [Translator's note: "Propaganda" refers to the Sacred Congregation for the Propagation of the Faith (*di Propaganda Fide*); also "the Propaganda."]

political in nature."[6] However, in the eyes of Monsignor Montini, it would be difficult, despite Costantini's intentions, to keep an exclusively individual image of the author separate from his prestigious ecclesiastical duties and from the authority he was granted in his capacity as a close aide to the happily reigning Pope.

Costantini did not consider the work he prepared to be the final text; in fact, he informed Mons. Montini that he had asked a well-known Jesuit at the time to re-evaluate it: "I asked Father Messineo of *Catholic Civilization* to review the book."[7] In a second letter, written on 1 June 1954, he made clear to the same pro-secretary of state that he had taken care of choosing three readers for his work: the aforementioned Father Antonio Messineo, the Hon. Alberto De Stefani, and General Umberto Pugliese. He reported also their respective observations and successively reproduced them in a concise summary. These observations explain how, as seen from various perspectives, a book on the Second World War might be evaluated differently. The book was the only one of its kind if one considers it the product of a principal representative of the Roman Curia.

The comments of the first examiner were rather lukewarm, as was his reply to the author on 28 February 1954: "I went through the manuscript carefully and have not found anything that is inexact in scholarship or that can generate theoretical observations. The facts are what they are, and H.E. does nothing but narrate events and personal experiences that are already common knowledge. Perhaps, in my humble opinion, one could tone down here and there some rather harsh comments regarding the past regime and its members." In the Celso Costantini Collection in the Diocesan Historical Archive of Concordia-Pordenone, some unsigned annotations – most likely written by Messineo and undoubtedly not written by the other two readers – suggest that the bulk of the manuscript be streamlined, thereby reducing it to one volume of reasonable size.

The Hon. De Stefani enthusiastically approved of the composition: "I read the typescript of his very noble work, *Ai margini della guerra*, with great interest; it is a work that contains an incomparable documentation of some very painful and tragic years that were made worse by a

---

[6] Copy of the letter quoted by Cardinal Celso Costantini, written from Rome on 6 January 1954 to H.E. Monsignor Giovanni Battista Montini.

[7] Ibid.

political crisis that reached an extreme and bloody outcome. In a noble and timeless way, this work is also evidence of the Church's abundant charity. The volume, owing to its fresh and simple style, its quantity and accuracy of material, and above all the religious spirit that inspires its interpretation of facts, deserves a very high and distinct position separate from the large amount of retrospective, often factious literature of those years."[8] The political representative, a former minister between 1922 and 1925 in the government that at the time was led by Mussolini, expressed only a few reservations about the very small number of opinions expressed about the key people in the Fascist Party.

Umberto Pugliese's answer, which was concisely summarized by Costantini, attests that the general had carefully read the text sent to him, regarding which he suggested only "a few stylistic revisions and, in general, some softening of the opinions expressed." [9]

The opinions expressed by the three readers caused the author to "take note of their evaluations and make additions and corrections to the text. The cardinal informed Mons. Montini of these changes in the same letter of June 1954: "I placed more emphasis on the enormous charitable work of the Holy Father and his appeal for prayers. I added other accounts of the work carried out by the Italian Episcopate ... I kept in mind the three readers' suggestions ... I did away with some common satirizations. Some of them seemed an adequate and timely way to convey the climate of war. Now I wait – 'without haste' – for what Your Excellency would like to tell me, ready to follow all instructions that will be given to me." [10] Then, almost appealing for a positive response, he stated that with the circulation of the book he would be defending the Church as well as providing the most extensive knowledge of the "marvellous work carried out by the Holy Father during the war."[11]

We have no information regarding the instructions which the pro-secretary of the pontifical state provided to Costantini. However, from a note dated 14 August 1954, signed by the cardinal and affixed to the first page of a typewritten copy of his diary, we have information regarding one of his various provisions: "*Ai margini della guerra*, 1938–1947, is to be published – if ever – after the death of His Holiness Pius XII and after

[8] Ibid.
[9] Ibid.
[10] Ibid.
[11] Ibid.

my own death. It is best to wait for the passing of the generation of those responsible."[12] This new decision was confirmed not only by a card[13] sent by Costantini to Don Ornella at Christmas 1957, but also by the account of his only living executor – his nephew Professor Giacomo Tasca – and by the 17 May 1958 letter that is quoted above.

Pope Pacelli died on 9 October 1958. Just eight days later the cardinal also passed away. Thus the temporal restraints that until then had impeded the publication of *Ai margini della Guerra* were removed.

Mr Giovanni Tullio, a long-standing close friend of Costantini, took steps to realize the publishing project and to fulfill the fervent wish of the author. In a letter to the vicar general of the Concordia Diocese, Mons. Leo Brevin, Tullio wrote that he had "the ready support of Count [Vittorio] Cini, which he expressed to me last November [1958] when the work of our venerated cardinal, 'Diario di guerra,' was printed."[14] In the same letter of 25 March 1959, Tullio stated that he and Brevin had told Cini of "our hesitation regarding the unabridged publication of the text and the advantage of a revision, which we knew would be difficult; we added that we would be grateful if he wanted to go through the manuscript and give us his opinion."[15]

Cini had answered in a letter sent from Venice on 1 March 1959, in which he expressed his understanding of the problematic aspects of the publishing venture, having carefully read the text that was submitted for his evaluation: "The doubts facing us, which we have paused to consider carefully, are more than justified and render even more demanding the task of publishing the diary of our noble and unforgettable friend ... I think that no one better than them can give suggestions and decide."[16]

---

[12] ASDCP, Celso Costantini Collection, a note on the cover of a typewritten copy of *Diario inedito del Cardinale Celso Costantini. Ai margini della guerra (1938–1948)* (Venice : Marcianum Press, 2010).

[13] Celso Costantini, in a card dated Christmas 1957, wrote the following to Don Antonio Ornella: "I have some manuscripts that will be able to be published after my death" (ASDCP, Celso Costantini Collection).

[14] ASDCP, Celso Costantini Collection, copy of the letter written on 25 March 1959 by Mr Giovanni Tullio to Mons. Leo Bravin, vicar general of the Diocese of Concordia.

[15] Ibid.

[16] ASDCP, Celso Costantini Collection, copy of the letter written on 1 March 1959 by Count Vittorio Cini to Giovanni Tullio Altan.

People such as Giovanni Tullio, who themselves admitted to being uncertain about divulging the contents of the unpublished work of the cardinal, are the ones whom he himself had recommended to the bishop of Concordia, H.E Monsignor Vittorio De Zanche, to the vicar general, Monsignor Leo Brevin, and to Professor Giacomo Tasca. In the absence of other written documents that we are not aware of, it can be reported, without arousing any possible interest in its publication, that the text was stored in the Seminary Library [Biblioteca del Seminario] in Pordenone.

In 1986 the director of the library, Don Antonio Ornella, who had always been committed to honouring the memory of his fellow townsman the cardinal, took steps to find the necessary funding and a collaborator with whom he could oversee the publication of the work. These were both found in Professor Ruggero Simonato who, after outlining an introduction and producing a. draft of the opening part of the book,[17] had to give up the task because of the death of Don Ornella.

Subsequent attempts to complete the project bore negative results until the closing events celebrating the fiftieth anniversary of the cardinal's death. In this period of commemorations, the proposal to publish the diary received a *nulla osta* [Certificate of No Impediment] on 28 March 2009 from the Congregation for the Evangelization of Peoples [formerly the *Congregation di Propaganda Fide*], since the text was written when Costantini was secretary of that ministry. The publisher of the proposed edition of the book, Marcianum Press, entrusted the editing to Bruno Fabio Pighin, a full professor at the Faculty of Canon Law, St Pius X, Venice, because of his expertise in the fields of history and law and for his knowledge of his very distinguished fellow citizen.

The reasons underlying the project are numerous. The first was born from the desire to give deserved prominence to a person who distinguished himself in the international sphere in both the Eastern and the Western parts of the globe – so much so that he placed himself among the actors, if not at the forefront, of the historical drama of the Church and the twentieth-century world.

The need to reveal features of his character and views that were previously not known is motivated by the fact that Celso Costantini does not belong only to the past, to a moment in history that has irrevocably gone. He has proved himself, in some respects, to be a teacher of the

[17] We found in the ASDCP, Celso Costantini Collection, the printed drafts of the diary years 1938–40.

present and sometimes a prophet of the future, as shown in the short profile given below.

The second reason is connected with the contents of the book. Although it does not produce new official documentation on the Second World War with respect to an impressive amount of acts and events that are already common knowledge, it does provide a previously unknown and unpublished consideration of the historical figures it presents – points of view regarding those who were close to the cardinal and in some way involved in the war. Finally, it provides unique snapshots of the events connected with the conflict. The originality of this cross-section derives, on the one hand, from the opportunities offered to Costantini by reason of his position in the Roman Curia as secretary of the Sacra Congregazione di Propaganda Fide [Sacred Congregation for the Propagation of the Faith], and, on the other, from his unique experience accumulated on national and international levels from the First World War onward.

Our objective is to make available to a wide range of readers a precious source of knowledge and interpretation concerning the last world conflict, a source that until now was inaccessible to those interested. For this purpose it seems obvious to publish – among the three existing versions – the typescript that was the product of Costantini's last revisions and received the comments of the readers he chose in 1954.

To assist the reader who is not familiar with the subject, numerous explanatory notes regarding the people, places, and events presented are included in the volume. Two different types of annotations are given: those that were written now and those that were provided by the cardinal. In order to distinguish between the two, the latter are prefaced with "cc."

This work, although its format mirrors the literary genre of a diary, boasts a unique theme that revolves around the title its author gave it: *Ai margini della Guerra*. The two characterizations provide just as many keys to its reading. On one hand, the progression of the story cannot be anything but chronological; on the other, the settings provided in its headings make sure that the storytelling, which begins in 1938 and ends in 1947, embraces a time span that is much wider than that of the last world war by including the period before it and the one immediately following the terrible conflict. In between these periods, one finds a greater amount of information and content that is more "heated" during the years 1943–45; the year 1944 reveals his greatest expressiveness and significantly warmer "degrees" of storytelling.

The phrase chosen for the title, as Costantini emphasizes in his preface, anticipates his position when he was writing down his thoughts: "These diary entries do not constitute the history of the war. They simply gather together certain events that occurred, as seen from a limited angle – that of a spectator on the margins of the conflict and outside any party affiliation. What comes to light in these entries are more the spiritual aspects of an enormous tragedy." The author is not directly involved in the fortunes of war – which is the subject of his comments – either as an actor or as a passive subject of the story, with the exception of a few events in which he was involved against his will. But he is a person inevitably involved in a horrendous disaster of proportions so terrible that they were once unknown to humanity. He allows himself to question the depth of his spirit as a man, as a Christian, as an Italian, and above all as a bishop, a bishop placed by Providence on a privileged observation point that was wide-open to the whole world and at the epicentre of a disastrous earthquake – namely Rome, a city that allowed him certain extraterritorial immunities, thanks to the duties he carried out in service of the Holy See. His field of vision, which was uncommon, allowed him to scan extremely wide horizons and at the same time to enter the remote recesses of a horrible and useless massacre and then to pinpoint those who in various ways acted as its coordinators, perpetrators, and collaborators. All of this was carried out in the historical-cultural context of a game that, through various actions and in different ways, would see all of them end up as its losers.

In such a catastrophic setting, the figure of Pius XII rises up with his inspiring teachings, with his pastoral guidance at a universal level, and with his charitable deeds – without any discrimination toward those in need of help. With his diary, Celso Costantini is able to make himself a staunch, credible, and convincing witness to Pius XII's interventions – which were often criticized after the war, not on the basis of historical facts but of widespread prejudice – as well as to the activities of the Church in Italy and in the world. Thanks to the precious interpretation he has left us, he is truly unique in his genre.

Bruno Fabio Pighin

Chronology of the
Life of Celso Costantini (1876–1958)

Celso Costantini, holding doctorates in philosophy and theology, became a priest and pastor in the parish of Concordia. During this time (1901–15) his artistic talent as a sculptor emerged, leaving us with more than forty of his works. He also proved himself to be both a scholar and critic of art: he wrote about thirty books and approximately two hundred scientific articles on art history, specifically, sacred art. He advanced archaeological discoveries in Concordia and Aquileia, both of which are Roman and Paleo-Christian sites of primary importance. In 1912 he started a movement in Italy, which then stretched overseas, for a productive synthesis between art, faith, and modernity. In 1913 he founded and served as editor of the magazine *Arte cristiana*, which is still published in Milan. He fostered the establishment of the Pontificia Commissione per l'Arte sacra [Pontifical Commission for Sacred Art], which was run by his brother, Archbishop Giovanni, and upon his death, by Costantini himself. As the vicar general of the Diocese of Concordia at the end of 1918, he became the strategist for the material, social, and moral reconstruction of Friuli after the destruction caused by the First World War, during which he had served as a military chaplain.

His artistic and literary talents led him to establish contacts with many men of culture, among them the poet and nationalist Gabriele d'Annunzio. When the nationalists conquered Fiume in Croatia, the Holy See sent Costantini there to establish the Diocese of Fiume – which today is called Rijeka – where he averted a bloodbath among the civil population and proposed an accord, which in 1921 brought an end to the occupation of the area by d'Annunzio, allowing him to leave the political scene unharmed.

This brilliant operation impressed the Pope, who chose him for a very difficult mission, that of the first apostolic delegate to China. Here, in the span of eleven years, he brought about a genuine revolution: he "decolonized" the Catholic religion by rescuing it from the rule of the European colonial powers; he "launched" the Catholic Church there with the ordination of the first Chinese bishops, with the assignment of responsibilities to the indigenous clergy and the secular faithful, and the founding of a Chinese religious congregation. He enculturated the message of the Gospel for the civilization of the Celestial Empire through a liturgy in the Mandarin language, through sacred indigenous art, and the establishment of Catholic universities and schools at all levels.

After returning to Italy, he served for eighteen years as secretary of the Sacra Congregazione di Propaganda Fide, the ministry that supervised Catholic communities in mission countries, which at the time were in Africa, Asia, Oceania, and parts of Europe and America. Through his office, he became the main promoter of the missionary policies of Pope Pius XII. In this role, his connections expanded intercontinentally and were striving to create a new connection between the East and the West.

During the Second World War he carried out an important role in Rome that aided the fall of the Fascist regime and prevented a civil war. He saved the life of the statesman Alcide De Gasperi by keeping him hidden in his residence while the Italian capital was occupied by the Nazis. He carried out humanitarian activities for those, including the Jews, who fell into abject poverty and desperation. He supported the democratic growth of Italy and its post-war reconciliation.

He was made cardinal in 1953 and was appointed chancellor of the Holy Roman Church in 1954. He carried out an important role in the construction of a "common European house" in the concert, or community, of democracies. He was the first and only high prelate of the Roman Curia to propose, even in 1939, an ecumenical council for church reform. He convinced his good friend, the future Pope John XXIII, of the effectiveness of such a project. He would not see his friend become Pius XII's successor because it was felt that the time had come to elect a non-Italian Pope in order to show the universality of Catholicism and to avoid the "curse" of the Italianization of the Church.

FROM BIRTH TO EPISCOPAL ORDINATION (1876–1921)
1876　On 3 April the second son of Costantino and Maddalena Altan is born in Castions di Zoppola and receives the sacrament of baptism in the town's parish church.

1882   He begins to attend elementary school in Castions di Zoppola.

1887   He begins an apprenticeship as a bricklayer in his father's building company.

1890   He suffers a serious work accident and must concede to a period of inactivity.

1891   He prepares for his admission exams to the seminary under the tutelage of Don Antonio Agnolutto, the cousin of Celso's mother.

1892   He enters the Diocesan Seminary of Concordia in Portogruaro.

1899   On 10 May he obtains a university degree in philosophy and on 14 July receives a degree in theology from the Pontifical Gregorian University in Rome. On 23 September he becomes a deacon in the seminary church in Portogruaro and on 23 December is ordained presbyter in the Chapel of the Bishop in Portogruaro. On 26 December he celebrates his first solemn Mass at Castions di Zoppola.

·1900   On 8 June he is appointed spiritual steward of Rorai Grande Parish in Pordenone.

1901   On 21 February he is appointed vicar of the Parish of Concordia Cathedral.

1902   He begins his work as a sculptor and continues this activity until 1914; his passion for art will always lead him to be attracted to sculpture, as his scientific publications in the field of art history demonstrate.

1907   He publishes in Florence the manual *Nozioni d'arte per il clero* with an original manuscript of Saint Pius X.

1912   On 24 October he founds the Società degli Amici dell'Arte cristiana [Society of Christian Art] in Milan.

1913   On 15 January he founds the magazine *Arte cristiana*, which he edits and which is still published in Milan.

1915   On 5 July he becomes regent of Aquileia Parish and custodian of the Basilica of Aquileia.

1917   On 12 December he becomes military chaplain of the Italian Army on the war front.

1918   On 3 November he is appointed vicar general of the Diocese of Concordia; during the month of December he breathes life into the Istituto S. Filippo Neri for infants in Portogruaro and founds in Venice the Opera di Soccorso [Foundation for the Assistance] of churches destroyed by war.

1919   On 30 October he is appointed director of the Archaeological
       Museum of Aquileia with managerial responsibility also for the
       excavations of ancient sites in the surrounding area.

1920   On 30 April he is raised to the position of apostolic adminis-
       trator of Fiume (which is now in Croatia) without the title of
       bishop.

1921   On 22 July he is elected titular bishop of Gerapoli and on
       24 August is ordained a bishop by the patriarch of Venice, Cardinal
       Pietro La Fontaine, in Concordia Cathedral. On 4 November in
       Aquileia he blesses the eleven bodies of unknown soldiers that are
       to be placed at the Vittoriano [the Victor Emmanuel II monument]
       in Rome.

THE MISSION IN CHINA (1922–1933)

1922   Between April and May he carries out the assignment given to
       him by Pius XI as apostolic visitor of the Tyrol. On 12 August he
       is appointed the first apostolic delegate to China, then is raised
       on 9 September to titular archbishop of Teodosia. During the
       month of November he arrives in China and sets up his tempo-
       rary residence in Hankow.

1923   In Beijing he sets up the official see of the Apostolic Delegation,
       far away from the Western legations; the office was purchased
       thanks to the financial involvement of Chinese Catholics.

1924   From 14 May to 12 June he chairs the first Chinese Plenary
       Council in Shanghai as a pontifical legate; on 12 December, after
       great effort, he establishes the Apostolic Prefecture of Puchi, the
       first of many ecclesiastical districts entrusted to Chinese prelates.

1925   He helps found Fu Jen Academy, the Catholic institution that
       grows to become Fu Jen University; it is currently located in
       Taiwan.

1926   On 24 October he is made an honorary citizen of Aquileia; on
       28 October he presents the first six Chinese bishops to Pius XI for
       their episcopal ordination in the Basilica of St Peter in the Vatican.

1927   With the approval of the Propaganda ministry, on 4 January he
       founds the Congregatio Discipulorum Domini, the first male
       Chinese religious institution, which begins to take shape in 1930
       and is still in existence, with an important and flourishing sacer-
       dotal program. Then, on 26 September in Beijing, he opens the
       courses at the Fu Jen Academy, which at that point has already

reached the status of a Catholic university – something he had wished for and constantly supported.

1929   During the month of January he is received at Nanjing by the head of the new Chinese national government, General Chiang Kai-shek, receiving honours that are usually reserved for ministers of foreign affairs; on 19 May he opens the l'Associazione Generale della Gioventù Cattolica Cinese [Association of Chinese Catholic Youth] inside the see of the Apostolic Delegation; on 31 May he acts as envoy extraordinary of the Holy See at the funeral for Sun Yat-sen, founder of the Chinese Republic, held at Nanjing. Beyond this, in Shanghai he oversees the publication of the provisions of the Chinese Plenary Council, which are approved by the Propaganda and His Holiness's secretary of state.

1930   He endures continual attacks from the Western press in China but is defended by the Holy See.

1931   On 14 January, in Pordenone, he chairs the events in honour of the Blessed Odoric from Pordenone, who died six hundred years earlier; he considers him his precursor and protector. Between June and July he is in the United States of America for an operation to remove a tumour; he returns to Beijing on 17 August.

1932   On 15 May he administers the sacrament of baptism to the painter Tcheng Yuandu, the future leader of the Christian Chinese Art movement. On 15 September he approves the final statutes of Catholic Action in China, which will be headed by Joseph Lo Pa-Hong.

1933   On 14 January he receives a visit from Colonel Galeazzo Ciano, the Italian ambassador to China, and in February he leaves China to undergo medical treatment in Italy.

THE MINISTRY AT PROPAGANDA FIDE (1934–1952)

1933   On 3 November, for health reasons, he resigns from his position as apostolic delegate. On 3 December he is appointed consulter to the Sacred Congregation for the Propagation of the Faith [*Propaganda Fide*].

1934   During the summer he makes a study trip to Greece, the Middle East and Egypt; he is also appointed consulter to the Sacred Congregation for the Oriental Church

1935   On 28 March he is invited to meet Benito Mussolini, who receives him at Palazzo Venezia. In May he makes a trip to Maghreb. On

29 June, in Belgium, he confers the presbyteral ordination on Célestin Luo Tseng-Tsiang, former premier of the Republic of China. Finally, on 17 December he becomes secretary of the Sacred Congregation for the Propagation of the Faith.

1936   He is appointed consulter of the Sacred Congregation of the Holy Office of Rites, and then also that of Extraordinary Ecclesiastical Affairs. On 19 January the title of Assistant to the Pontifical Throne is conferred on him. In the summer he goes to Holland to meet some bishops from Scandinavia. On 26 November, in Venice, he commemorates Cardinal Patriarch Pietro La Fontaine and takes over the job of rector of the Pontifical Urban University.

1937   In the month of July he carries out the duties given him by Pius XI as apostolic visitor in Spain, and in October he makes an official visit to France.

1939   On 8 December he countersigns the order that approves the participation of Catholics in rites that honour Confucius.

1940   On 5 May he countersigns the decree to abolish the official act against Malabar Rites, a reform that he supported.

1941   On 9 May he obtains, from the Sacred Congregation of the Holy Office, the translation of the Roman Ritual in modern Chinese and in other indigenous languages.

1943   On 19 July he is left miraculously unharmed after the bombing of the San Lorenzo Outside the Walls area.

1944   From February to June he offers shelter inside the residence of the Propaganda to the Hon. Alcide De Gasperi, a feared opponent of the Fascists and Nazis.

1946   On 18 February he rejoices because of the internationalization of the College of Cardinals and the creation of the first Chinese cardinal, a request he had made to Pius XII. On 11 April he brings about the establishment of the Episcopal Hierarchy in China, a request he had made to Pius XII on 9 May 1939.

1947   On 11 October he blesses the marriage of Maria Romana De Gasperi and Piero Catti, the first-born daughter of the statesman Alcide De Gasperi.

1948   On 6 June he presides over the Ceremony of Religious Clothing for Lucia De Gasperi, another of Alcide's daughters, as she becomes an Assumptionist nun. On 19 June, in Rome, he opens the College of St Peter for the clergy of mission countries.

1949 On 12 April he obtains from the Sacred Congregation of the
      Holy Office the translation of the Roman Missal in modern
      Chinese.

1950 On 9 July in Rome, he opens the Exhibition of Missionary Art,
      which he curated, with the participation of the prime minister,
      the Hon. A. De Gasperi.

1951 In May he goes to Madrid to open the Exhibition of Missionary
      Art.

THE PERIOD OF HIS CARDINALATE (1953–1958)

1953 On 12 January, Pius XII makes him cardinal deacon of Saints
      Nereus and Achilles. On 5 January he is appointed a member
      of the four departments of the Roman Curia: the Sacred Con-
      gregation for the Oriental Church, for the Council, for the
      Propagation of the Faith, and of Rites.

1954 Between February and March he gives lectures, previously
      approved by the Pope, in Turin, Genoa, Milan, and Rome; their
      theme is "Il pensiero di S.S. Pio XII contro i crimini di guerra"
      [the thoughts of His Holiness Pius XII regarding war criminals].
      On 22 May he is raised to the position of chancellor of the Holy
      Roman Church and to the dignity of presbyter cardinal of
      St Lawrence in the House of Damascus.

1955 On 14 March he is elected an honorary member of the Pontifical
      Roman Academy of Archaeology. On 19 December he acts as a
      representative for Pius XII at the event held in the Palazzetto
      Venezia in Rome by the Italian Society for International Organi-
      zation, on the tenth anniversary of the United Nations statute,
      giving an official speech for the occasion.

1956 On 30 June the high honour of Grosskreutz is conferred on him
      by the president of the Federal Republic of Germany. During
      the same month, Pope Pius XII appoints him honorary presi-
      dent of the Pontifical Central Commission for Sacred Art in
      Italy. On 22 September he is made an honorary citizen of the
      City of Pordenone. On 22 November he is appointed a member
      of the Sacred Congregation for Extraordinary Ecclesiastical
      Affairs.

1957 On 6 August he is notified by the secretary of state on behalf
      of Pope Pius XII that the latter, in response to his request, has
      issued a universal dispensation that allows, by discretion of the

Ordinaries, the use of older styles of vestments during mass; for example, one style of chasuble in place of another.

1958   On 17 October, on the eve of the conclave that will elect Pope John XXIII, he dies in Rome. On 23 October he is entombed in the Castions di Zoppola cemetery.

THE SECRETS OF A VATICAN CARDINAL

Cardinal Celso Costantini

Diary, 1938–1947

Nothing is lost with peace. Everything can be lost with war.
Pope Pius XII, 24 August 1939

Author's Preface

These diary entries do not constitute the history of the war. They simply gather together certain events that occurred, as seen from a limited angle – that of a spectator on the margins of the conflict and outside any party affiliation. What comes to light in these entries are more the spiritual aspects of an enormous tragedy. For reasons of documentation and objectivity, I have included the current thinking, cynical comments, and opinions of that era. Those perspectives and opinions were not always borne out by objective facts. Naturally, my views have nothing to do with the opinions expressed in the documents I have cited.

The reader will forgive me if in this diary I return many times to certain moral and political principles. The enormous tragedy of the war occurred precisely because those principles were forgotten. These recollections represent irrefutable documentation of that fact.

> Oh senseless strivings of the mortal round!
> How worthless is that exercise of reason
> that makes you beat your wings into the ground![1]
> Dante Alighieri, *La Divina Commedia, Paradiso*, 11:1–3

Although I am the secretary of the Sacred Congregation for the Propagation of the Faith, I have not referred to the sad repercussions that the world war has had on Catholic missions. That subject would require a substantial book of its own.

---

[1] Translator's note: Adapted from Dante Alighieri, *The Divine Comedy*, Trans. John Ciardi (Oxford: Oxford University Press, 1985), 686.

I would, however, like to offer my most cordial recognition and tribute to the apostolic spirit and strength with which our missionaries have endured the destruction, killing, imprisonment, and countless other sufferings caused by the war.

On the sea of humanity, overwhelmed by the fiercest storms and still blocked by the wreckage of an immense shipwreck, there emerges a helpless ship, battered but steady and strong. On its sail is a red cross. The Helmsman, whose commands unfortunately were not heeded by the shipwrecked, now kneels beside the helm and prays for the dead, inviting the survivors to accept the error of their ways and embrace salvation.

The Year 1938

CLOUDS ON THE HORIZON

Meminisse iuvat.[1] I preface my diary with several documents that constitute important points of reference. They offer a vision of a port from which the fragile small ship of peace had unfortunately become unmoored, only to be tempest-tossed on the stormy open sea.

The Thoughts of Benedict XV

"The equilibrium of the world and the prosperous and secure tranquility of nations depend on mutual benevolence and upon respect for the other's rights and the other's dignity, a lot more than on a great number of weapons and formidable walled fortresses" [message of Benedict XV, 28 July 1915].[2] On 1 August 1917, Pope Benedict XV wrote a letter to the leaders of the warring nations[3] proposing a peaceful compromise that would preserve each side's military dignity. The continuation of the war would have represented a *senseless slaughter*. The Pope's paternal invitation was not accepted – in fact, his words were met with derision.

---

[1] *Meminisse iuvat* [Sweet is their remembrance], quotation of a proverb from the poet Statius in his poem *Achilleid*, book 2, vol. 167.

[2] The message cited by Benedict XV is "Apostolica exhortatio ad populos belligerantes eorumque rectores," in Acta Apostolicae Sedis [AAS] 7 (*Bollettino Ufficiale della Santa Sede*, 1915), 367–8.

[3] The letter in question is that of Benedict XV, "Lettre aux chefs des peuples belligérantes," in AAS 9 (*Bollettino Ufficiale della Santa Sede*, 1917), 423.

Thus ensued the revenge of Versailles,[4] which kept alive the smouldering embers for a future conflagration.

The Judgment of Marshal Enrico Caviglia[5]

"Military operations were in a winter-stasis phase. During the long evenings, in a reasonably comfortable environment, there were many endless discussions. With me were intelligent and civilized officials such as [Mario] Caracciolo, now a colonel and a professor at the military academy; Captain Rotigliano, author of a good book on military policy, who is now a member of parliament; and others. They would have liked the Pope to side with Italy and the Allied cause because, they said, 'our case is the cause of justice and humanity.' I argued that since we were on one side, we could not be impartial judges and that the Holy Father would not take sides but instead had to seek peace. In all of his addresses, I heard a soul that was not simply in pain but was desolate because his words could not quell the passions that kept Europe in flames. His prayers to God and the prayers he asked of the people were his only hope. When the war ends and passions are quelled, the conduct of Benedict XV will be admired by all nations, because they will see how he was truly on the side of justice, humanity, and love."[6]

---

[4] The Treaty of Versailles, signed on 28 June 1919, contained 440 articles. The treaty was imposed by the Allies on a defeated Germany in 1918 after the tremendous global conflict. Germany had to cede part of its territory to France, Belgium, Poland, Denmark, and Czechoslovakia. It was also condemned to pay an enormous sum for reparations and to demilitarize various areas.

[5] Enrico Caviglia (1862–1945) was one of the main architects of Italy's victory at Vittorio Veneto in 1918. The following year he was nominated a senator for life. After being minister of war (1919–20) in Vittorio Emanuele Orlando's government, he was made a marshal in 1926. He briefly assumed command of Rome on 8 September 1943, negotiating with the Germans on the fate of the city. Retiring to private life in the city of Finale Ligure in his native region of Liguria, he wrote various works, among which was Diario (Aprile 1925 – Marzo 1945), published posthumously by Gherardo Casini Editore, Rome, 1952.

[6] E. Caviglia, Diario: April 1925 – March 1945 (Rome, 1952), 63.

The Prophetic Vision of P. Rosa,[7] SJ[8]

"On 28 June 1919, in the Hall of Mirrors at Versailles, the leaders embodying the knowledge and power of the century ended the war by signing a peace treaty. But at the same time a new and even more terrible phase was beginning – one of hatred, rivalry, and national and international struggle. Of this new phase, tomorrow's history will tell. As for us here and now, without giving ourselves the least claim to prophecy, we can see with certainty how the future will unfold ...

What matters and what will have a decisive effect on the history of nations is the absence of the spirit, of a high and serene sense of justice, civilization, and Christian generosity. It is the exclusion of God and of his eternal laws, where even the mention of His name is silenced. It is therefore the damaged disposition of souls that are all but becalmed. It is the intrinsic substance of those 440 articles of the peace treaty that in reality can be called articles of war, signed by more than thirty victorious powers against a vanquished one. It is, in sum, the entire famous Treaty of Versailles. That treaty will also be famous to a posterity that will be able to judge its value more dispassionately. Today, there are few who do not denounce its arbitrary nature and foretell its effects not only on the vanquished but also on the victors themselves. We can say it right now, and we repeat it loudly: We have sanctioned a new war by imposing on the nations a cynical 'peace treaty.' This is not what nations were expecting after so much suffering!"[9]

THE FOUR-POWER PACT OF 1933

The pact was signed in Rome on 7 June 1933.[10] Article 1 provided that the contracting parties agreed on all the settled questions. They undertook to do everything they could, in the context of the League of Nations, to collaborate, in effect, to maintain the peace among the signatory

---

[7] Enrico Rosa (1870–1938), Jesuit, writer, and editor of the review *La Civiltà Cattolica* from 1915 to 1931.

[8] The initials stand for Society of Jesus, the name of the religious order of Jesuits.

[9] E. Rosa, "La guerra Sociale dopo la pace di Versailles," *La Civiltà Cattolica* 70, no. 3 (1919): 262.

[10] The Four-Power Pact was negotiated between Italy, France, Germany, and Great Britain.

nations. Speaking to the Italian press, Göring[11] declared that Germany heartily supported both the idea and the policy of the Four-Power Pact. Von Papen[12] clearly expressed the real reason for Germany's cordial reception of the pact: "We Germans are committed to realizing a revision of the [Versailles] peace treaties …"

The pact was signed on 15 July (in spite of its official date of 7 June), but because only Italy and Germany signed, it never entered into force.[13] The pact was conceived by Mussolini with the intent of revising the Versailles treaties. Since those treaties were tied to the League of Nations,[14] which acted as a type of committee of guarantee among the Great Power signatories, the pact failed. It did, however, have a certain exemplary value – much like the Kellogg Pact[15] of 1928 – as a worthwhile initiative.

[11] Hermann Göring (1893–1946), Nazi leader, a minister in Adolf Hitler's first administration, air marshal of the Reich in 1938, and commander of the Luftwaffe during the Second World War. He was condemned to death at Nuremberg after Germany's defeat and killed himself in his jail cell before the sentence was carried out.

[12] Franz Von Papen (1879–1969), German diplomat and politician, a member of the Catholic Centre Party (Zentrum) who in 1932 headed a national coalition government. Von Papen was vice-chancellor in Hitler's first government in 1933, the year in which Germany signed the concordat with the Holy See. In 1934, Von Papen distanced himself from the Nazi regime and risked being killed on Himmler's orders. He was the next ambassador to Austria and then to Turkey. He was arrested in 1945 and stood trial at Nuremberg, where he was acquitted of all charges for lack of evidence. In 1947 he was condemned to eight years of forced labour by a German federal court for complicity with the Nazi regime. Released in 1954, he spent his remaining years outside the political scene. He published a memoir in 1968.

[13] CC: L. Salvatorelli and G. Miro, *Storia del Fascismo* (Rome, 1952), 628.

[14] The League of Nations was an international body established shortly after the First World War and headquartered in Geneva. Virtually all governments were members. Its objective was to avoid war by solving contentious issues between nations and to establish bilateral and multilateral relations on questions of justice and international law. The outbreak of the Second World War signalled the failure of the League and its subsequent dissolution.

[15] The name of the pact derives from Frank Billings Kellogg (1856–1937), a United States diplomat and public servant. Kellogg was secretary of state between 1925 and 1929 and became judge of the International Court of Justice in 1930. He was awarded the Nobel Peace Prize in 1929 for promoting the

The pact was an attempt at peace that reflects favourably on Mussolini. Treaties are not eternal, after all. They are contingent instruments for the peaceful coexistence of nations. If there had been a little bit of good faith, and if there had been time to reform that tragic Treaty of Versailles, this great war could probably have been avoided. A politician[16] once remarked to me that the Second World War was essentially a continuation of the 1914–18 war.

AUDIENCE WITH THE HOLY FATHER, PIUS XI

30 SEPTEMBER 1938

This text is not reproduced here because it was published in its entirety in C. Costantini, *Ultime Foglie. Ricordi e pensieri* (Rome: Unione missionaria del clero in Italia, 1954), 185–6. The text refers to an audience granted by Pope Pius XI to Cardinal Costantini and four other persons, among whom was Senator Vittorio Cini. Pius XI addressed part of his remarks to Senator Cini, saying, "Do you believe in peace? We cannot abandon ourselves to simplistic hopes because we have proof of the will of national leaders."[17]

TESTIMONY OF CHARLES-ROUX

François Charles-Roux,[18] French ambassador to the Holy See, offered the following version of our meeting with the Pope: "We were received by the Holy Father on 30 September at Castel Gandolfo. After my audience,

---

peace pact that bears his name. The Kellogg Pact was signed in Paris in 1928 by 14 states, with the objective of avoiding military conflict as a solution to international disagreements.

[16] In an early version of the manuscript, this person is identified as General Umberto Pugliese.

[17] The Pope was referring to the so-called Munich Agreement, a theme which the diary picks up on 27 January 1942. On 29 September 1938, a peace conference on the Czechoslovakian question was held in Munich with Hitler, Mussolini, Daladier of France, and Chamberlain of Great Britain. By conceding Sudetenland to Germany, Anglo-French foreign policy acquiesced in Nazi expansionism, dealing a hard blow to prospects for peace.

[18] François Charles-Roux (1879–1961), a French diplomat, historian, and businessman, held various ambassadorial postings before being appointed French ambassador to the Holy See (1932–40). In 1940 he was named general secretary of the French Ministry of Foreign Affairs. Between 1948 and 1956 he was president of the Universal Suez Ship Canal Company.

the Pope received three Italians – Mons. Costantini, Senator Cini,[19] and an architect [Marcello Piacèntini], who were there to present the plans for a prospective church, the Church of the Missions, for the Universal

[19] Vittorio Cini (1885–1977) was born in Ferrara but made Venice the centre of his activities. He died there at over 90 years old. Cini was an important representative of the world of industry and finance in the early 1900s. He collaborated with the great Venetian industrial and financial entrepreneurs of his day, a group headed by Giuseppe Volpi di Misurata, on a number of industrial initiatives, one of which was the creation of Porto Marghera. Cini was active in forming and guiding numerous associations, assuming the presidency of several navigation companies. One of these companies was Adriatica di Navigazione, whose endeavours brought Venice and its port great prestige. From 1953 he was president of the Società Adriatica di Elettricità (sade). Cini was invested with the title Count of Monselice and Senator of the Kingdom in 1934. He was tasked with overseeing the preparations for the Universal Exposition planned for Rome in 1942, but the project was subsequently cancelled because of the war. The preparations, however, led to the construction of the Roman neighbourhood eur (Esposizione Universale Roma). In February 1943, Cini was appointed minister of communications, only to resign in June because of his disagreement with Mussolini's policies and military organization. After 8 September 1943, he was deported by the Germans to Dachau concentration camp, from which he was subsequently liberated, thanks to the efforts of his son Giorgio. In 1946 he was acquitted of the charge of cooperating with the Fascist regime. At his trial, conducted in Venice by a commission of inquiry, the many people who testified on his behalf included Cardinal Costantini. After Cini's son Giorgio died tragically in a plane crash in 1949, Vittorio set to the task of memorializing his son by raising the Venetian island of St George, rehabilitating both the island and its magnificent monuments. Cini founded the Giorgio Cini Foundation, which was dedicated to his dead son. The foundation is involved in various cultural sectors and hosts first-class conferences that have garnered international fame. He was a great art collector, and at his death the works of art in the family palace in Campo San Vio were donated to the foundation. Cini also donated his castle at Monselice – a castle that he both owned and renovated. Cini was a great friend of Celso Costantini, as is borne out in Costantini's letters – especially in the correspondence between the cardinal and the count's wife, Lyda Borelli, who died in 1959. The Cinis had four children: Giorgio, Mynna, and the twins Ylda and Yana. In 1967 Cini married Maria Cristina Dal Pozzo d'Annone. Cini collaborated closely with the patriarchs of Venice (who are ex-officio members of the Board of the Cini Foundation). Between 1955 and 1967,

Exposition that was to be held in Rome in 1942. They were hoping to express to Pius XI[20] their delight at the fact that peace had been secured [by the Munich Agreement] the night before their visit. But it went badly. "That's a good one!" – replied the Pope, – "the peace achieved is at the expense of the weaker party – which was not even consulted! It is an unjust peace, with not all involved parties invited to the negotiations. You can tell that to the head of the Italian government from me."[21]

MUSSOLINI AND HITLER

It's worth noting that Mussolini was in reality averse to Hitler and the Germans. In the early stages of the Anschluss[22] he intended to defend Austrian independence. After the assassination of Dollfuss[23] [25 July

---

Cini headed the Procuratoria di San Marco [Procurator of St Mark] during a period of important restorations to St Mark's Basilica. Vittorio Cini was buried in the Certosa di Ferrara [the Carthusian Monastery at Ferrara].

[20] Achille Ambrogio Damiano Ratti (1857–1939), born at Desio and ordained in 1879, was the first director (for 24 years), then prefect (1907) of the Biblioteca Ambrosiana. He was called to Rome in 1914 to become the prefect of the Vatican Library. In 1919 he was appointed papal nuncio to Poland and became an archbishop. In 1921 he was promoted to the position of archbishop of Milan and made a cardinal. The conclave of 1922 elected him Pope, whereupon he assumed the name of Pius XI. Initially, Pope Pius XI had a benevolent attitude toward the Fascist regime, which in part resulted in the resolution of the "Roman Question" through the negotiation of the Lateran Pacts of 1929. With his 1937 encyclical *Mit brennender Sorge* (14 March 1937), he declared his opposition to Hitler's national socialism. In the same year, he declared his opposition to Communism with the encyclical *Divini Redemptoris* (19 March 1937). Pius XI devoted great attention to Catholic missions. To that end, he founded the Ateneo Urbaniano [Urban University] under the direction of the Sacred Congregation for the Propagation of the Faith. He also founded the Missionary Ethnological Museum of the Lateran. Pius XI died on the eve of the publication of an encyclical that condemned Nazi ideology – an encyclical that was never published.

[21] The original text was in French and was translated into Italian. CC: F. Charles-Roux, *Huit ans au Vatican* (Paris, 1947), 129.

[22] The political union of Austria and Germany, achieved by the annexation of the former by the latter in 1938.

[23] Engelbert Dollfuss (1892–1934), Fascist, leader of the Fatherland Front, became chancellor of Austria in 1932, seized power in 1933, and instituted one-party rule. He was assassinated in 1934.

1934], he sent two armoured divisions to the Brenner Pass. Then came the war against Ethiopia and the economic siege of international sanctions. England and France, of course without intending to, pushed Mussolini toward Hitler. Ambassador Charles-Roux wrote, "Day by day it's becoming more evident that Italy, alienated from England and France over the question of Abyssinia and the sanctions, has turned toward Berlin, and as a result of its hostility to London, Paris, and Geneva, it will abandon its defence of Austria to get closer to Germany."[24]

On 18 March 1938 Hitler's forces entered Vienna. Mussolini bowed his head and did not act. He delivered a pitiful speech in the Chamber in which he contradicted his previous solemn affirmations and tried to explain and legitimize Germany's actions. The Chamber then offered the contemptible spectacle of giving Il Duce's speech thunderous applause.

This background casts a grim light on the warning signals that led to the war of the Axis.[25]

---

[24] F. Charles-Roux, *Huit ans au Vatican* (Paris, 1947), 117.

[25] The term indicates the so-called Axis Powers – Germany, Italy, and Japan – united by a military alliance that provoked the Second World War against the United Kingdom and France, which were later joined by the USA and USSR, as well as secondary powers, co-belligerent nations, and satellite states.

The Year 1939

A MUTE PROTEST   10 FEBRUARY 1939
The body of Pius XI lay in state at St Peter's in the days following his death on 10 February 1939. On 12 February a sea of people visited the great basilica. The square was packed, yet nobody actually invited these crowds. Piety propelled them, but it was also the desire to offer a tacit demonstration against Fascist discipline, which took away liberty and offended human dignity. Pius XI had been the only person in Italy who could stand up to Mussolini, and the people knew it. Being barred from protesting, they wanted at least to vent their feelings by lifting their spirits toward the serene vision of peace, of which the Pope is the most legitimate and holy guardian.

The world is tired and disillusioned. After the Great War of 1914–18, all the promises and hopes of peace, justice, and well-being for the most suffering classes were betrayed. The human conscience revolts against the horrors of Bolshevik cruelty and against all tyrannies. In the name of freedom of the people, Nazism has established a hypocritical and far-ranging form of religious persecution. Dictatorships that once seemed temporarily necessary to re-establish order against social breakdown have become embittered and inflexible instead of evolving toward the law. The will of millions of people do not count. All that counts is the absolute will of a few.

FIRST AUDIENCE OF HIS HOLINESS PIUS XII 15 MARCH 1939
The Holy Father Pius XII received me with great and simple kindness. He seemed truly to be *Pastor angelicus*. He told me with great humility that he feels the entire weight of the formidable ministry which Divine

Providence has entrusted to him. I told him, "Holy Father, the entire world is praying for Your Holiness. And you can rely on the loyalty of the bishops and clergy, who have never been more united with the Pope than at this time." He was pleased about the promise of prayers. Turning to the dark situation in the world, I told him, "The world is falling apart, Holy Father; the only thing that remains is the Church, which is more solid than ever." The Pope replied, "In fact the reconstruction of order cannot be completed except on the foundation of the Gospel."

I reported on the work of the Congregation for the Propagation of the Faith and told him that this very day I was going to meet with the Hon. Cini to discuss the Catholic exhibition at the Universal Exposition.[1] The Holy Father replied that we should continue to work on what his predecessor had approved. He suggested that, while admitting the need to be modern, one should take care not to bring the Church of Saints Peter and Paul into the excesses of twentieth-century art forms, because sacred art had to serve devotional purposes and should not offend either the decorum of the faith or the *sensus fidelium*. I assured him on this point, adding that the plans for the church drawn up by the architect Foschini[2] were animated by a sense of refreshing modernity which conserved the high decorum and sacred character of a worthy place of worship.

AT ST PETER'S   9 APRIL 1939
In today's solemn celebration of Easter, at St Peter's, His Holiness addressed the world with the words of the Redeemer: "*Pax vobis. Largietur ille nobis quaemadmodum pollicitus es pacem, pacem suam, eam inquimus, quam mundus dare non potest, pacem*" [Jn. 14:27].[3]

---

[1] Count Vittorio Cini was the commissioner of the Universal Exposition. The exhibition would only be realized in 1950, when it was transformed into the Missionary Art Exhibition and officially opened by the Hon. Alcide De Gasperi, head of the Italian government.

[2] The architect Arnaldo Foschini (1884–1968), a university professor, was in charge of the plans for the church to which Costantini refers – the Church of Saints Peter and Paul – in the EUR district in Rome.

[3] The Easter homily of Pius XII is reproduced in AAS 31 (*Bollettino Ufficiale della Santa Sede*, 1939), 145–51. The passage in question can be found on page 148 and is translated as "Peace I leave with you, my peace I give unto you: not as the world giveth, do I give unto you." [All biblical citations are according to the Douay-Rheims translation of the Bible.]

MEETING OF THE FIDES AGENCY[4]   25 MAY 1939
[Translater's note: Fides is an Information Service of the Pontifical
Mission Societies.]

2 JUNE 1939
Today the Holy Father reminded the Sacred College of Cardinals of his
paternal concerns and initiatives "for a stable peace that will preserve
freedom and the honour of nations."[5]

THE HOLY FATHER'S SORROWFUL APPEAL
MURLIS DI ZOPPOLA, 24 AUGUST 1939
My brother Mons. Giovanni, bishop of La Spezia,[6] and I are at our
home in Murlis [Pordenone] for a brief period of rest. This fertile

---

[4] The text is not reproduced here because it was published in C. Costantini,
Ultime Foglie ... on p. 194. The passage explores the organization of the Fides
Agency, its mandate for the diffusion of missionary news and ideas, and the fact
that it comprised seven priests from six nations. It originated and continues to
operate under the Congregation for the Evangelization of Peoples (originally
called the Sacred Congregation *di Propaganda Fide*). In contemporary times
it operates as an international press agency across all media and information
platforms.

[5] This speech is published in *Discorsi e Radiomessaggi di Sua Santità Pio XII*,
vol. I (Milan: Società Editrice Vita e Pensiero, 1941), 151–5.

[6] Giovanni Costantini (1880–1956), born in Castions, Zoppola (Pordenone),
was a grammar-schooled graduate of the Diocesan Seminary of Concordia in
Portogruaro, after which he transferred to Rome for theological studies. Based
in the Diocese of Venice, he was ordained a priest on 18 March 1905. He
taught sacred scripture, archaeology, art, and patristics in the Patriarchal Seminary in Venice. Costantini was secretary to Cardinal Pietro La Fontaine, patriarch of Venice, and directed *Arte cristiana*, which is based in Milan and was
founded by his brother Celso in 1913. He also headed two institutions founded
by his brother Celso when the latter left for China to become the apostolic
delegate there: L'Opera di soccorso per le chiese rovinate dalla guerra [Foun-
dation for the Assistance of Churches Damaged by the War] and the Istituto
Filippo Neri per i figli della guerra (Philip Neri Institute for Orphans of the
War]. On 28 January 1927 he was appointed apostolic administrator for
the Dioceses of Sarzana and Brugnato, in Liguria, with the object of uniting
the two dioceses – a project that was accomplished with the publication of the

countryside radiates a great sense of peace. Our farmers tended to their work with their usual rhythm, but their spirits were troubled. "Are we heading toward war?" is their worried question. On 28 August we heard the mournful voice of the Pope: "The danger is imminent, but there is still time. Nothing is lost with peace, but everything can be lost with war ... Let the strong listen, so that they may not become weak through injustice. Let the powerful listen if they want their power to lead not to destruction but to support their people and safeguard tranquility in both justice and work. We beg them, in the name of the blood of Christ, whose worldly conquering power was gentleness in life and death."[7]

My brother and I looked at each other silently with anguished hearts: "We must leave." The next morning he left for La Spezia and I left for Rome. The Pope's fatherly and noble words struck an emotional chord in the hearts of the people, who see the Vatican as a great high barrier against whose ramparts break the frothy waves of humanity's tempests. But the Pope's warning was not heeded by those in power ... *tenebrae factae sunt super universam terram* [Mt. 27:45].[8]

To understand how these events unfolded, we have to go back to the recent past. On 26 March 1939 Mussolini delivered an address in Bari that contained the following mad assertions: "We consider perpetual peace a catastrophe for human civilization. My command is this: More artillery, more ships, and more airplanes, at whatever cost, by whatever means, even if we have to completely erase what we call civil life." *Completely erase civil life?* Never, to my knowledge, has a politician uttered such stupid, impudent, and harmful words. If occasionally war is a sad but terrible necessity, it is to protect civil life. The body does

---

apostolic constitution *Universi Dominici gregis* of 12 January 1929. That document brought into being the new consolidated diocese of La Spezia–Sarzana–Brugnato, with Giovanni Costantini as its first bishop (15 March 1929). On 26 July 1943 he was called to Rome to lead the Central Pontifical Commission for Sacred Art in Italy and was elevated to titular archbishop of Colosse. He died in Rome on 17 May 1956. He is buried in the crypt of the Cathedral of Christ the King at La Spezia. The crypt was built in his memory as the first pastor of the diocese.

7 Pius XII, "Nucius radiofonicus," in AAS 31 (*Bollettino Ufficiale della Santa Sede*, 1939), 334. The entire speech is on pages 333–5.

8 The expression is found in the recounting of Christ's passion: "there was darkness over the whole earth."

not exist for the pleasure of conducting surgery on it; but a surgical operation is occasionally necessary for the health of the body. It seems that Mussolini's psychological state has descended into a form of obsession.

What is also immensely sad and humiliating for Italy is the acquiescence of the press, a sort of criminal conspiracy of silence. How far we have fallen! Not one newspaper that I know of raised its voice against this criminal call to war.

31 AUGUST 1939

Cardinal Maglione,[9] secretary of state, delivered a message to the ambassadors of Italy, France, Germany, and Poland and to the minister of Great Britain, which read in part: "The Holy Father does not wish to minimize the hope that current negotiations may result in a just and peaceful solution, for which the entire world ceaselessly implores. His Holiness therefore entreats, in the name of God, the governments of Germany and Poland to do everything possible to avoid any incident and to abstain from taking any measure that might aggravate current tensions. He asks the governments of England, France, and Italy to support this request.[10]

In delivering this venerable document, His Eminence the Cardinal requested that the Most Excellent Heads of Mission take this message to their respective governments as quickly as possible and strongly commend to them this new and urgent invitation of His Holiness.

30 SEPTEMBER 1939

Assembly of the staff of Propaganda [Fide] and the Society for Missionary Cooperation. I urged them once again to use the greatest caution: to be innocent as doves and wise as serpents.

[9] Luigi Maglione (1887–1944), born in Casoria, Naples, was apostolic nuncio to Switzerland and then to France. He was made a cardinal in 1935 by Pius XI and became secretary of state in 1939, thus succeeding Eugenio Pacelli, who went on to become pope. Maglione was Pius XII's closest collaborator during the Second World War until his death in his hometown on 22 August 1944.

[10] The Pope's message is reproduced in *Le Saint Siège et la guerre en Europe. Mars 1939 – Août 1940*, vol. I of *Actes et documents du Saint Siège relatifs à la seconde guerre mondiale* (Vatican City: Libreria Editrice Vaticana, 1970), 271.

30 SEPTEMBER 1939

These are sad and dark hours. It seems as if a darkness of the spirit has spread across the land, thirsty for blood. Yesterday, the papers announced the dissolution of Poland and its partition between Germany and Russia. It is an injustice. It is a crime against law, against promises made, and against life. Every principle of justice has been trampled. It is even deprived of the least element of guilt for the crime itself.

Germany has vociferously denounced the Treaty of Versailles, and it is true that it was an unfair treaty. Russia boasted about its program of human solidarity and social justice. All this is now utterly crushed. Germany and Russia are committing a massive act of brigandage that exceeds even the injustices of Versailles. And the press remains silent. Only the *Avvenire d'Italia*[11] showed a hint of sympathy and voiced a hope for Poland's resurrection. It was announced that today the Vatican would meet with a delegation of Poles. They will hear some words of comfort from He who, like Christ, has words of eternal life.

It is a truly tragic time. It seems that we are participating in the collapse of so-called civilization. Our civilization has alienated itself from the spirit of Christ and returned us to the status of cavemen. The *homo homini lupus* [man is a wolf to his fellow man] has become much more wild and ferocious than ever. Not only does he have the club to strike with and teeth with which to devour the enemy, but he also has at his disposal all the scientific knowledge that has produced instruments of destruction. This is no longer civilization, much less Christian civilization. This is refined barbarism that is sustained by one thing: brutal egotism – unquenchable and bereft of any decency. Christ has been abandoned, and we are reaping a most bitter harvest as a result.

2 OCTOBER 1939

Mr Hsu Dau-Cin, the Chinese chargé d'affaires to Italy, came to see me today. He asked me to see whether the Holy See could promote peace between China and Japan. We must encourage the United States to mediate and stand beside it with our moral support: "China and Japan are weary. Russian policy has created a new situation in the Far East. Peace

---

[11] The Catholic Daily *L'Avvenire d'Italia* was founded in 1896 and based in Bologna. The paper is the oldest Catholic Christian daily published in Italy. Later, Pope Paul VI merged it (on 4 December 1968) with the Milan-based Catholic daily *L'Italia* to create *Avvenire*, headquartered in Milan.

has to be negotiated in a spirit of collaboration between Japan and China, 'saving face' – that is, maintaining the honour of both parties so that there are no winners and no losers. Today, in fact, we have reached this point because Japan could not conquer China, nor has China succeeded in driving Japan back."

29 OCTOBER 1939

The Chinese chargé d'affaires is most grateful for the Holy Father's paternal concern in favour of peace. He also appreciated the favourable disposition of [President] Roosevelt.

31 OCTOBER 1939[12]

Today, the same chargé d'affaires came to inform me that he had conveyed Roosevelt's response to his government and that his government had directed him to convey to the Holy Father its great respect and sincere gratitude. The Americans think, however, that Japan at the moment is not disposed to accept mediation.

PIUS XII'S FIRST ENCYCLICAL
FEAST OF CHRIST THE KING, 29 OCTOBER 1939

Two days ago, Pius XII's first encyclical was released. It is a magnificent document, clear and complete, and one that puts the Church above this low and dark human horizon. It sheds light on the true and divine meaning of life and on the salvific teaching of the Holy Church. They are words of instruction and words of warning for everyone. The encyclical gives one a kind of holy pride in belonging to the Church, to this divine institution that is more alive and more solid than ever. The political crisis of civilization has produced an admirable testimony of the values of the Church. This crisis appears to be a kind of earthquake that upsets and reduces a splendid city to ruins. In the vast, smouldering ruins, the only thing standing is the Church. The victims direct their eyes and their spirits toward that image of salvation.

29 OCTOBER 1939

Last night I passed in front of the Porta Pia with the engineer Milani. There is a plaque that proclaims the "free conscience of a free Italy" in

---

[12] It appears here (out of chronological order) in the original diary.

opposition to papal Rome. "Now," the engineer remarked, "if you want a little liberty, you actually have to go looking for it in the Vatican."

THE CONSECRATION OF MISSIONARY BISHOPS

29 OCTOBER 1939

The ceremony was held in St Peter's with all its ritual majesty. Mons. Streicher[13] and I assisted. The bishops came from seven countries and were heading for distant missions in Africa and the Far East. In the prayers, the era of the early Church came to life again, but not in an archaeological sense; rather, full of life and momentum, like an abundant and majestic torrent. It has remote ancient origins but flows rich, alive, and productive, satisfying the thirst of past, present, and future generations with its waters and giving life on its banks to flowers of eternal springtime.

At the point in the liturgy when the Pope and the bishops bow their heads with clasped hands, one conjures up, on the altar, the whole world both near and far: the Pope in his heart bringing universality, and each bishop in his heart bringing his own missions. You could also catch glimpses of a marvellous panorama of people filing past from distant lands – white, black, yellow – dressed in all kinds of fashion, speaking all kinds of different languages, nourished by various and different civilizations. Everything, however, came together at the altar.

The Pope personally gave communion to the twelve bishops. I thought to myself: They belong to countries that are at war with each other, but they drink from the same chalice, they eat of the same Eucharistic bread, a marvellous symbol of unity … *unus panis, unus corpus multi sumus, omnes qui de uno pane participamus*[14] [1 Cor. 10:17]. When the graduates of the Collegio Urbano filed past bearing the offertory gifts that the bishops would present to the Pope, you could see passing before you young devoted representatives of the races of the world. All the racial barriers come tumbling down before the altar of Christ. What majesty, what greatness, when compared to the anti-human diatribes and racial persecution!

---

[13] Henri Streicher (1863–1952), originally from the Diocese of Strasbourg, was a missionary in Africa, titular archbishop of Brisi and vicar apostolic emeritus of Uganda.

[14] "For we, being many, are one bread, one body, all that partake of one bread."

When we accompanied the Holy Father back to the Vatican, we stopped at the altar of St Peter – a deeply moving occasion. Mons. Respighi[15] sang the antiphon, *"Salvam fac populum tuum, Domine."*[16] The Cardinals replied, *"Deus meus, sperantem in Te."*[17] The Pope recited the *Oremus* for peace.

THE FEAST OF ALL SAINTS   1 NOVEMBER 1939
It is the feast of souls, living and dead, who encounter each other in the great immortal meeting place, at the foot of the altar. It is a feast of love that embraces the whole of humanity. But in what times are we celebrating? This Feast of All Saints very vividly and strikingly calls to mind images of the same feast day in 1917, when, in the defeat of Caporetto, I was travelling through Concordia Sagittaria, my parish. The town was in a state of panic and bewilderment, anxiety and confusion. The night before, I had seen from the bell tower bursts of flame from exploding enemy bombs at Portogruaro, while the dark, flashing sky was full of the sinister drone of airplanes. On the morning of All Saints, I celebrated mass in the cathedral, but the people, even though they were very devout, went in and out of the church as if they were captives of dark dismay without knowing where to turn. Leave? Stay? Will the enemy come today?

Twenty-two years have passed and Europe is still without peace. It is still torn apart by war and the fear of war. Why? Because Versailles established a peace that was not Christian but instead was inspired by egotism and the interests of the victors – and therefore was built on precarious foundations and undermined by subterranean currents. *Nisi Dominus aedificaverit domum, in vanum labouraverun qui aedificant eam*[18] [Ps. 126:1]. The invincible principles of justice and charity cannot be crushed with impunity. They form the only solid foundation of civilization. Benedict XV proposed a humanitarian peace, formulating those Christian principles of equity that were later taken up by Wilson.[19] He

[15] Carlo Respighi, prefect of Pontifical Ceremonies.
[16] "Save your people, Oh Lord."
[17] "My God, our hope is in Thee."
[18] "Unless the Lord build the house, they labour in vain that build it."
[19] Thomas Woodrow Wilson (1856–1924), jurist, Democrat, and president of the United States for two terms (1913–21). Wilson maintained the US's neutrality at the beginning of the First World War, intervening in 1917. He worked hard to realize a peace based on his famous fourteen points. The

brought those principles like merchandise from America onto the green carpet of the conference at Versailles; but Lloyd George and Clemenceau tore it to pieces like waste paper and threw it in the garbage.

But Benedict XV also said, "Nations do not die." You see that, as always, time has vindicated the Pope. He lives again today in the person of Pius XII. The new pope, however, does not take comfort from this high spiritual vindication. Saddened and imploring, he turns to face the horrendous spectacle of a superb civilization that is devouring itself. Why is this war being waged? Why are we throwing Europe into the abyss? Why do we deploy all the instruments of our civilization to destroy, to gratify, these sophisticated barbarisms that outstrip in both horror and cruelty all the barbarism of so-called savages? They say, "Why can't we have faith in the words of Hitler, and why can't we admit that Germany is making itself master of all of Europe?" This much is true: we cannot believe Hitler, who has ruthlessly crushed the principles that until yesterday he had preached, much less his solemn promises. We are face to face with a new Genghis Khan,[20] a new Tambourlaine.[21] Hitler deserves no confidence. Besides, he even assassinated some of his earliest collaborators. He railed against Versailles and then suppresses Czechoslovakia and Poland. He rose up against communism, and then embraced an alliance with Russia, throwing Europe's doors wide open to Bolshevik propaganda. All of this is, unfortunately, true; and it is very sad.

But the war being waged today is, if we can simplify the workings in order to get to the crux of the matter, a fight between Germany and England – a fight in which Europe itself is in play. We have essentially come back to where we were in 1914. At that time, Belgium offered England the opportunity to intervene; today, it's poor Poland. Of course,

---

Wilson Plan ran aground at Versailles, especially in the face of opposition from Britain and France. He was also a passionate advocate of the League of Nations.

[20] Genghis Khan, a nickname meaning "universal prince" inherited from Temuein (1155–1226), was a Mongol conqueror. Under his leadership his army established a vast and sprawling empire that included China, Turkestan, Persia, and Afghanistan.

[21] Timur Leng (1336–1405), or Tambourlaine as transliterated, was a Muslim leader who created a huge Asian empire, with Samarkand as its capital. After conquering Persia, Mesopotamia, Anatolia, and India, he set his sights on China, but ultimately in vain.

if one has to choose between the hegemony of Hitler's Germany or England, many believe that for us it's better to side with England, because Germany weighs heavily on Italy's shoulders and because the German style is harsher than the English style. In the overseas missions, it is England that treats our missionaries with the most open spirit possible. The Germans have made it clear that, if they emerge victorious, they will actively block Catholic missions.

Moreover, from the moment that France allied with England, we have been obligated to stand beside France. With Versailles, France has committed several political injustices against Italy, but it is a nation of great and generous spirit, capable of understanding the wrongs committed against Italy. It is, moreover, a nation with whom we share an affinity, not only because of a shared classical culture but also because of a great religious sensibility. Like Italy and Spain, France is the homeland of many saints. It will be a sad day indeed if we are compelled to descend into war against the French. God save us from this and other wars, because all of them are set against Christian civilization.

Then there is a horrible doubt about the conflict that has just begun. Who will win? What if England and France end up as losers? Both sides think they will win. But faith is not enough to win, and neither is the potential to win. Napoleon fell just when he thought he had victory within his grasp. But there are yet worse things to contemplate. There is the sneering spectre of communism. If the war lasts a year or two years, it's likely that the winner will be neither Germany nor England and France; it will, at least partly, be communism. It seems to be a sadly logical outcome. The anguish of a long war exasperates the multitudes and throws them into a type of desperation. They say, "Here is where our leaders have taken us. Let's rebel. It is we who pay with our own blood, we should govern ourselves." This reasoning has a depressing logic to it. But its conclusion represents a terrible illusion. But it is often grand illusions that move the multitudes. It is an illusion because it is never the people who govern. It is an elite that seizes power in its name. The names change and things remain as they were before, if they don't get worse. Russia under the Czar was not a worse tyranny than the one that governs now. The war, therefore, whatever its outcome, will only encourage the revolt of the nations. That revolt means opening wide the doors to an abyss directly in the path of Christian civilization. It is because of this possibility that I, personally, deplore the fact that there was no will to call a conference before the hostilities began. To be sure, that conference could not be held because of Hitler's program, but it seems that it might have been possible to accept at least the principle of encountering one another. At least the roles might have been reversed, and Hitler could not later have claimed that he had offered peace but England and France had refused to accept it. Besides, one small point may be conceded to Germany. A population of 80 million cannot be suffocated. Why wasn't the possibility of restoring the colonies to Germany ever discussed?

For Italy, it is a great blessing that, for now, she is not hitched to Germany's wagon. Let's pray to God that she doesn't get caught up in the vortex. Somebody told me that Mussolini recently said, "Let the Saxons of the land fight it out with the Saxons of the sea." Replying to England's question of whether he was for England or against England, it is reported that Mussolini replied, "I am against everybody."

7 DECEMBER 1939

Today the Holy Father received in solemn audience Dr Dino Alfieri,[22] the new Italian ambassador. His Holiness responded as follows to the ambassador's words: "The approval with which Your Excellency graciously received the fundamental concepts of Our recent encyclical – for the tranquility and fraternal union of souls and for peace with justice – inspires in Us the cheerful hope that the concerns that motivated such a noble purpose will always find faithful resonance in the valiant, strong, and industrious Italian people."[23] It was observed that the Pope did not refer to the government, but to the "valiant, strong, and industrious Italian people." In fact, how could he possibly have faith in Mussolini, who just eight months earlier had said that with war they could achieve a *tabula rasa* of civil life?

[22] Edoardo "Dino" Alfieri (1886–1966), born in Bologna, was a politician and diplomat. Elected to parliament in 1924, he served in various capacities as under-secretary in various ministries. He was appointed minister of popular culture in 1937 and became Italy's ambassador to the Holy See in 1939. A year later, he became Italy's ambassador to Germany. A member of the Grand Council of Fascism, he voted against Mussolini in July 1943. He was condemned to death in absentia in 1944. He returned to Italy from Switzerland in 1947.

[23] Pius XII, "Allocuzione," in AAS 31 (*Bollettino Ufficiale della Santa Sede*, 1939), 704–6.

THE SOVEREIGNS OF ITALY VISIT THE SUPREME PONTIFF
21 DECEMBER 1939
This was a great occasion. Pius XII addressed paternal words[24] to
Their Majesties the King [Victor Emmanuel III] and Queen [Elena of
Montenegro] of Italy. Filippo Meda[25] wrote a wonderful piece in
L'Italia of Milan today, which constituted a noble political testament.
Three days later, the old warrior passed away.

THE CHRISTMAS MESSAGE OF THE HOLY FATHER PIUS XII
24 DECEMBER 1939
Today I attended the audience in which the Sacred College of Cardinals
and the Roman prelature presented their good wishes to the Holy Father.
A melancholy shadow weighed on everybody's spirit, in contrast to
the joyfulness of the ceremony and the magnificent and austere dignity
of the Consistory. I relate here some passages of Pius XII's admirable
address and the supreme principles on which a future peace may rest:
"With inexpressible anguish, for four months I have been observing this
war, launched and carried out in such singular circumstances, piling ruin
upon tragic ruin. If until now – with the exception of the bloody soil of
Poland and Finland – the number of victims have possibly been lower
than We feared, the sum total of pain and sacrifice has reached the point
of causing great anxiety to those who worry for the future economic,
social, and spiritual state of Europe, and not just Europe."
    He went on to outline the fundamental basics for the peaceful
coexistence of nations: 1. The right of nations to exist; 2. Disarmament;
3. Institutions that safeguard and guarantee treaties; 4. Equitable reception of the just request of nations. 5: A high sense of responsibility on the
part of government leaders. The Holy Father continued: "Even the best
rules will be imperfect and definitely condemned to failure if those who
guide the destinies of the people, and the people themselves, do not
allow themselves to be infused more and more by that spirit that
can exclusively breathe life, authority, and duty into the dead-letter

---

[24] AAS 31 (Bollettino Ufficiale della Santa Sede, 1939), 708–9.

[25] Filippo Meda (1869–1939), journalist, Catholic politician, and banker,
was one of the founders of the Università Cattolica del Sacro Cuore di Milano.
He resigned his directorship from the Banca Popolare di Milano in a strong
protest against the policies and actions of Mussolini's Partito Nazionale Fascista
[PNF; National Fascist Party].

paragraphs of international arrangements." The Pope's words were greeted with tremendous approval around the world. But the avalanche of war, once it begins, does not stop.

Appointment of a Personal Representative of President Roosevelt to the Holy See

The *New York Times* of 28 December writes, "The Pope and the President are the spokesmen for peace who have the most influence in the world. If the closer ties that the President intends to establish with the Holy Father can result in a common expression of their shared ideals and launch the start of a timely and parallel action, we cannot possibly doubt the efficacy of their efforts."

THE POPE'S VISIT TO THE KING   28 DECEMBER 1939
A luminous day today that clarifies the past and projects rays of joy and hope toward the future, even if the sky is a little cloudy. The Holy Father Pius XII went to the Quirinale. I saw him pass by, smiling and blessing people, from the loggia of Santa Caterina in Via Nazionale. All along the route the people cordially cheered him. Pius XII, accompanied by the Royals of Italy and the impressive procession of the two courts, entered first into the Pauline Chapel and stopped to adore the Blessed Sacrament. On the altar were the relics of the blessed of the House of Savoy and the golden roses donated by the Popes to the Queens of Savoy.

He then entered the throne room. The words addressed to the King were stupendous: this speech was a masterwork of solid beauty; it was as lovely and solid as the entrance to a great castle full of history, within which the rites of hospitality close one period of life and open a new one. The Pope said, "The Vatican and the Quirinale, divided by the Tiber, are united in the bonds of peace with the remembrance of the religion of Our fathers and forefathers. The waves of the Tiber have swept away and buried in the deep churning waters of the Tyrrhenian Sea the hostile swells and surges of the past. Those waves have allowed olive branches to blossom on its banks." Today, in this splendid hall, for the first time in decades, the hand of a Roman pope is raised in a benedictory sign of peace. Italy watches and rejoices. The Catholic world watches and rejoices, and it even seems as if the two Princes of the Apostles who are seated motionless at the entrance of this place are pleased to see the dawn of this new era.

These Princes of the Apostles at the entrance of the Quirinale have been waiting for this day, because the worldly obstruction of temporal power had in the end to give the Church the freedom to act and raise herself in the eyes of the world above all earthly kingdoms. Today, the king of a small state did not visit the king of another: it was the King of Souls who visited.

Today's ceremony demonstrates just how immensely far we have come in recent times as a result of a certain maturity of ideas and accomplishments and as a result of the far-sightedness of Pius XI and Mussolini. It is a pity that Mussolini has been more opportunistic than sincere; nevertheless, this great event is one of Mussolini's honourable accomplishments. Never has the Church appeared more dynamic, more steady, and more divine than in recent times, even as we witness the ruin of a materialist civilization, as Europe is shaken by a political earthquake that has already caused so much death and so many ruins.

30 DECEMBER 1939

Senator Salata[26] wrote to me: "I feel the need to open up to you and to express my profound satisfaction as a Catholic and as an Italian for such auspicious events. They are very positive omens for the new year, so filled with possible destinies, that we will be able to confront them with a serene spirit."

How hilarious and pathetic these puffed-up, arrogant Masons from before the last war are! On 20 December 1920 Nathan, mayor of Rome and grand master of the Masons, declared in a speech, heavy with rhetoric, that he made in front of the Porta Pisa, that the Church could be compared to a meteor that had had moments of splendour, but then began to break up and would ultimately disappear. It all seems like a dream... Thank God for giving us the grace to see the Church triumph

[26] Francesco Salata (1876–1944) was a politician, diplomat, historian, Italian irredendist, and pre-Fascist liberal. By origin a Giulian [that is, from the region of Venezia Giulia around Trieste], Salata was born in Ossero on the island of Cherso when the territory was part of the Austro-Hungarian Empire. In 1920 he participated in the negotiations that led to the Treaty of Rapallo. He was then elected senator and became councillor of state and head of the Central Office for the New Provinces belonging to the regions of Trentino–Alto Adige and Venezia Giulia. He was also minister plenipotentiary of Italy in Vienna. Salata published numerous works of an historical nature.

over all its growling enemies, both large and small. That's how Hitler also will end up, and the Church will remain stronger than ever.

Mussolini did not attend the papal visit to the King. This is strange, but I think can be attributed to the fact that he never wants to put himself in a subordinate position. Vanity is a small and miserable thing that makes men small, even if they take their place on high. Mussolini has never paid a visit to the new pope. The son of a blacksmith can sometimes be a gentleman; Mussolini is not. A Chinese proverb states, "You cannot turn yourself into either a tree or a gentleman."

The Year 1940

THE HOLY FATHER PIUS XII TO ROOSEVELT 7 JANUARY 1940
The Holy Father responded as follows to President Roosevelt's message[1] sent on the occasion of the Christmas holidays: "As Vicar on Earth of the Prince of Peace, from the beginning of Our Pontificate we have dedicated Our efforts and Our concerns to the objective of maintaining peace and for its re-establishment. Heedless of temporary setbacks and difficulties, We continue to proceed on the path indicated by Our apostolic mission. On this often-bitter and thorny journey, the echoes that join me are those of countless people inside and outside the Church, and this gives me an ample and consoling recompense that my duty is accomplished.[2]

The Support of the President of the French Chamber of Deputies
On 11 January 1940 Monsieur Herriot[3] gave a speech to the Chamber in which he said, "Our conception of peace corresponds to the noble thoughts expressed by Pope Pius XII on Christmas Eve."

---

[1] Message of the President of the United States to the Pope, 23 December 1939, reprinted in *Le Saint Siège et la guerre en Europe, Mars 1939 – Août 1940* of *Actes et documents du Saint Siège relatifs à la seconde guerre mondiale* (Vatican City: Libreria Editrice Vaticana, 1970), 348–50.

[2] Pius XII, Letter to the President of the United States of America, in AAS 32 (*Bollettino Ufficiale della Santa Sede*,1940), 46. The text of the letter in English with Italian translation is reprinted on pages 43–7.

[3] Édouard Herriot (1872–1957), French politician, leader of the Radical Party, senator (1912–19), was consistently re-elected as deputy (1919–40), and

One could not have wished for a more supportive recognition than that of the President of the Chamber, leader of the Radical Party, and former leader of the Left.[4]

A few days ago I saw Count Galeazzo Ciano,[5] minister of external affairs. I found him to be easy and cordial, just as he was in China. I told him that one should not have pursued this war, because the victor would likely be neither Germany nor England: the victor will be Russia – that is to say, communism. He replied, "No. In a war like this there will be a victor and a vanquished, but most likely there will be two vanquished powers. The Church is the one that will prevail."[6]

---

from 1946 until his death. He was a minister in various governments of the Third Republic and was three times elected prime minister. President of the Chamber of Deputies (1925–28) and from 1936 to the fall of the Third Republic in July 1940, he was elected president of the National Assembly in 1947 and served until 1954. He was mayor of Lyon (1905–57), with the exception of the wartime period (1940–45).

[4] CC: F. Charles-Roux, *Huit ans au Vatican: 1932–1940* (Paris: Flammarion, 1947), 364.

[5] Galeazzo Ciano (1903–44), son of Constanzo (an admiral and politician), was a diplomat and politician during the Fascist period. In 1930 he was consul general at Shanghai and then minister plenipotentiary of Italy in China. In that capacity he met Celso Costantini, the first apostolic delegate to China, as Costantini himself wrote in his book *With the Missionaries in China* [*Con i Missionari in Cina*], vol. 2 (Rome: Unione missionaria del clero in Italia, 1947), 372–3. The two maintained contact and regularly exchanged correspondence. Count Galeazzo became Mussolini's son-in-law, having married Il Duce's daughter Edda. In 1935 he was appointed minister of popular culture and the following year minister of external affairs. In 1943 he became ambassador to the Holy See. In July of that same year he voted in favour of the overthrow of Mussolini in the Grand Council of Fascism, an action that led a special tribunal at Verona to condemn him to death. He was executed on 11 January 1944.

[6] CC: "Yes, Rome has won, but not the Rome of Mussolini: Christian Rome has won: its victory was not as a result of fratricidal arms but a victory of the spirit."

1 FEBRUARY 1940

Il Messaggero[7] published the following notice: "While the German soldier spills his blood for the defence of Italian soil and by so doing prevents the even greater devastation of Italian territory that is inevitably provoked by the war's advance, the great majority of the population of Rome has not yet understood the gravity of the situation caused by the proximity of the front."

But no! The people of Rome are not so stupid as to think that "the German soldier spills his blood for the defence of Italian soil." The Germans and the Allies are waging a "real war," and unfortunately Italy has to suffer the consequences.

4 FEBRUARY 1940

The dread overwhelming Italy as a result of the war weighs on minds here like a nightmare. The horizon is dark and menacing, as when a thunderstorm approaches. Our spirits are troubled and depressed. The organization of the party mobilizes around Mussolini and in a certain sense keeps him prisoner. The public is tired. They see certain merits in Mussolini, but they sense the lack of a feeling of confidence and serenity; they sense a lack of proper respect for human dignity. That dignity demands an honest use of liberty. It was to be hoped that the Fascist dictatorship would evolve into a regular form of governance in which the nation could freely express its own thoughts. Instead, this dictatorship has hardened and is becoming a tyranny. Who can succeed the dictator?

There is widespread malaise and discontent. The power of the Masons has been overthrown, but the favouritism of the party has replaced it, and a frightening corruption is spreading. The Empire has been created, but the financial structure of the nation has been shattered. The veins of taxpayers are sucked ... Taxes drain the veins of taxpayers, and then millions are squandered on unnecessary things: for example, many millions for German uniforms for clerical workers, fabulous salaries for certain party officials – some have an annual salary of over a million lire!

---

7 *Il Messaggero* was founded in 1878 and is still published. It is considered the "historical" daily newspaper of Rome and it has the greatest circulation in the Italian capital.

What is more, one has the contradiction and the doubly serious useless expense of the prefects and the *Federali*.[8] Aren't prefects enough?

There is discipline, but it is a discipline on the outside only, insincere and not actually felt. All of the newspapers are the same and all of them take an eternally panegyric attitude toward Il Duce and toward Fascism. It's natural and human to make an occasional error in judgment, but the result is always the same: praise, praise, praise.

If a little reasonable freedom were permitted, it would be of the greatest service to the government and to Mussolini. He himself, when he was on trial before assuming power, said that an opposition was a necessary and precious thing for the government ... Now, if you talk, you are sent to prison. One can understand this in a time of war, in a time of revolution; but it cannot be a regular measure of a government. The unfortunate Pinetti, the administrator of *Pro Familia*, citizen, father, and otherwise harmless worker, was condemned to five years in prison for giving his opinion on union with Germany. And the Hon. Martire[9] was sent to prison for having made, in the halls of Parliament, a remark about Ciano that showed little respect. These methods invite a revolt, one that could favour communism. Rather than being a social or political theory, communism is often an explosion of the people's discontent and the desire to possess the riches of others and to avenge themselves against those currently privileged.

Days ago Mussolini, speaking with reference to the promulgation of the new code, said that justice is the foundation of civil life. Very true. The law is the instrument with which justice is exercised; this is defined as *cuique suum* [to each his own]. But today, what use is the law? In the Statute it says that everybody is equal before the law, but the Jews, born and raised under the aegis of the state have been abandoned and stripped of all the rights that the law conferred upon them. One cannot even say

---

[8] A federal secretary was appointed directly by Il Duce, on the recommendation of the secretary of the National Fascist Party, for every province of the kingdom.

[9] Egilberto Martire, Catholic politician, was a member of parliament for the Italian People's Party [Partito Popolare Italiano], founded by Father Luigi Sturzo, from whose ranks he was expelled in 1923. Re-elected in 1924 on a national party slate, Martire became a supporter of Fascism. He disappeared from the political scene because of his opposition to the racial laws proposed by Il Duce.

that the Senate voted for this racial law; it was passed under intimidation, which among other things does not reflect honourably on the Senate. Worse, with money you can obtain discriminatory decrees. I could name names, but I am afraid to write them down because if this diary falls into the hands of others, I would not want harm to come to these poor, discriminated Jews. Worse still, a racial tribunal has been established. A wife only has to declare to have had a son as a result of an adulterous affair to have that son declared Aryan. It is the height of immorality. Nobody believes these disgraceful declarations; they are made as a juridical subterfuge that dishonours Fascist society. The Honourable Jung,[10] a convert from Judaism, told me, almost in tears, how this tragedy of disgraceful declarations anguished his conscience. He could have had recourse to this ignoble trick to save his two nephews, but he refused.

Is this civilization? All this is due to Hitler, who wants to replace religion with the myth of bloodline. Mussolini is Hitler's prisoner and is enveloped in the clouds of a poisonous flattery that isolate him from external reality. "We cannot take it anymore," a prelate told me. This is the feeling of the great majority of Italians.

THE ANTICHRIST   12 FEBRUARY 1940

Hermann Rauschning,[11] former leader of the Danzig government's National Socialists, has published in France a book called *Hitler m'a dit* [Hitler told me]. Chapter 7, entitled "The Anti-Christ," contains the following declarations: "One evening, in the Chancellery building, there

---

[10] Guido Jung (1876–1949), born in Palermo to a prosperous Jewish family, supported Fascism and was elected as a Fascist member of parliament. He was minister of finance and the treasury between 1932 and 1935. Although denied any government role in 1938 in the wake of the racial laws, he later became under-secretary and then minister of finance and the treasury from 11 February to 17 April 1944.

[11] Hermann Rauschning (1887–1952), conservative politician, born in Thorun, was part of German National Socialism and governed the free city of Danzig. In that capacity he had numerous encounters and discussions with Hitler, which later became the subject of his publication *Hitler m'a dit* (Paris: Coopération, 1939), translated into English and German in 1940 – a translation made possible by his escape to the United State of America.

were in Hitler's apartments two Bavarian *Gauleiters*,[12] Streicher and Wagner, along with other people. It was on that occasion I began to understand what National Socialism was, and most of all what it wanted to become. Responding to Streicher, Hitler declared, 'Religions? They are all the same. None of them has a future, at least for Germans. Fascism can, if it wishes, make its peace with the Church. I would do that too. And why not? That will not stop me in any way from *extirpating Christianity from Germany*. Italians are primitives; they can be pagans and Christians at the same time. But the German is much more serious; he is either Christian or pagan, but not both.' But Hitler wanted us to become pagan and to substitute the Christian faith with Nazi neopaganism. 'We shall see,' he added, 'if they will remain faithful to the Judaeo-Christian religion and to a morality that serves God's mercy, or whether they are capable of embracing a new faith, strong and heroic, in an immanent God in nature and in the nation, inseparable from his blood and resurrection.'"

26 MARCH 1940

Today, in the home of the former ambassador [Vittorio] Cerruti,[13] I met Marquis Imperiali,[14] master of the Collare dell'Annunziata, who had

---

[12] *Gauleiters*: district governors, functionaries of the National Socialist Party.

[13] Vittorio Cerruti (1881–1961) was born in Novara and entered the diplomatic corps at a young age. He met Costantini during his stint in Beijing between 1921 and 1926 as a chargé d'affaires and then as minister plenipotentiary of Italy in China. A deep friendship developed between the two, based on mutual respect, as is evidenced by the more than seventy letters sent by the Italian diplomat to the cardinal and archived in the ASDCP. He served as ambassador in a number of prestigious postings: Moscow (1927–30), Rio di Janeiro (1930–32), Berlin (1932–35), and Paris (1935–37). He was retired in 1938 by External Affairs Minister Ciano. In 1946 he assumed the presidency of the Banca Popolare di Novara, a bank founded by his father. Cerruti is considered one of the most illustrious diplomats of his era, both for the objectivity of his judgment and for his extraordinary foresight.

[14] Guglielmo di Francavilla Imperiali (1858–1944), diplomat from a noble Genoese family, was Italy's ambassador to Constantinople (1904) and then to London (1910), where he assisted in the negotiations of the Treaty of London of 26 April 1915. At the end of the First World War he was a member of the Italian delegation at Geneva, on hand to sign the Treaty of Versailles of 28 June 1919.

been ambassador to London during the Great War of 1914–18, and Marquis Salvago Raggi,[15] who in China in 1901 signed the Boxers' protocol on behalf of Italy. Speaking of the gloomy political situation, Marquis Imperiali said that he puts his faith in God and therefore is optimistic: "Providence has always been kind to Italy. From the establishment of the Kingdom of Italy onward, we have seen the manifest hand of God, who has saved us from many perils. Italy is a country of believers, and thus the family is honoured and healthy."

28 MARCH 1940

Navy General Umberto Pugliese[16] came to see me today, an Israelite with a high religious sense who was baptized a number of years ago. As a result of the inauspicious racial laws, he was deposed from his high command in the navy. The navy lost one of its greatest minds in naval engineering. He is not bitter for his own position as much as for Italy's and for the suffering of the Jewish people. He told me: "Two men [Hitler and Mussolini] met on a train at the Brenner Pass; heavy curtains were drawn behind them. The fate of millions of people was being decided and even the fate of nations. But those millions of people do not know anything about it. [These two men] determine the people's destiny without their having the ability to express their own thoughts."

He represented Italy in the Council of the League of Nations in 1921, a position from which he resigned after the March on Rome (28 October 1922). A senator since 1913, he was given the Collare dell'Annunziata in 1932, the greatest honour bestowed by the House of Savoy.

[15] Giuseppe Salvago Raggi (1866–1946), a marquis, a native of Genoa, diplomat, and Italian politician, was minister plenipotentiary of Italy in China, where in 1900 he lived through the terrible experience of the Boxer assault on the foreign legations in Beijing. After serving in a diplomatic posting in Cairo, he was governor of Eritrea (1907–15). He was ambassador in Paris (1916–17) and in 1919 he represented the Italian government at the peace conference at Versailles and then, in 1921, served on the War Reparations Commission.

[16] Umberto Pugliese (1880–1961), general of the Italian Navy who designed new models of naval warships and the more efficient underwater protection system bearing his name. Between 1930 and 1934 he was director general of naval construction and machinery. He became minister of the navy and therefore head of the navy. Closely tied to Costantini because of their mutual esteem and friendship, he was tasked by the cardinal to examine this diary.

He referred to a saying of Scialoia that was making the rounds: "Mussolini is a superior man, but he lacks an economic sense, a legal sense, and a moral sense." So what's left?

29 MARCH 1940

A few days ago *Il Giornale d'Italia*[17] reported on the capitulation of Finland, with not one word against Russia's brutal aggression. In the world today there does not even exist the decency of a moral sense. Only force is appreciated, criminality writ large.

HITLER, THE LIAR   30 MARCH 1940

A typed booklet has come to my attention authored by Mr Thyssen,[18] the great German industrialist who in 1932, with Von Papen, Krupp, Von Bolen, and Von Schroeder, helped put the National Socialist Party in power. He says, "In the course of the many years during which I have been able to observe the Nazi regime – and I have had ample occasion to do so as a government adviser and economic director – I have concluded, with growing anxiety and ultimately true desperation, that I made a grave error. Hitler represents the worst type of vile liar, capable of denying to your face what he said, did, or swore to do the night before. For him, neither objective truth nor subjective truth exists; nor do tradition or European spirit. He knows no other idea than his own "I," which gets bigger every day, and as long as his power lasts he will know nothing but the folly of grandeur, brutality, and aggression."

Hitler's Germany

[In a speech] to the Free Church Council,[19] Chamberlain stated: "Each day that passes offers fresh evidence of the absolute disrespect of the

---

[17] The daily *Il Giornale d'Italia* was founded in Rome in 1901 as the national voice of the political Right. During and after the First World War it was one of the most read newspapers in Italy. During the Fascist period, it was made to serve the regime and thus gradually lost its credibility and circulation numbers. It stopped publication in 1976.

[18] Fritz Thyssen (1873–1951), son of August Thyssen, was founder of the great industrial family of the same name. Fritz Thyssen was, like his father, among the financiers and principal supporters of the party created by Hitler.

[19] The Free Church Federal Council was established in England in 1940 to promote cooperation between Protestant churches, the Methodist community, and others.

Germans for religion, piety, faith, and justice. If they triumph in what they are doing, every rampart that civilization has built on the principles of Christianity will be destroyed, and the world will fall back into the barbarism that just a short time ago we believed was buried by centuries of progress. But this will not come to pass."

The things Chamberlain says are true. But when the victors united at Versailles to dictate the terms of peace after the war of 1914–18, they allowed themselves to be guided by a spirit of vendetta, betraying any Christian value.[20]

19 APRIL 1940

I went to lunch at Faccini's place. The Hon A. De Stefani,[21] member of the Grand Council of Fascism, and the former prefect Maggioni were also in attendance. I said that if Italy were to enter the war alongside Germany, they would have to reckon with the opinions of the Italian bishops and clergy. For us, Hitler is a persecutor of religion. He is the Antichrist. Maggioni said that he had listened to a speech given by a parish priest in Veneto: "If I were prefect, I would have interned him. However, as a private individual, I shared the opinions expressed by the parish priest."

THE NOBLE SENTIMENTS OF A CONVERTED JEW

21 APRIL 1940

Professor Mario Conigliani, a converted Jew, deprived of his teaching duties and thrown out onto the street, has found comfort in his faith. He has sent me a note, part of which I report: "An hour can change an

---

[20] CC: L'Osservatore Romano, 18 April 1940.

[21] Alberto De Stefani (1876–1969), was an economist and politician originally from Verona. He was a Fascist member of parliament from 1921, minister of finance from 1922 to 1923, and from 1923 he headed the Treasury. As head of the Treasury he balanced the State's books and reformed Italy's administrative and taxation system. A member of the Accademia dei Lincei and also of various foreign academies, he was invited by Chang Kai-shek in 1937 to act as an economic adviser in China. In 1943 he was condemned to death in absentia for having supported Grandi's motion in the Grand Council of Fascism. He stood trial on the charge of collaboration with the deposed regime but was absolved in 1947. His close friendship with Costantini is evidenced in the correspondence in the ASDCP between De Stefani and his wife with the cardinal. Costantini also entrusted De Stefani with the task of examining this diary.

existence, but God is higher than all the judges, and He alone is truth, justice, mercy, providence. Everything can be taken away, but not the faith in which we believe, not this gift of grace for which, though beaten, we feel so close to the Lord; we are prepared for the journey to the heights sublime."

Blessed are those who, though persecuted, remake between the thorns a humble trail for the salvation of their children, causing this trail to flower with holy promises.

Blessed are those who, though ignored and hunted, are able to regenerate themselves in work. Blessed are they who have resisted the storm, who did not hate anyone, who will not hate anyone, who will feel pity for their enemies and have lit in the deepest part of their hearts, as at an altar, the purest flame for authentic Christian faith, for their true beloved country.

And blessed are they who offer safe refuge and bread, a kind word, and a smile to those who have lost absolutely everything except their own precious lives. These are Samaritans of the spirit, offering the freshness of a charity that always renews itself.

APPEAL OF THE KING OF NORWAY   21 APRIL 1940
Yesterday's *Osservatore Romano* reported the noble appeal of the King of Norway: "In this hour, one of the most difficult that our country has passed through in a hundred years, I make the most urgent appeal so that everyone does everything in his power to rescue Norwegian freedom and independence. We have been the object of a lightning attack by a nation with whom we have always maintained friendly relations. The enemy has not hesitated to bombard the civil population, which has endured inhuman suffering ... I thank all of you who, with me and with the government, find yourselves today at action stations for the independence and freedom of Norway. I pray that all of you retain in precious memory those who have already given their lives for the Homeland. May God Save Norway."

                                                21 APRIL 1940
Yesterday evening's *Il Giornale d'Italia* resorted to this panegyric of Hitler: "Adolf Hitler is 51 years old today. The Italian nation salutes the leader of the National Socialist Revolution, the great chancellor of a resurrected and friendly Germany, the strong ally of Fascist Italy. The more the years pass, the more the person of Hitler is elevated in the

history of Germany and Europe as one of the great driving, constructive forces ... In vain today do the imperial democracies denounce this great German chancellor, who has such a proud sense of his nation, as the man responsible for this new war. History, which records the facts as they actually occurred and does not deform them in the polemics of the moment, knows that this war is the fatal epilogue of the armistice of Versailles and of its intolerable terms; it is the confrontation of the great, hegemonic imperial powers against national necessity and the righteous imperial anxiety of young and strong nations. Raising its salute to Adolf Hitler, the Italian nation turns its thoughts to the entire friendly German nation, which has understood your word and, following it with obedience, has rediscovered the path to resurrection."

All of this causes me a great sadness. Poor press! Poor Italy! Every moral principle has been eclipsed. But the real Italy, which will be the Italy of tomorrow, responds deep down against this cowardly action of the regime. Through this present catastrophe, Providence will prepare a victory of the spirit.

23 APRIL 1940

On 18 April 1940, Dr Adolfo Keller, professor at the University of Geneva and director of a Protestant seminary in Switzerland, came to see me here at the Propaganda.[22] He is a Protestant with deferential views toward the Catholic Church.

A PAPAL AUTOGRAPH FOR THE HEAD
OF THE ITALIAN GOVERNMENT   24 APRIL 1940

The news that has continued to reach us from many parts has demonstrated with ever greater clarity just how threatening the situation is and how much more founded is the fear of Italy's participation in the European conflict. With the desire to preserve peace in Italy, the Holy Father made a last attempt, writing a letter to the head of the government:

---

[22] The term "Propaganda" indicates the Sacred Congregation for the Propogation of the Faith [di Propaganda Fide, today called the Congregation for the Evangelization of Peoples]. It is one of the Roman congregations instituted in 1622 by Pope Gregory XV to promote and administer the missionary activity of the Catholic Church. The seat of this pontifical dicastery is situated in the historic palace called "di Propaganda Fide" in Piazza di Spagna in Rome.

"To my beloved son Sir Benito Mussolini, Head of the Government of Italy. Beloved son, health and apostolic benediction to you. Faithful to my mission to promote peace, which is among the main duties of Our pastoral ministry, We consider it timely, while the fears of a wider conflict grow, to open Our faithful heart to you. Without doubting your persevering work along the lines that were prescribed for you, We beseech the Lord to assist you at a time of great seriousness for all nations, a time of heavy responsibility for all those holding the reins of government. By virtue of the universal fatherhood that is vested in Our office, We express from the bottom of Our heart that as a result of your actions, your resolution, and your Italian soul, Europe be spared even greater ruin and deeper grief."

MUSSOLINI'S RESPONSE TO PIUS XII   28 APRIL 1940
"Most Blessed Father, please accept my profound thanks for the letter that you deigned to address to me. I understand, Blessed Father, your desire that it be given to Italy to avoid war. This has indeed happened until today, but I cannot in any way guarantee that this will last right to the end. The history of the Church, and what you teach me, Blessed Father, has never accepted the formula of peace for peace, of peace at any cost, of peace without justice. Of only one thing can I reassure you, Blessed Father, and that is that if tomorrow Italy is compelled to take to the field, this would mean that the evidence shows to all that its honour and future interests have absolutely forced us to do so. Please, Blessed Father, accept my expressions of devoted allegiance. Mussolini."

5 MAY 1940
Acclaimed by an immense multitude, the Holy Father Pius XII today went to the Basilica of Santa Maria Sopra Minerva to visit the chapel in honour of Saint Francis of Assisi and St Catherine of Siena, both proclaimed last year as patrons of Italy. He spoke admirably from the pulpit of the basilica.[23]

DARK HOURS   17 MAY 1940
There is an apocalyptic darkness spreading over Europe: it seems as if the sun has been deprived of its rays and its life and that the moon is

[23] The text of Pius XII's address can be found in AAS 32 (*Bollettino Ufficiale della Santa Sede*, 1940), 181–8.

coloured with blood. The beast of the Apocalypse, represented by all the greed and human cruelty, has emerged from the sea of misguided humanity ... He vomits a deadly smoke for mankind and curses against God. This war, which renounces every principle of civil cohabitation based on the honour of a person's word and on the rights of the other, is a continual insult to Christ and our Heavenly Father who made Him manifest. But above the darkness that envelops Europe shines the inextinguishable light of the Church. The darkness that today dims the light will pass, as a hurricane passes and one sees the light again, a light that will console great suffering, restoring to life the divine sense that is now hidden from view.

This is how we are tied to these long, sad, horrendous days in which once again Italy – though in peace – finds itself in a bad state because it is tied to Germany. *Abyssus abyssum invocat*[24] [Ps. 41:8]. England and France are paying for the error of having pushed Mussolini into the arms of Hitler. But regrettably everyone will suffer, just as a snowball rolling down a hill becomes an avalanche and sweeps away everyone – the innocent and the guilty. We are seeing here in Italy a campaign that promotes Hitler but forgets all religious and moral principles. It is an extremely hurtful spectacle.

We have even arrived at the idiocy of preventing the distribution of the *Osservatore Romano*, which has committed the crime of telling the truth, though it tells it in the most respectful manner. Didn't they think of the disastrous effect that this would produce in the entire world? How very bitter – but how right, even if offered in good faith – is the commentary of international opinion on the violence in Italy, which by touching the Papacy has not yet understood that it touches the entire world. I say the whole world because even those who do not believe look to the Vatican as the only beacon of light in this dark and tempest-tossed sea.

DENIAL OF THE *OSSERVATORE ROMANO*   25 MAY 1940

The Swiss *Neue Zürcher Zeitung*[25] [20 May] reported a rumour that the *Osservatore Romano* denied in its n. 24 edition of 25 May: "The Holy See sent to all diplomatic representatives in the countries that have

---

[24] The expression is "deep calleth on deep."

[25] *Neue Zürcher Zeitung* is the oldest Swiss paper still in circulation. It was founded in 1780 in Zurich by Salomon Gessner. The "Neue" was added in 1821, not having been part of the original title.

diplomatic relations with it a circular that categorically denies those biased reports circulating in various parts about the Pope and the Holy See abandoning Rome and Italy." Pius XII is resolved, in any eventuality, to remain in the chair that God has assigned to the Head of Christianity. The circular stresses that relations between the Holy See and Italy have not changed in the least and that isolated incidents, which in certain parts have been greatly exaggerated, have no importance and their actual effects have been minimal – almost nil.

26 MAY 1940

I was shown a little volume containing images of the sculptures of Ferruccio Vecchi.[26] In order to be heroic, Mussolini has degenerated into an animal. Disembowelled women are supposed to signify the mystery of life; it is said that this is Fascist art. I think it is actually the monstrous expression of the times in which we live, and Fascist art is a mirror that reflects what surrounds it.

Last night Cerruti told me that in St Mark's Square in Venice there was an anticlerical mob that burned a cross. Is this a symptom of communism? A mob is always ready to rally to any slogan to give vent to its basic instincts.

27 MAY 1940

The German grip in Artois and Belgium is increasingly tightening; it looks as if in only a matter of hours the Germans will be on the shores of the Channel, facing England. Poor heroic Belgium! All piety and good feeling go to the person who, though he may lose, embodies the utmost and holy defence of justice.

Today I lunched at the home of Marquis Salvago Raggi. There exists in everybody a desperate anxiety for Italy's predicament. Cerruti and the Romanian ambassador, Commene, apart from raising the apocalyptic spectre of war, reminded us of international law. They said that we cannot rebuild a new Europe if we do not return to respect for the law, which is both the expression and necessary condition for civilization. I said that we need to return to Christian principles and to the idea of human solidarity, otherwise we will revert to the status of cavemen.

[26] Ferruccio Vecchi was a sculptor born in 1894 and linked to Mussolini in his squadrist [Blackshirt] days. He was arrested along with Mussolini in Milan in 1919. Vecchi created works to glorify the Fascist regime and Il Duce.

"Worse," replied the Romanian ambassador, "because a caveman fought equal against equal and made an attack that was at the same time a defence. Today the stronger prevails over the weaker. "How are things going in Romania?" I asked. "At the moment, things are not bad. But tomorrow? We are at the mercy of the mighty. The malign prophet of this cataclysm of civilization was Nietzsche; he is one of the main people responsible."

Generally speaking, with the exception of a few diplomats and reasonable men of conscience, people admire the German successes. It's always this way; the world applauds success. An anguished preoccupation prevails over Italy's entry into the war. There is talk of a separate peace with France that would offer concessions to Germany and Italy. God willing that it be true, that we will be spared a conflict with France. Senator [Riccardo] Gigante[27] told me that the Hon. [Giacomo] Suardo confessed the following: "We must save Italy and the regime. If Mussolini can reach agreement with France, it will be an act of true salvation. We will then have to stop the disgraceful corruption that is spreading everywhere."

THE DEMEANOUR OF THE KING OF BELGIUM   1 JUNE 1940
To the frightening and immense tragedy that is overtaking Europe is added the personal and public drama of the King of Belgium. I think that he could no longer sacrifice his army solely to protect the Allied retreat; the battle had already been lost. Beyond the Byzantine politics of the situation, we see rising the humanity and Christian sensibility of a king both courageous and unlucky. He is still on Belgian soil, surrounded by the affection and loyalty of his soldiers.

A LETTER FROM BADIA DI CAVA [SALERNO]   1 JUNE 1940
And so, after thirteen years, I have come back here to my room, with windows that open onto the shady valley; I have rediscovered the silence of that past. But how worried and tormented I feel! How profoundly into my spirit has penetrated this terrible crisis that has shaken Europe!

---

[27] Riccardo Gigante (1881–1945), of Fiume in Istria, was a journalist by profession. He was mayor of Fiume and then of Podestà from 1930 until 1934, when he was named to the Senate. Costantini met Senator Gigante in 1918, after which they became friends. Gigante was executed at Castua on 10 June 1945, a fact to which this diary attests.

I left Rome to lift my spirit a little; I don't say to forget, which I neither want nor can do, but to seek to turn my torment away. For you, daily work absorbs and transforms that torment. Sometimes it is impossible for me to stay in the room or to leave, to read or write or even to do nothing without thinking of the millions of men who are being exterminated almost at our borders! And tomorrow our hour will come!

I would like to stay here a few days – as long as the anxiety of not knowing of or seeing you compels me to rejoin you. I have the feeling of being like a straw in the wind of this tempest of the times …

Giovanni Tullio.[28]

FROM A MEETING WITH MONS. PRINCIPI[29]
OF THE SECRETARIAT OF STATE   3 JUNE 1940
The heads of the religious order and the procurators general are making arrangements to remain in Rome in contact with the Holy See. For all others, it is recommended they leave. For the foreign employees of the Holy See, preparations are being made so that they may stay. For Sisters, the Italian government has given assurances that they will be treated with consideration; it is prudent, however, that they keep their passports at the ready. If it comes to it, there will be a phased exodus because they can go, for example, to Switzerland. If they want to stay and they are interned, we must ensure that they are not treated badly and that they are isolated.

---

[28] Giovanni Battista Tullio (1881–1979) was originally from San Vito al Tagliamento, where he was born and where he also died, after having travelled extensively, especially in the Far East. He was a close friend of Costantini and was with him at Aquileia, at Fiume, and for a time even in China. In the Celso Costantini Collection in ASDCP, there is documentation of an extensive correspondence between the two.

[29] Primo Principi (1894–1967) was attached to the Second Section of the Secretariat of State of the Holy See at the time when Italy entered the war. He then served on the Pontifical Commission for the Vatican City State and the Sacred Congregation of the Holy Office. He became titular bishop of Tiana in 1956 and became pontifical administrator of the Patriarchal Basilica of St Paul Outside the Walls, pontifical delegate of the Basilica of St Anthony in Padua, and pontifical administrator of the Basilica of the Holy House of Loreto.

3 JUNE 1940

Today I saw Ambassador Cerruti. It seems that events are coming to a head: either peace proposals will be put forward or war will ensue. In the first case, Mussolini would play the part of mediator, re-establishing a broader, more decisive, and presumably longer-lasting Munich Agreement; in the second case, Italy, by moving out of a non-belligerent status, will side with Hitler.

God willing that the first possibility comes to pass and that it prevents more slaughter of young lives and more destruction of cities and public works! Moreover, war is a match that is played; you can win and you can lose. Are we sure of winning? May Providence sustain us in this critical hour, which puts in play the existence of Italy, this beloved nation that has escaped the tribulation of many adversities and the traps of many enemies. But today, the foundations of our civilization – a civilization that is the fruit of a Roman culture, purified by the fragrance and the profound regenerative virtue of Christianity – is placed in danger.

5 JUNE 1940

The thoughts and sentiments of *La Croix* are noble and holy, but they are like a wreath of flowers that you put on a grave, on the rotten stone of the Treaty of Versailles, and they are not enough to overcome the stench. Why, then, don't they wish to remember the duty owed to their Latin roots or their duty to do justice to Italy? From [Versailles] comes the first error, aggravated later with sanctions. France bound Italy to itself, and the link was consecrated by blood; it should never have been broken under any conditions. I pray to God to save us Catholics from the pain and error of fighting against Catholics, against France, the mother of many saints, beacon of much religious thought!

6 JUNE 1940

Germanophiles, if they weren't so fanatical, would understand that by remaining neutral, we would safeguard our true interests and could be especially useful to Germany, something we cannot do by entering the war. For all these reasons and for others as well, I do not want to believe that Italy will enter the war.

ALEA IACTA EST [THE DIE HAVE BEEN CAST]   10 JUNE 1940

On 10 June the die were cast. We have gone to war against France and England. I listened to Mussolini's address at the Collegio Urbano on the

Janiculum for the Feast of Saint Jacinto, Martyr. On news of war that we
knew would come, a dark sadness weighed on our souls. The eyes of the
rector, Monsignor Brizz, filled with tears. I gave him this instruction: "Be
quiet and pray. No seminarian must leave the college." There are many
here who are natives of countries under English rule. How inconsistent,
contradictory, and false human civilization appears to be! The man who
roused Italy to intervene on the side of the Allies in 1915 is the same man
who today declares war against the same Allies and makes the nation
march at Hitler's side.

12 JUNE 1940

After two days, the first communiqué of the war was released today; it is
colourless and offers little satisfaction. Last night we woke to the menacing wail of the sirens. God help us! May he let the leaders of the peoples
see the light and save this troubled Italy! Privately, some people express
the most deeply pessimistic thoughts. If things go badly, we can expect a
period of communist excess. A poet's phrase comes to mind: "Tomorrow
has the face of a ruthless executioner."

One newspaper writes: "The Vatican maintains the most absolute discretion with respect to the situation created by the Italian intervention.
While it is true that the attitude and responsibility of the Vatican are
totally distinct from those of the clergy and Italian Catholics, and the
Holy See is answerable to Catholics of all nations and must conduct
itself accordingly, it is to be noted that the Italian clergy, who themselves
have specific responsibilities toward the homeland, carry out, as always,
those responsibilities unanimously and with every generosity."

One's thoughts turn again to the clergy, to whom mothers and brides
confide their secret suffering. But a month ago the Pope and the clergy
were insulted and rudely offended, and people were prevented from
reading the Osservatore Romano. This style of stirring up, this unleash-
ing of the mob does grave damage to Fascism; one hoped to have
returned to the rule of law, one had faith in civilization. Instead ... those
gangsters that beat up readers of the Osservatore Romano, among
whom were highly placed and respectable people, today are Fascists,
and tomorrow they will be communists; they are simply the lowest,
slimiest bottom level of society that muddies the waters when that bottom is stirred up. It is understood that Fascism in its first phase, in order
to succeed, had to resort to violence; it is said that revolutions are
not made with floods of honey. But what was necessary briefly, like a

surgical operation, cannot remain the norm. There are, regrettably, profiteers who don't serve a cause but have the cause serve them. The population of the Alto Adige, en masse, after twenty years under Italian
administration, opted for Germany, even overcoming religious feeling ...
Even conceding wicked Hitlerian propaganda, this happened above all
as a revolt against a regime of violence, of coercion, and deprivation of
fundamental freedoms.

12 JUNE 1940

These personal and secret notes contain perspectives that have been
prompted by the present urgent situation. I do not mean to offer judgment. These notes look a little like the screams of a man undergoing
surgery without anaesthetic. They will perhaps later serve to offer perspectives on future decisions. I appreciate the good that Mussolini has
done, but now I see him falling into an abyss.

13 JUNE 1940

It is a pathetic and humiliating spectacle for Italy that one man deter-
mines the destiny of 45 million people – their lives, their possessions,
their prestige, their history – without consulting the institutions of government, without listening to anyone. He who claims to lift up the name
of Italy does not not understand that he is now, before the world and
before history, inflicting on Italy the branding mark of slavery. And the
King? Poor King, hypnotized by Mussolini!

Freedom is *the* condition for human dignity. In the prayer of the Church,
we ask God every day *ut salvi e liberi esse mereamur* [as long as we deserve,
to be saved and free]. Today, freedom does not exist in Italy; nor does there
exist what Mussolini once defined as the *right to chatter*, because the chat-
terers are in jail. In vain is written on the banner before the monument to
Victor Emmanuel "*Patriae unitati. Civium liberati*" [To the unity of the
homeland. To the freedom of the citizens]. Mussolini has removed every
means available by which a free people can express their will. There is no
parliament; there is no press; Mussolini himself is a prisoner of his own
praetorian guard. For Mussolini, the Grand Council of Fascism is a joke.
A terrible war has been unleashed without even hearing from it ... How
useful it would have been if an honest opposition had denounced the corruption and the squandering of public funds! There was once too much
freedom – there was licentiousness, of which the worst kind of people took
advantage; but today we have gone to the other extreme.

THE APPEAL OF ITALIAN CATHOLIC ACTION
[AZIONE CATTOLICA ITALIANA]   14 JUNE 1940
The leadership of Italian Catholic Action has made the following appeal to its members, which will be published in the next edition of the *Bollettino ufficiale:* "In this grave and solemn time in which our homeland calls all of its sons to its side, the members of Catholic Action respond to the call with the profound sense of duty and a generous sense of giving that comes from their Christian formation. Their special duty at this time can be summed up in two words: *pray and work.* Pray for God to bless our dear homeland and protect its sons who fight valiantly. And act together with serene strength – each at his own post performing the duties assigned to him by the authorities in a spirit of sacrifice and perfect discipline ... Evasio Colli, bishop of Parma, director general of the ACI."[30]

It seems to me that this declaration is both opportune and well formulated: clear in its ideas, noble in its style. When the homeland is in danger, one does not discuss: one obeys. This is a human and Christian precept.

14 JUNE 1940
Last night enemy warplanes dropped the following leaflets on Rome: "Il Duce wanted war? HERE IT IS! France has nothing against you. STOP! France will stop. Women of Italy, nobody has attacked Italy! Your sons, your husbands, your fiancés did not leave to defend the homeland. They are suffering and dying to satisfy the pride of one man. Whether you are victorious or vanquished, you will suffer hunger, destitution, and slavery."

15 JUNE 1940
Last night we heard the ominous wail of the sirens; but more ominous was the high drone of the airplanes. Anti-aircraft batteries were engaged, and the Roman sky was full of explosions and flashes. We got out of bed and went down the passageway to the ground floor of the Propaganda. I don't believe I heard the peculiar rumble of the bombs being dropped. I still have in my ears the whistles and explosions that I used to hear in

---

[30] CC: *L'Avvenire d'Italia,* 14 June 1940.

Aquileia during the last war.[31] When the sortie ended, I opened the window of my office. Rome, enveloped in darkness, had a ghost-like quality. The great palaces, dark indistinct masses, had a funereal appearance. City life would have seemed dead if it hadn't been for the sound of a few whispers at ground level and a rare cry here and there; a nightmare weighed on the city.

I thought that although our hardship was small, it had nonetheless depressed our spirits. But what was happening in Paris? There, millions of people had hastily taken flight … So much suffering, so much ruin of lives on the front. What a sea of misery was flooding the streets that just a few days ago had seen the flowering of spring and the peaceful work of people! We have to ask ourselves: Are we civilized? Are we Christian? No.

15 JUNE 1940

Yesterday, Signore Apolloni, formerly attaché to the press office of the embassy in Shanghai, came to see me. He is now taking up the same post at the embassy in Berlin. He asked me, "What do you think of the war?" I responded, "Here we do not occupy ourselves with war, unless it is to deal with the many repercussions that war has on our missions. We are outside the conflict. At the Propaganda we breathe the pure air of the stratosphere."

16 JUNE 1940

This morning the radio reported the resignation of the Reynaud[32] cabinet in France and the establishment of a broadly based war ministry. Even Laval has joined. This news brings the hope that a separate peace can be made with France. God willing! Even for Italy this would be a great benefit. Before German military operations began on the western front (when many in Italy doubted the outcome of the war), Mussolini

[31] For these reminiscences, see *Foglie Secche. Esperienze e memorie di un vecchio prete* (Rome: Tipografia artistica, 1948), 183–240.

[32] Paul Reynaud (1878–1966), French politician, prime minister in March 1940, was forced to resign as a result of the failure of military operations. He ceded the leadership of the government to Marshal Henri Philippe Omer Pétain, who signed the armistice with Germany. Reynaud was put on trial and deported by the Germans (between 1942 and 1945). He later returned to politics and government, contributing as a convinced European to the formation of the Council of Europe and the European Economic Community.

had declared and categorically affirmed that Germany would be victorious. The King blindly believed him. Italy's action against France is criminal and cowardly. It is a stab in the back; it is a disgrace; it is an incredible folly, because the hereditary prince is involved. Didn't Victor Emmanuel III consider that whatever the outcome of the battle, it would compromise the future king in the eyes of France? This aggression, strategically speaking, is ill-considered from a military perspective, and the hearts of the troops and the country are simply not in it. Mussolini uttered his unhuman remark: "I need a certain number of dead to enable me to sit at the peace table." *Jupiter quos vult perdere dementat* [Whom Jupiter would destroy, he first makes mad].

17 JUNE 1940

Today came the unexpected news that France has capitulated. The news was met with confused feelings here, including a sigh of relief and the hope for peace. Rome spontaneously decked itself out with flags; it is a sure sign of the communal desire for peace. I am happy that hostilities with France have ended and hope that England, too, will in time decide in favour of peace. The message of Pétain is full of bitterness but shows a human and civil sensibility. Il Duce and the Führer are meeting today. In their hands they hold Europe's destiny.

COMMUNIQUÉ OF MARSHAL PÉTAIN[33]

BERN, 17 JUNE 1940, NIGHT

"By the invitation of the President of the Republic, I am assuming the leadership of the French government, beginning today. In these painful

[33] Henri Philippe Omer Pétain (1856–1951) was a French general with wide responsibilities extending back to the First World War. He opposed the diffusion of socialist ideas in the armed forces. He was minister of war in 1934, ambassador to Spain in 1939, and in 1940 he became vice-president and then president of the Council of Ministers. In the latter capacity, he signed the French-German armistice on 22 June 1940 and transferred his cabinet to Vichy in occupied France. He was proclaimed head of state and pursued a collaborationist line with Hitler's regime, though refusing to fight alongside Germany in the war. After the Allied landing in Normandy in 1944, his government was compelled to transfer to Belfort and then Sigmaringen, Germany. In April 1945 he fled to Switzerland but then returned to France to be put on trial for collaboration with the Germans. His sentence of death was commuted to life imprisonment.

hours, my thoughts turn to the wretched refugees who fill the streets of France, and I express to them all my compassion and sympathy. It is with a broken heart that I inform you today that we must cease military operations. Last night I approached our adversaries to ask if they were ready to seek with me, soldier to solider, after the conflict, honourable means to end hostilities. May all the French gather around the government over which I will preside during these hours, during this difficult trial, and may they silence their anguish by obeying solely their faith in the destiny of the homeland."[34]

GERMAN COMMUNIQUÉ   BERLIN 22 JUNE 1940
The Führer's headquarters issued the following communiqué: "On 22 June at 18:50 hrs German standard time in the forest of Compiègne, the Franco-German armistice was signed. General Kietel,[35] head of the high command of the armed forces, signed for the German side on behalf of the Führer, Supreme Commander of the armed forces; on the French side, General Huntzinger[36] signed. The armistice treaty does not provide for the cessation of hostilities. Cessation of hostilities will occur six hours after the Italian government informs the German High Command that the Italo-French armistice has been completed. At this moment, we know nothing of the contents of this armistice treaty."[37]

[34] CC: *Il Messaggero*, 23 June 1940.

[35] Wilhelm Kietel (1882–1946) was a German general and close associate of Hitler. He led the reorganization of the armed forces in 1929. In 1938 he became head of the armed forces and minister of defence of the Reich. In 1940 he led the military delegation that signed the capitulation of France. In the same year he was given the rank of Marshal and signed Germany's surrender on 8 May 1945. Found guilty by the tribunal at Nuremberg for crimes against humanity, he was condemned to death by hanging. The sentence was carried out on 16 October 1946.

[36] Charles-Léon Huntzinger (1880–1941), a French general in both world wars. In 1933 he commanded the French armed forces in the Levant and later became a member of the Supreme Council of War. At the beginning of the Second World War he commanded France's Second Army. On 22 June 1940, at Compiègne, he signed, on behalf of Pétain, the armistice with Germany and Italy. In 1941 he was minister of war in the Vichy government. He died on 1 November 1941 in an airplane crash.

[37] CC: Agenzia Stefani [An Italian Press Agency].

24 JUNE 1940

This morning, as I was thanking people after mass, my driver, holding
Il Messaggero in his hand, exclaimed outside the chapel, "The armistice
between Italy and France has been signed!" This wonderful and great
news made my heart leap and I offered to God an enthusiastic prayer of
thanks. In the mass, I had prayed for all the war dead, for so much
youth mowed down in the flower of their years. May God grant that
this great sacrifice will not be lost but that from it a true peace will
germinate, a Christian peace that re-establishes solidarity between peoples. For us Catholics, it is a great relief that the war with our French
brothers has ended. Christianity now has something very important to
say. Imolo Marconi put it beautifully in yesterday's *L'Avvenire d'Italia*:
"Catholics who have responded or intend to respond to the divine
vocation of the Apostles cannot turn away from the imperative of their
message: *to be the leaven of the future and not the ashes of the past.*"
May God inspire wise counsel to England. Poor nations must live.
Mankind was not made for the earth; it is the earth that was made for
mankind. Yesterday's class struggle between the rich and the proletariat
has been transferred to a national level, some members of the nation
being rich and others poor.

29 JUNE 1940

News has hit like a lightning bolt: Italo Balbo[38] has been killed in action,
crashing his flaming plane at Tobruk [Libya]. I suffer for the fate he
endured and for his family, and for the void he will leave behind. He
seemed to be a man destined for great things in civil life. He had moder-
ated his youthful exuberance, and his religious sensibilities, inspired by
his mother, were being reborn in him, giving him a sense of balance and
equilibrium in his actions. I remember the kind of general confession he
made to me when in 1935 I was his guest in Tripoli, and then the private
religious thoughts he confided to me in a meeting at the Excelsior Hotel
in Rome. He was the only man who knew how to resist Mussolini's

[38] Italo Balbo (1896–1940), an organizer of Fascist squads established to
perpetrate acts of violence against all opposition, was a politician and aviator
as well as being minister of the air force. He was made governor of Libya by
Mussolini, not least because he was a difficult personage and a potential rival.
He was shot down on 28 June 1940 by Italian anti-aircraft batteries "by mistake," according to the official version of events.

wishes. The sinister shadow of the assassination of Don Minzoni[39] hangs over him: we will know the truth. All the same, he seemed to be a circumspect man. *Requiescat in pace!* Today, 30 June, I prayed for him.

THE TIRELESS WORK OF PIUS XII   2–3 SEPTEMBER 1940
"As we mark the first year of the new European conflict, the *Osservatore Romano* [2–3 September] briefly recalled the efforts of the Holy See and the Pope to prevent the outbreak before it occured, to hasten its conclusion, and to alleviate the devastating effects of the war ... His paternal exhortations were accompanied by a vast, hidden, and tireless diplomatic effort of rapprochement and friendly mediation, glimpsed in the subtle allusions of the Holy Father himself, who never gave up hope that a 'just and honourable peace for all' might present itself, as wished for and defined in his Christmas address."[40]

ARE WE HEADED TO A WIDER WAR?   29 OCTOBER 1940
Yesterday the war against Greece began. Why? The pretexts are put forward, and there was not even a minimum of time allowed for Italy and Greece to discuss the situation. It is said that Mussolini wants to do this on his own. It seems to me that Hitler is extremely irritated by Mussolini's rash act, by the lack of military preparation, and by the first hard defeats.[41]

NAVAL DISASTER AT TARANTO   20 NOVEMBER 1940
After the naval disaster at Taranto in which several of our ships were sunk, General Umberto Pugliese was called back into service because of his great ability. He writes to me: "Taranto, 19 November. At 12, I was called by my under-secretary, and with Il Duce's authorization I was sent here for a very important mission, which I am fulfilling with the full commitment of my mind and heart. I have regained all the attention,

---

[39] Giovanni Minzoni (1885–1923), a priest of Ravenna, archpriest of Argenta and anti-Fascist, who was murdered by Fascist assassins.
[40] cc: *La Civiltà Cattolica* 91, no. 3 (1940): 466–7.
[41] cc: E. Caviglia, *Diario (aprile 1925 – marzo 1945)* (Rome: Gherardo Casini Editore, 1952), 293. "Now we shall see how the question of Greece is handled. At the beginning of June, Mussolini had the keys of fortune in his hands: all he had to do was remain outside the conflict. By entering the war against France he has ruined our excellent position."

reception, and above all authority of my rank, all of which permits me to carry out fully the mandate entrusted to me with the satisfaction of tackling all the technical difficulties. More than my right, it will now be my indispensable duty to seek once again the formal legal position the command entails. I have thought of Your Excellency many times and how you have helped me always to have a sure faith in the Lord." The recall of General Pugliese has been received throughout Italy with a general sense of approval, not only for a person who is unanimously appreciated for his great ability and rectitude, but also because his recall signifies a type of repudiation of the so-called racial laws that are not approved of and are in fact deplored by our Latin and Christian people. His patriotic and conscientious act has demonstrated how in him are extraordinarily combined the intellectual and spiritual gifts that derive from a great faith in God.[42]

An Englishman Who Tells the Truth

The Reverend Rowland Jones, stung by the Presbyterian homilies of Lord Halifax that call, in every passage, for religion and the most beautiful Christian virtues, has not hesitated to write a letter to the newspapers in which he takes to task the minister of external affairs of his country: "Ah, you say that this is a battle between Christianity and Nazism? Pray tell, can you clarify what you mean by Christianity? Can we say that England is an incarnation of the Christian love of neighbour? In 1927 there were two million people unemployed. Is this Christianity?"

A GRAND FUNCTION AT ST PETER'S   24 NOVEMBER 1940
The European horizon (and we can say the entire world's horizon), instead of clearing, is being covered with darker and darker clouds and lightning flashes of terrifying menace. The air is filled with anguish and fear. At this gloomy time, a shaft of heavenly light appears – the grand ceremony of penance, of conciliation, and for the suffering souls in Purgatory that took place yesterday in St Peter's and was celebrated in all the Catholic churches in the world. When I looked upon the dignified and high figure of the Pope at the altar above the tomb of St Peter, I thought that he was carrying in his Father's heart the entire Catholic

---

[42] For an appreciation of Pugliese, see Renzo De Felice, *Storia degli ebrei italiani sotto il fascismo* (Torino: Einaudi, 1961), 309 and 494. The text of this annotation was dictated by Pugliese to Costantini when the latter asked him to review the manuscript of the diary.

world; it appeared that his slender hands were offering to God the anxiety and prayers of the entire world. In the stupendous words of the homily, all people could recognize themselves because the words were the profound words of humanity itself. From one battlefield or another, from one church or another, of one religion or of no religion, all people were present because the sentiments of the Pope were the most profound sentiments of every individual. One can say that in this actual moment, the failure of every principle of right, justice, and peace found refuge in the Vatican. The Pope is the only sincere and authoritative defender of freedom – without which there is no dignity and no possibility of honest cohabitation.

This noble and eternal spectacle shines much more brightly over the gloomy horror of the moment. "We," said the Pope in his homily, "have omitted no measure for peace between nations, conscious as We are to be servants and ministers of a sublime King, peaceful and peacemaker not with the blood of battles but through the blood of his cross and the things of the earth and the things of heaven."[43]

The "Urbe" as Image of the "Orbe"
Giuseppe De Mori writes[44]: "Even in these circumstances the Urbe [city] was the image of the Orbe [world]. Rome's prayer was the prayer of all humanity. The central church of Christianity has reconstituted, as in blood-stained ages past, the right of sanctuary, where the belligerents can meet each other in peace."

27 NOVEMBER 1940
Monsignor Caprio,[45] who is from Benevento and knows the family of the late Senator Bocchini,[46] also from Benevento, tells me that Bocchini

---

[43] The complete text of Pius XII's homily can be found in AAS 32 (*Bollettino Ufficiale della Santa Sede*, 1940), 531–6.

[44] CC: *L'Avvenire d'Italia*, 26 November 1940.

[45] Giuseppe Caprio (1914–2005), originally from Avellino, studied in the seminary at Benevento and was pro-secretary of economy in the Sacred Congregation *di Propaganda Fide* at the outbreak of the Second World War. He entered the diplomatic corps of the Holy See and was sent to various diplomatic postings, including Nanjing. He was also substitute at the Secretariat of State between the pontificates of Paul VI and John Paul II. He was made a cardinal in 1979.

[46] Arturo Bocchini (1880–1940), a prefect of various Italian cities, a senator from 1933, and head of the police from 1926 until his death in 1940.

on his deathbed married a young woman with whom he was living, and that he left her an estate of many millions ... For a police chief who should be an exemplary gentleman, this is not a bad outcome. It is a sign of the times. It is quite true that human justice is like a spider's web: the gnats get caught up in it, and the blowflies tear through it and fly free. The homeland, like every form of government, needs gentlemen.

21 DECEMBER 1940

The hours pass heavily with a sense of tragedy. In the skies over Italy a cloud pregnant with storms and menace is spreading, and just as nature seems to shudder with the imminent arrival of a hurricane, that is how spirits in Italy are seized with a deep and bitter sadness. Almost two months after Italy's act of aggression, the Greeks are still on Albanian territory. Italy is in disgrace. The English have entered Libyan territory, overcoming the resistance of Graziani.[47] German soldiers have descended upon Italy in great numbers. Mussolini has informed the leadership that now more than ever we must make common cause with Germany. Ex-Minister Jung, a man of high and pure patriotic feeling, said to me yesterday, "If God does not save us, we will be on the road that Romania is on." The anguish of Italians is sharp and exasperated because of the moral recklessness and imprudence with which Italy was thrown into the Greek adventure. If all the materiel sent to the Greek front had been sent promptly to Graziani, perhaps even the outcome of the Libyan war would have been different. Why was Greece attacked? There was no discussion of the moral principle of whether it was legitimate to attack in this way a country that was certainly not a friend but had, in essence, conducted itself prudently.

Moral principles do not exist; only pride and force do. I was told that Hitler was against the Greek adventure and that Mussolini wanted to go ahead to acquire a pawn, to do just as Germany had done with its violation of many little nations. The sorrow for the innocent victims of the war and for the military reversals which have made Italy the subject of

[47] Rodolfo Graziani (1882–1955) was a general who commanded the forces of the southern front in the Italian-Ethiopian war. He was marshal of Italy and viceroy of Ethiopia (1936–37). He was head of the Italian armed forces (1930) and commanded Italian troops in North Africa (1940–41). He was also minister of war in the Republic of Salò (1943–45), after which he surrendered to the Allies.

ridicule and spite by the global leadership to which it had ascended (the proud man, victim of his arrogance, is always covered in ridicule and spite) is sharpened and poisoned by two other thoughts:

1 Where have we come to with this degeneration of the regime, with these delusions of grandeur, with this mad megalomania? Yesterday the former minister [Giovanni Maria] Longinotti[48] said to me: "The statutes of the regime establish that war may not be declared without the consent of the Grand Council of Fascism. Now war has been declared without having convoked the Grand Council, in which, one has reason to believe, several people, such as the Hon. De Vecchi,[49] would have opposed it. How did we get to this point!"

2 To this illegality is added a foolishness that would be unbelievable if it were not true. It is said that the Italian government had assurances that the Greeks, before a feigned resistance, would surrender and that the Albanians under Greek dominion would have made common cause with the Italians. These suppositions were based on a lot of money distributed in Greece as the price of treason … The Greeks pocketed the money and then inflicted on the Italians the most humiliating defeat.

The soldiers fight well, but there are too few of them and, what's more, they are badly equipped. Two months into this stupid and iniquitous aggression, the Greeks are solidly established in Albania. The Italy of Mussolini has fallen into the most bitter contempt: contempt for the

[48] Giovanni Maria Longinotti (1876–1944) was born in Brescia and received a degree in chemistry at the University of Parma. He later worked for the national metallurgical workers' union and was one of the founders of the Italian People's Party, which he later represented in parliament. He was a member of the government before the advent of Fascism, after which he retired from political life. He was a friend of his fellow townsman Giovanni Battista Montini, the future Pope Paul VI. In fact, it was Montini who informed Costantini of the death of Longinotti in May 1944 as a result of an automobile accident.

[49] Cesare Maria De Vecchi (1884–1959) was a Fascist politician, one of the "quadrumvirate" (with Italo Balbo, Emilio De Bono, and Michele Bianchi) of the March on Rome and a member of the Grand Council of Fascism, in which he voted against Mussolini in July 1943. He was condemned to death in absentia by the special Tribunal of Verona in 1944.

unbounded arrogance and for that attitude of defiance with which Fascism treated the foreigner. In neither case does the excuse of betrayal wash; they should not have resorted to this most cowardly force of arms, and if anything they should not have stupidly placed their faith in these false assertions. Wars are not waged with gossip; it was legitimate to expect that Mussolini would have learned, at least in this area, something from the Germans – that before beginning their formidable campaigns, they were well prepared.

Another unpardonable foolishness: Farinacci[50] has attacked the military in his paper. Badoglio[51] wrote to Mussolini to say that these insults must be withdrawn or he will leave; and Mussolini let him go. Worse still, instructions are circulating among the leadership to defame Badoglio, saying that he is a traitor.

21 DECEMBER 1940

Today the English reconquered the territory they had lost and entered Libya. Will they stop? Let's hope so. But the disaster is dreadful. Today *Il Messaggero* published the following passage: "No. 8 of the AROI writes, "We report that the forces of Great Britain, concentrated and engaged against Italy in various sectors of the conflict, amount to not less than 1,500 airplanes, 425,000 men, and half a million tons of warships in the Mediterranean. The troops were recruited and chosen in England, Australia, New Zealand, India, and other parts of the British Empire. As Prime Minister Churchill affirmed in his address to the House of Commons yesterday, "the armaments for this army were sent directly from Great Britain in July and August in a long journey via the Cape of

[50] Roberto Farinacci (1892–1945) was secretary of the National Fascist Party (1925–26), director of the daily newspaper *Regime Fascista,* and a member of the Grand Council of Fascism. Farinacci voted against the motion of non-confidence in Il Duce, later supporting republican Fascism and the Germans. He was later executed by the partisans.

[51] Pietro Badoglio (1871–1956), a general in the First World War, marshal of Italy in 1926, then governor of Libya (1929–33). He conquered Ethiopia in 1936, becoming its first viceroy. He was head of the armed forces until 1940. At the fall of Fascism in 1943, he was appointed president of the Council of Ministers by Victor Emmanuel. He formed two successive governments until the liberation of Rome in 1944.

Good Hope and comprised," according to him, "valuable tanks of the highest quality and modern artillery that were in short supply and were necessary to our own defence."

Shouldn't all this have been known? What are the intelligence bureaus doing? It would in any event have been so easy to determine the position and strength of England in Egypt! *Incidit in foveam quam fecit*[52] [Ps. 7:16]. The Fascist press has the impudence to write: "These are the days in which Italy is summoning the highest level of military valour, and not just of the military type. These are days of the greatest trial in which a people can put to the test both the strength and the virtues that constitute their defence and establish their power: courage, determination, the spirit of sacrifice, discipline." Clowns!

But facts speak louder than words. They tell us to have *faith in destiny*. What is this destiny? One must have faith in one's leaders: but they must be worthy of it. That faith has been shaken; this is also because the Italian people feel that they have been treated like children ... They talk of truncheons and castor oil. Do they think they will instill confidence with these measures? Last night the former Minister Longinotti said to me: "In the last war, the King convoked the Council of the Crown, and Parliament could express its views. The homeland participated in the most paramount decisions, extending the responsibility to the entire nation. Today Mussolini decides on his own, for his own ends, disregarding all the ways in which he could have consulted the nation; and they expect the nation *to have faith?* In the past, various successes justified this faith; but the stupid reversals of these recent days provoke criticism and recrimination."

And the King – what is he thinking, what is he doing? The former Minister Jung said to me last night, "As long as Mussolini dedicated himself to the homeland, living in moderation, everything went well. When in full view of the nation he crushed the morality and dignity of the family, unreservedly giving himself over to vice with women, the decline began. You cannot serve your country and abandon yourself to the pleasures of vice."

I also learned that German troops continue to arrive. We are headed toward the same fate as Romania. It is said that Farinacci is close to Mussolini and controls him. What is going to happen? We can see no light. We are left to pray that God will intervene. And in the meantime,

---

[52] "He hath opened a pit and dug it; and he has fallen into the hate he made."

in spite of everything, everyone must do his own difficult duty in a spirit
of discipline and sacrifice, because the honour and life of the homeland
are in danger.

THE FAILURE OF CIVILIZATION   22 DECEMBER 1940
I transcribe here several newspaper headlines:

From *Il Giornale d'Italia* of 20 December 1940:
OUR TROOPS SUCCESSFULLY COUNTERATTACK ENGLISH MOTOR-
IZED FORCES.
BOMBARDMENT OF ENGLAND / Bombs equalling 21 million tons have
been dropped on London.

From *Il Messaggero* of 20 December 1940:
HEAVY AERIAL BLOWS IN THE AREA OF AGIROCASTRO AND ON THE
SANTA MAURA CANAL.
VETERANS OF ALL WARS, indissoluble bulwark around IL DUCE/greet
soldiers of land, sea, and air who fight with icy toughness and indomitable
force.

From *Il Messaggero* of 22 December 1940:
THE OFFENSIVE AGAINST GREAT BRITAIN/Waves of assault on London
follow each other continuously for 36 hours/Flights over the entire island,
from the Channel to the Shetlands/An arms factory and numerous military
targets severely hit/Thousands of incendiary bombs and explosives dropped
on Liverpool.
SIX MILLION BOMBS DROPPED IN ONE MONTH AGAINST GREAT
BRITAIN.

Reading these headlines breaks one's heart and makes one take fright.
One gets the urge to cover one's eyes and refuse to contemplate this
spectacle of savagery, cruelty, and destruction ... Oh humanity, where
are you headed? Oh civilization, are these the fruits you were preparing
for us? We are tempted to despair of our wretched nature. The so-
called savages are substantially more civilized than we are; they have
less culture and hygiene, but they do not harm life in this way – the
greatest good that we enjoy in this world. This is how the Eskimos will
judge us.

HOMAGE, OR PERHAPS INSULT, TO MOTHERHOOD
24 DECEMBER 1940

I want to write down here my memory of the ceremony in which motherhood was celebrated and exalted in Rome, a spectacle that should lift the spirit and cast a ray of light onto the darkness that surrounds us. *Il Messaggero* of 24 December 1940 reports: "From every corner of Italy is raised today a hymn to motherhood. Motherhood is honoured because it is a moral, civil, and political value: it protects the young, it assists childhood because it is the spiritual foundation of the family. Family, homeland, state – these three elements perpetuate civilization, transmitting moral values that have been shaped across a thousand years of history. The family ideally embodies the past and heralds the prospect of the future."

But Mussolini's act, which welcomes and rewards prolific mothers because they produce sons for power and war, humiliates motherhood. Besides, his private life is an insult to the sanctity of the family and the home! What seemed like a dignified ceremony was transformed into the theatrics of a buffoon. One woman said to me, "They should at least have had the Queen or Princess Maria preside over this ceremony!" It is significant that the Holy Father, who is so generous in welcoming many, many people, declined – at least it is said – to receive this group of mothers. Motherhood is too majestic a thing to turn it into a lowly political exhibition.

SORROWFUL CHRISTMAS 1940   CHRISTMAS 1940

I remember three tragic Christmases: that of 1917 at Bassano, after the rout at Caporetto; that of 1921 in Fiume; and the *anti-Christian* one of 1927 in China. This Christmas we look out over a more vast and immense horizon: East and West are involved in a war that is implacable, ferocious, bathed in blood, smoking of ruins and fratricidal. It breaks one's heart. For almost two thousand years the divine message has been sung: "Glory to God in the highest, and on earth peace and good will toward men." A million and a half people have spent Christmas night underground in London; millions of soldiers are keeping watch on the battlefield, with their rifles close by; sailors of all nations set traps and seek to avoid the traps of others; ships laden with men and supplies sink into deep waters. Mothers, brides, and sons fear for their distant dear ones, and their Christmas is bleak.

Ubique luctus ubique plurima mortis imago.[53] The description which St Girolamo gives of the horrors of the barbarian invasion at the fall of the Roman Empire is overtaken by a reality that is immensely more tragic and vast. Nonetheless, humanity feels the need to kneel at the cradle of the Redeemer, understanding that He alone gives meaning to life, that He alone can console hearts gripped with so much anguish. Humanity perceives with a more acute feeling than usual that we have not been given life to cast it into the furnace of war, but to work in peace, to take delight in the holy joys of security, work, and family. We are Christians even if there are individual Christians, who no longer have Christian governments. This terrible experience demonstrates that if we wish tomorrow to rebuild a form of order that offers the possibility of living and working, we must return to eternal Christian principles. The world has ignored or rejected Christ, and this is where we have ended up.

The Pope's Christmas Eve Message
Yesterday on Christmas Eve the Pope delivered an address that was profound with Christian meaning and also courageous at such a time: "The Prophet speaks for the future: time will prove him right. I offer a few thoughts that in this asphyxiating environment give a healthy lift to our spirits. With a tragic and almost fatal persistence, conflict, once unleashed, proceeds on its blood-drenched way, creating ruins and not sparing venerable churches, great monuments, charitable institutions, blithely oblivious of the standards of humanity, indifferent to the norms and conventions of war, and at times going far beyond them ... A time less shattered and troubled than our own will record these events as some of the most painful and dark pages of the history of the world. But amidst the many disasters that have come from this terrible conflict, one in particular has burdened and continues to burden Our heart – that of the prisoners of war ... We were able to reach at least some of the Polish prisoners; but with some others, contact is more frequent, especially with prisoners and interned Italians, particularly in Egypt, Australia, and Canada."

He concluded his address recalling the five fundamental points for the peaceful coexistence of peoples that he proclaimed in his Christmas address last year, adding that "if subsequent events have pushed back their realization, the ideas have lost neither any of their intrinsic truth

[53] "Everywhere appears cruel sorrow, everywhere death in a thousand shapes."

and realism nor their value in practical implementation." He then recited the five indispensable conditions for a new international order that would guarantee a just and lasting peace:

1 Victory over hate;
2 Victory over mutual distrust;
3 Victory over utilitarianism conceived as the foundation and principle of rights;
4 Victory over inequality in the world economy;
5 Victory over egotism that easily leads to nothing less than the honour and sovereignty of states rather than the just, sane, and disciplined freedom of citizens.

Percipientes mercedem iniustitiae[54] [2 Pet. 2:13]
At the heart of this tremendous conflict is the struggle between greedy powers and insatiable ones, between poor nations and rich nations. The old class struggle between proletarians and capitalists has now been transferred to a national level. The rich did not want to yield gracefully. In vain did Leo XIII[55] raise his voice with *Rerum Novarum*. The rich yield when their backs are against the wall. Today, with immensely more vast proportions, the same conflict is being waged.

[54] "They who harvest the fruits of injustice will be paid back for the harm they have done."

[55] Gioacchino Pecci (1810–1903), who became Pope Leo XIII in 1878 and governed the Church for 25 years, during which he issued many encyclicals, among which perhaps the most famous is *Rerum Novarum* of 15 May 1891 (Rome: Libreria Editrice Vaticana, 1891), which dealt with the so-called social question. This encyclical launched a veritable corpus of pontifical documents on the social doctrine of the Church.

The Year 1941

This evening I encountered the journalist [Giuseppe] De Mori. He said to me, "Providence has always blessed Italy ... But with the attack on Greece, we have challenged Providence, and Providence has abandoned us for now."

It is feared that Tobruk[1] is falling and that from there England will direct its efforts against Ethiopia. And if isolated, will she be able to resist?

It is said that leaflets were dropped over Naples with the following message: "Mussolini is sending you to die; and he has fun with his lover. If you want to keep the Empire, liberate yourselves from Mussolini; Otherwise we shall take the Empire and will leave you with Mussolini."

Everybody deplores the lack of military preparation and the disorganization of the armed services in the war against Greece. The defeats were not the fault of the soldiers, who fight well and are truly admirable. They are the fault of those who send them to war without uniforms and ammunition. They say that one division of troops in Albania ate their horses and mules to avoid death by starvation. Others suffered from hunger, cold, and lack of ammunition. Who is to blame? Who is the minister of war? It is Mussolini's fault and the fault of systems inspired by arbitrary and idiotic absolutism. Not least, it is also the fault of the generals who were chosen and sustained on the sole qualification of their

---

[1] Tobruk, a city in northern Cyrenaica (Libya) was in Italian hands until 21 January 1941, when it fell to British forces. It was retaken by the Germans under the command of General Rommel in June 1942 and taken back by the British in November of the same year.

devotion to the regime, but who lack any military leadership and should resign from their positions rather than leading their soldiers to slaughter and the nation to mockery.

Fascism Is Lost

Around Mussolini there are plenty of low-minded people who inebriate him with smoke and with the easy living of the useless and gluttonous; outside, the entire press wears a muzzle. Fascism has devoured itself. There are three Mussolinis: the one before the revolution – and it is better to leave that one in the merciful and discreet shadows; the one from 28 October 1922 to the conquest of the Empire, when Italy rose to the heights of prestige; and the third Mussolini, infatuated by vanity and ruined by vice – he who was the wretched strategist of the war against France and Greece; he, the malevolent creator of the Axis; he, the sinister author of these dark and threatening days. What will happen? Will we be saved by the Germans? Will it fall to them to reconstruct the Holy Roman Empire? Was this the legacy of the Axis? Was this Mussolini's dream? Barring a miracle, today one cannot see how Italy can find a way to recover, stop, and lift itself away from descent into the abyss. Lord, illuminate the rulers of nations so that they will finally understand that one cannot rebuild with hate but only with love, promoting harmony between nations based on a justice and fraternity that is human, Christian, and blessed by peace.

Mundus totus in maligno positus est
[1 Jn. 5:19; The whole world lies in wickedness]
I pray every day to God that he will receive into the light of eternal life in heaven the youth cut down by war, the most beautiful flowers of life cut down on land, swallowed into the abyss of the sea. But unfortunately, I can no longer have faith in the counsels of men; experience has spread the poisonous gas of skepticism in the surrounding atmosphere; the soul does not breathe and cannot breathe. People speak of a "complete alignment of vision" between Mussolini and Hitler. But who can believe it? Mussolini went to Germany with a political-military record that was not only passive but ruinous. Among other things, it seems that Hitler warned against the criminal error of attacking Greece. Two leaders, two dictators, proud to the point of self-infatuation – how can they get along? One cannot accept or even stand the other. It is danger and necessity and not the heart that unites them at present. It is an artificial

union and one propped up from outside. Mussolini blows with the wind. He said a while ago that the Jewish question did not exist in Italy, and now he rages against the Jews and exaggerates to make his attitude seem original, while everybody knows that he is copying Hitler as a matter of affinity and because he has to.

The nations blame each other for responsibility for the war, but the truth is that the war originated in the rivalry between Germany and England, as in 1914. They did not want to restore the colonies to Germany; and Germany prepared for war to obtain not only its so-called living space but also to realize its continental plans. Around these major stars orbited the minor stars of Italy and France. Like an earthquake, the war has buried all the pillars on which modern civilization rested. The spectacle we see before our eyes is horrendous: destruction, death, suffering; all of civilization's means directed in an inhuman effort of nations to destroy life ...

The Church stands alone among the many ruins, unarmed and defenceless yet invincible. One thinks of Leo the Great, who in 462 stopped Attila on the Mincio; and Gregory the Great, who stood up, unarmed, against the Longobards. In contrast to the divine sincerity of the Church, Roosevelt, president of the United States, appears to be a questionable prophet. Is he rising against Germany and Italy to defend democracy ... or for other reasons? He has spoken out against Germany's racist persecution, but this preacher has not said a single word in defence of the victims in Mexico, Russia, and Spain. Many believe that in these cases the money and electoral influence of American Jews was not in play. The Church always exhibits a consistent position, a consistent spirit, and a consistent ministry of justice, peace, and love.

23 JANUARY 1941

What will happen? It breaks one's heart and one tries to find some kind of horoscope for today's situation. English radio announces that English forces have taken Kassala and have penetrated 60 kilometres into Eritrea, and that English troops are retaking previously abandoned positions in Kenya. May God have mercy on prolific, Catholic, and hard-working Italy! If there have been injustices committed on our part, the English have not had clean hands either. The behaviour that has accompanied many colonial adventures weighs on them, as does, in large part, the *responsibility* for Versailles.

Dark days, as if they were covered by a heavy and threatening cloud. Instead of thinning out, it just gets darker and bigger. As secretary of the Propaganda [Fide], I put myself above conflicts, on a plane that's simply Christian, in which all people, from whatever nation, encounter one another and recognize themselves as brothers. Every day I find myself with missionaries from the different warring nations; never among us has a hostile or bitter word been uttered. We work together in a spirit of high Christian understanding that surpasses wretched and fleeting political differences.

However, as a private individual, I remain an Italian citizen, and Italy's agony breaks my heart. I have always loved Italy, and now I feel that I love it even more because it is suffering from misfortune rather than being to blame.

It is the government that is to blame, not Italy. Italy has been deprived of any means of expressing its will. There is also the King, but even he – a man without a strong religious faith – has failed, yielding to the will of Mussolini. It is said that he has occasionally refused to sign decrees presented by Mussolini, but the fact remains that he has infamously burned the constitution on the question of the heir to the throne. In these awkward situations, the King could at least have looked to the old traditions and convoked the Council of the Crown and the Senate: nothing. Nor does Italy have any way of changing the government. At one time, a ministry that would have brought Italy to the edge of the abyss, as in the current situation, would have been thrown out and replaced. Instead, one man has claimed Italy for himself indefinitely. There is still the Senate, but even this great legislative institution has been terrorized and rendered impotent. Acquiescent commissions are created to vote for expenditures, and we are then told that the Senate has voted, etc.

What bitterness. What moral debasement. One must not forget that genuine liberty is an element of human dignity; although masters sustained their slaves, the latter were still slaves: they were treated as objects, not men. "*Paucis vivit genus humanum*," Tacitus wrote. The human genus was a minority compared with the great mass of slaves. This was a monstrous situation and was abolished. How is it that Mussolini did not understand this – he who fought and suffered for freedom? Is he acting in good faith? Has he a logical pattern of thought?

Yesterday I heard that a Fascist made the following paradoxical observation: "We hear too much talk about Italy, forgetting Fascism." It is as if Italy is for the Fascists, and not the Fascists for Italy. At certain times people lose their sense of shame, as happens to the insane.

I have had a letter from the painter [Francesco] Margotti, who has had no further news from his son who is fighting in Bardia: "We beseech God to put an end to these many evils. In Him alone rests our every hope." It is true: there is no other light in this darkness. With others I do not discuss the war, but if I do say something, I repeat the following phrase: "Prayer and discipline." Discipline: otherwise things will go from bad to worse.

Our poor homeland finds itself on the horns of a dilemma: either to lose the war or to win it with Germany's assistance. We are lost with either solution. If we lose the war, *vae victis*! [woe to the vanquished!] If we win along with Germany, Hitler will think about rebuilding a kind of Holy Roman Empire, where nothing will remain sacred. Mussolini will have handed Italy over to Germany.

For we Catholics, this is also a matter of faith. They say that they will publish German and Italian postal stamps featuring the images of Hitler and Mussolini. *Roma moritur et ride* [Rome dies, and laughs] ... We cannot divine God's mysterious plans. We do know, however, that He punishes pride. One is reminded of Napoleon. A future historian may well reveal that the beginning of Italy's defeat and its rush toward the abyss will be called 28 October 1940 – the attack on Greece.

31 JANUARY 1941

Marking the eighth anniversary of his coming to power, Hitler delivered a speech at the Sportpalast. Among other things he said, "Germany and Italy were practically excluded from the life of the world for three centuries, with the result that what held sway in Europe was a disequilibrium on the continent in favour of Great Britain, which acted to hold Europe in place in the name of the balance of power." In reality, it is necessary to establish a new order, in which all the powers have a chance to live and work. Men were not made for the earth; the earth was made for men. It is not right that one nation monopolizes, for its own profit, all the territories and riches of the world. Nor is it right that America and Australia close their doors to the immigration of young and dynamic people.

America, which is moving against the Axis, can examine its own conscience and see whether it has helped to lay the groundwork for today's catastrophe of civilization by prohibiting immigration. [Woodrow] Wilson was a false prophet: now Roosevelt is moving *to save democracy*, transforming America into an arsenal. But it remains to be seen what kind of prophet he is.

In Hitler's speech there is a fundamental equivocation. To give the nations of the Axis a better order and a more honest possibility of life, was it necessary to violently suppress many states? Is it necessary that a people renounce the incomparable gift of genuine liberty?

The Italian people have been reduced to a herd, where they are not even left freedom of speech in private. A few days ago I found myself in the office of Bishop Mons. Antonio Giordani;[2] before he began speaking, he took the precaution of switching off the telephone line.

2 FEBRUARY 1941

I was surprised to see a reprint of an article by De Bono[3] in which he states, "It is foolish to believe that you can suspend the time-tested principles of the art of war." Who, then, has suspended the time-tested principles of the art of war? Who is responsible for the stupid, disgraceful, and criminal action against France and Greece?

Mussolini was and is the minister of too many ministries and also wanted to be the chief strategist of the war. That is how the less senior officials were hampered; they lose their sense of responsibility, and the disorganization that emanates from the top permeates right down to every sector of the armed forces.

[2] Antonio Giordani (1877–1960), titular bishop of Mindo, was also the assistant general of the Gioventù Italiana del Littorio [GIL; Italian Fascist Youth].

[3] Emilio De Bono (1866–1944), a Fascist politician, one of the *quadrumviri* of the March on Rome, who had been minister of the colonies from 1929 to 1935, was among the signatories of the famous order against Mussolini presented by Grandi on 25 July 1943. He was subsequently put on trial and executed.

11 FEBRUARY 1941

On 11 February I was in Portogruaro[4] and Murlis[5] [Udine]. My two nephews Augusto and Luciano were drafted. One can say that Luciano, with brief intervals, has been a soldier for six years. He is now in Albania. Their mother, full of confidence in God and with a Christian sense of resignation, was calm and serene. At Murlis there are no men left. Aunt Geltrude left Portogruaro to keep Caterina company and comfort her.

At Portogruaro, Mrs Bonazza-Scarpa asked me to write a line or two in an album. I wrote: *Stat in adversis suo secura fato* – that is, Italy is strong in adversity and secure in her destiny.

I firmly hope that Italy, whatever the outcome of the war, will make a *good peace*. This will not be given it through benevolence or principles of justice, but simply because it will be in the interests of and beneficial to its enemies. A nation of 45 million people must have the resources that are necessary for life; otherwise peace will be nothing but a time bomb, ready to explode at a new point. The present is cloudy; but with hope we can see the future, even if we have to endure the occasional dark and stormy period.

12 FEBRUARY 1941

The bombing of Genoa is a very painful event. It is painful for the victims and because of the destruction, but also on account of the defeat inflicted on the Italian Navy and Air Force. It is said that the enemy ships were able to bombard Genoa for hours undisturbed. Where was the navy? Why wasn't at least a submarine or a torpedo boat mobilized? Why did the airplanes reach the fleet in the afternoon, after the bombardment was over? How could the enemy fleet circulate in the Mediterranean and the Tyrrhenian undisturbed?

[4] Costantini spent some of his vacations in Portogruaro [Venezia] at his sister Maria's home. Maria was married to Giovanni Pietro Tasca, a physician and director of the city's hospital. The couple was of great assistance in managing the Istituto San Filippo Neri for the so-called sons of the war [children orphaned by the war].

[5] At Murlis [now in Pordenone province], Costantini enjoyed spending his vacation in the country home that he and his brothers had purchased.

My heart breaks thinking that men or perhaps Providence did not come to their aid. Scripture says: "*Nisi Dominus custodiret civitatem frustra vigilant qui custodiunt eam*"[6] [Ps. 126:2].

They speak of disorganization. This is not an excuse, it is an aggravation. There are various reasons for it, already mentioned in these notes. But this situation undoubtedly derives from the arbitrariness, the centralization, of the new and stupid methods adopted in the mobilization under Mussolini's orders. If the mobilization had been done according to military science, the entire immense army machinery would have been put into motion. The high command, expert and precise, would have given a tone, a rhythm, and a sense of vigilance to the entire military leadership. Instead, the mobilization proceeded in dribs and drabs, with the overall effect that we all know and with the depressing result of creating an unfair situation. In fact, we see that in one family several soldiers were called up; in others, nobody or one – all of which results in a striking unfairness.

If the prosecution of the war does not change, Fascism will be overthrown, leaving a furrow and an outpouring of passions and vendettas. From Mussolini's work there will remain a few reasonable achievements, among which are the Conciliation, land reclamation, assistance to mothers and children, etc.

FOR THE TRUTH   16 FEBRUARY 1941

In one of the addresses the Holy Father delivered at the Wednesday general audience – in which the fatherly fervour of the Universal Pastor is rivalled only by the luminous clairvoyance of the Supreme Head of the Church – His Holiness deplored the fact that "in the great family of nations, the objective of destroying the fraternal relations between the sons of the same Heavenly Father seems to have established itself." [He] affirmed that "mendacious literature can become an instrument no less lethal than armoured vehicles and bombers."[7]

Only with time can we adequately measure the profound wisdom of these words, but it is certain that what is happening these days offers ever more abundant proof demonstrating just how this ringing denunciation is justified.

---

[6] "Unless the Lord keep the city, he watcheth in vain that keepeth it."
[7] cc: *L'Osservatore Romano*, 16 February 1941.

SUNDAY, 23 FEBRUARY 1941

From my bed, in which I find myself because of an attack of arthritis, I tried to listen to the speech Mussolini delivered at the Adrian Theatre on the military and political situation. I could not hear the entire speech because the radio was outside my bedroom. I therefore do not intend to offer any perspective on the long speech. But what I did manage to hear was a continuous roar of applause. Poor Italy, how low a state it has been reduced to! The homeland is in mourning under the weight and shame of the Greek and Libyan defeats; it is in mourning for the punishing uncertainty of what tomorrow may bring; and the councillors of the nation surround Mussolini with applause. ...

It is true that this is not the real Italy but a political clique that profits from Fascism; but even that is profoundly shameful. Among other things, foreigners will say that the Italian people have exalted Mussolini. Poor Italy! Whatever the contents of that speech, it was a speech of grief. They ought to have listened to it with discipline and dignity. Even this is now lost.

For the Polish Army

General Sikorski, prime minister and head of the Polish Army, delivered the following speech on the occasion of the honorary degree conferred on him by the University of St Andrews (England) [sic]: " I accept this honour as a tribute offered to the Polish Army, which fought well not only in defence of its own land but also at Narvik, Metz, Belfort, and on the Marne, and with great effort reached the British coast to continue by your side a struggle without compromise against the greatest evil that could ever have threatened humanity. The price that we paid on that land is enormous, but we persist in our resolve to spare no sacrifice in our effort to restore to Poland the greatness that belongs to it. The struggle we fight is for the triumph of our conception of the world; it is a struggle for the triumph of democracy, for fundamental liberty, for culture and civilization, and – as a consequence – it is a struggle for justice, because the law is fundamental to every freedom in an organized society and therefore a necessary part of any progress. We must build together a true *Commonwealth of Nations*, basing it on respect for the natural rights of man and of nations."[8]

[8] cc: *L'Osservatore Romano*, 3 March 1941.

21 MARCH 1941

The *Foglio d'Ordini* of the National Fascist Party [Partito Nazionale Fascista] contains the following address to Il Duce, delivered by the secretary of the party in the name of the Blackshirts: "Duce! The Twenty-second Anniversary of the Fasci finds the Italian nation under arms, protagonists of their new history. The courage of Fascist Italy, launched against the most powerful Empire in the world, consecrates the heroic spirit of the Revolution and the warrior-like temperament of the new generations of Fascism. From You, created for the struggle and driven by the purest ideals of life, the Party unfurls its flags in the sun of springtime and is proud of its contribution of blood and valour in this revolutionary war. Duce! The will of the Blackshirts is unconquerable: Victory! By your commands, as always, we will be Victorious!"

Reading this address I feel profoundly sad. The bitter words of an old Roman come to mind: *Roma ridet et moritur* [Rome laughs and dies]. We will be victorious! ... This is an ironic word to use. The Empire is dissolving and the Negus is marching toward Addis Ababa; in Albania there was in recent days a great initiative that came to nothing, with the negative effect on morale of a fresh defeat; the army appears disorganized; finances are adrift, and every day life inflicts new scarcities on the poorest classes; the Italian people, accustomed to twenty years of passiveness in the face of a tyrannical oligarchy, are distracted, disheartened, embittered, in voiceless revolt against the regime. And the Fasci say, "We will be victorious!"

Even if we could get the Germans to help us, we would still be defeated because we have hitched ourselves to the German wagon. This is the final outcome of twenty years of Fascist regime. In 1922, the Italian people, reacting against Communism, embraced Mussolini, desiring to assert the rights of victory won in the last war and to re-establish a little order and discipline in the nation. Later, the people submitted to being treated as a herd, deprived of any possibility of criticism, because Mussolini had in fact done a few good things. But the frenzy of the war and his infatuation with a stupid and boundless pride have led him astray, and with him have pushed poor Italy into the abyss. She deserves a better fate. Nobody speaks of the Crown: it does not exist. The King could have saved Italy and himself, but he did nothing. And Italy, suffering and blood-drenched, has detached itself from him. One has the overwhelming impression that God has abandoned the King and Mussolini. Mussolini's private life and the vileness of many of those who surround him have heaped dirt on the ruins of many great things. Mussolini is lacking the moral rectitude and foundation of religious and moral principles on which the future must be built. A thousand inconsistencies flake off the Mussolini structure. A thousand contradictions drain the authority from a man infatuated with himself. And today the vile words that he spoke against Greece and the Negus will backfire on him. What bitterness! And to think that the soldiers are admirable for their spirit of sacrifice. With those soldiers we could achieve miracles. But soldiers and civilians must have confidence in those who lead and govern them. Now nobody has confidence in Mussolini, the man who wanted to turn himself into a general and strategist.

Yesterday I was at the villa at Celio, the seat of the Geographic Institute. I read the beautiful inscription on the pedestal of an Egyptian obelisk. It reads: "This among many ruins, amidst the fall of the Roman Empire, remains intact. Such is virtue."

23 MARCH 1941

There was another large failed offensive in Albania. My nephew Luciano is there with the Alpini. We know nothing about him. Is he alive, is he wounded, is he dead? Lisetta, his sister, is reassured because a letter from Luciano arrived at Murlis. But that was before this offensive. I leave Lisetta in this illusion, but I cannot but be worried.

26 MARCH 1941

Monsignor Balconi, superior of the Missions Institute of Milan, tells me that Milan is champing at the bit, that they are reliving the memory of those five days, and how unbearable it is to put up with what seems in essence to be a German dictatorship. On the occasion of the celebration of the foundation of the Fasci, there was found in the Piazza del Duomo a poster showing Hitler standing and Mussolini polishing his boots ... Naturally, it was immediately removed. Discontent that cannot show itself publicly is like the drip, drip, drip of a rainshower that penetrates and soaks everything. One newspaper yesterday wrote these symptomatic lines: "Children, do not report outside what you hear said in the family ..."

THE PEOPLE FOR IL DUCE   1 APRIL 1941
"Yesterday in Piazza Venezia, Rome relived once again the grand and memorable Revolution, which continues and grows with its renewing

impetus for the necessities of life, and which cannot carry on without justice and by virtue of the Italian people. The entire Italian nation wants to express these convictions, renewing its most fervid and passionate expression of its inalterable devotion to Il Duce."[9]

Vitae postscenia celans [Lucretius]. We know how those gatherings in Piazza Venezia are organized. Fascists are enlisted by postcard, and in the crowd there are a few officials in civilian clothes with orders to call Mussolini to the balcony and then to initiate the applause.

2 APRIL 1941

Matsuoka, the Japanese minister of foreign affairs, arrived on 31 March.[10] He has apparently come to see how things are going in the West. What will he see in Italy? A lost Empire, Libya virtually lost, a new defeat in Albania, a fresh rout on the seas, for which they say Mussolini is directly responsible because he wanted to turn himself into an admiral … The toasts exchanged between Matsuoka and Ciano are nothing but words … The newspapers celebrate the popular rallies in honour of the Japanese minister and Mussolini, but this inspires a feeling of revolt. The demonstrators were invited, provided with flags, and instructed to applaud. It is painful to see that the Italian people, after twenty years of this regime, are reduced to this: to grumble *sotto voce* and then, if required, to applaud. Poor dear Italy! It deserved a better fate. Good sense is asserted through jokes; like the Roman parodies in earlier times, they represent popular satire.

2 APRIL 1941

Today Matsuoka paid a visit to the Pope. It is said that they met for an hour. The Roman newspapers did not want to publicize the visit. What pettiness! They are so seized with ill-temper that they would have preferred the visit not to be made. But the diplomats of the Far East know their business and with a little smile can confound rude behaviour.

---

[9] cc: *Il Messaggero*, 1 April 1941.

[10] Yosuke "Frank" Matsuoka (1880–1946) was a Japanese politician who lived for several years in Portland, Oregon, where he obtained a degree and converted to Christianity. As Japan's minister of foreign affairs in 1940–41, he was a supporter of his country's alliance with Nazi Germany and Fascist Italy. He was captured by Allied forces in 1945 and died in the United States while he was on trial for wartime crimes against humanity.

Matsuoka will have seen that only one thing stands strong in the midst of the present ruins: the Church. In fact, it is said that what most impressed and satisfied him was his visit to the Pope.

4 APRIL 1941

Yesterday the young Friulian Countess de Claricini[11] told me that she was totally disgusted with what she saw in Rome: full theatres, sentimental movies, and student demonstrations in favour of Matsuoka and Mussolini. While the homeland is in mourning for military failures and the Empire is almost lost, this mindless living truly offends decent sensibilities. It is also a spectacle of pitiful incomprehension. Whoever writes the history of this period will have to conclude that the Italian people are passive and grumble quietly but are not capable of determined reaction. In the murky outlines of the times, this is a shadow that covers the nation with shame; it is perhaps the saddest loss. Even after Caporetto, Rome offers this disgusting spectacle.

4 APRIL 1941

They say that this morning they found a cardboard suitcase around the neck of the Lion of Judah at the base of the monument dedicated to the Fallen of Dogali, which read: "I am preparing to return to Addis Ababa ..."

PALM SUNDAY   6 APRIL 1941

The beautiful liturgy of Palm Sunday is disturbed by the atmosphere of war that makes our breathing anxious. Today at 9 AM the radio announced the note that Germany sent to Yugoslavia yesterday. This is a new serious intention to go to war. The radio report did not mention Italy. May it be God's will that poor dear Italy, onto which is poured the entire might of England and America, does not become involved in this new war. Fiume would be quickly lost and perhaps a part of Istria, and we would have the Yugoslavs at our backs in Albania and Trieste.

[11] Costantini is likely referring to Contessa Giuditta de Claricini di Bottenicco, in the town of Moimacco, close to Cividale del Friuli. This noble family had been in Bottenicco since 1260 and obtained feudal status from Emperor Charles IV in 1368.

Mons. Nigris, the apostolic delegate to Albania, has written an extremely alarming letter but says that he will stay at his post. Good.

In the meantime, victories portend an improvement in the war in Libya. Benghazi has been retaken. It's too bad that this was not accomplished by the Italians alone ...

7 APRIL 1941

Italy has entered the war against Yugoslavia. What will happen to Fiume and Albania? Probably, the little King Peter will lose his crown, which itself was snatched from his grandfather by betrayal and assassination.

12 APRIL 1941

Today the *Corriere della Sera* published on its front page an essay entitled "Italy Is Great," which exalts the Italian armed forces and people. It is a sad time we live in when *vel nomina rerum confunduntur* [even the names of things are falsified]. Even the other papers are full of rhetoric lionizing Il Duce, the man who dishonoured Italy before the world, presenting Italians as if they were a nation of carefree people.

Everybody speaks up in private, but not even one voice has been raised to save the dignity of a free people ... There is no free press, no parliament, no king to demonstrate a will to defend the guarantees of the constitution and the crown. The Senate is terrorized. Every freedom of expression is suppressed by the spectre of imprisonment. And they say, "Italy is great" ... while Italy has never found itself as low as it is today ...

Many Italians loved and idolized Mussolini; now, they detach themselves from him, disillusioned, embittered. He was a paper giant. If only he had a little *fear of God*, an internal brake, he could have saved himself. *Dominatur homo homini in malum suum* [Eccles. 8:9; Sometimes one man ruleth over another to his own hurt].

13 APRIL 1941

I went to my family at Murlis [Udine] to spend the Easter holidays there – holidays veiled in sadness, also because we have no news of my nephew Luciano from Albania. We hope he is one of the 7,000 missing in this last disastrous battle. It has been a sad Easter for Italy, and even sadder for the many families who grieve for those fallen or injured or taken prisoner. The words of the Battle of Legnano come to mind: "For the Passion of Christ and for Milan!"[12] The descendants of Barbarossa now stroll through Italy as if they owned it.

THE POPE'S MESSAGE   13 APRIL 1941
After Mass we listened to the papal message. We were moved by the noble words of the Vicar of Christ, defender of liberty, justice, and Christian love. "Let us pray," he said, "for a quick peace. Let us pray for a peace for all, not a peace of oppression and the destruction of nations, but a peace that, guaranteeing the honour of all nations, satisfies their essential needs and the legitimate rights of all."[13] Amidst so much darkness shines a light that consoles our spirits.

                                                     17 APRIL 1941
News is circulating that advances are being made in Yugoslavia and Libya. But the advances are those of the Germans. They have the attitude that they are saving us, whereas instead they are saving themselves. They should be the ones who are grateful ... The Fascist press is troubled and has employed its violent and base style. Here is an example taken from *Il Piccolo* of Rome of 13–14 April: "There is still a puny minority of social garbage, people without a homeland and without honour, exhibiting attitudes and certain behaviours at odds with a state of war, who still appear to ignore the fact that the Italian people, on battlefields near and far, are writing in blood a page of glory in the history of the new Italy and the new world civilization."

                                                     19 APRIL 1941
The following is from a speech of Buffarini Guidi, under-secretary of the Ministry of the Interior: "Exceptional circumstances have put to the test the excellences and value of the Lateran Pacts. The Ministry of the Interior continues its policy of cooperation with the Holy See, interpreting the Concordat in its letter and above all in its spirit, because it is firmly convinced that this Concordat has become a profound part of the Catholic and Fascist conscience of the Italian people. As well, the Regime

---

[12] This passage is from verse 103 of the poem "Il Parlamento," by Giosué Carducci, which refers to the Battle of Legnano of 29 May 1176.

[13] Pius XII's radio message of 13 April (Easter 1941) is published in AAS 33 (*Bollettino Ufficiale della Santa Sede*, 1941), 112–17 (the cited passage is on page 113).

will maintain its attitude of absolute intransigence before any and all manifestations that attempt to mask, under doctrinal or religious pretences, principles that are political and in clear opposition to those sought and pursued by the Fascist Government. The guardianship of the public spirit at this extraordinary time will in any event be upheld energetically by state authority. (Applause)."

20 APRIL 1941

While I am quickly jotting down these thoughts during these morning hours of the octave of Easter, reaching me from the Via di Propaganda are the silvery voices of the singing children who accompany the Blessed Sacrament to offer communion to the sick. I face the window and see the beautiful orderly procession in which young boys and girls, with flowers in their hands, form an escort of honour to the Blessed Sacrament. There is also a nice group of men and women. The procession makes its way toward the Piazza di Spagna, and the beautiful singing fades into the distance. It will be for this that Christ the Consoler, Christ the Master of Truth, will return to earth. And humanity will welcome in him the one Saviour.

AFTER THE HOLY FATHER'S MESSAGE   20 APRIL 1941

The Holy Father's Easter message was broadcast everywhere on radio and was received with profound devotion by the faithful and with respectful attention and deference by all. Notable among the first responses was that of Le Temps,[14] for what it says and the times in which it writes, namely, in France's current circumstances, where it is possible to judge events through a most painful experience and with great objectivity. The paper defined the Pope's message as "the great voice of peace."

FOR HISTORY   20 APRIL 1941

A Roman newspaper published these shameless words. My pen trembles in my hand to quote them: "Today Germany celebrates, with the solemnity befitting an historical moment, the fifty-second birthday of Adolph Hitler, as the Italian people with profound cordiality share the joy of a great friendly nation and ally. From all the fronts of war there rises today a shared voice of good wishes and a single thought that exalts a heroism

---

[14] Le Temps was a French daily that ceased publication during the Second World War and began to publish again from 1944 onward as Le Monde.

in the certainty of victory, which is already taking shape and which brings with it the restoration of a long-suppressed justice."

Vidi impium (l'anticristo) superexaltatum et elevatum sicut cedros Libani. Et transivi, et ecce non erat, et quaesivi eum, et non est inventus locus eius. [Ps. 37:35; I have seen the wicked highly exalted and lifted up like the cedars of Lebanon. And I passed by, and lo, he was not; and I sought him and his place was not found].

COMMUNISM OR SUPER-FASCISM?   21 APRIL 1941

In truth, there is a particular anxiety: Mussolini has said that we still must close the gap between the rich and the workers. Where are we going? Some people talk of super-fascism, which would be none other than Communism. It is certain that returning war veterans will not accept this *Imperium in imperio,* this oligarchy of the privileged and gluttonous. Italy will no longer accept being deprived of any possibility of expressing what it thinks; it will no longer accept that more than 45 million people are at the mercy and unrestrained will of one man. This type of panicked terror into which Mussolini has thrown Italy must surely end.

21 APRIL 1941

I met with Senator Theodoli[15] outside the Senate entrance. He was speaking of the situation with bitterness. The senator told me, "In the corridors of the Senate, senators in groups of two or three criticize the tyranny and politics that have brought the country so many military and naval disasters and hitched us to Germany's wagon. Yet when they assemble in session and the bell rings, the senators no longer have the courage to oppose orders from above." This is how Italy, at low tide, has hit the muddy bottom ....

IL DUCE'S DECREE   23 APRIL 1941

Here is Il Duce's decree to the troops on the Greek front after the armistice with Greece: "Troops of all the Armed Forces on the Greek front! After six months of extremely bitter struggle, the enemy has laid down its arms. Victory consecrates your bloody sacrifice, which was especially

---

[15] Alberto Theodoli (1873–1955), Marquis of Sambuci, was adviser to the Bank of Rome and its *commisario* for a brief period during the Second World War. He was made a senator in 1934.

heavy for our ground forces, and enlightens your flags with new glory ..." Victory? Over whom? Over what? The Italians have only just retaken the positions they originally lost. At Giannina they encountered the Germans, who stopped the Italians in their tracks. The victory over Greece is Germany's doing.

Those words are rapidly disappearing clouds, even if they shine with light; the blood, the sacrifice, the cries of pain that were heard from the imposing Greek and Albanian cliffs echo in the hearts of all Italians and tighten them in a vise of endless suffering. Nothing is sadder than a sacrifice made in vain than blood spilled in vain and pooled in the dust of defeat. What remains of all this sacrifice? The crime of aggression remains; the defeat inflicted by the Greeks remains; the bitterness against those who wanted this action remains; there also remains a boundless pity and a heartfelt love toward the soldiers who showed such valour and heroism for nothing. I am in anguish thinking that my nephew Luciano may be among the fallen.

25 APRIL 1941

A serious person who is used to listening to radio dispatches from abroad learned that the Holy Father has approached the British authorities to obtain assurances that in any eventuality the lives of the civilians of East Africa will be protected. The British authorities responded that British troops, in collaboration with those of the Negus, will secure public order, guaranteeing protection for the civilian population. This protection is in fact one of the conditions attached to the Negus's return to Ethiopia.

29 APRIL 1941

Today I saw Mons. Haver [Luigi]. He was sad and anxious and said, "We are in a period of serious tension between the Axis and the Vatican. The Vatican is straightforward and proper. Naturally, the Pope is the Pope; he cannot be the chaplain of the Axis."

31 APRIL 1941

Today I saw posters in the city bearing a foul caricature depicting a Greek flattened by a coffin, upon which were the insignias of Nazism and Fascism. Underneath was written, "We have broken the backs of the Greeks." Mussolini is always right ...

Errare humanum est; perseverare in errore diabolicum est [To err is human, to persist in error is evil]. The Germans will plant on the

Acropolis at Athens only the German flag. Eight to ten days have passed since Greece was occupied by troops allied to Italy: not one word yet on Italian prisoners ... What a lack of mercy and psychological balance – and what disorganization!

THE FATE OF MY NEPHEW LUCIANO   10 MAY 1941
Father Luigi Faralli, chaplain to the 3rd Regiment, Alpine Artillery, writes to me: "Your nephew, much respected and appreciated in this Regiment, was chosen as OC observation and control on Mount Golico, along with Lieutenant Zuani. The Greeks were at 1615 m, while the Alpini occupied a position at 1534 m. Every day, especially at night, came an assault that never had a tangible result, while the Greeks shelled the position at 1534 m. Every time it occurred, it did light damage or resulted in a small advance. The Greeks attacked with vigour in the hope of cutting off the last line to reach Tepeleni and Valona. On the night of 6 March the Greek assault began once again. Luciano Costantini was in his tent at the position at 1534 m and was beginning to telephone the Conegliano unit when all of a sudden his voice was cut off and we feared the worst – or perhaps a hit knocked out the telephone line. The Alpini of the 8th Regiment reported after a few days that a mortar shell had landed on the tent and blown up the entire position. The Greeks came and remained for 15 days, after which they were chased off that position, where the shoeless naked body of Lieutenant Zuani was found, whom I buried on 23 March; but of Costantini nothing was found. We fear that perhaps he was taken prisoner, but based on the declaration of the Alpini he was hit full on; and as he would have remained for 15 days in enemy territory, nobody can determine if he was made prisoner or was buried by the Greeks. Right now, however, there is a detail to bury the dead, and therefore if he is found we will immediately inform the family, but we do not believe we will find him. In any event, if this action offers us some certainty it will be immediately relayed, but there is no hope because even if cadavers are found, it will be difficult to identify them. Your Excellency, if to the family I cannot reveal everything, to you I cannot hide anything, and I have told you what I know. Luciano was valorous and an excellent Christian – an example of courage to all."

Poor dear Luciano! He left determined to do his duty to the end, and he did. He held dear to his heart the dream of starting a family. And this monstrous Moloch of war has swept his dream away. His tragedy is the same as that of many other young people. I experienced great pity for the dead on the Carso and on the Piave. Back then, there was light. Back then, the sacrifice was being called for by Italy and was made for Italy. Today, it is imposed by a madman to satisfy his criminal megalomania.

25 MAY 1941

Yugoslavia has fallen under German and Italian military rule. On 18 May Pavelic,[16] the government leader, came to Rome with a Croatian delegation and obtained agreement that Victor Emmanuel III will appoint Duke Aimone of Savoy to be king of the Yugoslav territories under Italian occupation...The words of Jesus Christ come to mind. He said that a house will endure if its foundations are built on rock, but will fall if its foundations are build on sand: "And the rain descended, and the floods came, and the winds blew, and beat upon that house; and it fell: and great was the fall of it ..." [Mt. 7:27].

I have the distinct impression that in this murky whirlwind of war, in this disintegration of every right, the house of this new dynasty is built on sand ... It is certain now that the Holy See will not recognize the new King of Yugoslavia. In fact, the Holy Father Pius XII received Duke Aimone simply as a private citizen.

Painful news in the meantime comes from East Africa of the surrender of the garrison of Amba Alagi. The headquarters *Bulletin* recounted how "the enemy, in honour of the valour of our soldiers, conceded military honours to them, leaving our officials with their sidearms and allowing our garrison, with its weapons, to march out of the ruins of Amba Alagi up to the position of the English, who paid them honours." And as a last honour to the commander, the *Bulletin* added, "The Duke of Aosta followed the fate of his troops." The painful exit from the struggle seemed to have given even greater emphasis to the valour of those fighting men who, deprived of any communication with the homeland, faced with an overwhelming enemy in terms of numbers, arms, and resupply, driven

[16] Ante Pavelic (1889–1959), a Croatian politician and founder of the ultra-nationalist movement known as Ustasha, forged ties with Fascism and Nazism, becoming dictator in 1941 of the Croatian state formed by the German-Italian invaders. After the Second World War he lived out his remaining years in Generalissimo Francisco Franco's Spain.

only by their devotion to duty and inspired by the example of a Royal Prince, fought for the territory inch by inch, inflicting serious losses on the attacking force and sustaining heavy pressure to alleviate the pressure on North Africa.

27 MAY 1941

Yesterday evening I went to visit a hospital for the war-wounded that is at the mother house of the Brothers of Christian Schools in Via Aurelia. What a spectacle of suffering! Many soldiers were gathered in a hallway to sing a hymn to Mary; some were in wheelchairs, some with crutches, some were seated or kneeling, having had both feet amputated; a few were without hands. But for the most part the soldiers were maimed in the feet; one person got around on the stumps of his legs that had been amputated from the knee. They were singing with joyful voices hymns glorifying Mary. On their faces was no trace of rancour or bitterness; they were young faces, healthy, serene, I would say almost smiling. I went to say a few words of greeting and comfort, and I could not speak because I was so overcome and my voice kept trailing off in a sob. I steeled myself, remembering the soldiers of the last war, who were the fathers of these soldiers, and spoke of the richness of the sacrifice of Christ crucified: "You have given a part of your lives and your blood to fulfill your duty. May God remember your sacrifice, and your country will not forget you. Comfort yourselves in the thought of having done your duty and having returned, while many of your colleagues have remained there on the battlefield. You are alive. Return to your families. The Crucifix is the symbol of sacrifice and of painful victory – He is the Great Consoler."

I distributed little medals. Dear good young people! Their faces were full of innocence, like the faces of children. The old soldiers of my time were not like that: many were poisoned by anticlericalism and Communism. Leaving the hospital, I felt such regret thinking of all that torment, all that broken youth that could have been avoided. We should not have gone to war, but if anything we should have remembered the extremely bitter experience lived on the Alpine front and provisioned our soldiers in Albania with munitions and the necessary equipment. This carelessness and disorganization is not just a shame but a crime. Dear good young people! They were not thinking about such things. Youth is generous.

THE APOSTOLIC DELEGATE
OF EGYPT VISITS PRISONERS OF WAR   31 MAY 1941

"We have announced news of the visit of the apostolic delegate in Egypt [Monsignor Testa][17] to hospitals where the war-wounded are recovering. Information now follows of Mons. Testa's visits, at the request of the Holy Father, to prisoners of war."[18]

This news, so comforting to many families whose members are being held prisoner, is not reported in the press. Even in the past, news was cloaked in silence. Why? Either they do not want the press to report on prisoners of war or they believe that by remaining silent they will generate hostility toward England. This shows not only a lack of humanity but also a lack of psychological understanding. No news was released of the prisoners held by Greece, and this only served to engender a feeling of rancour against the Italian government.

If they think they can incite hostility toward England, they are mistaken. The resentment instead will be turned against the Italian government. Even in the depths of the tragedy of war, humanity endures. To ride roughshod over the deep feelings of this suffering humanity is an act of authentic and idiotic cruelty.

The news agencies and Vatican radio have offered extremely valuable assistance in the discovery and dissemination of news. The radio broadcasts, which began in June 1940 after the occupation of Belgium and France, started with a few hundred outlets per week, but slowly expanded to Australia, South Africa, etc. The Papal Office of Children's Aid, led by the valorous Mons. Baldelli,[19] has initiated and developed a magnificent relief program. The Holy Father has explained the immense work of both

[17] Gustavo Testa (1886–1969), titular archbishop of Amasea, was the apostolic delegate in Egypt and Arabia from 1934 until 1948, when he was also given responsibility for Palestine and Jerusalem. He was papal nuncio in Switzerland from 1953 until 1959, when he was elevated to cardinal by Pope John XXIII.

[18] CC: *L'Osservatore Romano*, 31 May 1941.

[19] Ferdinando Baldelli (1886–1963), an official of the Fifth Section (Emigration) of the Sacred Congregation of the Consistory, was made a bishop in 1959. He was president of the Pontificia Opera di Assistenza (POA), which before 1953 was called the Pontificia Commissione di Assistenza.

spiritual and material aid it carries out to assist prisoners of war, refugees, internees, and populations that languish in misery, the war-wounded, etc. It is also known that the Pope intervenes when possible to request clemency for those condemned to death. There is no misery that does not find a ready and affectionate response in the heart of the Holy Father, who, beyond any differences of race, religion, and nationality, carries out his marvellous work as an *alter Christus* [another Christ].

THE SANCTITY OF JUSTICE   1 JUNE 1941

In his great address today the Pope recalled a passage from the secular poem of Pope Leo XIII: "*Vae segregatis Numine legibus! Quae lex honestis, quae superest fides? Nutant, semel submota ab aris, atque nunt labefacta iura.*"[20]

12 JUNE 1941

The facts stand against Mussolini's presentation to the Chamber:

1 the Empire lost;
2 Libya lost and reconquered, thanks to the Germans;
3 the defeat inflicted on Italy by the Greeks, with over 13,000 dead and
   a great number of disabled;
4 the demonstrated lack of preparation and incapacity of the leadership;
5 the devaluation of the lira and the rise of the cost of living.

There is the gain of Dalmatia and Slovenia, but this is a small thing compared to the debit side of the ledger. And will these conquests last? These facts are more eloquent than words. One feels shame for the Chamber, which does nothing except applaud. These are times of incredible decadence. A Chinese proverb says, "When the sun is low, even small men cast a large shadow."

---

[20] "Woe to those condemned by God's laws. For honest people, what laws are superior to faith? Once separated from altars, they quake, and rights so enfeebled end in ruin."

THE DEPORTATION OF A HUNDRED THOUSAND CITIZENS FROM THE BALTIC STATES, 14–15 JUNE 1941 [21]

23 JUNE 1941

Yesterday morning the news that Germany is at war with Russia exploded like a bomb. The newspapers gave no hint of it. The news came on the radio. This is one of the most frightening developments of this terrible world war. Two giants confront each other and the duel is to the finish. The passage from Scripture comes to mind: *fallacia lonquuntur unusquisque ad proximum suum* [Ps. 18:3; They speak to each other with deceit].[22] Yesterday, Germany was closely tied to Russia to beat Poland. There were treaties and visits, and promises made to oppose England. Now the tables are turned. And England once again courts Russia. Russia will make common cause with England. If England and Russia manage to win the war, England will find itself faced with a competitor much more powerful than Germany. Even Italy will be bound up in this new war.

THE PAPAL MESSAGE   29 JUNE 1941

Beyond time and beyond ephemeral events, from the Vatican's heights, from the eternal rock of truth, the consoling voice of the Pope is raised. Jesus Christ is the Sole Consoler, and the voice of his vicar touches the

---

[21] CC: A religious service for the victims of Soviet rule: "*The twelfth anniversary of the Soviet deportation of 100,000 citizens of the Baltic States.* Yesterday with a religious service at the College of the Marian Fathers in Via Corsica, the Lithuanian and Latvian colonies of Rome commemorated the tragic days of 14–15 June 1941. During these two days the Soviets deported more than 100,000 people from three Baltic States: Lithuania, Latvia and Estonia. Serov – who replaced Beria – ordered the deportation of more than 700,000 people, but the Lithuanian insurrection and subsequent German-Soviet war prevented him from carrying out this crime of genocide. Many of those present were not only eye-witnesses to the manhunt but also lost numerous family members. The Holy Mass was celebrated by the venerable exiled Archbishop of Piepaja, His Excellency Mons. Urbisis, who spoke to those present in both Lithuanian and Latvian and offered emotional words of hope as well as wishes for the future. He offered prayers for the victims of Soviet rule in the Baltic States, who today total several hundreds of thousands" (*Il Popolo*, Monday, 15 June 1953).

[22] This is an error in Costantini's citation. His meaning, however, is clear.

feelings of all people. The Pope connects with the troubled and disheartened souls of the world, comforting them by setting forth the uplifting
nature of a divine Providence that stands above the conflicts of human
events and directs them to its own ends – even if men are not able to
understand them.

Between us and Providence there extends an immense tapestry. From
Providence's perspective, the tapestry has a great and harmonious design,
but from our position underneath this tapestry, we see only a knot of
differently coloured threads.

                                                          7 JULY 1941
The war against Russia, understood in particular as a crusade against
Bolshevism, has found a certain level of support in Italy.

One father told Monsignor Bernardi, "I have two sons in the war.
I tolerated their recall to arms with discipline but without personal
approval. Now my third son is called to serve to go and fight against
Bolshevism. I will accompany him to the train station because I am a
Christian, and I understand that we must fight against the enemy of the
Church." This good man did not consider that Hitler, too, is an enemy of
the Church.

THE COURAGEOUS SPEECH OF THE BISHOP OF MÜNSTER
                                                         20 JULY 1941
Monsignor Clement August von Galen,[23] bishop of Münster, delivered
an admirable speech in the church of Ueberwasser. It was sent to me
clandestinely. I quote a few passages:

[23] Clement August Von Galen (1878–1946), a count, bishop of Münster
from 1933 and a great opponent of Nazism for its neopagan ideology and its
persecutions. He publicly upheld the right of all people to life and freedom,
both the faithful and all his fellow citizens. By doing this, he put his life at great
risk for his outspoken denunciation of Hitler's regime. In the war's immediate
aftermath he continued to be a point of reference for those who had any need
whatsoever. Pius XII elevated him to cardinal on 18 February 1946, at which
time he was popularly nicknamed the Lion of Münster. He died on 22 March
1946. Pope Benedict XVI beatified him on 9 October 2005.

Von Galen's courageous speeches and their repercussions were the subject of
several dispatches of Apostolic Nuncio Cesare Orsenigo to Cardinal Maglione
from Berlin on 17 July 1941, 2 August 1941, 19 August 1941, and 23 September

On Monday, 14 July, I met the governor and asked him for protection for the freedom and property of innocent German citizens. He declared that the Gestapo[24] is a completely autonomous authority in whose operations he could not interfere, but he did promise to convey my concerns and my prayers to Gauleiter Dr Mayer. But nothing happened. On that same Monday I sent a telegram to the Chancellery of the Führer in Berlin. I telegraphed the same message to the Lieutentant for Prussia, to Marshal Göring, to the Minister of the Interior, to the Minister of Religions, and finally also the Supreme Command of the Armed Forces. I had hoped that, if not for reasons of justice, then at least in recognition of the consequences for the morale of the home front, these authorities could put a brake on the actions of the Gestapo and that they would not have refused the chivalrous protection asked of them for innocent German women. But the hope was in vain. Their actions proceeded apace, and what I feared would happen and predicted last Sunday has happened: we are facing the destruction of a community spirit that has in recent days become inexorably damaged.

I made it clear to the Governor, the Minister, and the Supreme Command of the Armed Forces that the violence against innocent German men and the violence against defenceless German women makes a mockery of chivalry and can only be derived from a deep hatred against the Christian religion and against the Catholic Church. Taken together, all these measures sabotage and blow up popular solidarity like an explosive.

Solidarity with men who drive out of our country, like wild game, our religious, our brothers, and our sisters – without legal grounds, without request, and without any possibility of defending themselves and without a judicial sentence? No, with them and with all who share responsibility with them it is not possible to maintain a unity of thought and feeling. I will not hate them and I truly desire that they repent and convert ... This is how, according to the

---

1941. Maglione replied on 2 September 1941, declaring that the Pope approved of the sermons of the bishop of Münster. For more information, see *Le Saint Siège et la guerre mondiale (juillet 1941 – octobre 1942)*, vol. 5 of the *Actes et documents du Saint Siège relatifs à la seconde guerre mondiale* (Vatican City: Libreria Editrice Vaticana, 1942), 88–9, 123, 143–5, 179, 194–6, and 245–6.

[24] The Gestapo were the secret police of the Third Reich. The name derives from the initials Geheime Staatspolizei. Established in 1933 for Prussian territory, it was responsible for the "Night of the Long Knives" of 30 June 1934, from which point it operated throughout Germany. In 1936 Heinrich Himmler assumed leadership of the Gestapo.

Lord's command, we will pray for all those who persecute and slander us. However, until they change, as long as they continue to despoil the innocent, to banish them from the country, to jail them, I reject any solidarity with them! I would be ashamed before God and before you, I would feel ashamed before our noble ancestors, before my chivalrous late father, who educated my brothers and me to venerate every woman and girl respectfully and to protect them chivalrously when they are unjustly oppressed, and especially those who as women are images of our own mother and the Mother of God in Heaven. I would feel ashamed, I repeat, if I maintained solidarity with those who banish from their homes and families women without guilt and without protection and drive them from their land without any means of support.

It is certain that we Christians do not make revolution. We will once again do our duty of obedience toward God and for the love of our people and our homeland ... We will continue to fight against the external enemy, but against the internal enemy that torments and strikes us we cannot take up arms. Here, there is only one way of fighting back: to hold on strongly, constantly, persistently. To become strong and remain firm! We see and clearly experience what lies behind the doctrines that for years they have wanted to impose – and, as a result, have seen the banishment of religion from our schools and the oppression of our associations. Now they even want to destroy Catholic kindergartens: an insurmountable hatred toward Christianity which they want to eradicate.

Become strong, remain firm. At this time, we are not the hammer but the anvil. Others – especially foreigners and dissenters are hammered, and by applying force they want to bend our people and our youth to abandon the proper attitude that we must have before God. We are the anvil and not the hammer. But look what is happening in the forge. Ask the blacksmith or have him teach you. That which is forged on the anvil takes the form not only of the hammer but also of the anvil itself. The anvil cannot strike itself, nor does it have any need to; it simply needs to remain firm and strong. However violent the hammer blows come, the anvil remains quietly firm and also serves in the long run to form what will be forged.

Today's victims between the hammer and the anvil are those without guilt who are unjustly imprisoned or banished and expelled. God will help them to maintain both the form and the behaviour of their Christian steadfastness when the hammer of persecution cruelly strikes them and inflicts on them undeserved injury.

In these days, what is being hammered is our religious community: fathers, brothers, and sisters. The other day I visited some of the expelled in their makeshift quarters, and I was energized by the edifying and courageous manner of these good men and women who are helpless and weak, having been brutally driven out of their convents, torn from the chapel and the area of the Tabernacle, and are preparing to go into an unjust exile with their heads held high, aware of their innocence, having faith in He who provides for the birds of the air and clothes the lilies of the field ... It could be that obeying God and remaining faithful to their conscience will cost me and them our lives, our liberty, and the land of our birth. But it is better to die than to sin. May God, without whom we can do nothing, give me and you this unmovable steadfastness.

Another Address by Bishop Von Galen
At St Lambert's Church in Münster on Sunday, 3 August 1941, Bishop Von Galen delivered a homily on the Gospel [Lk. 19:41–7], which recounted how Christ wept for Jerusalem, the capital of his people:

For several months reports have reached us that, by order of Berlin, those with long-term illnesses and those appearing incurable in sanatoriums and mental asylums are being taken away. After a short time, the relatives then receive notice that the sick person has died, that the body has been cremated, and they can pick up the ashes. Everybody now has a suspicion, which borders on certainty, that these numerous and unexpected deaths of the mentally ill are not occuring naturally but are being done deliberately, taking inspiration from the doctrine which affirms that it is right to destroy lives "that have no vital value"; in other words, to kill innocent people when it is believed that their lives no longer have any value either for the people or for the state: This is a frightening doctrine that seeks to justify the assassination of innocents and the violent death of those who are no longer able to work, the crippled, the incurable, and the elderly infirm.

When I learned of the proposal to take away the sick from Mariental to kill them, I immediately reported this on 28 July to the State Attorney's Office and to the Münster Regional Tribunal as well as to the chief of the Münster Police by registered mail ... I received no news of any action from the State Attorney's Office or the Police ... Once we allow the principle that men have the right to kill other unproductive men ... nobody's life is safe. Any commission can compile a list of the unproductive and declare that, in its judgment, they are "not worthy of living." And no police will protect them, and no tribunal will punish the assassin. If the situation is thus, who can trust a doctor? Perhaps he can report the sick person as unproductive and obtain the order to kill him.

The barbarization of morals and the mutual suspicion that will be generated even inside the family will become imaginable when such a fearsome doctrine is tolerated and applied.

Woe unto the men of our German people if God's sacred Fifth Commandment, "Thou Shalt Not Kill," proclaimed by the Lord amidst thunder and lightning and instilled by the Creator from the beginning in the conscience of man, is not only transgressed but if the transgression is tolerated and committed with impunity!

As for the Sixth Commandment, "Thou Shalt Not Commit Adultery," think of the instructions contained in Rudolph Hess's[25] notorious open letter, which has since disappeared. These were public instructions in all the newspapers that counselled freedom of sexual relations and illegitimate maternity. And what more shameful and vulgar things related to this subject can we read about, see, and feel even here in Münster? Our youth has become used to dressing shamelessly – preparation for future adultery. Modesty, that bulwark of chastity, has been destroyed ....

When it comes to the first three commandments, they have not applied to the German public for a long time. Sunday, along with other feast days, is profaned and removed from service to God. The name of God is abused, dishonoured, and sworn upon, and instead of uniting themselves to the one True Eternal God, other gods are created at a whim to be adored – idols that are called "nature" or "the state," people, or race. Moreover, how many as St Paul said, still have their belly as their god? [Phil. 3:19]. That is, sensual pleasures, the thrill of gold, the hunger of domination. It is no surprise that they even attempt to arrogate to themselves attributes of the divine and make themselves into the lord of life and death.[26]

[25] Rudolph Hess (1894–1987), a Nazi leader designated by Hitler as his successor. In 1941, for reasons still not clear, he fled to England, where he was imprisoned. Condemned to life imprisonment by the Nuremberg Trials of 1946, from 1966 he was the lone prisoner in Spandau Prison.

[26] CC: On 18 February 1946, Mons. Von Galen was made a cardinal. Inside St Peter's, when he was moving forward to receive the cardinal's berretta from the hands of His Holiness Pius XII, a long and very lively applause exploded from the audience when this tall and stately figure passed the cardinals. Unfortunately, Cardinal Von Galen died soon afterwards, on 22 March 1946.

10 AUGUST 1941

On 3 August at Concordia Sagittaria, we solemnly celebrated the Feast of St Stephen. I offered the saint a panegyric. My homily was simply and exclusively religious. Speaking of St Stephen, I offered the following thought of St John: *Haec est victoria, quae vincit mundum, fides nostra* [This is the victory that overcame the world: our faith]. But the papers offered an inexact summation. It is understood that the Ministry of Propaganda wanted to exploit the anti-Bolshevik implications of the homily, amplifying it, etc. They have a need to shake up the public indifference for the war. Cardinal Pietro Fumasoni Biondi[27] wrote to me on 8 August saying, "Your last homily has caused a stir in high places." When I returned to Rome, I amply justified myself and my explanations were accepted. Naturally, I could not personally make the required corrections in the press.

THE DENATIONALIZATION OF STYRIA   10 AUGUST 1941

A Slovenian priest gave me an extensive report on the barbarities being committed in his country. I offer here some passages. Hitler's order *"Macht mir die Südsteinermark deutsch, so deutsch wie die übrige Steiermark"* [Make Lower Styria German – as German as the remaining part of Styria] was executed in May. With this also began the annihilation of religion, of Catholicism, against which was pitted a strong principle, since for thirteen centuries the Slovenes had held their own against extremely strong national pressures from Germans, Italians, and Hungarians.

At the beginning of the summer of 1941, one heard a few voices amongst the German administrators responsible in Graz and Klagenfurt,

---

[27] Pietro Fumasoni Biondi (1872–1960) was a diplomat of the Holy See, a representative in India, Japan, and the United States before being elevated to cardinal in 1933 and named in the same year a prefect of the Sacred Congregation for the Propaganda of the Faith. Celso Costantini, secretary of this dicastery, appreciated the hospitality of Mons. Fumasoni Biondi at the Apostolic Delegation in Washington when Costantini had need of a period of convalescence after the operation he underwent in the United States in 1931. On this, see *Con i missionari in Cina*, vol. 2. (Rome: Unione missionaria del clero in Italia, 1947), 252. Constantini always enjoyed a very good relationship with Fumasoni Biondi, whose esteem for Costantini was such that he placed a great deal of faith in his direction of the activities of the Propaganda.

who counselled a gradual approach to denationalization – over a generation, for example, especially through education, as in the Germanization of the Third Reich. With respect to the annihilation of Catholicism, by contrast, the bureaucrats were completely in agreement; in fact, Stendi, the president of the Steierischer Heimatbund [Military Interest Club], put it this way: "In Lower Styria we need to make room for the new mysticism of blood and race, brought by the ancient Germanic race." In the meantime, during the summer, even on the question of national feeling they chose the radical method, and from June 1941 the annihilation of Slovenians in Germany has proceeded at the same pace as the religious one.

To achieve these objectives ordered by Hitler, measures for the "transformation of the Slovenes" are being used, through propaganda, enticements, and constrictions; but the main method remains the removal of the Slovenians by means of deportations and executions. Their objective is to render the territory German more than the population itself; the authorities are focused on depopulating and reoccupying the region with a German population, rather than making the Slovenian population German. In the occupied territory the only ones remaining are those whom they are sure can be removed immediately and quickly.

All the remaining children and young people are being removed without any reference to their parents and put into kindergartens, schools, and courses and educated along German and anti-religious lines. The majority of the population has been deported or has fled to Serbia, then to Germany, and probably also to countries of the East. These deportations are carried out on a strip of territory that is 18 kilometres wide but in places 50 kilometres wide. Even the so-called *Volksdeutsche*[28] are being targeted for deportation because the new despots do not trust even them, these people having been brought up in good religious circumstances and tolerant national conditions.

Measures against Church Officials
Right from the beginning of the occupation, almost the entire clergy were placed under arrest and detained for weeks in concentration camps. On 1 July 1941 in the Diocese of Maribor, of 250 parishes 180 were

[28] This term indicates Germans of German nationality but of foreign citizenship, resident in Southeastern European countries to 1945.

already without any ecclesiastical administration and 85 percent of all priests (340 of 410) were driven away. In the Diocese of Lublijana, of 240 there are only 9 old and infirm priests left – and even they were incarcerated this summer before being driven out. Among these were a 90 year old, a 73 year old, and a 72 year old. Consequently, in this diocese there are now 210,000 souls without a priest. In the two dioceses with 30 deaneries, 368 parishes, and 750,000 souls, of 618 priests there are only about 30 remaining. We assume that all the property and real estate of these churchmen have been expropriated. All the brothers and sisters have been exiled. The arrests and expulsions were carried out in a brutal fashion, often at night and with abuse. Some priests lost their lives because of this kind of abuse, as in the case of Jesuit Father Zuzek, aged 76. At Maribor, a young Gestapo agent repeatedly slapped and cruelly struck a priest until he repeated the words "I am a Slovenian Pfaff" (*Pfaff* is a pejorative term for priest, now very much in use). The guards forced priests to shine their boots.

The following fact is typical. At the end of April, the Franciscans and Jesuits of Maribor were forced to demolish a Serbian Orthodox church. The fathers carried out this work dressed in their altar garments that ordinarily would have been prohibited. A film was shot during the course of the church's demolition which was then shown in Serbia by order of the occupying authorities to demonstrate to the population "the Catholic priests' hatred of the Orthodox Church." Priests were often forced to transport garbage and do other dirty work, along with imprisoned Communists and common delinquents. Many priests were sent to Croatia, where some originally found work taking care of souls, but later the German authorities prohibited even this activity.

The moral and religious consequences of all these actions are extremely serious: baptism is given by lay people; only civil marriage is possible; to the dying, the Holy Sacraments are not administered; in the majority of churches, Holy Mass is no longer celebrated, and neither are funerals; prayer books are searched for in homes and taken away; the public cult of the person of the Führer is propagated. It is interesting to note that even in occupied territories one may observe the same events that have already happened in Mexico, Spain, and elsewhere: the fewer priests there are and the more difficult and dangerous religious life is, the more the entire population ardently desires the return of normal and ordered conditions. Religious life may suffer on the outside, but on the inside it gains.

Concentration Camps

The life of both clergy and lay people in these camps are a true martyrdom: miserable food and outrages and abuses by young agents of the Gestapo. Many of the detainees – and at the end of November 1941 there were in all tens of thousands – fell ill and died.

Deportations

All intellectuals were forced to leave the country. Some fled and others were deported. These deportations were carried out in truly barbarous ways and in a few hours, without regard for old age, advanced pregnancy, or grave illness. Young marrieds were forced to leave each other and to leave their children, even their littlest ones. Occasionally they could take RM 10,[29] but sometimes not even this small amount. The oldest made it to Serbia or Croatia; the young were sent to Germany as slave labour. The great deportations took place in Lower Styria from the end of April and in Upper Carniola in May and June. These wretched folk, left without food and water, were transported en masse in railcars sealed up for days. There were cases of death as a result of weakness and lack of water (especially among the old and among children) or because of hemorrhaging for lack of bandages.

Graz's *Tagespost* of 27 July 1941, p. 4, reported: "All those who did not want either German victory or a German future have voluntarily or involuntarily abandoned the region." By supreme order, 30,000 intellectuals in Lower Styria and 4,000 in Upper Carniola are to be sent to Serbia, and 65,000 farmers in Lower Styria and 30,000 in Upper Carniola are to be sent to Croatia. In all, there are 180,000 souls affected; they constitute, however, only the first phase, because there are sure to be others. To the end of November the following were deported:

94% of Slovenian church officials
84% of Slovenian engineers
66% of Slovenian professors
45% of Slovenian doctors and pharmacists
20% of Slovenian teachers, office workers, and lawyers.

---

[29] RM=reichmark, currency used in German lands, including occupied territory, 1924–48.

The majority of the German people are not aware of these events and these facts. The German press professes itself surprised that Slovenians are abandoning their homeland, their fertile territory, and are moving to Serbia. The property of these unhappy souls is given to Germans, who often are not aware that their predecessors were forced to abandon their homes and holdings. Terrifying scenes accompanied the rural deportations: some committed suicide, together with small children; others went insane ... In Serbia and Croatia many of them died when they arrived at their destination, for they were without any means of survival, without warm clothes, without food, without a place to stay and without medical attention. It was especially hard for urban people, who were not accustomed to the hardships of this new way of life. The deportations, up to the end of December 1941 affected the 20,000 inhabitants of a strip of land 18 kilometres wide along the new southern border. One can suppose that this strip will later be enlarged to 50 kilometres in width, probably in the spring of 1942. Such a move would certainly signify the liquidation of occupied Slovenia ... We know from solid evidence that deportees can be found in Poland or even farther east, and in western Germany. They also speak of cases in which Slovenian girls, before they are sent away, are branded with "F M" on their arms (*Freimädchen*).[30]

Executions

As a consequence of these deportations, crimes were committed by the population in their most desperate hour. At first – at the end of July – these were acts of sabotage and vendettas, crimes committed against renegades who offered themselves to the authorities as informers. The authorities responded to these acts not with investigations or judicial measures but by killing many innocent hostages. In Upper Carniola alone there were, up to December, 300 such executions along with the incineration of entire villages. Women were also killed. The recent "executions" (in November) were not carried out by shots fired by a firing squad but by the painful martyrdom of individuals, carried out by agents of the Gestapo, who for hours on end tortured the victims, shooting them with an automatic pistol – first the limbs, then the body, and finally the head. This took place in the presence of their comrades in misfortune, by day, in the open, in front of people forced to watch these scenes; nor were schoolchildren spared the scene, causing them a huge destabilization and

[30] *Freimädchen* means, literally, "free girl" or "marked girl."

nervous breakdowns. Similar atrocities took place in Serbia. At Kraljevo and at Kragujevac, two small Serbian cities, 60 percent of the male population was shot by machine gun, in groups of exactly 40 persons, without trial.

THE ATLANTIC CHARTER   12 AUGUST 1941

In the vast solitude of the Atlantic, Roosevelt and Churchill met on 12 August 1941 aboard the cruiser *Prince of Wales* and formulated the principles of the new world order. The document's inspiring principles were the four freedoms that Roosevelt, in his speech of 9 January 1941, established as the foundation of the new world order against Nazi thought: freedom of speech and expression, freedom of worship, freedom from want, and freedom from the fear of war. Where once, as a consequence of victory, there was a territorial expansion at the cost of the defeated states, now the United Nations declares not to have territorial aspirations.

The Text of the Atlantic Charter[31]

1 Their countries seek no aggrandisement, territorial or other.
2 They desire to see no territorial changes that do not accord with the freely expressed wishes of the peoples concerned.
3 They respect the right of all peoples to choose the form of government under which they will live; and they wish to see sovereign rights and self-government restored to those who have been forcibly deprived of them.
4 They will endeavour with due respect for their existing obligations, to further enjoyment by all States, great or small, victor or vanquished, of access, on equal terms, to the trade and to the raw materials of the world which are needed for their economic prosperity.
5 They desire to bring about the fullest collaboration between all nations in the economic field, with the object of securing for all improved labour standards, economic advancement, and social security.
6 After the final destruction of Nazi tyranny, they hope to see established a peace which will afford to all nations the means of dwelling in safety within their own boundaries, and which will afford assurance

---

[31] Reproduced here from the original charter available at www.nato.int.

that all the men in all the lands may live out their lives in freedom from fear and want.

7 Such a peace should enable all men to traverse the high seas and oceans without hindrance.

8 They believe all of the nations of the world, for realistic as well spiritual reasons, must come to the abandonment of the use of force. Since no future peace can be maintained if land, sea, or air armaments continue to be employed by nations which threaten, or may threaten aggression outside of their frontiers, they believe, pending the establishment of a wider and permanent system of general security, that the disarmament of such nations is essential. They will likewise aid and encourage all other practicable measures which will lighten for peace-loving peoples the crushing burden of armament.

These are beautiful affirmations. But can we believe them? Or will the Atlantic Charter end up like Wilson's 14 points? *Vani autem sunt omnes homines, in quibus non subet scientia Dei* [Wis. 13:1; But all men are ineffectual who have no knowledge of God].

The following countries subscribed to the Atlantic Charter: Belgium, Czechoslovakia, Greece, Luxembourg, Holland, Norway, Poland, Russia, France, Mexico, the Philippines, Ethiopia, Iraq, Brazil, and Persia. Here is Ambassador Maisky's[32] exact formulation in offering the adherence of the Soviet government: "The right of every nation to independence and the territorial integrity of its own country, and its right to establish the social order and form of government that seems opportune and necessary for the most efficient progress toward economic and social prosperity."

10 SEPTEMBER 1941

Between 25 and 29 August 1941, Il Duce and the Führer met at the German Military Headquarters. The meeting focused on "all problems of a military and political nature in relation to the developments and length of the war." It aspired to "strict comradeship" and the "common destiny" of the two powers, and the meeting was informed by the

---

[32] Ivan Michailovic Maisky (or Majskij) was the Soviet ambassador to Great Britain, 1932–43. The following year he was head of the war reparations commission. He participated in the Yalta and Potsdam conferences and authored several books of history.

"unshakeable will of the two peoples and their Leaders to continue the war until victory is achieved."

"The new European order that will spring from this victory," the official communiqué continues, "should eliminate to the greatest extent possible the causes that in the past led to European wars. The suppression of the Bolshevik menace on the one hand and plutocratic exploitation on the other will permit a peaceful, harmonious and fruitful collaboration in the areas of politics, economy, and culture between all peoples of the European continent."

Today the Benedictine Dom E. Giersbach, recently returned from Switzerland, told me: "Switzerland carries this hope: 'That every German soldier eats two Bolsheviks and then suffocates.'" Truly, the result of the German-Russian war does not look good for Germany, which advanced but now is confronted with a firm, organized, and formidable resistance. The dream of routing Bolshevism in a few months has vanished. Now comes the winter; military action will settle into a tight conflict of positions. There will be no relief from a long horrible winter. And then? Germany "will begin" to lose the war. The result of the war, in Italy, is terribly negative. The economic and spiritual hardship is ever more serious. The people do not feel the victory on the eastern shores of the Adriatic. The sacrifice of blood weighs heavier every day; the soldiers who return from the front, especially from Albania, say, "After the war they will have to settle accounts with us." And Mussolini and the King must shoulder alone the terrible responsibilities of the times. But the crippling weight of their foolishness keeps the people demoralized. The postwar situation looks dark and threatening, unless a great victory changes the psychology. But this victory is not at all in sight.

14 SEPTEMBER 1941

The Hon. Alcide De Gasperi[33] in a private conversation relayed to me the expression of a German official: "We have won and we will win. But because of our victories, we will be reduced to failure."

[33] Alcide De Gasperi (1881–1954), an Italian statesman and member of parliament in Vienna from 1911 until the defeat of Austria in the First World War. He was elected to the Italian parliament in 1921 for the Italian People's Party [Partito Popolare Italiano (PPI)]. For his anti-Fascism he was condemned in 1926 to 16 months in prison. He then obtained employment in the Vatican. During the Second World War, he reconstituted the PPI under a new name:

A Farmer's Observations

I note here the observations of a farmer, Mr Pelle, an employee of the Propaganda Fide. The plain folk who do not have their heads filled with cultural polemics reason with common sense that goes right to the essence of things. The farmer said, "I fought in the last war. Back then, we were fighting beside England against Germany. Today, twenty years later, we fight against England and beside Germany. Back then, the propaganda against Germany said more or less the same things that are now being said against England."

At the heart of things, for us Italians there is but one issue: change the master. Was it worth conducting this war, massacring our youth, and ruining the country by changing leaders? Is Germany a better master than England? To me it seems not! Wouldn't it have been infinitely better to stay out of the war? And if we had to do it, would it not have been necessary to hear the opinion of the nation first?

3 OCTOBER 1941

Hitler gave a speech in which, speaking against the Bolshevik threat, he said some things that are true. But there remains a worrying question about him: Why did he, a year ago, so warmly receive Molotov[34] in

---

Christian Democrats [Democrazia Cristiana (DC)]. He escaped being captured by the Germans thanks to the intervention of Cardinal Costantini, who sheltered him in the Palace of the Propaganda Fide, where Costantini himself resided. He became a minister in 1944, then head of government in eight consecutive cabinets, 1945–53. He signed the Peace Treaty of 1947 on behalf of Italy and focused thereafter on the reconstruction of a country destroyed by the tragedy of war. He emerged victorious from the confrontation with the Socialist-Communist front in 1946 by putting together a coalition of moderate forces around his party. On the international stage, he supported the Atlantic Alliance and promoted European unity, earning considerable prestige abroad. De Gasperi's and his family's relationship with Costantini were characterized by extreme cordiality and esteem, a fact borne out in the correspondence between them. See Costantini's *Epistolario* in Bruno Fabio Pighin's, *Il ritratto segreto del Cardinale Celso Costantini in 10.000 lettere dal 1892 al 1958* (Venice: Marcianum Press, 2012).

[34] Vjačeslav Michailovič Molotov (1890–1986), a Soviet politician and diplomat, whose original surname was Skrjabin; it was changed to Molotov (*molot* = hammer) as a *nom de guerre* among Bolshevik revolutionaries.

Berlin? The public doesn't remember much; however, one cannot push it too much against its common sense. Was Hitler sincere then or sincere now? Besides, Nazism is no less frightening than Bolshevism.

12 OCTOBER 1941

The press, all of it, has a false message. Reading newspapers is nauseating. Those who wanted this war have to speak this way or make others do so, but the Italian people are not a bunch of jackasses. I remember the thoughts expressed by the farmers of our fields at Murlis. It is an instinct that leads even uneducated people directly to the essence of things. Why are we waging this war? Who declared it? Why do we have to maintain, with our meagre bread, Greece and Montenegro? We will then have to return these countries.

The people keep their mouths shut for the sake of discipline and out of fear, but they clearly see the weak and distressing sides of the situation: the sacrifice of many young people, the leaders' lack of preparedness and foolishness, defeat after defeat, the destruction of the commercial fleet, the devalued lira, the runaway cost of living, etc.

I fear that the crowds (not of farmers, who will find a way to hide their wheat) of workers will react with riots. Woe betide us if a revolt starts!

12 OCTOBER 1941

A German official defined an Italian this way: "Personal valour, lots; organizational capacity, zero."

12 OCTOBER 1941

News of victory over Russia is received with satisfaction but without enthusiasm. The only thing that people care about is the struggle against Bolshevism, especially because of its anti-Christian content. But there is no active, positive, dynamic cooperation; one accepts destiny almost fatalistically.

I will try in the following points to characterize the various perspectives:

Molotov was USSR's minister of foreign affairs, and in that capacity became famous for signing the Molotov-Ribbentrop Pact with Nazi Germany. After the Second World War he was vice-president of the Soviet cabinet, and in 1956 became minister of state control, shortly after which he was forced to retire to private life.

1 A good many people are perfectly indifferent to the outcome of the war because they believe that, for us, it is just a matter of changing uniforms, and between Germany and England, England seems preferable.

2 Those who hope for an Axis victory hope that a defeated England will be obliged to pay an indemnity or at any rate help to shore up the ruinous state of Italian finances.

3 There are also many who hope for an enemy victory to liberate Italy from Fascism ...

4 Bread rationing has covered the nation in a dull malaise, and latent signs of revolt are beginning to appear. The measure has also been received badly because it is known that we had to send many foodstuffs to Germany, and because it is known that we are maintaining Greece and Montenegro because of the beautiful treatment they have offered and continue to offer our soldiers.

5 Some say that if we had remained non-belligerents, at a certain time, Italy could have acted as mediator.

6 Commendatore L.C. said to me that if Germany wins the war, thereafter secret societies will be established, as occurred before the events of 1848 to liberate Italy from the German yoke.

7 I personally see a murky future and fear upheavals.

The campaign against Russia has been prosecuted with valour and immense sacrifice. But one cannot see victory. Even if St Petersburg, Moscow, and Odessa fall soon, will the campaign be definitive? Will it end? No. It will be definitive only if Germany conquers the Caucasus and if it is provisioned with materiel and supplies. It will have gasoline, iron, and bread. But today one has the impression that the case of the Sino-Japanese War is being repeated. Japan took over half of China but is not able to make peace. And to remain on a war footing for five years and more is already a defeat.

20 OCTOBER 1941

Today Senator Calisse[35] came to see me and gave me a thousand lire for the evangelization of the faith. Seeing him so agile in both body and

---

[35] Carlo Calisse (1859–1945) was a jurist and historian who taught at various Italian universities. His academic merits earned him a nomination to the Senate in 1919, and thereafter he joined the National Fascist Party [Partito Nazionale Fascista (PNF)].

mind, yet knowing that he was at an advanced age, I asked him, "How old are you?" His response: "Eighty. It is one of the many blessings that the Lord has given me. I am working on a book on common law, Father Gemelli's[36] commission. By coming to see you, I took a break from my work. If God calls me, I am ready. In fact, I am waiting for his call."

I had a meeting with His Excellency Tucci[37] on the occasion of a cycle of missionary conferences at the Institute of the Middle and Far East. I proposed two regulations that were accepted:

1 that we do not discuss politics in any way;
2 that the conferences be of an absolutely orthodox and Roman character.

Tucci agreed. Speaking subsequently of the war, he said, "When you kill a young person, you destroy a world."

21 OCTOBER 1941

Today the Hon. De Stefani, member of the Grand Council of Fascism, came to see me. I note three things:

1 He brought a booklet in which, he said, it is argued that laws should be given a moral foundation, namely, the Catholic faith: something eternal and self-sustaining, independent of the vicissitudes of the war.

---

[36] Agostino Gemelli (1878–1959), a physician and psychologist, was active in socialist causes and founded the periodical *La Plebe*. He later converted to Christianity and became a Franciscan brother. He was president of the Pontifical Academy of Sciences and founder and rector of the Catholic University of the Sacred Heart, in Milan. He was friends with Costantini, as is demonstrated in the latter's correspondence (preserved in the ASDCP).

[37] Giuseppe Tucci (1894–1984), an orientalist, was appointed academic of Italy and organizer of scientific expeditions to the Orient, including Tibet. He was very active in cultural ties with Japan and in the promotion of the Middle and Far East Institute (Istituto Medio ed Estremo Oriente, ISMEO). He maintained a correspondence with Cardinal Costantini, as evidenced in the latter's correspondence in the ASDCP.

2 He then told me that in circles close to Mussolini they are upset with
the *Osservatore Romano* because it does not take a sufficiently decisive stand against Bolshevism.

I replied that there exists an encyclical against Bolshevism and that
the attitude of the Holy See is reserved because Nazism is involved; it
is no less an enemy of religion than Bolshevism. He admitted this and
recalled a phrase of Hitler: "Either Germans or Catholics."

3 He said that there are cells amongst the *fucini*[38] who believe they can
reconcile their faith with socialist theories, and who are anti-Fascist.
He fears the consequences this may have on the Italian Catholic
University Federation. As an old university professor, he loves young
people and follows not only their technical learning but also their
moral formation.

I responded that this is not something I didn't already know. There
are opponents of Fascism as a result of recent serious errors – for
example, the folly through which our young men were led to the
slaughter in Greece. The Hon. De Stefani admitted this sad fact. We
agreed that I could not be a spokesperson for his concerns because
these are developments that are absolutely beyond my office.

26 OCTOBER 1941

Count Prampero of Udine[39] was killed in Albania valiantly fighting
against Greece. Just before his deployment, he spent a little time on leave
and said to his father, "Now we fight. But when the war is over, we will
return to Italy with grenades and will make a clean sweep." This sentiment is widespread in the army. Colonel Scarpa, a veteran of Albania,
confirmed this to me. Poor Count Freschi expressed the same feeling.[40]

[38] The *fucini* were people who belonged to the Italian Catholic University
Federation [Federazione Universitaria Cattolica Italiana (FUCI)] founded in
1896, which still exists today.

[39] The noble family of the Counts of Prampero ruled Gemona [Udine] until
the twelfth century, when the territory became a municipality. At that time, the
family acquired the title and feudal right of the Bramberg, near Magnano del
Friuli, with jurisdiction over Montenârs, on the Canale del Ferro and other
places in the province of Udine.

[40] The noble family of the Counts Freschi of Cutanea, originally from Faedis
[Udine], owned a mansion in Cordovado [Pordenone].

A colonel told Giovanni Tullio, "One war raised up Fascism; another war will bury it."

The war being waged in Russia ought to be the tomb of Bolshevism and Nazism. The massacre of 100–200 innocent hostages committed at Nantes and in other cities as reprisal for the killing of one or two German officials has elicited a sense of horror in the entire world. Two nights ago, I understand, Cardinal Hinsley[41] delivered a noble protest. This massacre represents a lost battle for Germany.

A PROUD LETTER FROM THE DUTCH EPISCOPATE

12 NOVEMBER 1941

On 25 July 1941, the Dutch Episcopate disseminated a pastoral letter that was both vigorous and noble. It was sent to parish priests on the Friday so that it could be read on the Sunday in the churches. At 4 AM on Sunday, the Gestapo went to the residence of the archbishop of Utrecht to inform him that the letter must be withdrawn. The archbishop responded that it was already sent and it could no longer be withdrawn. He was then hit with a 500-florin fine. When the public learned of this, a Protestant sent the archbishop a cheque for 500 florins; and others, Catholic and Protestant, spontaneously sent him other donations. I managed, through clandestine means, to get this noble document:

> You already know, dear faithful, that we have many times warned against the harm that National Socialism inflicts on our faith. Sunday, 26 July, we ordered an announcement from the height of all the pulpits that the sacraments must be refused "to Catholics who are known to have given considerable support to the National Socialist Movement because this movement not only threatens to block the free exercise of the mission of the Church in certain fields, but also constitutes a grave danger to the Christian conception of life to which we adhere." It is clear that a Catholic association cannot be guided by men whose mentality is in direct contradiction with the Catholic vision of life and who strive to spread this spirit in the organizations they lead. As a result of this fact, these cease to be Catholic associations. But this is not all. The League of Catholic Workers, if it is placed in the service of the National Socialist Movement, becomes in reality one of their organizations.

[41] Arthur Hinsley (1865–1943), archbishop of Westminster [UK], was elevated to cardinal in 1937.

As a consequence, Catholics cannot remain members. In future, it is necessary to refuse the sacraments both to those who remain members of an organization affiliated to the workers' league in its new guise and also to members of any other organization associated with the National Socialist Movement.

Publicly and forcefully we raise our voice against the injustice committed to tens of thousands of people deprived of their social organizations. We protest against the unprecedented violence committed against their conscience in the wish to impose a conception of life that is in open conflict with their religious beliefs ... We know our people and understand how they would respond. Therefore, permit us to express here publicly our joy over the courageous fidelity of the leaders and their refusal to collaborate. We are proud of these men who have been able to prove, even in these painful circumstances, the marvellous qualities that constitute the greatness of our people: unwavering firmness, strength of character, faithfulness to honour, and conscience. Perhaps they will be made to face deprivation, but we are convinced that our Catholics will not abandon their brothers when they find themselves in need ...

We are united to our brothers in the German Episcopate. Last 6 July, the 29 bishops and ecclesiastical superiors of the Great Reich had a letter read in all their churches to protest against the injustice recently perpetrated against the Catholic Church in Germany. They declared, "We are dealing with the existence or extermination of Christianity in the German Church." They continued: "Recently there were circulated hundreds of thousands of copies of a book which argued that we Germans must today choose between Christ and the German people. With great indignation, as German Catholics we refused to make such a choice. We love the German people and we serve them, even if this means we have to sacrifice our lives. But at the same time, we live and die for Jesus Christ, and to Him we want to remain united now and forever." Dear faithful, to these words we have nothing to add; we make them completely our own ...

Given at Utrecht on the Feast of St James, 25 July 1941. [Signed] Dr J. de John, Archbishop of Utrecht; P.A.G. Hopmans, Bishop of Breda; A.F. Diepen, Bishope of Bois le Duc; J.G. Lemmens, Bishop of Ruremonde; J.P. Huibers, Bishop of Haarlem.

15 NOVEMBER 1941

A Dominican who has just returned from a vacation in Germany reports that Nazism is losing ground. It seems that the speeches of the

Führer and Goebbels[42] confirm this fact because they are straining to lift spirits.

20 NOVEMBER 1941

It is noted that Hitler remarked to Horthy,[43] "I respect the Italian solider, but he is badly led; I cannot respect [Italian] officials."

Today the Hon. De Stefani, member of the Grand Council of Fascism, came to see me. I note his observations:

1 Germany is pressuring to have Farinacci assume, beside Mussolini, a more active role in the government. The German authorities were made to understand that Farinacci is not popular in Italy.
2 Mussolini has fallen many steps from his original pedestal.
3 The *gerarchi* [Fascist party officials] believe that it would be better to effect a reform of the regime from the inside rather than from the outside. The latter would mean revolution.
4 This war was not wanted either by the Italian people or by the *gerarchi*; its unfavourable developments make it extremely unpopular.

I said to him, "It is awful that Italy was cast into the chasm of war without a gathering of the Grand Council of Fascism." He replied, "It would have been useless. Il Duce wanted war." I responded, "But couldn't the Grand Council find a way to make its views known? And the King, what is he thinking and doing?" He replied, "The Grand Council of Fascism is not unconcerned. The situation is a trial for every one of us. But what can we do? The members of the Grand Council do not have the authority to convene a meeting. Individually, they have not failed to make their views known, though with a caution imposed by the state of war. We are

---

[42] Paul Joseph Goebbels (1897–1945), a Nazi leader and minister of propaganda from 1933, who promoted the purification of German culture by a fanatical imposition of Nazi mythology. He killed himself after killing his family in 1945.

[43] Horthy von Nagybánya Miklós (1868–1957), an admiral and Hungarian statesman who served in the First World War as the commander of the Austro-Hungarian fleet. Regent of Hungary from 1920 to 1944, he supported Nazi forces during the Second World War, though he was nonetheless arrested during the occupation of the country.

in fact very unhappy about Il Duce's decision and about the defeat that is taking shape."

30 NOVEMBER 1941

Today I attended a solemn gathering of the Pontifical Academy of Sciences. Amidst this forum of scholars, the Holy Father Pius XII offered a marvellous synthesis of the infinitely large and the infinitely small, situating man before creation and God. The Vatican offers a marvellous scene. It appears as an oasis in a flame-filled desert. There continues undisturbed the beat of the heart, giving life to the limbs of the Church; there, the soul takes refuge and consolation in the contemplation of something that has the steadfastness of the eternal. Leaving the Vatican and returning to go back into the vortex of common life, I had a clear feeling of the vanity of our ephemeral unrest.

WAR ON AMERICA   11 DECEMBER 1941

Mussolini has announced from the balcony of Piazza Venezia that war is declared against America. "Today," he said, "the *Tripartito*,[44] in the fullness of its moral resources and its powerful material instruments of war, has a sure guarantee of victory. Tomorrow it will be the creator and organizer of a just peace between peoples. Italians, to your feet one more time! You are worthy of this great war. We will be victorious!" Mussolini truly must consider us idiots if he has the courage to denounce Roosevelt as a despot – he who by himself cast Italy into the chasm of war. Even if Roosevelt was one, we could say to Mussolini: "*Medice, cura te ipsum*" [Physician, heal thyself]. Hypocrite, take the beam out of your own eye if you want to remove the speck from the eyes of others.

I read today in the Breviary these words of Isaiah [chapter 24]: "The earth shall be utterly utterly emptied, and utterly spoiled ... The earth mourneth and fadeth away, the world languisheth and fadeth away ... The earth also is defiled under the inhabitants thereof, because they have transgressed the laws, changed the ordinance, broken the everlasting covenant." It seems that the Prophet paints a realistic picture of the present day.

44 *Tripartito*: the Tripartite Pact, or the alliance between Italy, Germany, and Japan in 1940.

Japan has declared war on America. While Italy and Germany have become allies, the nations of South America have allied with the United States.

YUGOSLAVIA   12 DECEMBER 1941
The lawyer Niels Sas de Gric, a Croatian native who has relatives in Croatia, paints a truly sombre and sad picture of Croatia and Slovenia. Those people want nothing to do with Italy. And that is natural. We Veneti did not want to have Austrians and Croats in our home. He says that Pavelić holds onto power through the violence of the Ustasha, who are like the early Fascists and carry out punitive attacks ... They are hated. Maček[45] has been interned. But 90 percent of the population is with him. He says that in their almost despairing suffering, the people take solace by turning their eyes to the Vatican.

Il Duce Speaks
Mussolini says: "The Italian people are sympathetic to the war; the Italian people are sympathetic to it in spite of how serious their privations and sacrifices are on the home front; these are – always – infinitely smaller that those that our soldiers confront, whether in the desolate Steppes of Russia or the sandy dunes of Africa ..."

To whom is he saying this? Either he is being deceived or he does not have his hand on the pulse of the people. "You cannot fight unless you hate the enemy before you. In wartime, several moral dictates that in normal times would be deeply respected appear superfluous and sometimes damaging. War demands both an extremely tough climate and tough men: we must be a single heart of steel."

Morality and the law are eternal. They are not a uniform that you take off and put on. General Chiang Kai-shek, in a message to the pagan Chinese people, said that the enemy must be fought but must not be hated. Christ taught the great lesson of forgiveness ...

In closing, Il Duce asserts "that in waging this war, which follows two others, only a truly strong and great people such as the Italian people could handle such a prolonged effort." What a great actor! A people

---

[45] Vladko Maček (1879–1964), a Yugoslav politician and head of the Croatian Peasant Party in 1939 became vice-president of the Yugoslav administration of Zvetkovic. Exiled after the war, he waged an active propaganda campaign against Tito's regime.

dragged into war without any possibility of expressing their own thoughts is called – irony? – a *great* people ...

MEETING WITH SENATOR CINI   19 DECEMBER 1941

Senator Cini said to me: "The devaluation of the lira is leading us to disaster, not just for all the capitalists but also for the most needy classes that the regime wanted to help and protect, creating social policies (insurance, assistance to mothers and children, etc.). But billions of capital in social insurance – billions that belong to the most needy classes – are used and squandered on the war. The Treasury is filled with paper that, if we do not win the war, will remain nothing but ... paper." He added, "I went to lunch with Federzoni[46] and Grandi.[47] If you had heard them, you would have sent them to prison. The former minister Guido Jung, returned from Libya, told me that his tenants refused to be paid in paper but instead asked for foodstuff. The war in Libya is going badly. Derna has fallen or is about to fall into the hands of the English. In Italy a sense of bitterness, distrust, and latent revolt is growing.

AUDIENCE OF PIUS XII   23 DECEMBER 1941

I had an audience with the Holy Father Pius XII. Speaking of Catholic missions in the Far East, I told the Holy Father Pius XII that the Propaganda ministry looks to the future of the missions without fear because the seminaries are flourishing, and even at Urban College [Collegio Urbano] there is an elite of young people that offers the highest hopes. The seminary accepted several seminarians from countries invaded

[46] Luigi Federzoni (1878–1967), an Italian politician who founded the Nationalist Party in 1910, which in 1923 merged with the National Fascist Party. He served as president of the Senate, 1929–39, and of the Italian Academy, 1938–43. In 1943 he voted for the resolution proposed by Grandi that expressed non-confidence in Mussolini's government. His ties with Costantini are borne out in the latter's correspondence, preserved in the ASDCP.

[47] Dino Grandi (1895–1988), an Italian political leader and one of the founders of the Fascist movement, who became foreign affairs minister (1932), ambassador to Great Britain, 1932–39, and then president of the Chamber of Fasci and Corporations [Camera dei Fasci]. He presented the resolution that expressed non-confidence in Mussolini on 25 July 1943 in an effort to save Fascism from imminent ruin.

by the Nazis. The attitude of these missionaries is equal to enduring the most recent ordeals.

23 DECEMBER 1941

I went with Mons. Caprio to visit the property of the Propaganda at Castel Romano. The shepherds had slaughtered a certain number of lambs. The sheep did not want to leave the bloody-stained place where their little sons and daughters had been killed and were lamenting continuously, bleating as if they could call back their offspring. The faces of these poor beasts, which normally have a stupid expression, seemed animated with a new expression. And their lamentation had something of a sad and touching quality. Even after we left the place, one heard in the distance that crying voice. Mons. Caprio remarked, "It is the great supreme instinct of maternity. And yet they tell us that children do not belong to the family, but to the state." I thought of the poor Italian mothers.

THE POPE'S GREAT ADDRESS   24 DECEMBER 1941

The august Pontiff directed his words as Father to the entire world. Speaking of the origins of the current conflict, he said, "In front of the vastness of the disaster ... there is no other remedy than return to the altar." He quoted the words of St Augustine, who described the folly of human devices:"*Bene currunt, sed in via non currunt. Quanto plus currunt, plus errant, quia a via recedunt*" [Serm. 141:4; They run quickly, but they do not run on the path. The more they run, the more they lose their way because they distance themselves from the path].[48] He concluded the radio broadcast by setting out and detailing the conditions of a new order founded on essential principles and the characteristics that alone can guarantee the world a true and lasting peace:

1 respect for moral principles, and for freedom, and for the integrity and security of all nations, large and small;
2 respect for the cultural patrimony of all peoples, including minority languages;

[48] Radio message of Pius XII, 24 December 1941, published in AAS 34 (*Bollettino Ufficiale della Santa Sede*, 1941), 10–21. The passage cited here is reported on page 11 and can be found in *Sermones discipulis*, reprinted in J.P. Migne, *Patrologia Latina* (Paris: Vrayet, 1844–64), 38 and 777.

3 respect for natural law in which all peoples share equally the natural resources of the earth;

4 respect for treaties freely ratified and for disarmament;

5 respect for religion and for the Church.

Comments on the Pope's Address
I collected the following comments. "At least one person speaks the truth that everybody feels"; "Everything has been said: there is something there for Hitler and Mussolini and for the Allies"; "These five points are fundamental for future peace. There will not be true peace if it is not based on these points"; "The most difficult and most necessary point is disarmament"; "It is the most incisive and realistic speech. Remember the words of Benedict XV in the last war"; "If they had listened to Benedict XV, this war would not have taken place."

THE THIRD WARTIME CHRISTMAS 25 DECEMBER 1941
Humanity better understands beauty, the human and divine significance of the great and sweetest Mystery. The churches are full of the faithful. Christmas is the sublime antithesis of the human savagery unleashed by the thirst for gold and from the beastly nature of man. The Pope's two speeches assert the rights of the spirit. No, the way is not the failure of Christianity. It is the failure of a so-called civilization that repudiates Christian principles.

26 DECEMBER 1941
Today it is said that the English have taken Benghazi. It is a victory that does not resolve the conflict. England remains hypnotized in the West, while its power is routed in the East. It is like a sick person who heals a pimple on his arm while gangrene spreads on his feet.

The Hon. Longinotti said to me, "Has the bell tolled for England's destiny? All nations live through this tragic moment: Carthage, Rome, Spain, Portugal. And couldn't America remain peaceful?"

26 DECEMBER 1941
The world war has taken on an accelerated rhythm with the explosion of hostilities between Japan and the Allies: America and England. Public opinion expresses itself more or less as follows:

"Japan has risen in the world of the Far East with formidable and decisive force. It has inflicted extremely serious losses on America; it has taken over the Philippines and the Pacific; it has taken Hong Kong; it has entered Borneo and is about to take Singapore. China can furnish iron and coal, Indochina rice and rubber, Borneo gasoline, and the Philippines other products, and these are lands in which Japan's surplus population can settle. They are trying to create a new order in the Far East, one that is organized by Japan and throws America, England, and even the Axis out of its territory. Other nations refused to understand that certain nations, rich in demographic vitality, cannot compromise forever: they are like a bomb that will explode, injuring or killing those who prepared it."

But the war is not over. What will be the outcome? Whatever the war's outcome, Italy and Germany will still have to have a place in the sun. Otherwise there will be neither justice nor peace. Japan committed the crime and the error of attacking China. China has a formidable capacity to resist. By retreating, she can weaken any aggressive force. The fate of Napoleon's troops in Russia could be repeated. Besides, China itself is overcrowded by excess population. We shall wait and see how events will unfold.

A small button is being circulated with enamelled wording: "GOD CURSE THE ENGLISH!" It is both a vulgarity and an impiety. English radio sent this response to Italians: "We instead say, 'GOD SAVE ITALY!'" There is style in this response, but it also has an edge of tremendous irony against Mussolini. History sometimes can be captured in little maxims.

The Pope's Marvellous Charity Work

Permit me at the sunset of this tragic year to lighten my spirits in the contemplation of the immense works of charity that have been and are being carried out by the Pope to alleviate much suffering. The Vatican has become a central workshop, a vast and multiplex organization that goes beyond the borders of Italy and embraces the infinite material and moral suffering of the world.

Where the storm of exterminating hatred has raged, or where there have been other calamities, comes the reconstructive love, the spiritual and material assistance of the Pope, and the breath of a calming peace.

News agencies and Vatican Radio provide an extremely precious outlet for the dissemination of news and for its research. The radio transmissions that began in June 1940 after the occupation of Belgium and France, with a few hundred listeners every week, eventually extended to

Australia, Egypt, England, India, Kenya, China, the Belgian Congo, Italian Africa, South Africa, etc. The Pontifical Organization for Assistance to Children, launched and run by the valorous Mons. Baldelli, has been delivering magnificent social assistance.

The work of delivering spiritual and material assistance which the Holy Father has deployed in aid of prisoners of war, refugees, internees, populations languishing in suffering, those wounded on the field of battle, etc., is also immense.

We well know that the Pope intervenes when he can to ask for clemency for those condemned to death. There is no suffering that does not find a ready and affectionate echo in the heart of the Holy Father who, beyond any racial, religious, or national differences, carries out his marvellous work as an *alter Christus*. I summarize from *La Civiltà Cattolica* of 1941 a few specific facts.

The Most Excellent Mons. Besson [Mario], Bishop of Lausanne, Geneva, and Fribourg, returning from an audience granted recently by the Holy Father, reported in *La Semaine Catholique de la Suisse Romande* how much he had learned in Rome about the work being tirelessly carried out by the Father of the Faithful to help the victims of war, no matter what city or country they are from. Above all, the Pope's paternal heart, moved by the especially serious trials to which Poland has been subjected, had many times expressed the desire to send a representative, even with a simple religious or charitable mission, who can acquire knowledge on the ground of the most urgent needs and the most suitable solutions. As this wish has so far been in vain, the Supreme Pontiff has opened his beneficent hand to help Polish refugees in various countries, including Germany, Portugal, Hungary, Latvia, Lithuania, Estonia, Romania, Sweden, and Algeria. For refugees in Italy, given the more favourable circumstances here, the works of charity have been much more considerable, and the Apostolic Nunciature has become an important centre for aid.

For Polish prisoners in Germany, the Pope published a large number of copies of a prayer book; for the numerous refugees in Romania, the Pope arranged for a bountiful shipment of clothing and drugs from Argentina; as well, there was the aid spontaneously offered to bishops to spread among the victims of war the entire amount of Peter's Pence which they had at their disposal. Other considerable sums, by the Pope's generosity, are distributed by the [papal] nuncios or by his other representatives to the French, Belgians, and Dutch; to this latter group was given the lion's share of the Peter's Pence collected in Holland.

Many steps were taken to aid prisoners; most recently, through the representatives of the Holy See in India, Egypt, Palestine, Australia, and elsewhere, the Pope hastened to make the holidays of Blessed Christmas more enjoyable. But charity does not just mean bread; and at the beginning of the war the Holy Father instituted the Office of Information in the Vatican ... Mons. Besson adds that the Holy Father spoke movingly of the profound suffering of his heart when faced with the difficulties that confront this beneficent work. While during the last war everything seemed to contribute to make the actions of the Holy See more effective and widespread, today almost everything conspires against its development, given the complex diversity of circumstances. Among the difficulties are the scarcity of foodstuffs, the obstacles to crossing national boundaries, the problems of banking regulations, of which the demands become more and more complicated, and the blockade, whose mesh progressively tightens.[49]

The arrival of Christmas offers the Holy Father an occasion to give fresh examples of his munificence to so many people hit hard by the war. By the wish of the Holy Father, a special Pontifical Mission was created in Italy for prisoners of war, headed by the Most Excellent Nunzio Borgoncini Duca, whose mission was to give, along with the august benediction and words of comfort, a Christmas present to those in the various prison camps – including civil internees. Between 24 and 26 December, members of the mission visited prisoners in Sulmona, Pollenza, and Treia and those interned at Arezzo and Parma, and they were received with gracious hospitality by the Italian authorities and with sincere emotion by all.

The apostolic nuncio – who can speak freely to everybody – distributed pictures, care packages, and monetary subsidies, recalled that the Holy Father would like to be among them at the Feast that all people long to spend in the bosom of their own families, and offered each of them greetings and blessings. French and English officials responded with expressions of genuine gratitude, and everybody showed the heartfelt recognition for the Universal Father. From Albania, His Excellency Mons. Leone Nigris reported that with the kind agreement of the authorities, Christmas gifts had been distributed to Greek prisoners, while the same care and attention was given to the many Greek families who are interned.

---

[49] cc: *La Civiltà Cattolica* 92, no. 1 (1941): 161–3.

In Jerusalem, it was H.E. Mons. Gustavo Testa who was able to visit a few thousand of the Italian prisoners and internees in Palestine, bringing them words of comfort and signs of the paternal concern of the august Pope, and receiving the most genuine expressions of filial gratitude. In Canada, H.E. Cardinal Villeneuve,[50] archbishop of Quebec, and the apostolic delegate had already begun their relief mission. But especially for Christmas, H.E. Mons. Antoniutti[51] visited several prison camps of Italians. He celebrated Holy Mass, preached and distributed gifts, for which the internees responded by promising a spiritual treasure of prayers for the Holy Father.

In Australia, the apostolic delegate had already organized for spiritual and religious aid for the Italian and a few German internees through the bishops in whose dioceses the prison camps are situated. Priests who speak Italian carried out this work. On 30 July 1940, he visited the prison camp in Brisbane and on 4 September that in New South Wales – for Italians and Germans – while the families of the internees were entrusted to the care of chapters of the St Vincent de Paul Society. On the occasion of the Christmas holidays, however, Mons. Giovanni Panico[52] sent everybody a precious keepsake of the constant thoughts and interest of His Holiness.

Here one must remember the words with which the *Osservatore Romano* concluded the foregoing partial account of the good works of the Holy Father: "There will come a day when it will once again be given to the world to appreciate fully what it means, in the middle of a war, to know of the survival of the flame of love or a voice of faith and comfort. For everyone today, even as they feel greater need, it is enough to know that that flame burns, that the

---

[50] Rodrigo Villeneuve (1883–1947), of the Oblates of Mary Immaculate, named archbishop of Quebec in 1931, was elevated to cardinal in 1933.

[51] Ildebrando Antoniutti (1898–1974), presbyter of the Archdiocese of Udine, entered the diplomatic services of the Holy See and in that guise collaborated with the first apostolic delegate to China, Mons. Costantini, to whom he remained close – as the latter's correspondence attests, with 45 letters from Antoniutti to Costantini. Antoniutti was ordained a bishop in 1936, was apostolic delegate in Canada, apostolic nuncio in Albania, and then in Spain. He became a cardinal in 1962. The following year he was named prefect to the Sacred Congregation for Religious. He died in a car accident in 1974.

[52] Giovanni Panico (1895–1962) was made archbishop and apostolic delegate to Australia in 1935. He was aspostolic nuncio to Peru in 1954 and to Portugal in 1959 before being elevated to cardinal in May 1962; he died suddenly a month later.

voice does not cease, feeding the most living and fertile seed of a civil and Christian blossoming that will lead to the day of a just peace."[53]

On that subject, the *Osservatore Romano* published the following note: "In the charity works that the Holy See, not without encountering difficulties, carries out to alleviate as much as possible the painful consequences of the present conflict, there is a special place for the concern expressed to ensure that the faithful are not without the spiritual comforts that religion provides and that are so vital in helping both individuals and groups to put up with their trials with dignity and conscience, and to spur an enhancement of life and of Christian piety. This concern is felt even more with regard to Catholics resident in occupied territories; among other measures of aid is the concession made by the Holy Father giving the bishops of those regions special and specific powers, with the object of avoiding obstacles to the conduct of religious life should exceptional circumstances occur and normal contact with the Holy See be lost."[54]

The Most Exc. Mons Orsenigo,[55] Nuncio in Germany, was able, thanks to the courteous permission of the German authorities, to visit on 26 January a group of 190 priests and 60 theology students detained in a barracks not far from Munich. During the Holy Mass, celebrated in the barracks and accompanied by sacred music composed by Father Lartisien, Master of the Chapel of Arras Cathedral, the nuncio offered words of comfort in the name of the Holy Father and ended the Holy Sacrifice of the Mass by blessing a rosary painted by various imprisoned French artists. In mixing casually with that group of ecclesiastics, he discovered how they organized their daily routine: meditation every morning with instructions from one Father Camilliano, chanting of Compline [last evening prayers] at night, and even Vespers on Sunday, on which day was sung two Solemn masses, with their respective homilies.

[53] cc: *L'Osservatore Romano*, 18 January 1941.

[54] cc: *L'Osservatore Romano*, 20–21 January 1941. The full quotation is taken from *La Civiltà Cattolica* 92 no. 1 (1941): 241–2.

[55] Cesare Vincenzo Orsenigo (1873–1946), a priest of the Archdiocese of Milan, entered the diplomatic corps of the Holy See in 1922, thanks to the esteem in which he was held by Pope Ratti. He was apostolic nuncio to Holland and then to Hungary. In 1930, as a result of a sudden death, he was sent to the nunciature at Berlin, from which he sent thousands of informative reports to Pius XI and then to Pius XII. He distinguished himself in aiding those in need during the Second World War.

Even though the nuncio could not personally convey the Pope's benediction to all 20,000 prisoners in that camp, he had the comfort of learning that they willingly flocked to religious functions and that in around two months there had been more than 28,000 Communions offered. Even H.E. Mons Godfrey,[56] apostolic delegate to Great Britain, began the visit to the prison camps, in honour of the wishes of the Holy Father, starting with the one near Liverpool, which held around 200 interned Italians and Germans. They greeted the representative of the Pope with lively manifestations of joy, who then had the grace to speak separately to each one of them and to arrange for the distribution of aid sent by His Holiness for prisoners of war and those interned in the British Isles.

In Palestine, as a second shipment of Italian soldiers arrived, Mons. Testa returned to the prison camp, where, in the name of all, the officials among the prisoners expressed their united gratitude for what the Holy Father was doing, especially in reassuring the families of the prisoners. Mons. Testa also comforted the Italian prisoners interned near Cairo, where he was received with the same demonstrations of exultation and gratitude, and was happy to find that there, as in the prison camp he visited in Palestine, the conditions of the soldiers are satisfactory and religious services conveniently organized.

As well as the comfort of prisoners of war, the concern of the Holy Father turned to assistance for the city of Santander, which had been struck by a terrible disaster. During a furious storm, an electrical transmission line felled by the storm had landed on a gaseline depot, causing a fire that spread rapidly, destroying about 400 homes and their contents. Upon learning of the disaster, the Holy Father sent through Nuncio H.E. Mons. Gaetano Cicognani,[57] along with other generous assistance, his special condolences and the expression of his heartfelt sadness for the victims, united with the paternal benediction for all those who have had to suffer in this distressing calamity.[58]

[56] Guglielmo Godfrey (1889–1963), titular archbishop of Cio and apostolic delegate to Great Britain, was made a cardinal by John XXIII in 1958.

[57] Gaetano Cicognani (1881–1962), a priest who trained in the service of the diplomacy of the Holy See, became apostolic nuncio to Bolivia in 1925, to Peru in 1928, to Austria in 1936, and to Spain in 1953, when he was created cardinal. His younger brother, Giovanni Amleto, became a cardinal in 1958 and was named secretary of state during the pontificate of John XXIII.

[58] CC: *La Civiltà Cattolica* 92, no. 1 (1941): 474–5.

To comfort those who feared for the fate of their relatives left in East Africa, news from His Holiness's secretary of state reassured them that "women and children of Italian families in Addis Ababa are in good health and would like this news, together with their good wishes and greetings, to reach their respective spouses, parents, and relatives." We know from Asmara that the quarter in that city where the women of Gondar were recovering was spared aerial bombardment, with the result that there were neither victims nor damage.[59]

Among the expression of filial gratitude for just how much the Holy Father has done and is doing to help prisoners, the *Osservatore Romano* of 6 June 1941 published an affectionate address of 2,218 French people detained in Silesia. After a mission of three weeks, concluded by a general Communion, they expressed their heartfelt gratitude for the words spoken by His Holiness in his Christmas homily at the Sacred College, in which he pointed out how much has been done and how much more he wanted to do for prisoners of war. To this, the Most Eminent Cardinal Secretary of State responded in the name of the Holy Father, expressing his deep-felt appreciation and exhorting them "to make these days of moral suffering days of grace, through a general and complete faith in the designs of Providence, which has not permitted this trial to happen without a merciful and salvific end."[60]

[25 September–8 October 1941] Even several centres holding Polish refugees in France had the comfort of a visit, made on behalf of the Holy Father by Mons. Alfredo Pacini, counsellor of the Apostolic Nunciature of Warsaw. The first centre they visited was that of Hyères, where in four houses are hosted persons of every class: the titled, diplomats, clerks, magistrates, and professionals. Staying a few days, Mons. Pacini sought ways for everybody to approach him to reveal their individual needs, distributing among other things subsidies, especially for the children and those left disabled by war and recovering in the hospitals of the area. As an expression of the collective feeling of gratitude, a solemn presentation was held in honour of the Holy Father, acclaimed by all as their consoler and benefactor. From Hyères, Mons. Pacini went to Lourdes, where there are two centres of Polish refugees taken in by the Red Cross housed in two hotels. Here also the representative of the Pope was received with demonstrations of reverential respect, and often it was

[59] cc: *La Civiltà Cattolica* 92 no. 2 (1941): 232.
[60] cc: *La Civiltà Cattolica* 92 no. 2 (1941): 476–7.

recalled, during a religious function in the major basilica at Lourdes and also in a presentation session, just how much the Holy Father had done both for the Poles still in Poland and for those who were far away; their Christmas and Easter gift is to make haste to reunite dispersed families, to find prisoners, to provide assistance to the wounded, and to give aid to the needy.[61]

These events have outlined the three dimensions of Pius XII that correspond to a triple providential mission, especially in these years *in quibus vidimus mala* [in which we see evil]: that of Teacher, Judge, and Father, almost as a new symbol of the illustrious tiara. Instead of diminishing and almost closing himself off in desolate mourning, the activities of the Supreme Pontiff have prodigiously multiplied.

His Excellency Mons. Castellani,[62] apostolic delegate to Addis Ababa, through the Information Office of His Holiness's secretariat of state has offered good news about the general population and the missionaries and ensured that the missionary work has continued with relative normality and that all Christians blessed the Holy Father's works of peace and charity. In particular, he noted that the seminary in the capital was proceeding comfortably, to which it was hoped to call other religious [priests and nuns] who are presently working in Asmara.[63]

[61] CC: *La Civiltà Cattolica* 92, no. 4 (1941): 144–5.

[62] Giovanni Maria Emilio Castellani (1888–1953), of the Brothers Minor was ordained bishop in 1929 and became apostolic delegate in Italian East Africa in 1937 and apostolic vicar of Addis Ababa.

[63] CC: *La Civiltà Cattolica* 92, no. 2 (1941): 232.

The Year 1942

9 JANUARY 1942

Monsieur O. Lavalette comments in *Lyon-Soir*[1] on the message of the Holy Father on the feast of peace and hope: "The Vatican, the head and heart of Christianity, the inexhaustible font of every truly human civilization ... And from the Vatican on that sweet and starry night was offered a lesson directed not so much to the people but to their leaders. With the peace and precision that the Apostles in their prayers expressed throughout the pagan world, which reflected the order that Christ instilled 2000 years ago, Pius XII – Saint Peter's successor – defined the terms of the new order that needed to be established in a world shaken by the worst atrocities of war, a new order that finally would be able to find peace, a well-deserved peace, a long-lasting peace. This new order would be identical to the one that Christ wanted – it would only have to be rebuilt. It can be re-established, but it must be done only with a deep-felt faith in a personal God, a faith that is not only virtuous but also represents the divine corridor through which different virtues enter into the temple of the soul, creating a strong and steadfast character."[2]

20 JANUARY 1942

This is a war of regimes, even though they frequently speak of democracy, plutocracy, totalitarianism, etc. This war is a crisis of civilization; it

---

[1] A French daily paper published in Lyon.

[2] CC: *L' Osservatore Romano*, 7–8 January 1942.

is the failure of materialist civilization. It was believed that material well-being, perfect technology, and culture would produce a new type of society, but instead we have arrived at the abyss, to the hideous conclusion that all the discoveries of science are being used today to destroy life and prosperity. The Pope said in his Christmas message, "The Church, mother of many universities in Europe, that still celebrates and gathers together the most advanced scientific experts and researchers of nature, does not, however, ignore the fact that from every good and from the same freedom of will, one can produce results that are worthy of respect and reward or those that deserve censure and condemnation. This is how the spirit and tendency with which technological progress is often used. As it emerges, technology should make itself expiate its own errors and virtually punish itself for creating instruments of destruction that destroy today what it built yesterday."[3]

Dante wrote:

> For where the argument of intellect
> Is added unto evil will and power,
> No rampart can the people make against it
> [Dante Alighieri, *The Divine Comedy, Inferno*, 31:55–7,
> Longfellow Translation]

20 JANUARY 1942

The United States is mobilizing 15 million men. All of America is an arsenal. Within a short time there will be a great and possibly decisive offensive.

21 JANUARY 1942

It is said that the command of the air force is now in German hands. It is also said that Hitler has sent forces to Italy to eventually defend the regime.

RELIGION IN GERMANY   22 JANUARY 1942

The *Osservatore Romano* had the following note: "Several newspapers have published reassuring news items about the situation of the Catholic

---

[3] This passage of Pius XII's message is quoted in AAS 34 (*Bollettino Ufficiale della Santa Sede*, 1942), 14.

Church in Germany. We are truly saddened to declare that unfortunately it is not possible to confirm these opinions." The note is followed with a long passage taken from the second chapter of *Gott und Volk: Soldatisches Bekenntnis.*[4]

25 JANUARY 1942

Japan goes from victory to victory. But the game is not over. Whatever the result of subsequent conflict between Japan and its enemies, I think that the face of the Far East has already been changed profoundly and irremediably. I hope that Japan is capable of understanding China's rights and will conclude an honourable peace. There are a few encouraging signs from both sides.

I note that there is irritation in the government because the Italian bishops are not encouraging the faithful to support the war. Bottai,[5] in his commemorative speech of 5 January, compared the American Episcopate, which is at one with the President, with the Italian Catholic Episcopate, which is almost absent. I had an opportunity to clarify this fact, saying that the Italian Episcopate, guided by its Christian sensibility, feels that the people are enduring the war without having wanted it and without having clearly understood it. The Episcopate cannot but have consideration for the delicate morale of the people.

Besides, the union with German Nazism, enemy of God and of the Catholic Church, naturally keeps the Italian Episcopate on the sidelines. One can also add that Mussolini has lost contact with the bishops, and he receives none. My brother, bishop of La Spezia, asked three times to be received and was never successful. Mussolini showed consideration for the suffering of all, but he forgot the poor clergy ... I don't know whether the American Episcopate supports the war waged by the United States. But in any event, the American Episcopate sees in this war the supreme religious defence against Nazism.

---

[4] CC: "God and Country: The Profession of Faith of the Soldier."

[5] Giuseppe Bottai (1895–1959), a Fascist politician, and minister of corporations (1929–32) and national education (1936–43). He voted against Mussolini in the famous July 1943 session of the Grand Council of Fascism.

27 JANUARY 1942

Senator Cini, along with Piacentini, Oppo, Saladino, Foschini, Castelli, and other engineers[6] of the E42[7] and from the Church of Saints Peter and Paul, came to my place for luncheon. Cardinal Fumasoni Biondi was also in attendance. The audience with Pius XI that had been held to show the scale model was recalled and remembered, as were the tough words that the Pope had spoken to Hitler, underlining that he could not have faith in the so-called Peace of Munich. Now we understand the prophetic sense and the bitter sadness of the former pontiff.

I note that Prince von Bismarck, the German ambassador to the Italian court, said that within a year or two the Vatican would be a museum that you can visit for a ten-lire ticket of admission. Another German of the Embassy to the Holy See said that he goes to the functions in St Peter's because they are interesting, and above all he thinks that they will soon be abolished.

12 FEBRUARY 1942

I note that at a meeting granted to the Tuscan *Federali* in recent days, Mussolini said these words:

1 Those who have money we will make them spit it out;
2 We will roast lukewarm Fascists;
3 We will settle the score with the Vatican.

16 FEBRUARY 1942

The newspapers announce that yesterday Singapore was taken. The English, unable to resist the hurricane of steel and fire unleashed by the Japanese, had to surrender. Churchill announced this funereal news to the British parliament. With the fall of Singapore and Hong Kong, that of Manila seems imminent, and with Japan's taking several Indonesian

---

[6] Senators Cini and Foschini have already been mentioned in these notes. Marcello Piacentini (1881–1960) also merits attention, as he was an official representative of the monumentalist architecture of the Fascist period and the director of the entire urban project of the EUR in Rome. The painter Cipriano Efisio Oppo (1891–1942), is also worthy of mention here.

[7] E42 signifies the Esposizione Universale di Roma [EUR; Universal Roman Exposition], which was supposed to be held in 1942.

islands and several Pacific Ocean islands, the political, commercial, and cultural equilibrium of the Far East is changing. The West is threatened there. But the war continues, and outcomes cannot be predicted. The world admires the skill of the Japanese; yet the formidable resources of America and England suspends any judgment. Besides, Japan is in China like a bull immersed in a deep and vast swamp from which it does not know how to escape. Attacking China, so populous, was both a crime and a mistake.

But, leaving aside the imperialism of the Japanese military, Japan raises a great problem. Japan, by observing the divine precepts *crescite et multiplicamini* [be fruitful and multiply] is more Christian than certain Western nations. Every year it has to find places outside the restricted borders of the home islands for hundreds of thousands of people who represent the annual demographic growth. America, Australia, Canada, etc., have closed the doors to Japanese immigration, and that compressed bomb has exploded, overturning Western imperialism, at least for now. I do not want to offer a judgment on this current conflict between two imperialisms. But I believe the greatest problem is a legal one. It is commonly held among jurists that a people, when they can no longer live because of a demographic surge or because of poverty or the lack of their own territory, have a right to find a place to live elsewhere. This concerns a crucial exigency that is like that of the man who, reduced to extreme poverty, rather than dying of hunger takes bread where he finds it. St Thomas Aquinas says, *"in casu extremae necessitatis omnia sunt communia. Unde licet ei qui talem necessitatem patitur, accipere de alieno ad suam sustentation, si non inveniat qui sibi dare velit."*[8] Japan's drama is the same drama as Italy's.

I look at the future of the missions with confidence. Japan has recognized the Catholic Church. Perhaps it will prefer that the missions be managed by indigenous leaders; but this is also the Christian program. And that which missionaries, who for centuries have led foreign missions, hesitated to understand must now understand and acquiesce with

[8] CC: "In cases of extreme necessity, everything is shared by all. That is why it is acceptable for those who suffer this need to take things necessary for their survival if they do not find anybody who wants to offer them" (Thomas Aquinas, *Summa Theologica*, II–II, q. 32 a. 7 ad 3).

good grace; as for the rest, their spirit is generous and magnificent, and they will not create any difficulties in yielding to the new requirements.

THE POPE AND GREECE   20 FEBRUARY 1942

Having been informed by the apostolic delegate of the conditions of great poverty in Greece, especially the lack of foodstuff, the Holy Father has sent a conspicuous sum of drachmas to create and supply several types of inexpensive meals for the people and ultimately, through the representatives of the Holy See, to send the apostolic delegate in Greece[9] powdered milk and ovomaltine from Switzerland and flour from Hungary, all to alleviate, even if in small measure, the suffering of many unfortunates and, most of all, children.

Death of the Duke of Aosta in Africa

The sad news has reached us that Prince Amedeo of Savoy, Duke of Aosta,[10] died on 3 March in Nairobi, Kenya, in the presence of Military Chaplain Boratto, Dr Borra, and General Nasi. Sensing he was near his end, the prince expressed his satisfaction for a life spent in the service of the homeland. Requesting and receiving the sacraments of the Church, he made known his desire that the Holy Father be so informed – he who had often asked after the health of the prince, comforting him with his benediction ... In acknowledging the ill-fated valour of this Prince of Savoy and wanting to connect his fate with the heroic group he had

[9] The apostolic delegate in question was H.E. Mons. Angelo Giuseppe Roncalli (1891–1962), the future Pope John XXIII (1891–1963). Roncalli became a bishop in 1925 and was sent to Bulgaria, where he remained for ten years as a representative of the Pope. In 1935 he was apostolic delegate to Turkey and Greece and then apostolic nuncio in Paris (1944–53). He was elevated to cardinal in the Conclave of 1953, along with Celso Costantini, and in the same year became patriarch of Venice. His pontificate is of course marked by the convocation of the Second Vatican Council (1962–65), a proposal advanced by Costantini twenty years earlier which was later pursued and championed by Cardinal Roncalli. He was beatified in the year 2000 by Pope John Paul II.

[10] Amedeo of Savoy (1898–1942), an Italian general, became Duke of Aosta in 1931 and in 1936 viceroy of Ethiopia and therefore governor general of Italian East Africa.

commanded, the enemy rendered military honours to his remains, which now rest in the Nairobi cemetery.

The Stefani News Agency published the following in *Il Messaggero*: "Roosevelt was named Supreme Commander of the Land, Sea, and Air Forces of the United States." After the experiences of Pearl Harbor, Manila, and Java, this mandate entrusted to the strategic mind of Roosevelt is an act of courage on the part of the North American people. Some might actually consider it an audacious act. Audacious or irresponsible? And Mussolini? This paper strategist who has led Italy to so many defeats?

The missionary A.B. Badoni of Milan tells me that there are many Italians who desire the defeat of our armies in order to liberate Italy from Fascism ... This is an awesome sign of the times, however painful.

It is announced that Japan will send a representative to the Holy See. This is a significant fact. The Propaganda ministry receives this news with satisfaction.

WARNING TO A STAFF MEETING OF THE PROPAGANDA
I said, "We are passing through a most delicate period. Each one of us must therefore have a sense of dutiful discipline and abstain from any opinions of a political character. This caution is all the more urgent in that we are in the service of an eminently international congregation. Our conduct must be inspired by the prudence and extreme impartiality of the Holy Father."

With a letter of today's date the Holy Father, sorrowful for the terrible tragedy that bloodies the world, has written to the Most Eminent Cardinal Maglione, his secretary of state, a letter which, putting every faith in God, exhorts all the faithful to unite their prayers. Therefore, as the month of Mary approaches, he invites all, especially children, as he has done in the past, to a crusade of prayer, interposing the effective mediation of the Mother of Jesus who, because of the prayers of Mary, worked his first miracle. And to these prayers are to be added "salutary works of penance and charity that go toward satisfying divine justice, so violated by many and with such grievous blows."[11]

THE XXV ANNIVERSARY OF THE EPISCOPAL CONSECRATION OF HIS HOLINESS PIUS XII   13 MAY 1942

On 13 May 1917, in the Sistine Chapel, Mons. Eugenio Pacelli was consecrated bishop by Holy Father Benedict XV. Mons. Achille Ratti was also present at the sacred rite. The Holy Father said in his radio broadcast[12] that this jubilee is "a dear remembrance that, while it makes a hymn of praise to God spring in Our heart, also moves it to implore with forceful ardour the heavenly benediction on the Lord's flock that is entrusted to Our pastoral concern, and on the work and the struggles of the Church for the salvation of the world." Thus did the Holy Father transfer his personal joy into the vision of his most noble ministry: "This auspicious date surpasses the personal and projects itself onto the entire Church."

In this great address the Pope revealed for the first time the important and decisive archaeological discoveries regarding the tomb of St Peter: *saxa loquntur* [the rocks speak]. The Holy Father, always mindful of the exigencies of the moment, ended his address with the following courageous appeal: "To the Leaders of the Nations, We would therefore like to direct a paternal voice of warning: The family is sacred ... Unanimous is the cry that reaches Us from the family front: Yield to our desire for peace! If you have the future of humanity at heart, if your conscience before God gives importance to what matters for man, if the names *father and mother* are important, and if what makes your children happy is also important, return the family to its work of peace!"

I, who have the grace to be close to the Holy Father in these regular audiences, remain ever more amazed and edified by his immense activity, his sense of the moment, the clarity of his thoughts, how precisely he is informed of events, and the serenity that his character draws from intimate communion with God. I sometimes see him distressed, but this

[11] Pius XII's letter to Cardinal Luigi Maglione, his secretary of state, is reproduced in AAS 34 (*Bollettino Ufficiale della Santa Sede*, 1942), 125–7.

[12] The text of Pius XII's radio broadcast on the occasion (13 May 1942) is reproduced in AAS 34 (*Bollettino Ufficiale della Santa Sede*, 1942), 154–67.

distress seems to be that which Christ endured before the tomb of Lazarus: it comes solely from love. The addresses, dense with thought and elevated in form, delivered by the Holy Father in varying circumstances, constitute a synthesis not only of theological and pastoral learning but also of social and political learning. In considering this ideal work, one recalls the speeches of St Leo the Great and St Gregory the Great, delivered and written in times no less troubled than our own.

The theme of peace in justice – *opus iustitiae pax* – is the polar star, or better yet the star of Bethlehem, to which the eyes of the Supreme Pontiff have constantly and faithfully been fixed. But beyond the solemn affirmations in numerous public manifestations, the Holy Father has carried out a vast initiative through the Secretariat of State to make his august views known to various governments through diplomatic means. His Holiness Pius XII's body of thought is supported and enlivened by a pastoral activity that appears to be miraculous. Just think of the multiform and vast charitable activities that reach beyond the borders of Italy and alleviate so much physical and moral suffering in the entire world.

The Natural Law

The laws of life cannot long ensure the crystallization of privilege and the armed protection of gold. One clairvoyant statesman from the hegemonic empires would have anticipated and avoided catastrophe by moving closer to proletarian states. The disparity could have been corrected before they reached the precipice. But the leaders in London and Washington cannot, alas, cite one, one single equitable and spontaneous concession during two decades of royal global and societal dictatorship. On the contrary, they must confess – and they have in fact confessed many times – to the most serious omissions and the most baleful errors.[13]

And I want to hope that there will be a just peace at the end of this war, which will take into consideration the inalienable right to live which all peoples have, even if the fate of their armies are not at all favourable for them. But the current situation does not permit excessive optimism. General "Time" and General "Space" are against the Germans. In Libya, the breakthrough offensive has become a series of actions to slow the advance of the Allies.

[13] CC: Imolo Marconi, in *L'Avvenire d'Italia*, 10 June 1942.

In the Anglo-Soviet treaty of alliance – beyond the mutual undertaking not to conclude a separate armistice or peace and to give mutual support by all possible means during the war and economically after the war, as well as similar articles concerning the "postwar period" – there are certain aspects that concern mutual approaches to ensure peace and to suppress any type of aggression on the part of Germany or any power allied to her. Among these, article 5 is important, in that it affirms that Russia and England, in working together for "the security and economic prosperity of Europe," .,. "will act in conformity to two principles: not to aspire to territorial acquisitions for themselves and not to interfere in the internal affairs of other states."

A letter arrived from home for me that announced the conferring of the bronze medal in memory of my late nephew Luciano. The sadness for the death of this good and honest young man, cut down in the most beautiful flowering of his years [twenty-seven], is tempered by his honourable end. As an educated person in the full religious sense of that term, before rushing to an almost certain death he would certainly have turned his thoughts to God, and the sacrifice of his young life would have earned him the reward of eternal life. May God grant that his sacrifice and that of many young lives benefit the good of our homeland.

Remembrance of Zuani and Costantini
"On the afternoon of 3 March 1941, while rallying the men of his unit, Zuani paid tribute to the members of his unit with these words: 'Forward those in love with death.' Luciano Costantini was the first to answer that call: 'I will go, Mr Lieutenant.' Costantini, like Zuani, normally said little. After him, another five artillery men made their way toward Elevation 1615. That night, at 2000 hrs, the first telegram arrived: 'It is freezing cold, but all is well.'"

The morning after, on [Mount] Golico, a storm of snow, ice, and wind. We were looking up. We knew that Zuani had pitched a tent on the ice above a rocky overhang. He was there all day. On the morning of the 6th, before dawn, that elevation became a hell. Hundreds of explosions, hundreds of strikes. It was artillery and mortar fire. They were shooting at our men, and they were on target, horribly on target. But our men resisted in the dark of night, amongst the icy lashings of torment. At

6 [am] the first telegram [arrived], and until 1300 hrs they continued to transmit. At 2130 hrs the last telegram arrived, interrupted in mid-sentence: 'Extremely urgent stop. Attacking forces overwhelming ...' At this point Luciano Costantini's voice was cut short by a mortar shell. Zuani and Costantini were showered with hand grenades and went down in a supreme act of bravery. Above, the inferno continued. At dawn on the next day, calm returned with the light. Elevation 1615 is no longer white with snow but all black from explosives, black and yellow as if it was a gas attack."[14]

20 AUGUST 1942

It is a remarkable fact that Italian youth, although very carefully molded by Fascism, has an attitude of intimate rebellion. It is also a disconcerting fact that serious people are asking themselves whether victory or defeat may be better for Italy. Massimo Bontempelli, in the *Corriere della Sera* of 15 July 1942, writes that the French Revolution failed to achieve its objectives largely because it was revolution without God; Galileo's revolution in the conception of the universe is, by contrast, full of God.

NOBLE WORDS FROM THE POPE TO THE MEN
OF CATHOLIC ACTION   20 SEPTEMBER 1942

A magnificent address by the Pope to the men of Catholic Action on the spiritual rebirth of society. Conclusion: "Move forward, persevere in your sacred and social fervour, which is both right and a defence of the greatness of the nation, imploring virtue and comfort from on high where, with the ascent of fervent prayers, spiritual weaponry and power descend, which in every struggle for good sustain the weakness of the Christian hero."[15]

21 SEPTEMBER 1942

I encountered the surveyor Colle. He said to me: "We will win." "Will we?" "Yes! because we will lose." Il Duce went to Libya to be ready to

---

[14] cc: From the letter accompanying the conferral of the medal.

[15] Pius XII's speech to the men of Catholic Action of Italy is reproduced in AAS 34 (*Bollettino Ufficiale della Santa Sede*, 1942), 282–93. This citation is at p. 293.

enter Alexandria, Egypt, on a white horse. He wanted to see Rommel.[16] The latter did not respond, making it understood that he received orders only from Berlin.

22 SEPTEMBER 1942

I received a letter from my sister Maria, who lives in Portogruaro. She writes, "Here it's like 1917" [the period of Austrian occupation].

Speaking with SDA regarding the confusion that reigns in the Roman command, she writes: "It's an advantage at this time, offered also by confusion … Do you know how Fascism was defined? A tyranny tempered by confusion."

28 SEPTEMBER 1942

There is anxiety and enormous trepidation for the young men called to military service from work. One Italian official said, "How can we win if many combatants hope to lose? They consider the worse defeat would be to fall under German domination."

A military chaplain returning from Germany told me, "Militarily, Germany has reached its maximum performance; politically, it considers Italy within the context of its own hegemony and imposes its own will on Italy, threatening to leave it without coal. Religiously, it is in a battle against Rome."

15 OCTOBER 1942

In recent days I met with Prof. Castellani.[17] We talked about tropical diseases, of which he is a world-famous expert. At one point he said, "Life is a mystery. We know nothing."

[16] Erwin Johannes Rommel (1891–1944), a German field marshal and one of Germany's non-Prussian generals. He was nicknamed the "Desert Fox" for his exploits in the conquest of Tobruk and other areas of North Africa when he commanded the Afrika Korps during the Second World War. Deprived of resupply from Germany, he had to abandon Libya before the advancing British forces commanded by General Montgomery. He then commanded an armed battle group in the battle for Normandy. He was arrested and charged with having participated in a plot against Hitler in July 1944 and was driven to commit suicide in order to avoid trial and sentencing.

[17] Aldo Castellani (1874–1971) was an Italian physician and parasitologist. He was responsible for important research and discoveries on tropical diseases.

Senator Prof. Alessandri,[18] a clinician and surgeon, told me the same thing at the inauguration of the medical school for missionaries. On 12 October I found myself with P. Stein, SJ, director of the Vatican Observatory at Castelgandolfo. We spoke of astronomy, and he concluded, "We are profoundly ignorant of the universe."

24 OCTOBER 1942

News has spread rapidly that Mussolini is sick as a result of an acute intestinal ulcer. The news produced two effects: fear that he would be gone and Italy would fall under the dominion of Hitler; joy for the hope that his death would hasten the end of the war. In all this there is extreme fatigue.

25 OCTOBER 1942

The entire press is playing the fanfare for the celebrations of the regime's twentieth anniversary. It seems that a psychological understanding is lacking: Italy is at war, the population is sombre, worried, and seized with a generalized panicked terror, and we put on festivals, celebrations, speeches ... Don't they notice that they are creating exactly the opposite effect? What is the result of twenty years of this regime? If Mussolini had been stopped after the conquest of the Empire, he would be truly famous. Today he has fallen to earth from the pinnacle to which he brought Italy. Does anything positive remain? The lost Empire, a seriously threatened Libya, the defeat suffered in Greece, the stupid and unjust action taken in the Alps against France, the flower of youth mown down or dragged into war, Italy yoked to Germany, the riches of the nation squandered, the terrible enemy incursions into Milan, Genoa, Turin ...

25 OCTOBER 1942

"Il Duce has given precise directives to the minister of corporations, on the basis of solidarity and justice, to continue his defence of the work that fights the great battle for the conquest of the new European order." I am ignorant in economics. It seems, however, that all these provisions are a swindle. What is the lira worth? What will it be worth when we demobilize?

[18] Francesco Roberto Alessandri (1867–1948), professor of clinical surgery at the University of Rome and president of the Italian Association of Surgery, was named a senator in 1939.

29 OCTOBER 1942

The markets in the morning are full of queues. I asked the housemaid what is said in these queues. She answered, "Nobody speaks of Mussolini and the war. They are scared. They speak only of food, of the prices that always go up, of the difficulties in getting provisions, etc."

One newspaper had the following title: *Soldiers of Christ and the Homeland.* "Abnegation and heroism of military chaplains. They fight without taking up arms; they move forward together with their soldiers to comfort them and take immediate care of the injured without regard of danger and death."

EXCHANGE OF MESSAGES BETWEEN HITLER AND MUSSOLINI

31 OCTOBER 1942

Il Duce responded to the message of the Führer as follows: "I thank you very cordially, Führer, for your message, for sending a delegation headed by Dr Ley, and for the lively participation of National Socialist Germany in the celebrations of the first twenty years of the Fascist Regime. During this relatively long and very important historical period, the Fascist Regime has attempted to resolve the fundamental problems of the Italian people – that is, their right to life – by peaceful and constructive means, but always and everywhere we were confronted with absolute hostility from the old plutocratic states, a hostility that culminated in an assault on [our] society. From that moment, it appeared clear to everybody that our two revolutions should band together in a fraternal pact of solidarity for peace and war, and answer the challenge of the old world. It is thus in the *Tripartito* that we march and fight together ... Mussolini."

Prattle! After the Empire, we could have remained outside the war; but in any event, one needed to be prepared to wage it and needed to know how to wage it.

31 OCTOBER 1942

At the Propaganda we discussed savages. One bishop returned from Africa said, "Are the savages the blacks or are they us?"

A SECRETLY DISTRIBUTED PAMPHLET   1 NOVEMBER 1942

ROMANS! Terror is about to be unleashed on our city. The thugs of the ss[19] have orders to deport to Germany able-bodied men for the

[19] ss is an abbreviation for *Schutzstaffel* [Protection Forces], the name of a special militia in the service of Nazism. The ss controlled the internal

army and for labour. In one night, Rome will become a desert. ROMANS!
FELLOW CITIZENS! Will we allow ourselves to be subjected to so
much havoc? Are we doing ourselves any favours by remaining inert and
silent before this vicious design? NO! It is necessary for everybody, from
the Roman Pontiff to the last commoner of Trastevere, to offer resistance, even physical, against those who want to line us up like cattle and
drag us into slavery and death in Germany. The inhabitants of Rome
must shut themselves in their homes and offer armed resistance against
this barbaric violence. Among them, the Bishop of Rome must get
involved, made strong by those spiritual weapons that repulsed Attila
from the walls of Rome, and by the invincible fact of that heroic charitable virtue for which CHRIST died on the Cross. ROMANS! Let each of
us arm ourselves with spiritual and material power! Let us no longer
allow ourselves to be deluded by lying promises that have too often been
torn to shreds. He who is not willing at this moment to fight with all his
individual energy will himself be responsible for his own destruction and
that of his dear ones, and of the indelible offence committed against the
Holy City. ROMANS! The tragic hour is about to strike. From the Vatican
to San Lorenzo, from Trastevere to Testaccio, let each of us prepare to
defend the life and liberty of all!

ALL SOULS DAY   2 NOVEMBER 1942
Yesterday, the Feast of All Saints, today All Souls; the spirit is lifted in the
contemplation and awareness of the Communion of Saints. We live with
the dead; the thought of the continuation of life beyond the grave makes
sweet the inevitable sadness of death. In life, according to the words of
Job in the liturgy, "*quais flos egreditur et conteritur et fugit velut umbra.
Ecce nunc in pulvere dormiam; et si mane me quaesieris, non subsistam.*"[20]
(But I know that my Redeemer lives, and on the last day I will rise again.)
These anniversaries of All Saints and All Souls make me recall those of
1917, in the rout of Caporetto. But now these days are even sadder. Back
then, under the outward collapse of the armed forces, one felt the spirit

---

administration of the Reich, including the police and counterespionage. The
Nuremberg Court defined it as a criminal organization that actively participated
in the persecution of the Jews. During the Second World War, the SS was formed
into military divisions on the orders of Himmler.

[20] Job 14:2, "who cometh forth like a flower, and is destroyed, and fleeth as
a shadow, and never continueth in the same state."

trying to raise itself; external appearances to the contrary, there was in everybody a painful, bitter feeling for the homeland and the will for resurgence. The armed forces seemed in disarray, but the spirit was united, and one rallied under a common will of revival and return. The weather then was rainy and gloomy, while today it is beautiful and warm, but then there was light in our spirits, while today there lies on the spirit a weight, a sense of sadness, of distrust and bitterness.

Yesterday a Friulian who hailed from the lands conquered in the last war illustrated in dark colours the mood of ex-Austrian Friulians. He said, "They want Italy to lose." What sadness there is in this statement that is, moreover, confirmed by other significant proof. It is also confirmed by the vote of the people of the Aldo Adige who, after twenty years of Fascism, have opted for Germany. All of this occurred as a result of violent propaganda and methods that humiliated the people. They did not know how to win hearts. To this is added privation, poverty, the sufferings of war and its less-than-reassuring progress. Even the Albanians are rising up, doubtful that Italy will win the war. The action on the Russian front has ended up being a moral victory for the Russians. We have lost the Empire, and Libya is in danger.

As I write, it seems as if a naval battle looms: an English convoy has crossed the Straits of Gibraltar. What will be the outcome? In Libya the army is holding, but how long can they resist against the formidable pressure exercised with total superiority of men and equipment? The valour of our soldiers always shines brightly. Yesterday news arrived that two brothers of the Ruspoli[21] princes went down fighting like heroes. We hear talk of American troops massing in the Lake Chad region; we hear talk of Moroccan and de Gaullist troops at the ready around Tunisia. If these troops attack, engaging the Italians from the rear, what will happen? Italy seems absent from this war. It obeys and is disciplined but without being interested, its spirit frequently being in mute revolt. It is said that this is not Italy's war, but rather Fascism's war. They wanted to celebrate the twentieth anniversary of Fascism, thinking that spirits would once again be galvanized with parades and press rhetoric. The opposite effect was achieved: it was not a resounding effect, but an intimate one.

[21] The noble family Ruspoli is of Florentine origin and became prominent in the middle of the thirteenth century. It divided into two branches, one of which transferred to Rome, where it acquired the title of marquis in the eighteenth century before being elevated to princely status by Pope Clement XI.

Spirits are secretly in a state of revolt. To this is added grief for the incursions into Genoa and Milan, and the conviction that they lacked any means of defence.

It is said that Mussolini is like a mountain: there are heights illuminated by sunshine, and there are abysses full of dark shadows; today he is enveloped in the shadows of the abyss. What is more, he is ill, and it seems gravely so. It is certain that the celebrations prepared at the Adriano have been suspended, for which they say the preparations cost one million. The King gives the impression of being uninvolved or of being Mussolini's servant. Yesterday evening an old diplomat said to me, "Twenty years of Fascism have morally ruined the Italian people. There is a latent but diffuse reaction, but nobody has had the courage to raise his voice. And so the swindle continues. They authorize millions in spending without observing any of the usual constitutional formalities. Senators murmur under their breath. But there is not one who has the courage to move a motion for the convocation of the Senate, to say nothing of the Chamber. It was well conceived, but then it fell under the will of Mussolini, who changes national councillors on a whim ... It is a colossal mockery. The Germans act as landlords of Italy. German troops in Italy call themselves an army of occupation."

I would like to close these quick and melancholy notes with a religious reflection. In the shipwreck of so many precious things there remains a light that consoles people's souls: the light of God. Many people have today come back to the thought and practice of religion. Just yesterday evening the architect Professor Fasolo told me of a very nice and unusual project: to hold on Saturday evenings intimate gatherings of artists to read the words of the Fathers of the Church. The architect said, "We have need of spiritual nourishment, and it seems that we cannot find a more substantial and interesting source than in the ideas of the primitive Church."

I promised to organize these *lecturae patrum apostolicorum*. When I think of the tragedy of humanity, my thoughts naturally rise up to God and become prayer. This morning, at the Mass for the dead, I focused on remembering and recommended God's clemency for many dear souls; and I almost had a vision of the countless formations of servicemen who had fallen on land, sea, and in the air. I saw these youths, cut down by death, colouring many lands with blood from East to West, and the waters of almost all the seas. And I commended all of them to God, without distinction of race, nation, or religion. I prayed also for pagans, that He may show them mercy. All have fallen to accomplish a difficult duty, to be loyal to a severe discipline. And behind them the cry of the mothers and orphans. Lord, have mercy on this great suffering and hasten the days of peace! *Parce, Domine, parce populo tuo; et ne in aeternum irascaris nobis* [Have mercy, Oh Lord, have mercy on your people; do not be angry with your people forever].

5 NOVEMBER 1942

On the occasion of the twentieth anniversary of Fascism the *originality* of the Mussolinian conception was discussed – that it came before the National Socialist Movement and that Fascism is called to exert its influence in the world, etc. I ask myself in what element does this presumed and magnificent originality consist; after twenty years of experience, one should easily be able to distinguish the outlines of this originality! I don't see it. In fact, I see the disappearance of all those facts that in the past led one to confuse novelty with originality. Experience has shown us that Fascism is in essence nothing but dictatorship. Now, there is nothing original about that. There is a certain originality in the tribunals that handled workplace conflicts between employers and workers; it rejects the class struggle and establishes the reasonable principle of collaboration. But professional associations, unions, etc., are an instrument that has been used since the Middle Ages: associations for mutual assistance, etc. The corporations parliament [Chamber of Fasci and Corporations] would have been an original idea if it had not been reduced to a swindle.

Let's talk facts. Mussolini has accomplished some works that are genuinely impressive and bear the mark of his personality. But these accomplishments are due to his dictatorial powers. They are not original forms of government but are original conquests of the will of a dictator: thus the [via della] Conciliazione, the reclamation projects, etc. As for the rest, the balance sheet is disastrous because the riches of the nation have been squandered, and a crazy war has been taken on without comprehensive planning, without resources, and without great leaders ... An ambassador said to me, "If war had to be waged, the Alps and Greece should have been left to one side and in due course we should have placed men and munitions in Libya, with serious preparation and not with haste and improvisation. And at the right time we would conquer the Suez Canal and from there, across Sudan, reach Eritrea and save the Empire. It seems as if this was the plan of Balbo and the Duke of Aosta.

But Mussolini was jealous of the glory of others. And such wretched jealousies unfortunately find parallels in history.

8 NOVEMBER 1942

Catastrophic news reaches us from Africa. One feels one's heart breaking thinking especially of the dead and for the future of Italy. Yesterday G.C. said to me, "I am glad we are losing; that way, we will free ourselves from this tyranny. And many think as I do." What sadness in these words! This evening I went to Piazza Venezia. Rome looks the same: people on the streets, people in the cafés, people on the streetcars. Everything is calm, ordinary, and seems indifferent. It seems as if the outcome of the war in Libya does not elicit interest. Even this is sad, as when a sick person no longer feels his own sickness. What will happen? Will peace have to be made – a beggar's peace? Will the regime fall? Mussolini is ill, moreover, and it seems seriously so. If there is a separate peace to be made, the victorious nations will not want to deal with Mussolini. And what will Germany do? The King is a sphinx. These are days full of threats. It is possible that the mob will be unleashed. But against whom? Fascism is bankrupt. The people, and especially the class that thinks, sees today's situation and its failure, easily forgetting the merits of the past. Yesterday an old prelate said to me, "Mussolini thought he could rule a nation without letting it breathe a little freedom … He failed to understand that tyranny cannot last forever … Now events are overwhelming him." There is nothing left to do but pray. This morning, at Mass, I reflected on the vision of the many dead lost in the sands of Africa.

Leaflet Dropped by Allied Aircraft
ALLIED AIRPLANES WILL BLOT OUT THE SUN OVER ITALY. Today, the war is at Italy's doorstep. Did you ask for this end? Do you want it today?

8 NOVEMBER 1942

Today, reading in the Breviary the prophecies of Ezekiel, it seemed to me that his voice was directed at Italy: "*tabescet omne cor et dissolventur universae manus: ut, occupante pavore mentis hominum, nullus audeat repugnare.*"[22]

---

[22] Ez. 21:7: "And every heart shall melt, and all hands shall be made feeble, and every spirit shall faint, and nothing can stop it."

15 NOVEMBER 1942

The King has been absent from Rome for several days now. Nor did he participate in the *Te Deum* celebrated in the Church of the Sudario[23] on 11 November. His absence from the capital in such terrible and decisive times for the life of the nation seems like an abdication: he is doing *de facto* that which one sees must happen *de jure*. What sadness! Last evening I met Senator Francesco Rota.[24] He was mournful, with almost a sense of desperation for the fate of the homeland. I said, "Permit me to speak with complete sincerity. There is a widespread feeling that the Senate has not fulfilled one of its high responsibilities, a function that goes beyond forms of government. The nation is on the brink of a precipice. Why isn't a motion made for the convocation of the Senate?" He replied, "Yes, some have had that idea ... But we are not under the rule of law. They immediately speak about truncheons." They are afraid, therefore. This does not reflect honour on this high assembly.

Last evening, going to Chiesa Nuova, I saw many line-ups of people at the doors of butcher shops. They were muttering softly, but without anger, with an inert passiveness. The sad conditions of Italy are on everybody's mind, but they seem almost outside the homeland itself. People

[23] The church of the Sudario in Rome, close to its more famous counterpart Sant'Andrea della Valle, was the church of the Piedmonetese, Niçois, and Savoiards in the city and in 1870 became the church of the House of Savoy.

[24] Francesco Rota (1870–1957), a count, landowner, and lawyer, was mayor of San Vito al Tagliamento, his city of origin, as well as administrator of the province of Udine; he was a Liberal member in the Italian parliament for 15 years (1904–19) and then senator of the kingdom from 1924 onward. In 1925 he joined the National Fascist Party [Partito Nazionale Fascista]. He became an in-law of General Pietro Badoglio, who was head of the Italian government (1943–44), when his daughter Giuliana married the general's son, Duke Mario Badoglio. In 1945–46 Count Rota had to defend himself for not resigning his Senate seat. In the documentation of his defence there is a letter from Archbishop Celso Costantini (6 January 1945), who testified to Rota's patriotic and gentlemanly conduct. Confronted with the guilty verdict of 30 November 1945, Costantini wrote a similar letter (on 21 March 1946) to the president of the High Court, which was to pronounce on an appeal to overturn the verdict carried forward by Rota on 24 June 1946. The second verdict of 9 July 1946 went in Rota's favour, as can be seen in F. Rota, *Memorie della mia vita politica* (Treviso: Arti grafiche Longo e Zoppelli, 1950), 451–3.

are almost indifferent, not knowing whether to celebrate Italy's victory or its defeat. They can no longer take a regime that has so profoundly injured human dignity, rendering citizens virtual servants or automatons. This is an extremely painful fact. Mussolini wanted to put himself above everybody, and everybody is abandoning him, including certain Fascists who are concerned with landing on their feet. The Chinese wise man Lao-Tze[25] once said, "By luck a man can govern the world for a short time. But if he knows how to make himself loved, he can govern eternally." Mussolini could not make himself loved. Surrounding him is still the comedy of forced acclaim. In the Gospel there is the expression *potestas tenebrarum* [the power of darkness]. We are at the mercy of this power; it has eclipsed the light of love, of justice, of a sense of honour for keeping one's word.

16 NOVEMBER 1942
Ambassador Cerruti tells me that Himmler[26] came to Rome and told Senise[27] that in Germany two things preoccupy them: the health of Il Duce and the swarms of Communist infiltration. He recommended that they prevent Il Duce from flying and that they intensify the repression against Communist cells. He made it known that if they do not, Germany will take care of it. Senise replied that the "Italian police are up to the job." If the German Gestapo intervene, officially it will mean that Italy would fall under the control of the German police. It would be a type of German occupation of Italy.

[25] Lao Tze is the oldest and possibly greatest of the "wise men" Chinese thinkers; he lived in the sixth century before Christ.

[26] Heinrich Himmler (1900–45), the German politician who in 1929 was tasked with organizing the ss, first as a personal guard for Hitler and then as a larger military corps. From 1934 he was the head of the police services in the entire Reich and also principally responsible for Nazi crimes. In 1945 he became minister of the interior. After being captured by the English he killed himself in 1945.

[27] Carmine Senise (1883–1958), an Italian politician and first-class prefect from 1939 who was named to head the police in 1940, a position from which he was removed in April 1943. He was among the conspirators who on 25 July 1943 voted against Mussolini in the Grand Council of Fascism. He was interned in a German concentration camp, returning to Italy in 1945.

Yesterday I said goodbye to Monsignor Moro,[28] who is returning to Benghazi. He was returning from the Ministry for East Africa. He was told to go to Lecce, where he will be lent a military aircraft. God save this good bishop!

20 NOVEMBER 1942

Dark days. Life outside goes on with its usual rhythm, but if two friends meet and chat, their thoughts go to the sadly threatening military situation. Notwithstanding the truly heroic valour of our soldiers, it seems that the outcome is certain: Libya will be lost. The Mediterranean, which in past centuries was the dynamic centre of civilization, will again assume an almost decisive importance in this war, at least for Italy. Beyond the Adriatic, the Slavic populations and even Albania are rising up in anticipation of the war, ready to pounce on the Italians. The occupation, maintained by terror, has generated terror. Moreover, it is natural that all peoples aspire to their own independence. The annexation of Slovenia and the aggression against Greece always seemed to me to be an error and an injustice.

In recent days, reading the Breviary, I came across the dream of Nebuchadnezzar, in which there was a great and sublime statue with a fierce look; his head was of pure gold, his chest and arms of silver, his stomach and ribcage of bronze, his legs of iron and of steel and clay. A rock that came loose from the mountain hit the feet and broke them, which then also broke the legs of iron, the ribcage and stomach of bronze, the chest and arms of silver, and the head of gold. Mussolini had a golden head in the first years of his government. But he had feet of iron and clay; that is, he did not have a moral and religious foundation, solid and secure, on which to stand. The colossus, struck at his feet, is being destroyed ... God help us!

20 NOVEMBER 1942

I encountered Archbishop Mons. Giardini,[29] serene and calm as usual; he told me that he views the future with a certain serenity because

---

[28] Domenico Candido Moro (1880–1952), of the Order of Brothers Minor, was bishop of Uzita and from 1931 vicar apostolic to Cyrene, an ecclesiastical region that was renamed Benghazi in 1939.

[29] Mario Giardini (1877–1947), of the Barnabite Fathers, became titular archbishop of Emessa in 1921, and in 1931 he transferred to his residence at

while men agitate, God guides them. He consoles himself with a profound faith in God.

CONVERSATION WITH AMBASSADOR CERRUTI
20 NOVEMBER 1942

I said, "I think that at the right moment, Providence will say Enough! Hitler has committed too many crimes against humanity and the Church, and he will not remain unpunished. The punishment of God is a mill that grinds slowly, but does not stop." The ambassador responded, "I have never had any doubts about the faith. I thank God that he has given me a perfect adherence to the revealed truth. I do not know the torment of doubt. I do confess, however, that if Hitler were to win, I would begin to find myself in interior anguish."

21 NOVEMBER 1942

News reaches us of an incursion into northern Italy resulting in severe damage, above all, of dead and wounded at Genoa, Turin, and Milan.[30] And we are only at the beginning! The newspapers cry about barbarity, and truly these are acts of outright barbarism. Civilization has devoured itself and is destroying itself because what is being destroyed is the human and Christian sense of civilization. Our newspapers, however, have no right to cry about barbarity. They are all tied to Fascism, and they themselves have published idiotic words: *they were asking that Italy also be given the honour of going to bomb England.* And those planes went, returning in a pitiful state. To say nothing of the aggression against

---

Ancona. In 1940 he became titular archbishop of Laodicea in Syria, maintaining a base in Rome to carry out his responsibilities as apostolic examiner of the clergy of the Roman vicariate.

[30] The bombardments referred to here are discussed in the report that the nuncio in Italy, Mons. Borgoncini-Duca, sent to Cardinal Maglione. The report was the result of a meeting of the nuncio with King Victor Emmanuel III, as referred to in *Le Saint Siège et la guerre mondiale, novembre 1942 – décembre 1943* of *Actes et documents du Saint Siège relatifs à la seconde guerre mondiale* (Vatican City: Libreria Editrice Vaticana, 1973), and in *Actes et Documents du Saint Siège relatifs à la seconde guerre mondiale*, vol. 7 (Vatican City: Libreria Editrice Vaticana, 1970).

France! With arrogant idiocy in Italy a verb has been coined – "conventrizzare" – alluding to the destruction of Coventry.[31]

23 NOVEMBER 1942

A lady returning from Germany told me, "The cult of blood and race has led German youth to bestial aberrations. They send girls onto playing fields to have fun [have sex] with the boys. They are making men for Germany. Any sense of morality has been abolished. The government has taken on the task of raising bastards."

24 NOVEMBER 1942

The following writings have been found: "The Castle falls; the red flag is ready." Some think that this is a ploy of certain Fascist elements who are preparing to use the truncheon.

Mons. Balconi told me that a workers' chaplain in Germany recounted the following: "A worker in a laboratory who was using a pen splashed a drop of ink on an image of Hitler. The worker said that it was an accident. The Gestapo took him away, and we have heard nothing since. The chaplain looked into the matter, alerting the Italian consul, and succeeded in finding the worker and saving him while he was waiting to be shot along with two others."

26 NOVEMBER 1942

In the parish of s n s the pastor spoke to the children about the Pope. He added that if they heard talk against the Pope, they should not believe what was being said. One child raised his hand: "What do you want?" "Father," responded the child with an attitude of someone who has made a discovery, "Nobody speaks badly about the Pope; everybody speaks badly about Mussolini."

28 NOVEMBER 1942

I spoke on the second epistle of the Confessions of St Augustine to a group of artists. Tomorrow I will explain the Gospel to the artists, for the third time. These spirits are hungry for the truth. This evening I encountered Abbot Ricciotti; he told me that his *Vita di Cristo* [Life of Christ] is in its seventh edition, and he reminded me of the success of

[31] The destruction of the English city was carried out by German aerial bombardment in 1940.

Carnelutti's interpretation of the *Pater Noster* [Our Father].[32] I am reading Bruer's most beautiful booklet *Gesù nel secolo XX* [Jesus in the 20th Century].

29 NOVEMBER 1942

Today the architect A. said to me, "If Mussolini, after giving the Empire to Italy and creating new cities on reclaimed marshland, had offered the King his resignation, this would have led Italy to govern itself with the usual forms of honest freedom, and he would have risen to mythical status." I think this is true. Unbounded personal infatuation defeated him. And now, as a Chinese proverb says, everybody is voluntarily hitting the falling wall.

1 DECEMBER 1942

Sad and threatening hours. The clouds that obscure Italy's horizon are becoming ever more dark. No light has the power to overcome this evil gloom. Yesterday the former minister Jung came to see me. He was defeated and heartbroken, having come from Africa, where he had a vast concession. He had left last, after his farmers. This is the third time that his riches and promising holdings have fallen to the enemy. But this did not worry him excessively: he was mournful for Italy. Yesterday I received letters from Mons. Facchinetti,[33] vicar apostolic in Tripoli, and Mons. Moro, vicar apostolic of Benghazi. Mons. Moro says that no Italians remain in the vicariate except missionaries and the sisters. Even Mons. Lucato,[34]

---

[32] Francesco Carnelutti (1879–1965), an eminent lawyer of Friulian origin, was a university professor in a wide range of juridical subjects, especially trials and penal law. He authored numerous important works on law. He was among the founders of the Union of Catholic Italian Jurists, which was founded in 1948. In the last part of his life he wrote books of a religious nature in keeping with his Christian faith.

[33] Camillo Vittorio Facchinetti (1883–1956), of the Order of Brothers Minor, became titular bishop of Nicio in 1936, with pastoral responsibility as the vicar apostolic of Tripoli in Libya.

[34] Giovanni Lucato (1892–1962), a Salesian, became titular bishop of Tigia in 1939, with pastoral responsibility as vicar apostolic of Derna. He was transferred to the Italian diocese of Isernia and Venafro in 1948.

vicar apostolic of Derna, who returned to his post, is thinking of coming back to Italy.

Yesterday Churchill delivered an extremely fierce speech. Italy cannot but expect more pain, fresh destruction, and new defeats. It is the common opinion that Italy will shortly be expelled from Africa. It seems that Greece, Yugoslavia, and perhaps Albania are stirring and preparing for an uprising. Genoa, Torino, and Milan have been terribly hit. We are powerless to respond. And we must see Italy fall to pieces while remaining tied to Hitler? *"Salus reipublicae suprema lex"* [The good of the public is the supreme law], the Latins used to say. At base, this commitment was undertaken by the Fascist regime; it was not done with the consent of the nation. If the regime falls, the nation remains. Naturally, the King, who compromised himself, will know what duty awaits him. Meantime, he and the Senate remain silent ...

4 DECEMBER 1942

Mussolini's speech, whatever the Italian press says about it and in spite of the stupid applause of the parliament, has left a sense of bitter disillusion and increasing resentment toward the man who, alone, is primarily responsible for having brought Italy to ruin. To be noted is the absence of any sign of the monarchy, the outrageous mockery of the *intelligent Italian people*, the discordant note of hatred, the allusion to the valour of the Italian soldier *if well led* ... But the thing that truly brought it to the height of disgust was the spectacle of the abject cowardice of the Chamber, which could not do anything but applaud ... The mercenaries applaud the master.

Leaflet Distributed by University Students
The students have retrieved and republished an old speech by Mussolini, of 3 May 1918: "*Mussolini is always right.* If Germany wins, we must get it into our heads that total and certain ruin awaits us ... Germans have not changed their basic instincts ... They are the same as those whom Tacitus described to perfection ... Strong in war, armed with spears, well furnished with horses, they preferred to acquire what they needed with violence instead of by working the land ... Between Britons and Germans, that same Roman historian established a difference that even today is as valid as it was nineteen centuries ago: while the Britons fought for the defence of their homeland and families, the Germans fought out of avarice and lust."

Desperate Hours

A man said to me, "When I get up in the morning, it doesn't matter whether I find myself with the Germans or the English." Terrible, desperate apathy. Mussolini wanted to do it all himself, keeping Italians at a distance. And Italians abandoned him. They care neither for him nor for Italy.

CHRISTMAS MESSAGE FROM GENERAL CHIANG KAI-SHEK
25 DECEMBER 1942

"Today, the day Christ was born, is a day of universal joy. Our wise men have said, 'Those who fight for law received help from all sides, while those who work in error find little sympathy.' Today, 31 nations are united in their struggle against the Axis. The United Nations fight for international justice and for the freedom of humanity … I have the firm conviction that at the end of this war, the world will be based on equality and mutual assistance and on the construction of a new world order of peace and happiness … This new world order must be created through the love that Christ spoke of. And it is for this that while war rages, I welcome with all my heart the return of Christ as Prince of Peace; and I pray for an early shared victory, so that oppressed people can quickly obtain their liberation and freedom."

The Great Christmas Message of the Holy Father

As always, the Pope, the Universal Father, is the avenger of the truth: *liberat animas testis fidelis* [Prv. 14:25; a faithful witness delivers souls]; he is the avenger of freedom, *qua libertate nos Christus liberavit* [Gal. 4:31; by the freedom wherewith Christ has made us free]. His great message[35] discussed the double elements of peace within social life: "Any social cohabitation worthy of the name, since it derives its origins from the desire for peace, inclines to peace." He amply explained these ideas and concluded by establishing five principal points for the order and pacification of human society:

1 the dignity and rights of the human person;
2 defence of social unity and especially of the family;
3 the dignity and prerogative of work;

[35] This Christmas radio broadcast of Pius XII is reproduced in AAS 35 (*Bollettino Ufficiale della Santa Sede*,1943), 9–24; the citation is on pages 17 and 20.

4 reintegration of legal order;
5 a conception of the state inspired by the Christian spirit.

IMPRESSIONS OF THE HOLY FATHER'S CHRISTMAS MESSAGE
28 DECEMBER 1942

The editor Calogero Tuminelli commented to me: "Noble and courageous words with an intuition about the needs of the times and the serious dangers of the postwar era. It is necessary to prevent the unhappiness
of the people, who will be disillusioned in their political hopes and in
need of economic assistance." The maid in our house, who is intelligent
but not cultured, said, "The Pope should speak to us often to console us.
He spoke to each individual's situation." A worker of mine said, "*That* is
a speech – not the hot air of Mussolini."

Senator Salata: "We in Italy have already achieved a good measure of
responsible social policy. But as the Pope says, a little freedom is required,
even if it must be disciplined." The Hon. Longinotti said to me, "The son
of the Hon. S., a Communist, told me that he was enthusiastic about the
Pope's speech and that his father passionately defended him in an argument against the ideas of an old uncle." The director of *Il Popolo di
Roma*, after editing the paper, said, "Did you hear the Pope's Bolshevik
speech? An old senator and big landowner wrote to one of my friends
saying that the Pope delivered a Bolshevik speech."

The government and the Ministry of Popular Culture were dissatis-
fied. That is natural, because the Pope spoke about freedom and the
dignity of the individual. Some hypercritical Romans who belong to
the wealthier classes said that the speech was too socialist. Liberals,
especially the remnants of the old masonic liberalism (the Masons are
reviving and reorganizing) believed they saw in the Pope's speech a
certain preoccupation with re-establishing the People's Party [Partito
Popolare]. They think this way because certain points coincide with
the old party's program.

The Pope's Works of Charity

Lux in tenebris lucet [Light shines in the darkness]. The Pope's marvellous works of charity continue everywhere. Over the furrow of the misery and suffering dug by the war passes the smile of the bounty of God,
the image of Christ's Samaritan, which curves around the turns and
pours out the oil of fraternal love. The Vatican's information centre is
working at an accelerated pace. All the Pope's representatives have been

mobilized to this army of charity. I must limit myself to just a few points. Mons. Antoniutti, the apostolic delegate in Canada, recently visited a thousand civilians, Italians and Germans, in internment camps in Fredericton and 700 Japanese in an internment camp in Anglar, bringing to all the greetings and comfort of the Holy Father and distributing gifts and sums of money in his name. And Father Hughes[36] of the White Fathers, who heads the Apostolic Delegation of Egypt and Palestine, by continuing visits to the internment camps in Egypt was able to get to know the prisoners and internees, both the civilians and the religious, all of whom expressed the most profound gratitude for the charitable kindnesses of the Universal Father.

[36] Arthur Hughes (1902–49), a priest of the Missionaries of Africa who was named head of the Apostolic Delegation in Cairo and in Palestine on 16 June 1942.

The Year 1943

9 JANUARY 1943

Monsignor Aurelio Signora,[1] secretary general of the P.O. [Pontificia Opera/Pontifical Works] of St Peter the Apostle [for Indigent Clergy], writes: "One of the phenomena – among the most painful – of the current time is the moral atonality of the masses as individuals. Events that in other times would have agitated spirits are received with indifference and passiveness. A single force is perhaps – as never before – alive and operating in everybody: the spiritual power of the Supreme Pastor. His acts and words inspire a vast resonance in all social classes. The Christmas message of 1942 was listened to on the radio or searched for in the newspapers with urgency. Immediately after the broadcast, Dr Ugo D'Andrea, political editor of *Lavoro Fascista* and political contributor on EIAR radio news,[2] wrote to me: "I have just heard the most noble message of Pius XII. This offers comfort and hope for the future.""

---

[1] Aurelio Signora (1902–90) was born in Budoia, in the Diocese of Concordia-Pordenone. After serving as secretary general of the Pontificia Opera di San Pietro Apostolo, he was named in 1957 titular archbishop of Nicosia, prelate of Pompei, and pontifical delegate of the Sanctuary in the same city. He retained these responsibilities until 1978, when as a result of age he retired to his hometown, where he later died.

[2] EIAR is the acronym of the Ente Italiano per le Audizioni Radiofoniche, or the Italian Radio Program Company, established in 1927 by the Fascist government. The EIAR had a monopoly on radio broadcasting facilities and programming in Italy. In 1944 it was absorbed by a company called RAI (Radio Audizioni

A headmaster, G.P., declared to me: "Everybody, even those who do not belong to the Church, felt in the Pontiff's address anxiety for genuine freedom and find in its reading the infallible promises of order and peace."

A Gold Medal recipient of the 1915–18 war, D.C., affirms: "When the Pope speaks, one has total assurance that his teaching is superior, founded exclusively on justice and truth. It is a great comfort to hear him in times like these."

In Venice the most fanatical Fascists saw in the papal message a political meaning contrary to their convictions, declaring, "It's better like this. We know what we should think and what we have to do."

In many circles, especially the intellectual ones (the family of one senator, a minister of state, and university professors), there exists an uncertainty about how to interpret "crusade." They ask, "What should we do to give practical effect to the noble words of the Supreme Pontiff?"

P., an illustrious physician – a Gold Medal recipient – and a very high-profile person, breathlessly searched for a newspaper carrying the Pope's message because, he said, the Holy Father said things that are "very important and indispensable to know."

THE LOSS OF TRIPOLI   26 JANUARY 1943

Il Messaggero of 24 January 1943 reports: "And if it is true that today we must report the abandoning of Tripoli, it is just as true that we have annexed the three provinces of Dalmatia and that the Italian flag flies over Nice, in Corsica, on the Jonic Islands, and on the Aegean Islands at Cefalonia and Zante. The fight continues, and in certain ways it continues in more advantageous conditions: in a homogeneous and hospitable space from a population perspective, and with the security of more certain and rapid resupply."

Verbal acrobatics. What was lost [Libya and the Empire] belonged to Italy. The presumed annexations in the Balkans are *sub judice* and seem exposed to imminent danger. The saddest fact is the apathy of Italians, some indifferent or unconcerned or – and this is truly painful – even a few who are happy. Only certain select minds suffer, seeing many sacrifices, and much prestige, and many riches irretrievably lost. And the

---

Italiane), which exists today. But with the addition of the television component and the loss of its previous monopoly, RAI currently stands for Radiotelevisione Italiana.

Senate remains silent: it does not exist. Mussolini once served Italy; he then put Italy at his service, with catastrophic results.

28 JANUARY 1943

Raffaele Guariglia,[3] Italy's ambassador to the Holy See, asked me one day if one could hope that the Holy See would in some way recognize the government of Nanjing, created by the Japanese. This would have given the Japanese the satisfaction of legitimacy.

I responded that this question was not in my area of competence, but I could privately inform him about the position that the Holy See maintains in similar situations. The Holy See does not usually confer official recognition to governments established during a war that is being waged. It sometimes deals with these governments on a *de facto* basis because of urgent necessity. But a *de jure* recognition is always left until after the peace. He observed, "But don't you think that the Holy See could take a more conciliatory position for the sake of missionary opportunities?" I responded, "No. Look what is happening in the territories closest to us. The Duke of Spoleto, named King of Yugoslavia, was received by the Pope, but purely and simply as a private person, without anything in the accompanying ceremony to allude to his new position. The Holy See has a consummate experience and does not usually compromise its utter impartiality to please one side or the other."

1 FEBRUARY 1943

On 28 January, the superior of the Marists, a Frenchman, came to see me. We discussed missionaries in Oceania, some of whom had been massacred. Then we talked about conditions in France and the legal status of the Religious. He told me of a meeting with [Pierre] Laval in which he reminded him of the principle of freedom and common law that protect the Religious, to which the government leader made the following remark: "I look at facts. Principles interest me little. I went to Rome to pay homage to the Pope because the Catholic Church is a fact."

[3] Raffaele Guariglia (1889–1970), Baron of Vituso, an Italian politician and diplomat, was Italy's ambassador to the Holy See between February 1942 and February 1943. He was minister of foreign affairs in the government led by Pietro Badoglio from 28 July 1943 to 11 February 1944. After the Second World War, he headed the Italian Monarchist Union during the exile of King Umberto II and was a senator on the Italian Monarchist Party list.

THE GOOD SHEPHERD GIVES HIS LIFE FOR HIS LAMBS
2 FEBRUARY 1943

"The tragic and also sublime death of the archbishop of Reggio Calabria shocked and profoundly affected not only the multitudes who venerated His Excellency Mons. Enrico Montalbetti[4] as one of the most splendid glories of the Episcopate and one of the most noble sons of the nation, but also affected all Italians, and with them all Christian consciences, and even the fundamentally secular. The bishop, distinguished in doctrine and science, in his apostolic generosity and love of country has fallen victim to his vigilant care for his flock, as falls the Good Shepherd. This death, heroic in the most pure and holy sense, which is one of an ultimate sacrifice of love, aggrieves while at the same time building up, illuminating with beauty and a saving power that offers a theme of healthy meditation."[5]

A CHANGING OF THE GUARD   6 FEBRUARY 1943

Today, unexpectedly, a radical restructuring of the ministry was announced. Ciano, Bottai, Grandi, Pavolini,[6] Buffarini-Guidi, etc., have been "defenestrated." I heard this expression used to indicate the sudden and decisive way with which these ministers were fired. One has the impression that Mussolini wanted to prevent and thwart a "palace conspiracy." They say at the same time that Ciano was more anglophile than

---

[4] Enrico Montalbetti (1888–1943), born in Venice, was named coadjutor bishop of Trento on 5 May 1935 and titular bishop of Bova in 1941. He distinguished himself by being very attached to the city and its problems and was attentive to the needs of his ecclesial community. He was fearless in his criticism of the Fascist authorities when necessary; nor was he reluctant during the Second World War to hurry to where his presence was needed. He died at Melito Porto Salvo on 31 January 1943, not even 54 years of age, killed during an Allied bombardment while he was giving lessons of formation for some seminary students at Bova.

[5] CC: *L'Avvenire d'Italia*, 2 February 1943.

[6] Alessandro Pavolini (1903–45), an Italian politician, son of the Indianist Paolo Emilio, was as a young man part of the Florentine Fascist Action squads. He was minister of popular culture from 1939 to 1943, when he became director of *Il Messaggero*. After 8 September 1943 he was secretary of the Republican Fascist Party and a close collaborator with the Germans. He was captured by the partisans along with Mussolini and was shot on 28 April 1945 at Dongo.

germanophile, that he was already letting things drift and was preparing his own succession at the time when Mussolini, for sickness or other reasons, would have had to leave the government. Along with Ciano, his trusted friends Bottai, Tavolini, and Grandi are also eliminated. Some say that OVRA must have relayed to Mussolini intelligence about suspect conversations and meetings and that Mussolini then delivered one of his blows.

The public is indifferent, although they do show a certain interest for the eviction of Ciano, who is held in large part responsible for the war against Greece. One gentleman observed, "Fascism is finished. Better that the demolition starts from the inside rather than the outside."

A batch of Fascist senators are rewarding many of their faithful and seek to create a friendly environment in the Senate. Perhaps Mussolini fears that the Senate will make some kind of move or show some sign of life.

Ciano, Ambassador to the Vatican

He fell on his feet. And in practice, he may render service to the Holy Church and equally to Italy. It is too bad that his presence in the Vatican casts a Fascist shadow on the Rock, illuminated by a divine sun. It also shows little respect on the government's part for so frequently changing the ambassadors to the Holy See for internal and opportunistic reasons. Much more disrespectful is the fact that – as they say – the naming of Ciano to the post was made public without first having obtained the approval of the Vatican.[7]

FIERCE PASTORAL LETTER FROM THE BISHOPS OF HOLLAND
17 FEBRUARY 1943

Another letter from the Dutch Episcopate has been secretly delivered to me:

---

[7] In reality, the requested approval of Ciano by Ambassador Guariglia was given, but with the following notation relayed to Guariglia and offered by Mons. Montini: "The Holy Father has observed that this too-frequent change of Italian ambassadors is not considerate of the Holy See." (*Le Saint-Siège et la guerre mondiale*, vol. 7 of *Actes et documents du Saint Siège relatifs à la seconde guerre mondiale ...,* (Vatican City: Libreria Editrice Vaticana, 1973), 219.

We would be remiss in our duty if we did not publicly raise our voices against the injustice that is being perpetrated against many members of our people. In this we follow the path of our Holy Father.

We especially recall those principles that are at the base of the Christian life of our people: justice, mercy, and freedom of conscience. They must attest that even those who govern are subject to divine law and must abstain from actions condemned by this law. The Churches would be guilty if they failed to reprimand the governors for the sins committed in the execution of their governance; if they did not, they might well bring down God's judgment upon them.

The Churches have already spoken about this: the ever-increasing lack of justice and security; the persecution to death of our Jewish fellow citizens; the imposition of customs and doctrines that are diametrically opposed to the Gospel of Jesus Christ; the impairment of the freedom of Christian education; the violent deportation of Dutch workers to Germany; the execution of hostages; the arrest and imprisonment of many, even Church officials, in such circumstances as to cause the death of a frightening number of them in the concentration camps. To all of which, raids have now been added, as if we were slaves, with the capture and deportation of thousands of young people.

By all these actions, divine law has been ever-more-gravely violated. Brothers, among so much injustice and suffering, we hold a special compassion for those young people who have been violently dragged far away from their paternal home, and also for the Jews and the Catholic faithful of Jewish origin, exposed to much suffering. Moreover, we feel deeply mortified that the measures targeting these two groups of people are imposed on our own countrymen; that is, against our magistrates, clerks, and directors of institutes.

Brothers, we know what kind of torments of conscience such persons have endured. However, to crush any doubt and any uncertainty on this point, we declare with the utmost energy that this cooperation is against one's conscience. And if the refusal to cooperate demands sacrifices from you, then be strong and unwavering in the conviction that you are doing your duty before God and man."

THE MINISTER FROM CHINA PRESENTS HIS CREDENTIALS
TO HIS HOLINESS PIUS XII   25 FEBRUARY 1943
Haec est dies quam fecit Dominus [Ps. 117:24; This is the day the Lord has made]. It is to be noted how official relations between the Holy See and China have been vigorously resisted. But time is a gentleman. Today, Minister Dr Cheon Kan Sié presented his credentials to the Holy Father with expressions of gratitude and deferential homage. It is natural that

this event, relating in some way as it does to my work as apostolic delegate in China from 1922 to 1933, has created a great joy in my heart.[8]

1 MARCH 1943

Mussolini is not thinking of the succession. In fact, if he were not there, everything would collapse. He has imposed the heavy harness of the party on the nation; and the nation waits to liberate itself from this harness.

Fascism or Communism?

The general engineer Umberto Pugliese tells me: "The Fascist leadership that governs us has posed the dilemma: either Fascism or Communism. Both are pernicious in concept. Outside and above them there are the principles of Christianity, founded on the freedom of the individual, on love, on mutual tolerance. The great majority of Italians, who long to be liberated from Fascism, are not attracted to Communism, a fact that today is both understood and declared.

COLLECTIVE LETTER OF THE BELGIAN EPISCOPATE,

READ IN THE CHURCHES OF BELGIUM   21 MARCH 1943

To your suffering at this time we must add another that will be very painful: the occupying authority has informed us that it is about to requisition the bells of our churches ... Now we solemnly declare that we oppose with all our episcopal authority this measure, which has no other purpose than to transform our bells into instruments of war and instruments of death ...

Compulsion of body and will is serious; violence against one's conscience is more serious still. Belgian citizens are obliged to cooperate, directly or indirectly, with the military operations of a foreign power that unjustly subjects their homeland to an extremely harsh regime of occupation without offering the least assurance regarding its future. Male workers, and especially female workers, are often placed in moral and religious situations that are seriously harmful. Even your bishops, notwithstanding their repeated requests, are unable to obtain

---

[8] Pius XII's address for the occasion was in French and is reported in Costantini's diary. It is also accessible in *Discorsi e Radiomessaggi di Sua Santità Pio* XII, vol. 4 (Milan: Società Editrice "Vita e Pensiero," 1943), 399–401.

authorization to send chaplain-priests to exiled members of their dioceses to help with their priestly ministry.

It is said that these measures are necessary to protect European civilization. But is it defending civilization – or eliminating it – to apply policies that violate the essential principles of every civilization? Human reason and Christian morality condemn and brand these policies as unfair and barbaric. Any collaboration in carrying out these measures is gravely against one's conscience.[9]

A PATERNAL WARNING FROM THE ARCHBISHOP OF MILAN[10]

30 MARCH 1943

"Reports reaching us from various parts fill us with pain and worry us greatly for the future. There is once again talk of the profanation of the Eucharist, of organizations for promoting blasphemy, of atheistic movements, etc. There is one sole origin of these movements, and it is easily discovered. To our good Ambrosiani [the people of Milan], to whom the archbishop can still speak face to face and with a noble and serene openness and sincerity, we offer words of confidence and frankness."

---

[9] CC: This magnificent document has been given to me in great secrecy.

[10] The archbishop of Milan was Cardinal Alfredo Idelfonso Schuster (1880–1954), who joined the Benedictine Congregation of Cassino in 1904, became abbot of Saint Paul Outside the Walls in 1918, and was named archbishop of the Lombard capital and then cardinal in 1929. For 25 years he led what is considered to have been the diocese with the most faithful in the world. He was inspired in his approach by his predecessor St Carlo Borromeo. He built a diocesan seminary in Vengono Inferiore (inaugurated in 1935) and carried out numerous pastoral visits. He strongly supported the reconciliation of the Church and the Italian state, but distanced himself from the Fascist regime when the racial laws were promulgated. At the fall of the Italian Social Republic, he proposed a meeting in the archdiocesan palace between Benito Mussolini and representatives of the partisans, with the aim of avoiding a bloodbath. He proposed to Mussolini, who did not accept the suggestion, that Il Duce remain in the archdiocesan palace and then surrender himself to the Allies. He blessed the bodies of Il Duce and of the Fascist leaders hanged in Piazzale Loreto in Milan, as he had done on 14 August 1944 for 14 partisans executed by the Germans. He was beatified by John Paul II on 12 May 1996.

VISIT OF COUNT CIANO, AMBASSADOR TO THE HOLY SEE
30 MARCH 1943

With me, he was cordial and candid as usual. He read me a few pages of his diary, referring to the days immediately before the war. Hitler had promised that for three years there would be no war, at least as far as Italy was concerned. Instead, with the Danzig affair, events were precipitated in Germany and Poland. Germany acted *motu proprio* [on its own initiative] without consulting Italy beforehand. Mussolini had, in spite of everything, accepted to go to war. Galeazzo Ciano said, "My father-in-law deceived himself, underestimating the military might of America." The encounter with Ciano, however, left me with a sense of real bitterness. He was against the war, so why didn't he resign?

4 APRIL 1943

Some predict some kind of reaction and revolt in the north of Italy. The King, skeptical and closed, is inattentive; the people have detached themselves from him. Perhaps the monarchy – if the King does not intervene with a coup d'état – has its days numbered. And I think that that would be a bad thing for Italy. The monarchy represents a point of stability.

LENTEN STATION AT THE VATICAN   11 APRIL 1943

Today, in the afternoon of Passion Sunday, the Holy Father entered the Vatican Basilica to participate in the procession and the supplications of the Lenten Station … At the ceremony, beyond the great representation of Roman patricians and nobility and the Diplomatic Corps, at a special kneeler Her Royal Highness the Princess of Piedmont[11] attended.

13 APRIL 1943

A day of anguish. Italy is heading toward the precipice. All prestige has been lost, the honour of arms, the backbone of our finances, and above all "the soul of the nation." Italy is like a sick person who no longer realizes her sickness. Mussolini blames the people because they do not follow him. He has demoralized them, distanced them, terrorized them, made them into a herd of sheep. When you take away freedom from people, you kill their souls. Now the people are realizing they have been

[11] Maria José of Belgium (1906–2001), of the Saxe-Cobourg-Gotha family, was Princess of Piedmont from 1930 to 1946, when she became Queen of Italy for about a month, as consort to King Umberto II of Savoy.

swindled. The Parliament of the Corporations was created, an idea that was a good one, reconnecting in some way to the corporations of the medieval period. But the idea was betrayed. The national councillors are nothing but extras and comedic masks; that is, mercenaries who are obliged to applaud. If anybody reacts, either he is dismissed or fears to be dismissed. Not one voice is raised from the Senate. Everybody mutters, everybody deprecates the regime; nobody dares say a word.

. The architect Foschini told me today: "Some say that Hitler and Mussolini believed, more or less in good faith, to wage war for the good of their own countries. But today, as they realize they have brought their countries to ruin, they must withdraw and save what can yet be saved. If at first they deceived themselves, today they are committing a crime." There is talk of the Allies landing in the south of Italy. Leaflets were dropped on Naples with the words "Easter of blood. Christmas with us." It is feared that Tunis will capitulate any hour now. The game is lost.

20 APRIL 1943

The horrendous massacre of Katyn[12] gives rise to a feeling of loathing against the unprecedented barbarism of the Communists; history has not yet recorded anything so brutal and loathsome. Nero, by contrast, was a lamb. But if we have the right to raise our voices against these inhuman acts, official Germany must remain silent: it has equalled and even surpassed such nefarious cruelty. I have seen the picture of crowds of Jews who, after having dug ditches, were killed wholesale and thrown into the ditches; there were women, children, old people, men. A cold-blooded massacre, a barbarism that is equal to and greater than that of the Bolsheviks. But there are rumours that Italians have also been committing acts of ruthless cruelty against their own countrymen because they belong to opposing factions ... When reason and a Christian sense are eclipsed in man, he becomes an animal more ferocious than a wild beast, because he puts his reason in the service of his cruelty. Let us bow our heads, sad and ashamed, praying to God that he stops the war, which Leonardo defined as "an extremely cruel insanity."

27 APRIL 1943

I am told that a Russian soldier hurled this crude remark at Italian soldiers on the Ukrainian front: "You are soldiers of gold, your officials are commanders of iron, and your munitions are lead."

---

[12] Costantini drew this news from Il Messaggero of 20 April 1943.

28 APRIL 1943

From day to day the fall of Tunis is expected. And then? Attempted invasions of Italy and the Balkans are expected. This year, I did not go to spend Easter at my house in Friuli for fear of being cut off from Rome. There is in everybody a profound sense of bitterness and lack of confidence, but nobody reacts. Plenty of murmuring, plenty of apprehension, but a desperate and passive inertia. Considered individually, senators are lions; together, they become rabbits. The Senate has reproduced the spectacle of the Venetian Senate on the eve of the fall of the Republic. However, everybody notices that one thing remains standing: the Catholic Church. And many spirits, until now inattentive and hostile, today turn their eyes to the Vatican.

Europe offers the image of a vast countryside in which the valleys and plains are covered with a sinister cloud cover that flashes and thunders in a dark storm: but over this dark and threatening cloud cover, there rises in the sun a luminous peak: the Catholic Church. The sun that kisses this peak makes the spectacle of the dark storms that cover the earth even more striking by contrast. The encyclical of Pius XII of 20 October 1939 and his successive speeches reflect the light of the supernatural, the light of eternity. The Pope has spoken with the knowledge that comes from the Gospel; he speaks words that have touched the most profound sensibilities of the entire world, Catholic or not. Humanity, even if misguided or absent from Christ, preserves in the depths of its conscience the need for justice and charity that finds its code in the Gospel. Outside the Gospel, we see the foundations of civilization and domestic life fall. Last night an emotional Italian academic, Pietro Canonica,[13] said to me: "The Pope has conquered the world. Without wanting and without being aware, the enemies of the Gospel are working on a great apology in favour of the Church because they are digging an abyss in the path of humanity; and that necessarily turns all eyes to where there is the light of salvation, where there is a power superior to all deficiency and weakness, where against everybody and everything the truth is proclaimed."

[13] Pietro Canonica (1869–1959), an Italian sculptor and acclaimed international portraitist who produced grandiloquent works, many of which adorn the Vittoriano in Rome, as well as the monument of Benedict XV in St Peter's Basilica in the Vatican. Luigi Einaudis, president of the Italian Republic, named him senator for life in 1950.

12 MAY 1943

Today Allied airplanes dropped leaflets on Rome. On them was written: "ITALIANS! We bombed your ports and your industries that work for the sole interest of Germany. We will bomb these objectives without ceasing until the day Italy separates its destiny from this GERMAN war. We do not hate the Italian people. We are fighting only against your Fascist leaders who have identified your country with Nazi Germany."

The people read these leaflets with indifference and nurture an ill-concealed resentment against the Allies. The common thinking is as follows: If the Allies had had the least consideration (I do not say love) for the Italian people, they could have and should have landed in the north, bottling up the Germans who were in Italy and without reducing all of Italy to a battlefield, destroying certain areas with so-called carpet bombing. They say that the Allies, especially England, wanted to punish the Italian people because an exhausted Italy will no longer cast a shadow over its hegemonic plans.

12 MAY 1943

A sealed letter addressed to me was deposited at the reception desk of the Propaganda. It contained this letter:

TO HIS MAJESTY VICTOR EMMANUEL III

Sire, many Italians still have faith in the monarchy. But their numbers diminish with every day and every hour that passes. The sinister influence of a cross that is not the cross of Christ has reached from the Alps all the way to Sicily, where your subjects die under the blows of people who never wanted to be an enemy. Only one cry will capture the act that everybody awaits. Sire, the regime governs illegally against the will of the country. The war of Fascist imperialism is irretrievably lost. God willed that Fascism would boast of this war as a war of the party. Today, in the hour of Italian defeat, Sire, only if you desire it, it will not be Italians who lose a conflict that has never been their war. Sire, separate the fate of the country from that of a brutal and megalomaniacal faction. Sever all ties between the dynasty that gave unity and the constitution to the homeland and those who have taken away freedom and citizenship from civilized people. Sire, history will say whether the Savoyard monarchy watched impassively the great moral and material ruin of our country, or if at the eleventh hour it heard the cry of those who today still turn to You.

Turin, 9 May 1943

The Central Executive Committee of Monarchist Associations of Italy

14 MAY 1943

Tunis has fallen. The bulletin that announced this painful epilogue of the war in Africa was delivered with fierce words. In defeat, the honour of arms was preserved; over the mangled corpses shines the light of souls. A thought of love and homage and a prayer to God for the dead and for the prisoners.[14]

20 MAY 1943

The Duca del Mare, Thaon di Revel,[15] considered it his duty to go to the King to inform him of the morale of Italians. Some time ago Marshal Caviglia also went. In the morning, the duke approached the Blessed Sacrament to draw courage and light from God. The King listened to him. Then he thanked him, concluding, "The situation is difficult." In truth, it is too simplistic to say – as everyone does – that we must make a separate peace. But is it possible? This is a question of honour not only for Mussolini; Italy will have Germany opposing it and will be paralyzed by the lack of coal that comes from Germany. Only if Mussolini – who is responsible for the alliance with Germany – leaves can one think of a separate peace.

Everybody's state of mind is sad, worried, and extremely disturbed by the destruction in the city. If we lose our artistic patrimony, poor Italy! May the God of Mercy save it! The Senate sleeps! From day to day the people wait for anything that will drive away the storm that is

[14] CC: Cf. the passage in E. Caviglia, *Diario (aprile 1925 – marzo 1945)*. (Rome: Gherardo Casini Editore, 1952), 412–13.

[15] Paolo Emilio Thaon di Revel (1859–1948), an admiral and Italian politician, received the title 1st Duca del Mare [First Sea Lord] on 24 May 1924 and that of Grand Admiral in November of the same year. Before then, he was head of the Italian Navy, 1913–15, promoting the development of light cruisers and naval aviation. Near the end of the First World War he organized the rapid occupation of the islands and coastline of Istria and Dalmatia. He became a senator in 1917 and admiral in 1918. From October 1922 to May 1925 he was minister of the navy and confidant of Victor Emmanuel III. He was president of the Senate from 1943 to 1944. He received many high honours, among which were Knight of the Supreme Order of the Most Holy Annunciation [Ordine Supremo della Santissima Annunziata] and Knight Grand Cross of the Order of Sts. Maurizio and Lazzaro.

gathering over Italy. But in everybody there is an attitude of passiveness that is almost fatalist.

20 MAY 1943

In a conversation with a friend I learned that Admiral Thaon di Revel returned some time ago from the Quirinale – where he had gone as secretary of the Maurizian Order to have several decrees signed – sad, moved, and almost crying. To affectionately posed questions, he answered all of them by shaking his head in grief. He finally said, "There is no remedy. The King cannot do anything; he is being blackmailed by Mussolini. The truth is that the King is weak ... Let Mussolini say, do, and publish what he wants, but save Italy! If the King goes on like this he will lose everything – honour, homeland, kingdom, family."

IN COLUMNA NUBIS ET IGNIS ...[16]   2 JUNE 1943

In responding to the greetings of the Sacred College, His Holiness Pius XII spoke of the Church's concern about the extension of this terrible conflict. I relay here some of his thoughts: "We want to hope before it is too late that the Church can say with a heart full of joy and gratitude: '*In columna nubis ductor eorum fuisti per diem, et in columna ignis per noctem*' [Ex. 9:12].[17] Before such obstacles, the Church never forgets the responsibility that weighs on it for the care of souls. And it deeply feels the need to guard against and thwart any attempt to tarnish the purity of its doctrine and its teaching, to restrict the universality of its mission, and to negate the open disregard of its love, which nonetheless it extends with equal concern to all people, almost as if it were to let itself be drawn in and swept away in the swirl of exclusively earth-bound ideals and in the vortex of entirely human differences ..."[18]

[16] From scripture: "To lead them the way, I guided them by a pillar of cloud by day, and by night by a pillar of fire."

[17] The updated scripture reference can be found in Ex. 13:21: "And the Lord went before them to show the way by day in a pillar of a cloud, and by night in a pillar of fire: that he might be the guide of their journey and both times."

[18] The cited speech, by Pius XII to the cardinals on the occasion of his saint's day [*onomastico*], is reproduced in AAS 35 (*Bollettino Ufficiale della Santa Sede,* 1943), 165–71.

Impressions of the Speech of His Holiness Pius XII
To my knowledge, this most noble speech has elicited everywhere in
Italy a great and sympathetic response. Especially noted were the references to Poland, the protest against the inhuman forms of warfare, and
the assertion of the rights of small states.

The 3 June minutes taken by the Propaganda ministry revealed the
strong and linear character of the speech, its heartfelt tone, and its reference to the trials to which the Church may be exposed. Recalling the
gossip circulating – that the Pope was said to have wanted the war to
occur – one person said, "The Nero episode is repeating itself exactly –
which sought to put the blame on Christians for the fire of Rome."

General Pugliese, who in embracing Catholicism with the clear vision
of the harmony and continuity of the [Bible's] two Testaments, completely agreed with this insight, telling me that there is a spreading
general appreciation of the lofty thoughts of the Pope and the work of
the Church as a bulwark against any attack on the rights of civil society.
With his high moral principles, he offers the most secure sanctuary
against aberrations of the spirit. The sadness and faith of the Pope are
moving. I also believe that the Holy Church will emerge from this conflict better understood and everlarger.

The Portuguese ambassador said to me, "The horrible evils of war will
certainly bring good. We have a proverb: 'God even writes on crooked
lines.' We shall see, after the war, that we must return to the eternal principles of the Gospel; that will be a great recompense for much pain."

The Spanish ambassador said to me, "A most elevated speech, noble in
form, but strong in content."

The minister Baron Giovanni di Giura[19] agreed: "Impressive and
favourable without reservation. All look to the Vatican. One hopes that
the Pope at a certain point can intervene. This is also very important in
order to cut off in time the rise of Communism. This represents a latent
threat even for America. I know because I was there for two years. This
speech will serve to dispel the stupid rumour that the Pope wanted this
war. It is a rumour circulated by the Communists."

[19] Giovanni di Giura (1893–1989), a baron and Italian diplomat, acted as
minister plenipotentiary first in Lithuania and then in Venezuela between 1938
and 1946. He published various volumes on diplomacy, history, and art.

The former minister Jung, just arrived from Sicily on the 6th [June], came to see me looking for the Pope's speech. It had not arrived in Sicily, but he had heard good things about it.

Monsignor Polvara[20] of Milan said to me, "It is a simple, brief, and complete speech. Everybody also enjoyed it for its clarity and brevity."

WORKERS VISIT THE HOLY FATHER   13 JUNE 1943

Impressive representation of the workers of Italy in Rome on the occasion of the twenty-fifth anniversary of the episcopal consecration of the Holy Father. The workers were gathered in the courtyard of the Belvedere, and the Holy Father gave them a fatherly and courageous speech, illustrating the necessity of collaboration between classes; this is the hope, and is the guarantee of an effective social renaissance.

CONDITIONS IN SICILY   14 JUNE 1943

The former minister Jung tells me, "In Sicily life is paralyzed, and there are absolutely no means of transportation available; but this has a good side, because the wheat cannot be taken away. The harvest is excellent, and even the olives are promising. We will be eating bread soaked in oil. I will return, even if my house is destroyed, to be ready for any eventuality, even in the case of invasion. The spirit of the people is extremely pained and depressed, but there are no symptoms of revolt. The enemy are bombarding the ports in particular to free the Sicilian Canal."

15 JUNE 1943

These are sad days, full of heavy threats; spirits are feeling oppressed by a weight of anxiety, fear, and pain while our nation's lands are being mutilated. And we expect worse. It feels like living in the terror of a sad dream. The National Fascist Party has sent an SOS, just as a ship takes on water and is about to sink; but the cry of danger dies in a vacuum. Our thoughts are for the homeland, not for the party that is

[20] Giuseppe Polvara (1884–1950), presbyter of the Diocese of Milan, a teacher, architect, and painter, was involved from 1917 in the Milan review *Arte cristiana*, which was founded and directed by Fr Celso Costantini. Monsignor Polvara then became director of this review until his death. His charisma manifested itself in the foundation of both the religious community called the Family of the Blessed Angel and a school of the same name, whose objective was to give a new impulse for liturgical art.

responsible for the destruction into which Italy has fallen and is sinking. They say that the text of the proclamation is from Mussolini. Payments made with the Treasury Loan leaves everybody cold and skeptical. One [right-wing] leader said to an anti-Fascist friend, "Our fear is bigger than your expectations."

General Umberto Pugliese says to me, "The war is evidently already lost. Decided by one man alone, through erroneous impulses, without preventive, adequate preparation, it was badly led by him who wanted to hold all the reins; and it was not judiciously stopped in time. Mussolini is above all a victim of his scant knowledge of men and of his exaggerated confidence in himself, which was extended to areas in which he did not have any competence."

It seems that the words of Ps. 51:6–7 have come true for him: "*Dilexisti omnia verba praecipitationis lingua dolosa. Propterea Deus destruet te, et emigrabit te de tabernaculo to: et radicem tuam de terra viventium.*"[21]

COURAGEOUS WORDS   21 JUNE 1943

I am at lunch at the home of the Hon. Senator Vittorio Cini, minister of communications. The senator told me that in the Council of Ministers on 19 June he spoke clearly to Mussolini, telling him that if the ministers had to be associated with the responsibilities of this tragic hour, they desired to collaborate by offering their thoughts and actions, but they had to be brought up to date on what was happening. If we must continue the war, we must put our faith in the technicians of the military arts; if we cannot continue the war, we must turn our thoughts to the peace and not allow ourselves to be caught unprepared.

It is the first time that an honest and courageous voice has told Il Duce the truth. I agreed with the Hon. Cini that it was necessary to write to Mussolini, articulating the thoughts he expressed at the Council of Ministers so that they would not be twisted and distorted. He wrote the following and most noble document:

Rome, 24 June 1943 – XXI

DUCE, I meditated for a long time and hesitated before making the decision that I am submitting to you. I state a few details that I could not make in the session of the Council of Ministers of the 19th past, which ended before I had

[21] "Therefore will God destroy thee for ever: he will pluck thee out, and remove thee from thy dwelling place: and thy root out of the land of the living."

the time to speak once again. In that session, I denounced the extreme gravity of the moment, affirmed the necessity of changing the methods that have so far produced unfavourable results, proposed to pursue an in-depth examination of the general situation in its various aspects, and clarified that I did not intend to anticipate solutions, which can and must emerge exclusively from the objective examination of the actual situation. You, Duce, did not accept my proposal. You referred to it only to exclude its practical usefulness with reference to the "academies"; you dwelt on the theme of "peace," almost as if I had promoted such a discussion, while not only did I not present the problem, but I said quite clearly that we could not reasonably think of any solution without having the elements necessary to make a judgment. The sole object of my reference to peace was to alert us that it should not find us unprepared, in the same way that the war had found us unprepared. You also excluded the utility of the discussion because you judge that the situation is such that it does not admit any possibility of choice, and you repeated this view with your determined, peremptory expression "to burn the ships behind us." Permit me to think that this imperative may work for individuals, but not for peoples. One burns one's ships when all alternatives are impossible, when one has reached the point of desperation; but this is not the case for us. In any event, I repeat that my proposal did not intend to open a discussion about peace: its intention was to determine whether you, or at least your collaborators, would consent to an examination of general policy, which I believe to be an indispensable premise for taking any conscious responsibility. What emerged clearly was your intention to limit collaboration only to the technical field. I will not discuss this, but I would be reticent if I did not express my disagreement on this essential point.

Everybody, or almost everybody, thinks as I do; nobody wants to tell you. But I prefer to displease you rather than betray your confidence.

With these necessary details laid out, Duce, I renew my petition to you to exonerate me from the responsibility which, as you know, only a sense of discipline and duty has compelled me to take in an already serious situation. Leaving aside health reasons, which remain, reasons of hardship compel me to insist in my petition. While emphasizing my same duty of loyalty toward you, which I still feel most profoundly, how much more has been the confidence and affection that you have always demonstrated toward me. The knowledge, however, of the current situation and of my responsibilities demands that I, though insisting in my request to depart, leave you as the judge of the timing when this should take place. Please interpret my decision in the same spirit in which it is inspired.

Devotedly, V. Cini

FROM MUSSOLINI'S SPEECH   24 JUNE 1943

"The Italian People deserve all our respect and all our love because they offer a simply marvellous example, and in fact I do not know what more I can ask of our people. They give their soldiers, they give their money. Tighten your belts and remain fearless under the bombardments ..."

The Italian people should have been asked for their approval before being thrown into the chasm of war ... And Mussolini has the courage to say that the Italian people "deserve our respect." Is this how you respect? At least their passiveness was not insulted!

18 JULY 1943

Tonight the Allies dropped on Rome a rainfall of leaflets containing a proclamation with the signature of President Roosevelt and British Prime Minister Churchill, who in substance invite the Italian people to throw off the Fascist yoke and hold onto the "only hope" for survival that Italy has, namely, "a capitulation that will not be dishonourable, given the overwhelming might of the military forces of the United Nations," and warning that "only by abandoning Germany and the Fascist leaders can a renewed Italy acquire a respectable place in the family of European nations."

But this flattery contrasts with the conditions published on 13 July by Italian newspapers and presented as the objectives of the enemy. Beyond the political humiliation of Italy, deprived of its colonial empire and expelled from the group of Great Powers and permanently disarmed, they in fact were even contemplating the loss of a part of the national territory, of the Ionic and Dodecanese Islands, the suppression of metallurgical industries, etc.

These are nightmarish days: Sicily invaded, Italian cities bombarded, the people apathetic. One Italian radio station from Tunis applauded the occupation of Sicily. Others, even in Italy, desire the victory of the Allies to free them from this horrible and desperate situation and liberate them from Fascism. The masses blame Fascism for this debacle. They no longer want to put up with an oligarchy that has divided the nation and excluded it from decisions and responsibilities; the nation is called upon only to give its blood, its life, and its wealth. Discipline is observed in a material sense, but without conviction. Italy is on the verge of the abyss. The King does nothing, and the Senate does not meet. This spectacle of cowardice is the saddest thing. Moreover, some ask, "What can be done? Nothing! Poor Italy, reduced to a dilemma: either on Germany's side or that of the Allies!" Germany has already set foot in Italy!

UNDER THE BOMBS OF THE FIRST AIR RAIDS ON ROME

19 JULY 1943

On 19 July 1943 at 10.35, Mons. Giuseppe Caprio, economic pro-secretary of the Propaganda, and I were waiting at Bagni di Tivoli station for the train to return us to Rome. The train, composed of *littorine* [smaller railcars], arrived on time. We tried to board the forward cars, but they were overflowing with people. We boarded one of the last cars, where we remained standing and pressed on the terrace of the railcar. As soon as we passed the station of Roma-Prenestina, the train stopped suddenly with a formidable jolt. The siren scream and a hellish clamour filled the air. Shouts of fear rose in the railcar, while everybody tried to jump off. On a parallel track I saw emerging between the cars a stream of artillery fire and smoke with the crackle of mortar shells as if the mouth of a volcano had opened suddenly. The sky was filled with an ominous sound. Thuds and crashes repeated in every direction, and a dense cloud of black acrid smoke surrounded us in a darkness that took away our sight and began to suffocate us.

Mons. Caprio and I jumped from the train and were sprawled on the ground behind a low wall that protected the railway line. I saw a piece of a concrete gate, and I instinctively pulled it over me, deluding myself that I could protect myself from the shrapnel that filled the air. I put my faith in God, with a contrite thought and with the invocation to Mary, refuge of sinners. I was prepared to die and was extraordinarily calm. In a moment in which the blasts of bombs and machine guns seemed to stop and the smoke cleared somewhat, I got up. With Mons. Caprio I walked along the wall to find an opening and exit from the railway line. We finally jumped into the gardens. The travellers on our train were all dispersed, running here and there. I saw a man who was holding his hand to his head, all bloodied. Mons. Caprio and I reached a little house and entered. It was empty. Outside the bomb explosions and anti-aircraft artillery bursts continued; the little house shook as if it were a box.

"Monsignore," they said, "give us absolution." We knelt in front of them and we absolved them *in articulo mortis* [at the point of death]. We then left and saw people lying on the ground, and two small houses reduced to two heaps of rubble. We made our way between houses and gardens and arrived at the house of some farmers who had remained there, trembling and shouting and crazy with fear. I spoke calming words to them. I had them recite the *Pater Noster* [Our Father] and asked God to forgive their sins. And I absolved them. We continued, going farther away from the epicentre of the strikes. The latter were coming in waves; we were deafened by the percussion of the bombs and anti-aircraft artillery and from the crackle of machine guns. An occasional fearful voice could be heard in the brief intervals of that infernal fury. We tried to move forward between the houses. Everywhere there was destruction: houses destroyed, houses still standing with their shutters unhinged. To reach a road that appeared to be safer, we passed over the ruins of a house. Blocks, rubble, pieces of furniture, and telegraph wires all blocked our path. We thought there were perhaps people buried underneath our feet. Mons. Caprio fell and got up again. We reached a small house in front of the Braccio di Montone road. There was a subterranean refuge that was perhaps an ancient cellar. It was full of people who were moaning and praying. We went down, and I told them in the darkness that I was a priest and that they should say the *Pater Noster* and I would give everybody absolution.

But I was not tranquil. That refuge was like a catacomb. If a bomb were to fall at its opening, we would all be buried alive. I got out into the open. My breathing and throat were beset by smoke inhalation. I was spitting out black saliva. I was choking from thirst. The bomb explosions and anti-aircraft fire continued. The surrounding area was a desert: collapsed homes, homes destroyed to the foundations, windows and doors blown out. At a little fountain I sought some water, but the fountain was dry. The owner of the small house where we took refuge brought me a glass of water, which I greedily downed. In a moment of calm, between waves of airplanes, I went down a road and saw a small house razed to the ground. Two men were intent on creating an opening among the ruins. At a certain moment I saw a little girl of about two years of age, all blackened, emerge from that opening. I picked up the girl and brought her to a house across the way that I found empty. I placed the girl on a sofa and tried to clean her eyes, which were caked with black dust. The girl, stunned, did not cry, and let herself be cleaned up. A little later two men brought a young woman into the same room. She was the mother. She had wanted to save the little one, pushing her over her head and out of the opening. She was thus also saved. I removed the girl from the sofa and the woman was placed on it. All dishevelled and dusty with her clothes in tatters, she had a bloody cheek and arm. I sought to comfort her: "You are safe. The girl is safe." "But where are we? It is day or night? What happened?"

With a supreme effort, the woman had tried to save her little one and herself, but then she could no longer resist, appearing faraway and withdrawn. A man arrived at the empty house and not finding anybody began to beat his head with his fists: "Where is my wife? Where are my children?" A horrible doubt seized me that his wife and children may have gone into the small house opposite and might be buried under the rubble. Mons. Caprio and I continued our journey to distance ourselves from the railway centre. We did not come across other railway lines. They say that we were between Borgo Tiburtino and Porta Maggiore. Everywhere solitude: collapsed houses and houses that remained standing but with their foundations destroyed; on the road, rubble and the detritus of the bombed houses. I remember that while walking, I stepped over a blanket for a cradle, all white and embroidered: a testimony to maternal love and a pitiful indication of a cradle destroyed. We continued on, pausing three or four times in one doorway or another when the destructive bursts resumed. The women (there were few men in those makeshift shelters) were blessing us and thanking us for having stopped among them; they prayed and asked for benediction and absolution. Everywhere I was having them say an act of contrition, after which I imparted absolution, remaining there to pray with those good people. It struck me how the religious sense was the only comfort in those terrible hours. And to my surprise, I did not hear any curses against those responsible for these horrible events. Only one man said something threatening, gritting his teeth.

It was around three in the afternoon. We passed over a bridge over the railway line; some homes were damaged, others destroyed. Nothing was sadder than those intimate places swept away and destroyed: broken furniture, mirrors in pieces, pictures and frames still hanging on the wall, upended beds falling from floor to floor, curtains that blew in the open air … Beyond the bridge over the railway line lay a dead horse still attached to his cart, his bloody tongue extended out from his jaws. People were walking and began to venture onto the road. The all-clear signal had not yet sounded, but life began to resume. Police and Red Cross vehicles began to arrive in the affected areas. I gave them the address of that woman pulled out of the ruins.

People were watching, dumbstruck, as if emerging from a nightmare. The roads were strewn with detritus. I tried three times to telephone home, but the telephone was not working. Advancing in the direction of St John Lateran, we found the familiar sights of Rome. The all-clear sounded. And all the people reversed and headed toward their own homes.

Mons. Caprio and I found a public transport vehicle that brought us and other travellers to the Piazza di Spagna. On board the vehicle was a man who had been on the same train as we were. He said that the railway carriages at the front of the train were hit or reduced to pieces, with many dead. Mons. Caprio and I remembered that we had tried to board those carriages, but as they were overflowing with people, we had boarded one of the last railcars. We thanked God with a profound sense of comfort and gratitude: *Misericordiae Domini quia non sumus consumpti* [The mercies of the Lord that we are not consumed].

THE POPE'S VISIT TO SAN LORENZO   19 JULY 1943
The Holy Father Pius XII, in whose heart reverberates the pain of Rome and the entire world, went to San Lorenzo Outside the Walls, where he knelt on the ruins and remained in prayer before the basilica torn apart by bombs. Around this white figure quickly gathered a crowd of bewildered and anguished people, and the voice of suffering and protest was raised, the voice of confident love that recognized in their own bishop the human transfiguration of Christ.

"Father, Father, bless you!" And each person clung to Him, wanted to touch his garments and tell him of their suffering and their own troubles and the depth of their gratitude. I hope that a noble artist will be able to recreate this wonderful event, outlining the white figure of the Pope kneeling against the dark background of the gutted basilica.

20 JULY 1943
I said Holy Mass *pro gratiarum actione* [to give thanks]. Rarely have I celebrated with so much devotion. Toward evening, with Cardinal Fumasoni Biondi, I went to see San Lorenzo Outside the Walls. Its face has collapsed. Inside one sees the platform of the room and the lateral walls of red stones. The movement of air has torn the plaster, pulverizing the frescoes of Fracassini, Mariani, and other noble painters of the nineteenth century. The destruction of the church induces a sense of profound sadness and angry indignation. A few days ago Roosevelt publicly promised the Holy Father Pius XII to respect sacred monuments. There is no excuse for this sacrilegious and stupid attack against the Basilica of San Lorenzo Outside the Walls. There is an extremely visible cemetery there. A simple honest and noble thought should have sufficed to hold back the airmen. On no account, even if they were searching for military targets, should they have exposed themselves to

the possibility of destroying such a signal monument of art and faith and also the possibility of firing on graves. They had thus achieved the significant result of offending the graves of the Pope's parents. We, though much poorer, feel infinitely more noble than these sportsmen of massacre and vandalism. The Huns, the Longobards and the Vandals have certainly not been rehabilitated – they have been surpassed in destruction; that is, they have lost their sad primacy in this field.

The cardinal and I knelt on the ruins in front of the gutted basilica and said a fervid prayer. In the Tiburtine quarter, one can see the same spectacle of destruction that I saw yesterday near Porta Maggiore. Soldiers were working to clear the ruins. They say that there are cadavers lying underneath and that at some sites they hear the moans of living people. Water ran into one hole created by a bomb. People and soldiers flocked to drink. The little garden in front of San Lorenzo and a part of the cemetery are both damaged.

A DISTANT VOICE OF COMFORT   20 JULY 1943

I comfort myself reading *The City of God and the City of Man*, a book in which the many ideas of St Augustine are discussed.

THE POPE'S LETTER TO THE CARDINAL VICAR[22]

20 JULY 1943

Signor Cardinal, to You, who so closely participate in Our Government and in Our Pastoral activities for this Diocese of Rome, centre and Head of the Catholic world and of Christian thought and faith, We want to add Our word in an hour of particular bitterness, in which Our soul is immersed ...

---

[22] The cardinal vicar was at that time Francesco Marchetti Selvaggiani (1871–1951). He had been nuncio to Venezuela and Austria from 1918.to 1922, then secretary of the Sacred Congregation for the Propagation of the Faith from 1922 to 1930. In that capacity, he had frequent contact with Costantini, who had been the first apostolic delegate in China. He was made a cardinal in 1930 and the next year became the Pope's vicar for the Diocese of Rome, a position he held until his death. In 1939 he was named secretary of the Sacred Congregation of the Holy Office. In 1948 he became dean of the Sacred College of Cardinals. Pius XII's letter reported here can be found in AAS 35 (*Bollettino Ufficiale della Santa Sede*, 1943), 252–54.

As bishop of this dear city, with an assiduous interest, We endeavour – and she, Signor Cardinal, has followed all of Our footsteps – to spare Our suffering Rome the horrors and the damage of bombardment...

But unfortunately this, Our most reasonable hope, has turned to disillusion. And now what We feared has happened. How fearfully what We foresaw is now a very sad reality, as one of the most eminent Roman basilicas, that of San Lorenzo Outside the Walls, venerated as sacred by all Catholics for its ancient memory and for the most noble sepulchre of Our venerated predecessor Pius IX, is already in large part destroyed. In reflecting upon the ruins of this eminent church, the words of the prophet Jeremiah came to mind: "*Quomodo obscuratum es aurum, mutatus est color optimus, dispersi sunt lapides sanctuarii*" [How is the gold become dim, the finest colour is changed, the stones of the sanctuary are scattered].

PIUS PP. XII

22 JULY 1943

The words of the Pope, so noble, so human and Christian, were immensely successful. The *Osservatore Romano* sold like hot cakes. It is a voice of consolation and life when everything is falling into darkness and earth. The world looks to the Pope as the only custodian and defender of justice, freedom, and peace. The people of Rome turn to Him with a filial affection, turn to Him as their very protector, as a Father who calms the anxiety of his children, as their undaunted bishop who, to everyone's face, carries out his ministry of mercy, encouragement, and justice. Even for the situation in the city of Rome, as an open city, the people know it is the Pope's duty to safeguard it.

MEETING BETWEEN MUSSOLINI AND HITLER   22 JULY 1943

It is said that Mussolini and Hitler did not agree. In fact, the communiqué of their meeting does not conclude with the same phrases of hypocritical agreement. It is said that they agreed to shorten the front and to prepare to resist in the Po Valley. The people can no longer bear it. The Senate remains silent. The King is non-existent. Poor Italy! But there are imperceptible signs that indicate we are moving toward a crisis and an epilogue.

Guerrilla Warfare

It is suggested that we resist the Allies in Sicily with guerrilla warfare. Two weights and two measures. When a moral sense is missing, one applauds in one's own house what one condemns in the house of others. The guerrilla warfare of the Slavs and Greeks is on the same level as the guerrilla warfare in Sicily. But does this guerrilla warfare even exist in Sicily?

24 JULY 1943

I saw a serene Senator Cini. He has the knowledge of having rendered a service to the country by speaking clearly to Mussolini. In fact, amid the flood of cowardice among all public power and its collaborators, he – uniquely and first – dared to raise his voice, asking Mussolini for the rationality of his plan and provoking him to reveal his thoughts and discuss them. He tells me that this evening a meeting of the Grand Council of Fascism is planned. We left the restaurant because he evidently does not want to be found – if indeed he is being looked for.

There is talk that at 17 hours the Grand Council of Fascism met. War has been waged and led with much foolishness – for three years – without the Grand Council of Fascism ever having met. Today, the dictator has been reminded that the Grand Council of Fascism exists. The chickens are coming home to roost. They say that there is the smell of dust at the Grand Council of Fascism. May the Lord enlighten the men responsible to find the path of honour and peace. In the meantime, even yesterday there were terrible strikes on Bologna.

In the World, Serious Indignation Persists for the Outrage on Rome
The newspapers of Dresden and Saxony have reproduced pictures of the devastation caused by the enemy's barbaric attack on the Basilica of San Lorenzo, on Verano Cemetery, on University City, and on working-class neighbourhoods, and they exalt in the spirit of resistance of the Italian people. The spokesman for the Japanese government was interviewed in Tokyo by a representative of the Agenzia Stefani and expressed his views on the letter addressed to the cardinal vicar from the Pope after the bombardment of Rome in the following terms: "The letter of the Pontiff to his Vicar is the most solemn monument ever written by a man. It constitutes the most reasoned and most dispassionate appeal to those who hold high a sense of dignity, honour, and respect for the inviolability of peaceful citizens and of monuments of faith and civilization. The document fully expresses not only the most intimate sentiments of Christian peoples, but of all humanity, without regard to religious confession, colour, or race."

The entire Spanish press commented on the letter addressed by the Pope to the cardinal vicar of Rome. *Informaciones* wrote as follows: "Spain, accustomed to seeing its Catholic soul tortured and its land covered in ancient ruins, feels with filial pain the bombardment of Rome. Today's cry of the Pope over wounded Rome has profoundly moved all Spanish people and raises their filial solidarity toward the Head of Christianity."

Heartfelt messages were sent to Pius XII by Archbishops Mons. Caro[23] of Santiago, Chile, Mons. Farfan[24] of Lima, and Mons. Barbieri[25] of Montevideo. Speaking on behalf of their respective faithful, the prelates reaffirmed their attachment to the Pontiff. Special religious functions were held in all the countries of Latin America for the safety of the Pontiff.[26]

25 JULY 1943

Just now the Hon. A. De Stefani, a member of the Grand Council of Fascism, was here. He told me, with necessary reserve, that the meeting of the Grand Council of Fascism was provoked by the special action taken by Giurati: "The meeting of the Grand Council was extended from five in the afternoon to two this morning. The meeting of the Grand Council resolved, in what was more a retrospective requisition, to justify Grandi's order of the day as a means of regaining for Fascism its lost adherents by regenerating respect for parliamentary functions and the statutory prerogatives of the Crown. They proceeded with great discipline, and their criticism of the policies of the leader of Fascism was respectful, but frank and legal. Mussolini could offer no serious argument in rebuttal of Grandi's proposals, the criticism of his policies, and the events that substantiated them: thus, his impotence to respond with adequate arguments, and his air of a man who is failing; it truly made us

---

[23] Giuseppe Rodriguez Caro (1866–1958) was titular bishop of Milaso in 1912 and promoted to archbishop of Santiago de Chile in 1939. He was made a Cardinal in 1946.

[24] Pietro Pasquale Francesco Farfan (1870–1945) was made bishop of Huaraz in 1907 and promoted to archbishop of Lima in 1933.

[25] Antonio Alfredo Barbieri (1892–1979), a Capuchin Brother, was made titular archbishop of Macra in 1936 and became archbishop of Montevideo in 1940. In December 1958 he was made a cardinal.

[26] CC: The reported news was taken from *Il Messaggero*, 25 July 1943.

all feel pity, aware of his past and his great prestige. The approval of Grandi's order of the day was in fact a condemnation of the regime in its Mussolinian construction. The King was made aware of the order of the day. Now the King can lean on a constitutional fact, and he must reflect. How? Mussolini needs to withdraw in an orderly manner so as to avoid being thrown out."

The Hon. De Stefani tells me that the Holy See must be informed of the proceedings at this meeting of the Grand Council in order to reinforce its efforts to obtain from the Germans an armistice that will save Italy from further war-related disasters. The new government must be an evolutionary government, not a revolutionary one, so as to avoid a fratricidal war.

I expressed my thoughts in the following three points:

1 Ask for an armistice, legally informing Germany.
2 Germany might accept the armistice on condition that Italy declares and maintains absolute neutrality. It could withdraw its troops from Italy and from the borders of the Tirol.
3 The Allies have made it clear that they will not deal with Mussolini. It is therefore necessary that a constitutional government be formed.

The Hon. De Stefani then had to go to the King, bringing him the order of the day.

THE VENDETTA OF THINGS   EVENING OF 25 JULY 1943
St Ambrose writes in *De Officis*: "*Male se rectum putat, qui regulam summae rectitudinis ignorat*" [It is much more their dishonour to be ignorant of the universal government and laws of God]. Inebriated by his successes and overwhelmed by the frenzy of the war, Mussolini had ignored the *regulam summae rectitudinis* [the laws of justice], and today he is reaping the terrible consequences. Today, justice is avenged and has seized in its formidable grip the man who unleashed in Italy the whirl-wind of war, with its sequel of destruction and pain.

THE ARREST OF MUSSOLINI   25 JULY 1943
This evening, around 10 PM, the radio announced that Mussolini has submitted his resignation and the King accepted it and has named Marshal Pietro Badoglio as head of the government, with full powers. Thus one cycle of history closes and another opens. A sense of relief and

respite has liberated us from this police-state nightmare to which the politics of Mussolini had degenerated. Even the other day, while I was at Cini's place with the son of Orlando, while we were talking the Count Orlando motioned to be careful on the telephone. We could no longer go on like this. Mussolini, a mixture of brilliant qualities and incredible defects, could in his infatuation think to substitute himself – like an idol, like a magic fetish, omniscient – for the dignity and life of a nation of 45 million people. He has gone. He collapsed like a false idol, like the one Daniel referred to, which fell into pieces in the presence of the Holy Ark [of the Covenant].

Finally, one can breathe! Writing these notes, I was always terrified that this notebook would fall into the hands of the Fascists. I have conducted no smear campaign or propaganda against them; on the contrary, I always offered words of moderation and calm. But we were reduced to the following: that one was afraid even to think or write anything that went against the idol served by a clique of cowards and corrupt men. Finally one can breathe! I pity him. And one cannot and must not forget the good he has done; but today, he has fallen in the mud of rancour and contempt. The cowards who served him will be the first to renounce him. *Sic transit gloria mundi!*[27] A Chinese proverb comes to mind: "everybody willingly strikes a falling wall." Later we learned that Mussolini did not resign of his own accord but was trapped and arrested at the King's villa, and brought as a prisoner to a barracks. The arrest is to be applauded, but the method and the place where the arrest took place gives one pause.

THE KING'S PROCLAMATION   25 JULY 1943
ITALIANS, I am assuming command of all the Armed Forces. In this solemn hour that impinges upon the destiny of the homeland, every person must resume his place of duty, faith, and combat. No deviation can be tolerated, no recrimination can be allowed. Let every Italian bow before the great wounds that have torn the sacred soil of the homeland. By the valour of its Armed Forces, by the decisive will of all citizens, Italy

---

[27] The passage belongs to the *De Imitatione Christi* (1:3,6) in *L'imitazione di Cristo* (Venice: P. Loslein, 1483) and is taken from the liturgy for the coronation of the Supreme Pontiff, during which one burned select cloth and fabric and repeated the celebrated Latin phrase that in English is translated as "Thus passes the glory of this world."

will rediscover the path of recovery through respect for the institutions that have always accompanied its rise.

ITALIANS, I am today more than ever indissolubly united to you through an unshakable faith in the immortality of the homeland.

Signed: VITTORIO EMANUELE

Countersigned: BADOGLIO

THE WAR CONTINUES   NIGHT OF 25 JULY 1943

Marshal Badoglio, charged with forming a new government, spoke on the radio, and in concluding his broadcast he said, "The war continues." This statement creates a feeling of dismay, clouding the joy of the great news. It gives one a pang in the heart. But how? Once Mussolini fell, Fascism, which had declared war, also fell – not the Italian people, but the regime that had allied itself with Hitler. Once the regime fell, the iniquitous program it had undertaken must also naturally fall. The Axis has been broken! Have not the King and the little councillors who surround him thought and weighted the fact that, with this statement, we have declared war anew against the Allies? Or was it thought to fool Hitler with a lie to buy time?

Qui nititur mendaciis, hic pascit ventos [Who trusts in false promises throws his food to the winds; Prv. 10:4]. Hitler will certainly not be fooled, and he will think to take all possible action against Italy. They probably wanted to act in a Machiavellian manner: *Posuimus mendacium spem nostram* [Is. 28:15; We have placed our hope in lies]. What would have been sufficient instead was an ounce of honesty, to take the straight path: establish relations with the Allies and declare honestly to Hitler that, by not being able to continue an already-lost war and by the fact that the regime that wanted it has fallen, Italy would repudiate its alliance with Germany and ask for an armistice, assuring Germany of an honest neutrality. Naturally, it would have been necessary to immediately take action to block the incursion into Italy of new German forces and at the same time to gather all Italian forces to prepare an effective defence. This would have spared Italy from much destruction. Badoglio and the Hon. Vittorio Emanuele Orlando,[28] who are the likely authors of that

---

[28] Vittorio Emanuele Orlando (1860–1952), a jurist and Italian politician, was president of the Council of Ministers, 1917–19, after the rout of Caporetto. He participated in the Peace Conference at Versailles, which he abandoned in the face of U.S. President Wilson's opposition to Italian territorial claims on

incredible message, have cast an indelible stain on their names. In such a manner does Orlando conclude a long, industrious, and noble career.

OPERIBUS MANUUM SUARUM IRRETITUS ES PECCATOR [PS. 9:17]
[The sinner hath been caught in the works of his own hands.]
                                                 26 JULY 1943
If Mussolini had had a little Christian sensibility and self-critical sensibility, he could have saved himself by saving Italy, for he had brought it a high degree of prestige. He thought he was a god, and he was nothing but a miserable man, subject to the basest passions. From three sources it was confirmed to me in the last few days that, on returning from the conference with Hitler, he went to console himself with Petacci, a pathetic and disgraceful character. But it is done. And Petacci remains an anonymous Lupescu,[29] whom today is crushed in ruin.

Last night, around two o'clock, there was a little disturbance at the Piazza di Spagna. The Casa dell'Artigianato [the House of Artisans] was broken into near the stairway and this morning piles of paper can be seen scattered on the ground. While I write (it is 8 AM), in the distance one can hear voices: there is another demonstration of a hundred or so people ... The voices are coming closer. I go to the window and see groups of men and women processing, waving tricolour flags and

---

Dalmatia and Fiume. Before then, he had served in many ministerial posts: Education (1903–05), Justice (1907–09 and 1914–16), and the Interior (1916–17). He adhered to Fascism for a brief period. He left parliament in 1925 in protest against a government decree that limited freedom of the press. From then on, although he had retired to private life, he maintained relations with the King and also in politics, to the point of taking an important role in the actions that brought down Mussolini. After the Second World War he was elected to the Constituent Assembly in 1946 and was named senator for life in 1948. In his activity as a university professor, he worked in the field of constitutional law, especially administrative law, publishing numerous important works.

[29] Elena Lupescu (1895–1977), a charming Romanian woman, twice married and divorced, offered much fodder for the scandal sheets of her country and beyond for her easy mores that led her into the practice of high-class prostitution under the assumed name of Magda. After the abdication of King Charles II of Romania, she became his wife.

shouting, "Show your flags." One or two flags immediately come out from a few balconies.

A meeting between Federzoni and De Stefani was convened at my house for this evening at 19 hours. But events intervened, and I don't know if the meeting will take place. May God help Italy! May He enlighten its new leaders so that their work may be not of vengeance but of reconstruction. At last, the *federali* and all their parasitic superstructure that placed Italy in the service of Fascism will be abolished. The people who just passed under our windows were shouting, "Long Live Italy!" Lord bless it because it is a good, prolific, and Catholic nation; bless it because, in Italy, You placed the centre of Your Church!

26 JULY 1943, NOON

The city is rapidly covering itself with flags. The people have gathered on the streets, with a serene air; they speak quietly, commenting on the events with joy. The Fascist symbols have disappeared. A man in a black shirt, probably unaware of developments, was forced to disembark from the tram and was stripped; his black shirt was burned. Fascist symbols and images of Mussolini are sought out, torn up, and trampled on. Father Wang[30] tells me that a group of demonstrators took possession of a bronze bust of Mussolini, tied it up, and dragged it in ridicule through the streets. In everyone there is a sense of relief, as if they had emerged from an anguished dream: Mussolini and Fascism have not understood – this mental obtuseness is incredible – that one cannot permanently govern a people with the gag and the noose.

I went out on foot, walking toward the Vatican. Everywhere there is a lively gaiety, everywhere joyful voices, everywhere the fluttering of the tricolour. Everybody speaks against the Fascist tyranny. I saw a banner fixed above a tram. It said, "Long Live the King – Long Live the Army – Long Live Freedom."

---

[30] Joseph Wang (1911–85), a Chinese Christian, was a member of an institute of consecrated life called Congregatio Disciplinorum Domini (CDD), founded by Celso Costantini in China, with statutes approved by the Holy See in 1927. Wang was a valuable collaborator of the cardinal, for whom he was secretary when Costantini was secretary of the Sacred Congregation for the Propaganda of the Faith.

The King, who has alienated himself from the affection of the people, has become popular once again and perhaps may save the monarchy. God willing, it represents an anchor of salvation, as we see today.

When I was returning by tram, an old man said to me, "It seems that Mussolini has been taken to Fort Aurelio. He unleashed a useless war; he filled Italy with mourning; it is right that even he should suffer. I keep as a relic the red shirt of an uncle of mine. It was high time we turned our thoughts to the homeland, throwing away these parasites who had attached themselves on us like bloodsuckers. We should hang them by the cheek and cut their skin one centimetre at a time ... Many, many cry for him ..."

26 JULY 1943, AFTERNOON

In the afternoon I made a tour of the centre of Rome. The lively gaiety and sense of joy for freedom had been regained. It is, however, strange that even though pictures of Mussolini were torn and trampled upon, not many raise their voice against him. I saw only the following, written on a wall: "Death to Mussolini, Sold to the Germans."

A group of people were holding high a sign that said, "Piazza Matteotti."[31] Evidently, these demonstrators were intending to put the sign on top of some sign with Fascist names. Piazza Venezia was empty, with two vehicles and cannons in front of the Victory monument and with a cordon of soldiers around its perimeter.

One hears talk of rifle shots at the Viminale in a house of the Fascio in which some Fascists had barricaded themselves. Unfortunately, they say that there are a few dead, a young man and two women. We can already say that the ending of this armed and diehard regime, sustained by Germany, came quickly, decisively, and innocuously. The coup was conducted very well, even though one doesn't like the way Mussolini's arrest and treatment occurred while he was the King's guest.

[31] The name refers to Giacomo Matteotti (1885–1924), an Italian politician, former secretary of the Socialist Party, who after a speech in the Chamber of Deputies in which he had accused the Fascists of violence and electoral fraud, was assassinated by a band of Fascist supporters. Matteotti was considered a martyr for liberty, an emblematic personage in the fight against Fascism.

27 JULY 1943

Rome remains festooned with flags. Work has begun once again. In everybody one notices a new liveliness: the people feel they have regained their freedom and dignity. They say that the president of the Stefani [a news agency] committed suicide. Mussolini is held prisoner at Fort Aurelio, not far from Fort Bravetta, where executions are held. Even Scorza, they say, has been arrested. Farinacci has sought safety in the German Embassy.

The crisis appears to be resolved in the most radical and peaceful way; a skirmish here and there by militia in Rome and elsewhere will not change the broader picture. From Italy has been removed a heavy and threatening structure and nothing remains: *etiam ruinae periere* [even the ruins have been ruined]. This structure was built on sand. They say that Mussolini went to Villa Savoia with the insignias of an imperial marshal; he left in a Red Cross ambulance as a private person on his way to prison. He blithely sowed much, much suffering; he sent many innocent people to jail, their only crime being having their own thoughts. Finally, he's been repaid in the same currency. In the multitudes is diffused a sense of justice that at last has been done.

This fact represents the fall of one of two pedestals on which the Axis rested. What will happen in Germany? Hitler's time will not be far off.

Nisi Dominus ... [Unless the Lord build the house, they labour in vain that build it (Ps. 126:1). He who injures with the sword shall die by the sword].[32]

Patriotic Demonstrations in the Streets of Florence
Just yesterday evening the radio broadcast the news of the nomination of Marshal Badoglio to be head of the government, and notwithstanding the late hour, an enormous crowd of citizens quickly gathered and, walking the streets of the city centre, stopped in front of the headquarters of the Army Corps singing songs of the homeland. After having sung hymns to Italy, to the King, and to Marshal Badoglio, this imposing column of people headed toward the city's outlying neighbourhoods, renewing wherever they went demonstrations of fervid love of country.

[32] Refers to Mt. 26:52.

Political Prisoners Liberated
We are informed of the release from prison of a group of political detainees. Among them are Professor Guido De Ruggiero,[33] Professor Calogero,
Professor Fiore, Professor Rizzo, and Dr Stangoni, the lawyer Fenoaltea,
the lawyer Comandini, and many young students.[34]

The Communist Danger
Underneath lurks the Communist idea. Our tenant Pelle [via Nomentana]
tells me that the farmers are feeling this infection. Count Volpi[35] was
booed in Venice, and he is now at Farfa. Count Volpi is a great benefactor of Venice. Why was he booed? The common folk, who know him
little, may have wanted to react against his luxuriant splendour.

3 AUGUST 1943
Yesterday from my office I observed a mason who, hanging from a ladder, was dismantling the Fascist signs on the building in front of the
headquarters of the Stefani Agency. The same thing has happened everywhere. Where Fascist symbols have been chiselled into stone or marble,
they are encrusted with Augustan lime or hammered off.

Certain piazzas are changing their names. Piazza Montecitorio,
renamed for Constanzo Ciano, has reassumed its old historical name.
These are signs of the reaction. Sometimes people go overboard. In shop
windows there are many pictures of the King and of Badoglio.

Thinking about Tomorrow
There is in the newspapers a sense of elation for freedom regained; and
there is a certain euphoria that it will almost be enough to reconstruct

[33] Guido De Ruggero (1888–1948), a philosopher and historian of Italian
philosophy as well as a university professor and author of many publications,
was imprisoned for his declared anti-Fascism. He became minister of education
in the first Cabinet led by Ivanoe Bonomi in 1944. Identifying others in this list
is difficult because Costantini mentions only their surnames.

[34] CC: This information is taken from *Il Giornale d'Italia*, 27 July 1943.

[35] Giuseppe Volpi di Misurata (1877–1947), a financier, industrialist, and
Italian politician who established among other concerns the Adriatic Electric
Company in 1905, which furnished electricity to 15 provinces of the Triveneto
and in Emilia. Between 1921 and 1925 he was governor of Tripolitania and then
became minister of finance. In 1922 he was named to the Senate.

Italy by returning to the liberalism of old. This will not suffice. The Fascist phenomenon, the Communist phenomenon, which on certain points converge, are a symptom of the crisis of the old civilization, and they act as a warning about the renewal of certain antiquated forms, offering a civilization that is more life affirming, more just toward workers, more human in its conception of patriotism.

Nationalism was placed as a foundation for patriotism, a conception that gives excessive importance to territorial and political reality. This was also one of the most tragic errors and most serious of Mussolini's blows. We need to leave behind this narrow conception of peoples barricaded behind certain borders, at war with one another. We need to "Christianize" patriotism, lifting it from its excessively materialistic limits and purifying it in a bond of cordial relations with its neighbours.

The last terrible wars were born of this nationalist exasperation. What is needed is an environment that is more ample, more sane, more human; in other words, Christian. What is needed is the creation of a Christian front in which the patriotic concept can travel beyond materialistic confines and create the foundations of a new public sociology and economy. With universal suffrage it is not so much intelligence that governs, in spite of the numbers. Power already belongs to the masses. It is necessary to build a large Christian front. It seems that the Hon. De Gasperi is working effectively within this sensibility.

3 AUGUST 1943

Today the feast of St Stephen, the proto-martyr who, while he was being stoned, prayed God not to assign guilt to the stone throwers. Let us hope that a broad spirit of understanding, freedom, and love will purify this toxic atmosphere. Common crimes must be punished, and the possibility of a return to Fascism must be made remote, but political vendettas must not be pursued – one must not add suffering to suffering. Freedom must be defended, even against men's rancour. We must look ahead, not back.

In the shops of Rome, Marshal Badoglio's picture is circulating. Will he be up to the arduous job of the reconstruction and pacification of Italy? The untruth – "the war continues" – reveals a narrowness of thought and spirit and the absence of an elementary honesty that cannot leave us with a peaceful feeling.

4 AUGUST 1943

Today's *Il Messaggero* writes: "Certain people have created too much confusion about the licit and illicit for things not to be changed. Moral values consist of that which must remain intangible."

Agreed, but what are these "moral values"? It is a vague phrase if they do not refer to the "moral values" of the Gospel. There is no other positive value capable of governing an entire life, whether individual or social. If Mussolini had had a minimum of moral sensibility, namely Christian, before declaring war he would have asked himself if it was legal.

It then says that fortune abandoned the Grand Council of Fascism. It is a phrase that means nothing; by contrast, he abandoned the principles of justice and humanity. Then came the "debacle." Instead of breaking Greece's back, Greece broke his. *Vidi impium elevatum sicut cedros Libani ...; transii et ecce non erat* [Ps. 36:35; I have seen the wicked highly exalted and lifted up like the cedars of Libanus ... And I passed by again, and lo, they were not].

5 AUGUST 1943

At least I can now commit to paper these intimate thoughts without the fear of their falling into others' hands. Previously, I was truly anguished by this fear. At the end, Mussolini imposed a regime based on police information and the terror of jail. And he collapsed, just as a construction worker falls from the pinnacle of a building because the foundations are crumbling. I even feel sorry for him, because people forget the good he has done and do not see the phenomenon of Fascism as being the wrong cure but as something that lets a serious illness spread in the organism. I think that the old liberals are deluding themselves if they think all that is required is to return to those "immortal principles" polluted by antireligious sectarianism.

Today the Holy Father has convoked the Sacred College of Cardinals. This means that grave events are coming to pass. I would like to hope that the Pope can be a mediator to a just and honourable peace.

9 AUGUST 1943

I spoke with the Hon. Cini and Ambassador Cerruti. The situation is serious. We depend on the will of Germany. The foreign affairs minister R. [Raffaelle] Guariglia met with Ribbentrop and Keitel in the Brenner [Pass]. Guariglia informed them of the conditions of extreme privation in which Italy finds itself; it absolutely cannot continue the war. The response was hard. War will be waged in Italy by Germany. Germany considers itself master of Italy. It has an interest in keeping the enemy far from its soil. Germany sees two divisions, from the Tyrrhenian to the Adriatic. If the first line of defence is breached, German forces will regroup in the Po Valley; already there are many armoured divisions there. They are now coming from Germany. Who will maintain them? Guariglia said that Italy has no recourse. If Germany makes requisitions, Italy will be reduced to hunger!

All of this is the consequence of the solemn untruth: "The war continues." Panic had spread that the Germans wanted to take Rome, make the Pope and the King prisoners, and prop up a Fascist government. The threat has been thwarted temporarily. But what is next? We are in the hands of the Germans. I do think, however, that they will touch neither the Pope nor the King; there would be too much clamour in the world.

Even the German plan to transform Italy into a battlefield can be overturned. If the Allies land in France, Hitler will be forced to run for cover. This is how the Balkan volcano could flare up.

There is in Italy a strong current favouring peace. It seems that the Hon. Bonomi[36] represents this current.

NEW BOMBARDMENT OF ROME   14 AUGUST 1943
Yesterday, at 23 hours, a new incursion of American airplanes over Rome! The thunder of the planes filled the sky; it was as if trains were running in the sky. Having crossed Rome, the airplanes headed to the outskirts, toward via Casilina and via Tuscolana.

The employees of the Propaganda gathered in the corridors; a few went down to the basement. I remained in my office.

---

[36] Ivanoe Bonomi (1872–1951), an Italian politician who with Bissolati founded the Reform Socialist Party. During the First World War he was minister of public works (1916–19). In the two following years he was minister of war and in 1921 and 1922 was president of the Council of Ministers. Defeated in the elections of 1924 and blocked by Fascism, he retired to private life on 8 September 1943, when he became the president of the Central Committee of National Liberation [Comitato centrale di Liberazione Nazionale]. In 1944–45 he headed liberated Italy's first government. He then was a deputy in the Constituent Assembly, a senator from 1948, and president of the Senate, 1948–51.

The Pope at the Bomb Sites
The Holy Father hastened to get to the affected sites: a magnificent act, truly worthy of the Bishop of Rome and the Pastor of Pastors! Disconcerted among his children, beaten and defeated, in front of churches devastated by the violence yet protected by the eternal bestowal of the divine promise, Pius XII knelt on the ground. Then, rising, he opened his arms in that supreme gesture that unmistakably brings him close to the Crucifix and made the divine sign of benediction over the kneeling crowd. Then, on His white garments, everybody could see a red stain that bears witness to the tenderness of the embrace with which he had gathered close to his heart his wounded and bloodied sons, while the crowd, anguished and bewildered, pressed around Him. He offered words of comfort for the living and the dead.

THE WORK OF PRIESTS   14 AUGUST 1943
In each of these two terrible days, marked by constant mourning from the ferocity of the air raids on 19 July and 13 August, everybody has seen priests in stricken parishes go out, still under the fury of deadly explosions, hastening to bring their work of spiritual succour, to give help and benediction where the wounded and dying were crying out for the comfort of that sovereign charity that Christ transmitted to his priests in his divine remedy to all human miseries.

This is how, beneficent angels of comfort amidst horror and death, the parish priests and clergy of San Lorenzo Outside the Walls, of the Immaculate, of St Fabian, of Ste Helen, and that of Santa Croce all moved among the ruins in the manner of those who have just begun to recover from a serious surgical operation.

Father Raffaele Melis
He was the parish priest of St Helen. He went out under the rage of the bombardments with his stole and holy oil to reach the railway line in front of his church where a train, hit by the first wave, had crashed with its suffering load of wounded and dying. While Father Raffaele was carrying out his merciful ministry, laying down his life for his sheep, he was struck and killed.

The People of Rome at St Peter's
An afflicted and disheartened people turn their eyes and hearts to the Vatican. Rome knows that its bishop, the Pope, at the rock of St Peter, is

vigilant, paternal, courageous, full of every concern to save the city. *Il Messaggero* writes: "The last editions of the afternoon newspapers had just announced that Rome had been declared an open city and the crowd, coming from everywhere, gathered in a compact mass in St Peter's Square to call the Pope to the Loggia ... and the Pope appeared."[37]

QUAM PARVA SAPIENTIA REGITUR MUNDUS![38]   15 AUGUST 1943
The Fasci are being destroyed in an exaltation of freedom. Today one fights what yesterday was celebrated! It seems right to have this sense of joy for the liberation from a tyranny whose police-state methods had become intolerable. It is human dignity that in the end feels vindicated and restored. But often things get out of hand. History cannot be cancelled. The Chamber of [Fasci and] Corporations was a good reform. Mussolini had made it spiritless and deformed with his stupid judgment. But the concept was sound. The national councillors could have been sent home; the Chamber itself could have been preserved and, if anything, modified. Instead, they talk of the same old elections. What an uproar, what a wind of rebellion after the war!

Today I was at the Pincio. Passing before the bust of Oberdan, I thought that, apart from the intentions and obfuscation of Oberdan's conscience, he remains a bomb thrower, a failed assassin. He is on the same level as that Albanian who tried to assassinate Victor Emmanuel III.

There is only one morality, both on this side and that side of jail. And governments must guard themselves against stupid excuses for the worst crimes, because the people have their own fundamental good sense and must not be incited to assassination.

23 AUGUST 1943
Today, Commendatore Cartoni, attached to the person of the Prince of Piedmont, came to see me.[39] He told me that in visiting the churches of

37 cc: *Il Messaggero*, 15 August 1943.

38 The eighteenth-century saying, which has ancient roots, means "How little it takes to obtain the admiration of the world."

39 The Prince of Piedmont in that era was Umberto of Savoy, who held the title from 1904 to 1946. The title, an ancient prerogative of the House of Savoy, became his title as the hereditary prince when Victor Emmanuel II assumed the title of King of Italy. This prerogative, however, was alternatively shared with the Prince of Naples. This was done to reinforce national unity. Therefore, if the

the south, the Prince was very disturbed by the multiplicity of statues, pictures, artificial flowers, etc., that clutter the altars, lowering the decorum of worship. Since many churches have to be redone, the need to purge them of such rubbish must be kept in mind. I answered that for years my brother and I have fought a lively campaign to maintain the decorum of worship and art, and that this justifiable wish shall be kept in mind. I gave him, for the Prince, my book *Sacred Art and 20th Centuryism*.[40]

PRINCEPS PACIS [IS. 9:6]   1 SEPTEMBER 1943
Today, on the fourth anniversary of the beginning of the world war, the Supreme Pontiff Pius XII delivered his message to the world.[41]

SPIRITUAL PROBLEMS   3 SEPTEMBER 1943
Meeting with Senator Cini. We talked about the dark situation, full of threats. We talked about spiritual subjects, before which everything that is agitating the world appears truly ephemeral.

4 SEPTEMBER 1943
[What a] tragic situation this poor dear Italy is in! Peace cannot be made; war cannot be waged. And the Allies, implacable and cruel, who said they were fighting to abolish the Fascist regime, rage against Italy, a victim of Fascism and of Germany. It is, however, honest to say that our cynical King did declare war afresh against the Allies: "The war continues." At any rate, I believe and hope that God will not abandon this good people "of many lives." The Pope is an immense moral force in the protection of the weak.

---

heir to the throne carried the title of Prince of Piedmont, his son assumed that of Prince of Naples and vice versa.

[40] The title in Italian is *Arte Sacra e Novecentismo*, by Costantini (Rome: Libreria Francesco Ferrari, 1935). CC: The Holy Office released on 30 June 1932 an *Instruction* to all Catholic bishops in the world, detailing precise norms for the decoration of ecclesiastical art and for the purging from churches of pseudo-artistic trash.

[41] The Pope's radio message of 1 September 1943 is reproduced in its entirety in AAS 35 (*Bollettino Ufficiale della Santa Sede*, 1943), 277–9.

INTUERE ET RESPICE OPPROPRIUM NOSTRUM [LAM. 5:1][42]

10 SEPTEMBER 1943

Yesterday was a day full of uncertainty, menace, and fear. Badoglio and the King absent. Almost all the ministries completely deserted. One had the impression of breathing the air of Caporetto. The journalist O. Rizzini of the *Corriere della Sera* and a diplomat came to me hoping to learn something. Everybody had gone to the Ministry of Propaganda; it was deserted. Nobody is answering the telephone at the other ministries. General U. Pugliese tells me that at the Ministry of Marine he found nobody but the ushers.

Yesterday evening, airplanes and gunfire on the outskirts of Rome. Today, in the morning, the same atmosphere of uncertainty, full of alarmist and even catastrophic voices. A soldier, Cantarutti of Castions, came to ask me if I had any civilian clothes. To my protests, he observed that military officials had advised him to go home. This is Caporetto in full; actually, worse than Caporetto.

However, at midday there was news of certain declarations published by Marshal Caviglia. I ran out of the Propaganda and went to the editorial offices of *Il Popolo di Roma*.[43]

Somebody said that he, Caviglia, was taking command of Rome, since Rome was without government and he was the highest-ranking official (this was a task not delegated to him but one he assumed purely out of patriotism).

Another said that Rome is peaceful and that negotiations are in train with the German Army to have the army move north. Great relief; confidence regained. But where are the King and the government? Voices are beginning to circulate that the King, the Prince, and the royal family fled on 8 September during the night, without leaving any arrangement for the maintenance of order in Rome or for its military defence. King and army in flight ...

At 13.30, south of Rome there was formidable shellfire that seemed gradually to be getting nearer. We went down to the shelter at the

---

[42] This prophetic expression is addressed to God and can be translated as "*Remember, O Lord, what is come upon us:* consider and behold our reproach (Italicized portion not quoted in the diary but forms part of Lam. 5:1).

[43] *Il Popolo di Roma*, a pro-government daily paper, began publishing in 1925, taking the place of *Il Popolo d'Italia* of Milan, which had begun publishing in 1914 and had an impossible existence with the rise of Fascism.

Propaganda. Amidst those frightened people I recited the rosary. One shell, in Via della Vite, blew up a house, demolishing it right to the ground floor. No human victims. A few windows of my bedroom that look onto Via della Vite were broken. Another two shells landed in Piazza di Spagna. Now, it's evening, and the sound of shellfire is rare and distant. But who defends Rome?

11 SEPTEMBER 1943

Last night at 22.00 hours I was telephoned with the news that the German forces had given an ultimatum to the Italian forces. It had to be accepted before midnight. The conditions were extremely tough. The city was to fall under German control; Italian soldiers were to be disarmed; only the *carabinieri* [police] were to remain for the maintenance of order. The Vatican would be put under German protection. The proclamations of Caviglia turned out to be apocryphal.

I spent a restless night, preoccupied with fears for the Holy Father, for the Propaganda, and also for the terrible humiliation that is being inflicted on Italy and Rome.

This morning I celebrated Mass, offering everything to God's mercy. At 7 AM I listened to Radio Roma, which was broadcasting news of an accord reached between the German troops and the Italian authorities, according to which General Calvi di Bèrgolo[44] has assumed command of Rome. I heaved a sigh of relief, elevating my thoughts to God and thanking him for the visible protection he exerts over the city.

ROME UNDER THE GERMANS   11 SEPTEMBER 1943

With a bitter heart I went out for a long walk in the city: Piazza San Silvestro, Piazza Venezia, Corso Vittorio Emanuele, Piazza Navona, Corso Umberto I, Piazza di Spagna. The city is peaceful; the stores are closed; all work has been suspended. Groups of people gather on the

---

[44] Giorgio Carlo Calvi di Bèrgolo (1887–1977), a count and an Italian general, was King Victor Emmanuel III's son-in-law, having married the King's first child, Iolanda Margherita, in 1923. According to the agreement between German General Kesselring and General Caviglia for the command of the "open city" on 10 September 1943, Calvi assumed, by virtue of the armistice, the control of public order in Rome, which had passed under German control. The Germans arrested him shortly thereafter, but he was liberated by the Allies in June 1944.

sidewalk with an air of astonishment and a kind of contained anxiety. There is not one smiling face. A kind of nightmare weighs on everybody's soul. Not one *carabiniere*, not one public security guard.

When I arrived at Piazza Venezia, I saw a column of a great many German armoured vehicles with machine guns levelled and with an arrogant attitude shown by the soldiers. The vehicles were going in every direction. One got the impression that they were joy-riding without a plan or a direction or any purpose. I thought that the Germans were parading, an ostentatious show of force, a type of triumphal celebration in the streets of the Eternal City.

12 SEPTEMBER, 0700 HRS

A peaceful night. The city is beginning to move. In Via della Vite the work continues to clear the ruins of the house demolished by a bomb on the 10th. I did see a line up in front of a shop – a good sign. Life continues. They say, however, that the general markets were looted. Let's hope that the news is not true or that it is exaggerated. Here *carabinieri* or public security guards are nowhere to be seen.

0800 HRS

Radio Roma, now in German hands, broadcast the proud communiqué of the commander of the German forces in the south of Italy. Afterward he made an announcement on behalf of the Roman authorities. Tram services will resume. Give way to trucks, especially those designed for provisioning. Not so bad. At the end, the radio announced: "Listeners are advised that radio service can be interrupted for technical reasons." I think that means because of warfare.

13 SEPTEMBER 1943

A relatively calm day, except occasional gunfire in the outskirts. A good number of shops have reopened. There is talk of some looting, but these seem to be sporadic incidents. The trams have resumed service. There lurks in one's spirit, a cloud of uncertainty and anxiety. The phrase "Rome, free city" is a happy diplomatic formula, and it brings with it a few good results. The Vatican is respected. But, *de facto*, one feels the dominance of German military will.

The Liberation of Mussolini
The newspapers confirm that Mussolini was freed and is now in Germany. What a mockery of the poor Italian Army! To external defeats

is added even this defeat, which heaps ridicule on the armed forces! For Mussolini, death would have been more merciful. Now he must contemplate the dismantling of his work and, most of all, the dismantling of Italy. But he is already nothing but an exhumed cadaver that smells of decomposition.

15 SEPTEMBER 1943

Rome has returned to work and breathes an air of substantial confidence. Alarmist voices circulate, but they do not merit attention. Rome is under German control. They have said that one cannot make requisitions without the required permits; a certain spirit of respect for the law has therefore returned. The authorities deplore certain incidents and as an example have severely punished soldiers who commit wrongdoing. We are at war. I have confidence, however, that the Holy See and Rome will be respected.

Poor, dear Italy, torn limb from bloody limb and now also stained in its honour! If what the newspapers are reporting is true – and what is revealed has the appearance of being true – the King and the government conducted themselves disloyally, for the German authorities deny that there were negotiations for the armistice on the same day that the armistice was being signed. The King and government could have said to Germany that Italy was exhausted and was in danger of being overthrown by a popular insurrection; and consequently the necessity for an armistice was unavoidable and final. One must act loyally, as an unfortunate people can do, but be noble and spiritually proud. Ambassador Cerruti came to see me; he was dismayed!

16 SEPTEMBER 1943

This morning my brother Mons. Giovanni left Rome for La Spezia. He is still the pastor of that people and has done well to return to his seat. He has a safe-conduct pass from the German Embassy to the Holy See. In 1942 he was named president of the Central Pontifical Commission for Sacred Art in Italy and lives with me in Rome. But until the new bishop of La Spezia is named, he remains apostolic administrator of that diocese. Last night the maid left, fearful about the events of recent days. She went to Friuli.

17 SEPTEMBER 1943

The radio confirmed the story of the liberation of Mussolini. It is a huge slap in the face for Badoglio; it is a disgrace for Mussolini himself and for Italy. Ridicule is heaped on the army and, perhaps, culpability. Rome is externally peaceful, but spirits are oppressed by a dark anxiety and sorrow. At least the authorities are currently preoccupied with replenishing food supplies. In this, even the Germans have some merit. During the night, there was the occasional explosion and other sounds that indicate we are in a period fraught with danger. German armoured vehicles continued to circulate in Rome, inflicting a grave humiliation on the Eternal City.

If I take in a panoramic view of Latin people, I cannot escape a painful impression: the Latin bloc is in decay. Spain, torn apart by civil war, has been more or less reconstituted but is still without a clear and secure peace: France, defeated, is occupied by the Germans, who currently dominate her. Italy is, *de jure*, with the Allies who are invading it, but the army has for the most part been dissolved. *De facto*, it is under German domination.

If the proclamations of Mussolini succeed in exerting some influence in Italy, it could lead to civil war … Mussolini speaks as if he is the head of government or president of a fictitious republic. He is no longer himself; he is a tragic shadow of a cadaver. The son has revolted against the mother. If Mussolini had had a little moral sensibility, he would have withdrawn, even before becoming embittered, rather than taking up arms against Italy. May God help us! *Deus fecit sanabiles Nationes* [Wis. 1:14; God made the nations of the earth for health]. Will Italy rise again? Will the Latin people rise again? Let us hope and pray God that it may be so. But history teaches us that there are declines from which there is no return, like that of ancient Greece, like that of Egypt. Italy has reason for hope because of its healthy demographic position. Art, that has been so great in Italy, now reflects this decadence, this confusion of spirit.

One person alone rises high, with the sign of the Supreme Keys – Pius XII, who is no longer the uneasy and world-bound prince of an insecure statelet. He turns to the world and to all says great words of truth. People look to him in anxious hope. Even the movement of contemporary thought orients itself toward Christ.

17 SEPTEMBER 1943

The work of the Propaganda Ministry continues, although with a rhythm slowed by transportation difficulties and the blockages of the postal service. In the morning the office heads come to me and bring the latest news, which is often contradictory or exaggerated. They are, however, sincere echoes of the voices that are circulating in the city. This morning they speak of a terrible bombardment that happened last night at Ciampino or at Pratica di Mare. Evidently, the Allies – who now hold Sardinia and Corsica – are striking airfields that have fallen into German hands.

A LETTER FROM LA SPEZIA   19 SEPTEMBER 1943
On Friday I tried to return to La Spezia, but heavy gunfire near the mouth of the Magra led me to think that the English were landing; instead, these were exercises in the powerful new German positions. I therefore remained at Sarzana. Yesterday, Saturday, I went to La Spezia, where in the Curia and at home everything is in perfect order. At German Command – where I went to request an automobile to take me to Brunato – I let them know that mine was absolutely useless because it had no tires. The Command immediately provided me with an automobile from those it had requisitioned. I spoke immediately to the prefect, who was waiting for me and was happy to see me, and within the week I will have an automobile. I think this was the result of the document given me by the German Embassy; I thank the Lord, because as a result I can be present in many places in the diocese.

Yesterday afternoon a good German driver drove me here to Bugnato … Many Germans have stopped here for two days; they occupied the seminary, and an official slept in the Bishop's Palace in the room where the maid had slept. Neither in the seminary nor here has anything been touched. Now we will see how events unfold; if there is a respite, I will return to Rome.

+Giovanni Costantini, Bishop

AFTER THE SPEECHES OF MUSSOLINI AND PAVOLINI
20 SEPTEMBER 1943
Fascism's record can be divided into two parts: the one before this war and the one after the war. In the first, one can find some good things, even if they are infested with corruption and by a tyrannical oligarchy; in the second part, there is the ruin of Italy and of the army.

Mussolini and Pavolini dwell on the first part and skip over the second, confounding facts and ideas and implying that the armistice was responsible for Italy's catastrophe. The two orators were served by an able dialectic, but it cannot change the severe judgment against Fascism, which has brought Italy to complete ruin and civil war. They are like a gambler who remembers the first lucky games, skipping over recent and total losses. The nation takes stock of Fascism's balance sheet and finds it to be bankrupt. Mussolini appeals to the people, but the people – with their instinct – look at recent facts, feel the pain brought by the war, and curse the dictator. If Fascism once again succeeds in recruiting fanatics and profiteers, it will not be able to do so without the help of German arms; and that is its condemnation. Certain dead things cannot be revived.

21 SEPTEMBER 1943

Last night I heard on the radio the message of Marshal Graziani, who has renounced his oath of loyalty to the King and has put himself at Mussolini's service – or rather, at that of the Germans. What misery! Poor Italy! How low it has fallen!

There used to be an army, but with its leaders fled, it has collapsed like a house of cards. Now they incite Italians to engage in guerrilla warfare, imitating the example of the Slavs. The Balkans an example to Italy! The old Fascist leaders appear here and there, protected by the German army. What confusion, what debasement! In the meantime, like a subterranean current that eats away at the foundations of an edifice, the Communist idea spreads.

This evening Marshal Graziani, minister of defence, read a long proclamation on the radio. What misery! The proclamation also gives the impression of a personal grudge against "a man with the name Badoglio." The grave words of the Book of Wisdom come to mind: "For they were all bound together with one chain of darkness" [Wis. 17:17].

A LETTER FROM SENATOR FRANCESCO SALATA

26 SEPTEMBER 1943

"My soul, saddened by illness and by the disaster befalling the homeland, longs for peace, which can be found in the mysteries of God. I feel the need of His word of guidance and comfort. Perhaps my days are numbered. I always hoped that my friend Father Celso would comfort me. Would you like – if it doesn't weigh too much on you – to come and see me? I am at the Grande Hotel [Via delle Terme], because, for many reasons, my house is at present not inhabitable. With great bitterness I remember Aquileia and the truly holy war of redemption."

I brought him my book on the Gospel: *Jesus Christ: The Way, Truth, and Life*.[45] He told me that reading it has comforted him immensely.

27 SEPTEMBER 1943

This evening, when returning from visiting Senator Salata, I saw from the little garden in front of Termini Station a painful procession pass: men, women, old people, and children marched past with tired steps, gazing around with astonished and uncertain eyes, and bent under the bags they were carrying on their shoulders. A woman, still young but with a face marked by suffering, pulled along two reluctant and crying children. They were dressed like farmers and their general appearance revealed them to be foreigners. Some women were walking in bare feet. I asked, "Where are you from? Where are you going?" A young girl responded, "We are coming from a concentration camp and we are returning to Dalmatia."

Poor people, they did not know or think that their miserable procession through Rome was a triumph. They were returning to a liberated homeland. They passed in front of the Abyssinian Lion affixed on the monument dedicated to the fallen of Dogali. But in those poor people and in that lion I saw the fall of Italy, not as a result of any lack of valour of our soldiers, but because of the foolishness of our leaders and, in the final analysis, because of the offence committed against justice and humanity.

ANOTHER LETTER FROM THE APOSTOLIC ADMINISTRATOR
OF LUNI   LA SPEZIA, 28 SEPTEMBER 1943

Here things are taking a rather serious turn, and for that reason I have decided to establish myself at La Spezia, where my presence is absolutely essential. The people say that the only true authority is that of the bishop; we do not know if the others have any authority left and from whom they have it. Yesterday, Monday, 27 [September], I lodged near the chaplains of the Civil Hospital in the house and church that I had built. The president and all the doctors are happy to have me with them, and last night they expressed this in a way that was full of affection. The secretary and I go there only to eat and sleep; we spend the rest of the day in

45 The book cited by Costantini had a run of one hundred copies. Containing his comments on the Gospel, it was published by Tumminelli (Rome, 1943).

the bishop's headquarters or in the curia. The rectories of the city have been more or less destroyed, the pastors do not have any service staff, and the male and female religious communities have all abandoned the city. So I was left with only this solution if I wanted to reside in La Spezia. I am happy to have secured this accommodation. I know that the diocesan clergy are very happy because of it. Under the hospital, secure shelters have been built.

+ Giovanni Costantini, Bishop

29 SEPTEMBER 1943

Mussolini has proclaimed himself head of the Fascist Republican Government. What an aberration! To pit Italians against Italians! It is a crime of patricide. Mussolini was condemned, like Cain, to live ...

The synagogue of the Jews has been requisitioned. In addition, they have been commanded to collect among them the sum of 50 kilograms of gold, otherwise they will be deported to Poland. The sum has been collected and submitted. They say that the Holy Father contributed to this collection. But the Jews are painfully anxious because they fear being persecuted all the same. This is nefarious blackmail.

THE DEATH OF ANTONINO ANILE   29 SEPTEMBER 1943
Today's *Osservatore Romano* notes the news of the death of Anile.[46] This news pains me deeply because we were united in good friendship. He was a very noble spirit in which medical science, faith, and love of nature gave wings to a poetic inspiration.

29 SEPTEMBER 1943

I saw the Hon. Salata again, in bed, pale, thin, very down. He said to me, "I don't sleep, I don't eat; the homeland is in the abyss. I swore fealty to the Savoy, and I want to be loyal to that oath. You understand what

---

[46] Antonino Anile (1869–1943), a celebrated anatomist and author of numerous scientific publications in his field, was also a man of letters and a politician. In the latter guise he was elected as a deputy to parliament in 1919 for the Italian People's Party [Partito Popolare Italiano; PPI] and was re-elected in 1921. He served as undersecretary of education, 1921–22, and then as minister in the two ministries led by the Hon. Facta. With the advent of Fascism, he retired from political life.

loyalty means for the *irredenti* [Italians living in "unredeemed" Italian lands] who have suffered greatly for Italy. And we are in a civil war …"

Salata is a Fascist, but he is also a gentleman. Mussolini has sent Minister Mazzolini[47] to give him 100,000 lire because he knows that Salata is poor. But the proud senator refused the money. He gave me 50 lire for the Propagation of the Faith, lamenting that he could not give more.

30 SEPTEMBER 1943

The landing of the American Fifth Army at Salerno was strongly resisted by the Germans. At a certain point, the Americans were pushed back toward the beach. But then they rallied. They overtook and shattered the enemy positions in the hills. And today it is announced that the Germans are retreating and the Allies are advancing toward Naples. They say that Naples is being put to steel and fire and is being sacked by the retreating troops. The English [British] Eighth Army has conquered Foggia and is marching north. Airfields constitute an important strategic point for the Allies.

This news is received with relief in Rome, and everybody desires the Allies to arrive quickly in the capital. This is very painful. But poor Italy has been reduced to this extreme misery, to need – that is, to desire – the arrival of other foreigners to liberate us from the Germans. The Germans have made themselves detestable with their arrogance, their disrespect, and with the use of force. Besides, the masses no longer want to hear about Fascism and know that it is propped up currently with German bayonets.

In many families where there are young men or officials or soldiers, an anguished tragedy is being lived out. The young men do not want to

---

[47] Serafino Mazzolini (1890–1945) was an Italian politician and diplomat, as was his older brother Quinto. He took part in the seizure of Fiume with Gabriele D'Annunzio in 1919. In 1922 he participated in the March on Rome. He was vice-secretary of the National Fascist Party [Partito Nazionale Fascista] in 1925. The next year he became a member of the Grand Council of Fascism. A deputy in parliament from 1924, he held diplomatic responsibilities and among other things was a minister plenipotentiary to various countries. In Italy he was director general of staff and general affairs in the Ministry of External Affairs. He was under-secretary of external affairs in the Italian Social Republic, founded by Mussolini, with whom he remained a loyal collaborator.

enlist in the "Little Republican" army of Mussolini because of fidelity to their oath of loyalty to the King and because they feel an insurmountable repugnance to joining the Germans and Mussolini against their brothers. Workers fear deportation to Germany. There are accounts circulating about railway cattle cars loaded with young workers who are locked in and then sent to Germany. I have seen mothers and brides crying disconsolately for their own family tragedies. Many youths live their lives in hiding, or they are hiding in the bush. But the uncertainty, anxiety, and danger are oppressing many families. I have enrolled various young men in our Urban Atheneum to save them from conscription. Amidst much confusion and anxiety, two things lift the spirits:

1 The "Little Republican" government has once again declared Rome an "open city."
2 The Germans have conducted themselves correctly and respectfully toward Vatican City. The Pope can correspond with foreign countries at least via radio.

Poor Italy

If the Allies had a little respect for Italy, they would have landed at La Spezia or Genoa or Trieste, bottling up the German army distributed in the peninsula and liberating and saving our unhappy country. They landed at Salerno. How much time will they need to go up north? They rage at a lifeless body. Italy should be treated, Churchill said, as one treats a donkey: with a stick behind and a carrot in front ...

They are punishing us, and our wrongs are not unknown to us. But we know that vendettas have long aftermaths of rancour. The Allies, by offering a friendly hand to liberate Italy, would have seen their moral superiority affirmed and would have won the hearts of Italians. Instead, this possibility is closing.

THE CONTRADICTIONS OF THIS INHUMAN CIVILIZATION
1 OCTOBER 1943

In the last decade – as the Gea Agency reported from Rio de Janeiro on 30 September – Brazil destroyed over 65 million sacks of coffee. Even in this current year, at least eight million sacks of coffee have to be sacrificed, equivalent to a third of total production. But the quantity that must be destroyed will be even higher if the United States destroys its entire coffee order: 1,700,000 sacks.

One hears from everywhere news of plundering, raiding, and pillaging. One prelate tells me, "The Germans are doing in Italy what they did in France, in Holland, in Belgium, etc. They are not mindful that they are generating great hatred."

Having gone out into the city, I saw two trucks loaded with young men. These are the young men rounded up from the streets. They are being deported to work in Germany. What a miserable spectacle! Many families this evening are waiting for a loved one to return, and instead he is leaving Italy!

Conte C. says to me, "I ask myself if there is a difference between these young men and the slaves that the Egyptians engaged to work on construction of the pyramids."

A prelate says, "If one takes the individual German, he is full of finesse and manners. But if you find him in an armed group, the Longobard and Vandal in him rises to the fore." He adds, "The modern-day Longobards are much more frightening because they are educated barbarians and formidably armed."

The newspapers are emphasizing Rome's status as an open city. And that is good. The Allies until now have respected the city centre. And even the Germans, truth to tell, have respected the neutrality of the Vatican. The Pope is virtually a prisoner because he is at the mercy of the Germans. They have, however, at least until now, understood the convenience of respecting Vatican City. They have posted sentinels outside the Vatican, in Italian territroty. The German ambassador to the Holy See, who is understood to be a worthy person, has frequent contact with the secretariat of state. The Holy Father can communicate with foreign countries, especially through the radio; this too, both in theory and practice, is of great value. God willing, the Germans will not deviate from this line of conduct! Even they understand the greatness of the Papacy. I thus have great hope that nothing unpleasant will happen. The Conciliation is one of the best achievements of Mussolini. And he is "personally" interested in demonstrating its perfect efficiency and its greatest probative success.

The Pope Will Not Leave Rome.
A rumour was circulating that Hitler wanted to take the Pope prisoner. I then had an audience. His Holiness was sad but serene. He said to me,

assuming a grave expression on his sweet face, "Whatever happens, I am not moving from Rome. If I am forced to yield to force, I will protest. My place is here, with my sons, but I hope that nothing serious will happen."[48]

2 OCTOBER 1943

Last night around midnight I was still awake. I heard some noises and some whispers in the hallways of the house. Then came a light knock at my door. A sister, a little dismayed, told me that all of Rome was illuminated, and it seemed almost on fire because of balls of fire that were descending from the sky. I reassured the sister and went up to the little terrace on the roof of the Propaganda. Rome was a dark mass of buildings, and it seemed immersed in sleep. There were, however, a few windows timidly being opened in the darkness, and one could hear a few muffled voices. In the sky about fifteen fireballs cast over Rome an immense light, almost like the *aurora borealis*. The fire balls descended slowly, leaving streaks of smoke in the sky.

In the distance one could see flashes of light. But this was probably due to the return of cloudy and stormy weather. I heard the explosion of a distant bomb. I thought that the airplanes of the Allies had come for reconnaissance and perhaps were taking photographs. I reassured the sister and we went back to sleep.

Lieutenant Dr Sandrini then told me that in the pinery near Anzio, where he was in hospital, he saw the same spectacle; it seemed to be an amazing phantasmagoria of fireworks. But one's heart was seized by these dark threats.

2 OCTOBER 1943

Senator Count Vittorio Cini has been deported to Germany. Last night I saw his wife, Countess Lyda. She is profoundly sorrowful, but calm. Her face is marked by internal pain. She knows nothing of her husband's fate. She sustains herself thinking about God and reflecting that her husband has nothing to hide. She tells me that he will be able to put up with

---

[48] CC: They say that if this program had been prevented it was because of the wise comportment of German General Stahel, who retained direct responsibility. It is certainly because of the great influence that the Pope had over him and over the entire world.

his predicament with strength, taking comfort from his deep Christian sense and from his noble spirit.

She spoke of missionaries, citing the following thought from the message that I prepared for the day of the missionary: "Poor missionaries, suspected, often mistreated, many interned, deported, who endure with invincible courage their tough condition, hoping against hope with the same heart with which St Paul said, 'Joy abounds in all my tribulations.' The following expresses the divine character of missionary work: to endure suffering with joy for the love of God and your brothers. Nothing similar has ever been found in any idolatrous religions."

2 OCTOBER 1943

I have been shown a flyer dropped from an airplane that contains a proclamation by Badoglio. It says:

> After more than three years of struggle, ITALY has CONCLUDED AN ARMISTICE ... Because continuing to fight now means only to SACRIFICE OUR COUNTRY FOR THE CONVENIENCE OF GERMANY and that is to keep, as far away as possible, the horrors of war from German territory ...
>
> Therefore there is one demand for everybody, one commandment: GERMANS OUT! It is they – don't forget it – who since the time they became our allies – or said they were – subjected us daily to harassment and oppression, which for a long time we had to suffer. They are the ones who began the fight against us, and demasked, they have finally declared themselves our enemies and want to prolong the war indefinitely in our house.

How many words! But Badoglio himself said, "The war continues." Now he revolts against the Germans, to whom he promised collaboration. Naturally, the Germans understood that "The war continues" was a miserable lie. The armistice should have immediately followed the overthrow of the regime, which is solely responsible and solely involved, and it should have been arranged by legal means, speaking to Germany equal to equal. Badoglio should never have allowed even a hint of the appearance of so-called treason. I have the clear impression that Badoglio's government and the King were not equal to the task. Men have been infinitely smaller than the events befalling them. In sincerity, there is power, prestige, and dignity; it is the premise for an honest freedom of action. And then we complain when a Machiavellianism of the basest kind returns once again!

Today the Little Republicans speak of the treason of Badoglio as if Fascism – which has brought Italy to ruin – was innocent. What a confusion of ideas, what a moral collapse. We have therefore arrived at the following paradoxical situation: yesterday with Germany against the Allies, today with the Allies against Germany; and one part of Italy is still on Germany's side. Hungary and Romania tremble, and tomorrow, if they do not decide otherwise, will suffer the same fate as Italy: destruction upon destruction. Japan will remain with Germany, but it is very far away and thinks above all of its own interests in the Orient. So Germany is closed in a circle of hatred and iron within Europe. How can it overcome this circle that is reinforced by the power of America and England? One must pay for iniquity. It seems that the scales are tipping, ready to overflow. One cannot spread so much injustice and so much pain with impunity. At a certain moment God says, "Enough!"

For us, in this tragic picture, is added the pain of seeing that a group of Italians have been made available to Germany to fight against their own brothers. Yesterday some leaders, together with German officials, after the Adrian conference, went to pay their respects to the "Unknown Soldier." The irony of things: the Unknown Soldier was killed by the Germans in the last war!

THE REMOTE CAUSE OF OUR RUIN   2 OCTOBER 1943

If I consider the horrendous picture in which I see Italy flounder, bleed, and rattle, with the ruin of the army, the civil war, the Anglo-American occupation, the German occupation, etc., I ask myself: how could all this happen? What remote causes have provoked this tragic decomposition? The Italian people are not less intelligent than other peoples, they are no less hard working and no less patriotic. So then?

What was and is missing is a solid moral structure and the great quality that is character. D'Azeglio[49] has already said, "We have made Italy; we must now make Italians." National conscience, unfortunately, was still being formed. Then Fascism proposed the use of force at the base of its ideology. The education slogan of the child became "Book and

---

[49] Massimo D'Azeglio (1798–1866), a politician, Piedmontese writer, and moderate liberal, was president of the Council of Ministers. He had the merit of calling Camillo Benso Cavour to become part of his ministry and then yielded the presidency to him in 1852. His historical novels are famous, among them *Ettore Fieramosca* (1833).

musket." Religion was often reduced to an external parade. A strong moral conscience was not formed. Its followers were not taught "This is right, this is wrong." The barbaric cult of power prevailed. Neither Mussolini nor the King reflected on whether the war was more or less right; they arrogated to themselves alone the right to proclaim it, throwing into the abyss 45 million inhabitants. Franco saved Spain from the horror of the Communists but was guided by his religious and moral sense.

Fascism had become a rat's nest of corruption. Everything has collapsed in Italy because both at the top and the bottom there was no moral architecture left. Italy will rise again, because it not only has a great demographic capacity but also because of many other spiritual qualities granted to it by Providence. We do not forget that the same Providence wanted the Seat of the Church to be established in Italy. But we must re-educate it religiously and morally. Nor is it thought that morality can exist without religion. The work of rebirth will take two or three generations. But the rebirth will come; on condition, however, that it starts on the inside, that is, with the re-education of souls.

4 OCTOBER 1943

This morning a column of German tanks passed slowly through the streets of Rome. They go, they come, they stop. With ostentation and an act of defiance. In Piazza di Spagna an enormous tank, perhaps one of those extremely modern ones that are called tigers, stopped at the Barcaccia with its gun pointed at the Galleria of the Quirinale. Another was stationed at the wall of St Joseph's College.

People see this with cold and hostile curiosity. German soldiers have an air of arrogance and indifference that is contempt. Poor Rome! The Eternal City endures the humiliation that was suffered when Alaric the Goth came in 410 and sacked the city; and when Genserico did the same with the Vandals in 455. But then the Roman Empire was in decline, and the young barbaric peoples were on the ascent. Today, although Italian Rome has fallen, Christian Rome, eternal Rome has not fallen! And the descendants of the barbarians are at the point of being destroyed by their own brutal force. The spirit will once again be victorious.

Yesterday evening, passing by the Piazza of the Quirinale, I saw affixed to the great door of the Royal Palace a poster in German. Pathetic King – he deserved this nice compliment.

4 OCTOBER 1943

The newspapers are reporting that the Tribunal of Rome has sentenced a group of looters, imposing extremely severe penalties; almost every one of them received 12 years of prison and a 20,000 lire fine. Good. We must strike at the thieves. But the greatest and most ruthless looters are not these little delinquents but, rather, the Germans. The sentences have provoked in everybody this striking difference between the "poor folk" targeted and power unpunished. There is a single morality.

Fascism decreed: "All works of charity and social assistance are devolved to the *fascio* [branch of the Fascist Party]." But the people do ·not forget that the rings given by Italian women were – from what is commonly said – used in part to enrich certain Fascist officials.

Some say that German troops are leaving for the north; some say instead that they are going south. There is in all Romans a bitter sense of aversion toward these new *Landsknecht*.

I learned from a reliable source that the Holy Father Pius XII helped the Jews in collecting the fifty kilograms of gold which the Germans demanded for their release. He gave two and a half kilograms. What magnificent charity! *Lux in tenebris lucet.* [A light shines in the darkness].

Today, Cardinal Pietro Fumasoni Biondi, prefect of the Propaganda Ministry, gave me a document in which the Vatican City State declares that "the Palace of the Propaganda Fide is the property of the Holy See and enjoys the privilege of extraterritoriality. As such, this building cannot be touched." The declaration bears the signature of Governor Serafini[50] and the approval of General Stahel,[51] commander of the garrison of the Roman district.

9 OCTOBER 1943

The engineer Iesi, not a Fascist, has thrown himself against Badoglio for his foolish, disastrous Machiavellianism. He also has bitter words for the King and Mussolini – those responsible for the ruin of the homeland.

---

[50] Camillo Serafini (1864–1952), a marquis and Italian numismatic, was governor of the Vatican City State from 1929 to 1952.

[51] Rainer Stahel (1892–1950), a major-general of the Luftwaffe, was the military commander of Rome in September–October 1943. He was an "Old Catholic" by religion and established close ties in the Italian capital with the Pancrazian Father Pfeiffer, superior general of the Society of the Divine Saviour, who served as an intermediary of the Pope in humanitarian interventions.

He says that Badoglio, along with other leaders of the army, has added to his dishonour the shame of fleeing Rome. As for the rest, continued the engineer, for twenty years music has been in chaos, poetry has been a hermetic and barbaric exercise, and art a deformation of the beautiful. Behold the mirror of our decadence.

The details of the stupendous action of the bishop who liberated hostages destined to be executed are as follows. It was Monsignor Francesco Petronelli, bishop of Trani and Barletta. Together with the Podestà [head of the local administration], he went to the German authorities saying that he and the Podestà would offer themselves to save the 20 hostages. It seems that the proposal was not accepted, but only just. The hostages were gathered at the Bishop's Palace. Before the execution, the bishop placed himself in front of the lineup of hostages and said, "Execute me too!" This magnificent act saved the lives of the hostages and of the bishop as well.

Action of Phony Squadrists and Illegal Requisitions
The Roman federation of the Republican Fascist Party has alerted the population against *agents provocateurs*, swindlers and the like who, using the spoils of the squadrists, are committing rogue acts such as the illegal sequestering of vehicles, tires, and other material. The citizenry have been informed that any operations directed by the relevant organs of the Republican Federation must be confirmed by express and specific documents, which from time to time are issued by the federation itself for carrying out certain operations. In case of emergency, interested parties may telephone the federation's guard at telephone number 50031.

12 OCTOBER 1943
The days pass slowly and grey. The Allies are still on the Volturno and in the Termoli region; the Germans are offering fierce resistance. Rome has, externally, its normal aspect, but faces are serious, and men are taciturn and worried. A thousand families are living the tragedy of having young men and officials who remain in hiding and fear being exposed and forced into the service of the Germans or the pseudo-Fascist republic. Every day people come to the Propaganda asking for temporary shelter for themselves or their children. Women cry, men grit their teeth for their own anguish. Naturally, one cannot accept all requests. The German authorities have shown themselves to be correct and even attentive toward the Holy See, and we must be and want to be honest. This is also

necessary to avoid offering the least pretext for reprisals. As for the rest, Urban College [Collegio Urbano] is overflowing with refugees and patients, and in many other buildings of the Holy See are hidden politicians, Jews, young people, old people, etc. Even the catacombs are reliving a new and strange life, receiving many "wanted" people.

13 OCTOBER 1943

The airplanes over Rome dropped a great number of cards. The text:

THE ALLIES' ACCEPTANCE OF ITALY'S DECLARATION OF WAR.
The Governments of Great Britain, the United States, and the Soviet Union recognize the State of the Royal Italian Government as led by Marshal Badoglio, and they accept the *active collaboration of the Italian Nation and its Armed Forces as co-belligerents in the war against Germany.* Military events that occurred after 8 September and the *brutal treatment of the Italian people inflicted by the Germans,* followed today by the Italian declaration of war against Germany, has in fact put Italy in the position of a co-belligerent.
THE THREE GOVERNMENTS GIVE NOTICE TO THE ITALIAN GOVERNMENT OF ITS OBLIGATION TO RECOGNIZE THE WILL OF THE ITALIAN PEOPLE TO HAVE THE GERMANS EXPELLED FROM ITALY. NOTHING CAN PREJUDICE THE ABSOLUTE AND INDISPUTABLE RIGHT OF THE ITALIAN PEOPLE TO CHOOSE BY THEIR OWN CONSTITUTIONAL MEANS THE FORM OF DEMOCRATIC GOVERNMENT THAT MUST DEFINITIVELY BE ADOPTED.
   The relationship of co-belligerency between the Government of Italy and the United Nations cannot by their actions prejudice the terms of the recently signed armistice. These terms remain fully in force and can be modified after agreements between Allied Governments in relation to the help which the Italian Government can offer to the cause of the United Nations.

Senator Professor Perez[52] tells me that as well as the tragedy of the many families who are hiding officials, soldiers, and young men to

---

[52] Giovanni Perez (1873–1959), a university professor of surgical pathology, head of the Faculty of Medicine and Surgery at the University of Rome, was also a senator from 1939. He was deprived of his senatorial role because he was held responsible for actively collaborating with Fascism and making the war possible both by his vote and by his individual actions in spreading propaganda inside and outside the Senate.

prevent them being deported to Germany or forced into the service of the pseudo-republican government, there is also the unknown tragedy of some senators. These are poor senators whom the Senate assists with a monthly indemnity of 2,000 lire. Frequently in the morning they used to go to the Senate to drink a cup of coffee with milk. Now the Senate building is closed. And these poor but discreet senators, coming in large part from the teaching professions, find themselves hungry.

14 OCTOBER 1943

This morning three ladies came to see me, weeping for the tragedy of their relatives in hiding. Naturally, I tried to comfort them as best as I could. One lady told me that last night two German soldiers, one of whom spoke Italian, entered her villa looking for one of her young sons. They did not find him, and they took a purse containing 850 lire.

Engineer Mariani tells me that the other day a group of blackshirts, kids of about 16 to 18 years old, broke into his brother's house and stole an automobile. They are a reckless and dangerous lot because they are armed and believe – because they are Fascists – that they can do whatever they want.

15 OCTOBER 1943

An air force captain confessed the following to me: "I do not want to go with the Germans. I have a wife and children and do not have the means of supporting them. But they will immediately give me 10,000 lire and then a stipend with an indemnity, and I agreed to enlist, even though this burned me up inside."

At Urban College, which is on the Janiculum in an area just outside the city, various Jews and officials who do not want to be part of the so-called social republic of Mussolini have taken refuge.

I took a walk around Rome, passing by Piazza Venezia. On the balcony of the palace the Italian tricolour is flying, with the Savoyan coat of arms stripped from it. On the balcony's balustrade there is a picture of Mussolini giving the Roman salute. On the square in front of the great entrance, there is a tank as well as four German armoured cars. There is a notable movement in all directions of automobiles and German tanks. There is no hint of the Germans leaving. The war on the Volturno, on the Adriatic coast, and in the Apennines is being very bitterly waged.

16 OCTOBER 1943

A dark day for the Jews, a sad day for Christians and for civilization. A dazed Quirino, the usher, told me this morning that in Piazza di Spagna a German military transport was parked full of women, men, children, and old people all crying ... They were Jews torn from their homes who are now being deported. It is a spectacle of infinite misery! The clerks tell me of other truckloads of human misery. Then, at the office, there is a flow of Jews and others seeking help. Msgr. Signora tells me that two women and a girl took refuge, crying inside the precincts of the Propaganda, entering by the side door.

The round-up operations are being conducted by a company of the s s, which specializes in acts of cruelty.

St Joseph College, in Piazza di Spagna, reports that it rescued the child of Professor Conegliani, who was not at home when his parents were deported. I replied that they should advise the parish priest, because the mother is Aryan and the child has been baptized. The parish priest went to the barracks where the Jews are being held and clarified the situation. And the Jews gave the Germans 50 kilograms of gold as the price of their salvation! The visits to the Propaganda continue of people trying to save themselves from military service or work detail.

WHEN THE SON OF MAN COMETH, SHALL HE FIND FAITH
ON THE EARTH?[53]   16 OCTOBER 1943

These terrible words are coming to pass, unfortunately in our time. Nothing is more anti-Christian than war. For many, Christianity had become a habit, for others merely a culture, for the government a competing idealism with the so-called *sacred egotism* and something to be kept far from positivist [government] ministries! If there are any Christians left, one cannot say that there are any Christian governments. Christ remains in the churches and still lives in pious souls and in the liturgy, but does not live in public life. That life is actually, with its greed and cruelty, the exact antithesis of Christianity. Nazi ideologies are absolutely the opposite of the spirit of the Gospel. And the world receives its wages. Jesus Christ, however, said, "*In mundo pressuram habebitis, sed confidite: ego vici mundum*" [Jn. 16:33; These things have I spoken to you, that in me you may have peace. In the world you shall have tribulation. But have confidence. I have overcome the world].

[53] Lk. 18:8.

Our life is an ephemeral thing. But God is patient and marks time not in years but in centuries. Even if we do not see the victory of Christianity, it prepares us for the hard struggles of life, and its moment will come.

Pure Victims
The *Giornale d'Italia* of 14 October reports: "American artillery have attacked the city of Campobasso that had just been violently bombarded by enemy warplanes. The bishop of Campobasso was killed by an enemy grenade in front of the altar as he was celebrating a Mass for the victims of the bombing." The bishop's name is Msgr. Bologna.[54] *Requiescat in pace!* [Rest in peace!] This is the second bishop who in this terrible war has fallen victim to enemy bombing while he was carrying out his noble ministry. Monsignor Montalbetti, who was slaughtered by enemy bombs at Reggio Calabria, was 55 years old; Monsignor Bologna was 45. Two vigorous plants uprooted by this unjust maelstrom. But even when dying, these two noble pastors fulfilled their holy office. They demonstrate how the Church associates itself with the pain of the world and of the people. It reminds me of the three bishops and forty missionaries who fell in China when carrying out their work during the time I was apostolic delegate to Beijing.

THE TEARS OF CHRIST OVER JERUSALEM   17 OCTOBER 1943
Jesus Christ wept for the imminent destruction of Jerusalem.[55] This terrible prophecy is coming true for Rome. Today I went to Vatican Radio to deliver a missionary message. Along the street there was a rumbling column of German tanks. At the border between Italian territory and the territory of Vatican City were two German guards and a group of German soldiers stationed nearby. What shame for Eternal Rome, for the Rome that has dominated the Western world and was the cradle of civilization. What shame for Christian Rome, protected – or rather, besieged – in Italy by German arms.

17 OCTOBER 1943
A German soldier said to a high prelate: "Everyone everywhere hates us. The evil is that those responsible for this war do not feel this wave of hatred. We, who are in contact with the people, feel it."

54 Secondo Bologna (1898–1943), the bishop of Boiano-Campobasso from 1940, whose diocesan seat was in Campobasso.
55 Referred to in Lk. 21:20–4.

The resistance of workers, officials, and soldiers against the enticements and threats of the Germans grows more and more tenacious and
decisive. Those being sought remain hidden in houses, moving from one
place to another.

One general said, at a meeting after a heated exortation (so I am
assured by a reliable source): "If you do not accept the invitation, there
will be in Rome a St Bartholomew's Eve" [massacre in Paris, 1572, of
Huguenots]. Miserable servant, making himself an ignominious instrument in the hands of the enemy, who lays waste to Italy and terrorizes
and deports Italians. They say that the enemy has taken over the machinery of our main bank to print new paper money as it sees fit.

SAD HOURS   19 OCTOBER 1943
"The Command insists on the invitation of officials and Italian soldiers
to enlist in the German army." Supreme shame and humiliation for Italy.
As for the rest, the Germans are logical: in the Hitlerian plan, if Germany
emerges victorious from this war, Italy will be considered more or less a
borderland united with Germany.

And what are Mussolini and Graziani saying and thinking? Have blind
pride and personal resentment left them blind to the point of not understanding the defacement that is being done to Italian honour? An atrocious mockery is added to all this. The Germans say that "German troops
are spilling their blood to defend the sacred soil of the Italian homeland."
Clowns! They wage a war they have won, and to keep their enemies far
from Germany they submit Italy to steel and fire. A wave of hatred has
enveloped them for the nefarious arrogance, the destruction and cruelty
that they commit in Italy. They themselves understand that anybody who
has personal dignity cannot accept their invitation. And therefore –
supreme humiliation – they entice Italians with salaries, salaries that cost
them nothing because they have plundered the funds of the Bank of Italy.

Poor Italian Army! It could not have fallen lower than this: collaborating with the enemy by force or by hunger. Is this where the stupid and
emphatic *bluffismo* of Mussolini was supposed to arrive? And he is silent?
His vain infatuations and his physical and moral suffering have turned
him into a rag, with which the Germans buff and shine their boots.

                                                 19 OCTOBER 1943
A nun says to me: "This is a period of great tribulation. We offer God
our sufferings, and we shoulder them willingly. Death itself appears to us

like an open door onto an eternal garden. But those poor people who do not have faith, how much must they suffer! A pain without hope – a horrible thing." The poor humble nun, who is not a person of learning, says it just like that, simply, a great truth.

The same nun recounts that a Jew knocked on the door of a convent. He was accompanied by a woman who had a child in her arms. "Take him," he said, "and if you like, baptize him. If you don't take him, I will kill him and kill myself." The child remained with the nuns. And the two forlorn Jews vanished, looking to escape from the Gestapo.

It is said that on the outskirts of Rome shots are frequently fired in the night. They say it is Communists.

19 OCTOBER 1943

Five thousand members of the Gestapo have descended on Rome. It is said that Rome has been divided into 48 sectors, and that the vampires of the Gestapo must:

1 first, complete the plundering of the Jews;
2 capture officials who have not responded to the invitation;
3 seize young men to put them on work service;
4 take noted Freemasons.

The German Army knew nothing of this invasion of crows. And many of them are apprehensive because they believe that the Gestapo want to watch over German troops. The fact is that certain German officials have procured civilian clothes to save themselves for whenever the German failure comes and they have to prepare for the danger of release. These soldiers believe that if the Allies had offered good terms to Italy when the Fascist regime fell, even Germany would have been enticed to imitate Italy. But they say that Italy was very harshly treated: "Surrender unconditionally." And they became inflexible in war. This, in good measure, derives from the foolishness of "The war continues."

The wife of Prof. Ronchi showed me a circular by Barracu[56] that warns state functionaries to obey their respective ministries. Very severe

[56] Francesco Maria Barracu, the under-secretary of state, released circular no. 25393 of the presidency of the Council of Ministers, with which he directed all state employees to place themselves in the service of the Italian Social Republic according to their ministry. The penalty for not doing so would be

and inhuman penalties are threatened, among them this one: "Reprisals against the assets and families in the case of the persisting resistance of a deserter." Nazism and Fascism will go down in history stained not only by nefarious tyranny but also by remorseless barbarism. They threaten reprisals on innocents! And they find, unfortunately, some Italian cowards who place themselves at the service of the German executioners.

21 OCTOBER 1943

The Allies advance slowly. If they continue at this pace, it will be a few months before their arrival in Rome. And everybody here is anxious for fear of German bullying. Officials, functionaries, young people hidden in homes are full of trepidation, and Jews suffer the greatest anguish. M. showed me a note in which he marked the various locations where he has hidden money and valuables. Everybody is seeking to hide whatever they have that is either precious or compromising. I have received two packages of precious items to hide. The Allies have deployed a "small strategy," losing sight of the large strategy: everybody thought that they would have landed north of Rome; they would thus have quickly liberated Rome and southern Italy from the Germans. But perhaps the Allies thought to keep the German troops occupied here to lighten the pressure on the Russian front. And Italy pays the bill. There is no consideration for this disgraced Italy, overwhelmed in the destruction of people, riches, and monuments ... The Allies have not forgotten that stupid declaration: "The war continues."

I think that unfortunately the stories of nefarious cruelty committed by the Slavs are true. It is horror-inducing. And no reason suffices to pardon them. But there are motives that serve to explain these savage crimes. Fascism had assaulted Yugoslavia for no reason. They say that General Roatta[57] was denounced in the British parliament for acts of cruelty against Greeks and Slavs. He who sows the wind will reap the storm.

---

immediate arrest, removal from office, and notification to the Germans – which as a consequence might bring about any type of reprisal.

[57] Mario Roatta (1887–1968), a general and Italian secret agent, was head of the armed forces from 1941 to 1942 and was then sent to Croatia as commander of the Second Army. In 1943 he was commandant for Rome and surrounding area, from which he later fled with the King and Badoglio. Stripped of any responsibility on 12 November 1943, at the end of the war he was charged with

In the newspapers they now speak of Badoglio as if he were the only person responsible for the Italian catastrophe. The people mainly responsible are Mussolini and the King. Even Badoglio has much responsibility because he did not resist Mussolini and then was incapable of stopping the catastrophe. What was needed was manly readiness when the regime fell. But it is unjust and stupid to attribute to Badoglio the crimes against the Slavs; they were provoked by Fascism.

Clandestine Proclamation of the Christian Democrats
I have been given the 23 October 1943 edition of *Il Popolo*,[58] the clandestine newspaper of the Christian Democrats. I am told that this proclamation was written by Alcide De Gasperi.

25 OCTOBER 1943
There continues at the Propaganda the painful procession of mothers, fathers, functionaries, Jews, officials, young people, etc., who seek and implore help. Unfortunately, there are not sufficient means to satisfy everybody. We recommend hiding and we seek to console the suffering people with a less catastrophic vision of the times. Many young men ask to be taken into the Pope's Palatine Guard, but for 200–300 positions there are many thousands of requests. As best as I can, I make active recommendations.

The war on the Russian front is taking on catastrophic proportions for Germany. Many are enjoying this fact. Some think that at the end there may come a twist – peace between Russia and Germany. They say

---

having hunted down and procured the elimination of anti-Fascist leaders; for having contributed to a war against Yugoslavian partisans in Croatia, without cease and with every violent means; and for not having been able to handle responsibly and with competent leadership the difficult period from 25 July to 8 September 1943. He avoided serving his sentence because he took refuge in Spain and subsequently benefited from an amnesty.

[58] *Il Popolo* is a daily founded in 1923 by Giuseppe Donati as an organ of the Italian People's Party, led by Father Luigi Sturzo. It had a brief life because the Mussolini regime shut it down as a result of its anti-Fascism. It resumed publication clandestinely in 1943. The next year it became the organ of the Christian Democrats and as such continued to publish until 2003; that is, until the Christian Democrats once again became the Italian People's Party.

that Japan is working on this assumption. I hope that Hitler will be constrained to recall part of his forces from Italy. One is assured that there are already some symptoms of this in northern Italy. It would seem, therefore, that the troops active in the south may be recalled and that Rome might soon be cleared.

Yesterday along the Corso I passed an open truck full of young men in black shirts. Sad spectacle! These young men have been educated to hate other Italians; they exalt themselves because they possess weapons, and they are coddled by the Little Republicans as if they have been called to save the homeland. They can – poor victims – stoop to acts of brutal ferocity. What a pity! Don't they know that they are toys in the hands of the Germans?

26 OCTOBER 1943

I would like to note two things:

1 The troubles of the war and of the revolution until now have been contained within the political and military arenas; there is not the usual insurrection against the Church. In fact, the Little Republican press of Rome has always used deferential language toward the Pope. "Romanus" writes serene and sensible articles in today's *Il Giornale d'Italia* about Rome, centre of Christianity, and about Vatican City.

2 The German and Little Republican authorities have so far acted in a correct manner toward the Holy Father and the Holy See. In exempt premises, as a result of the Lateran Pacts, there have been posted little papal flags and an advisory signed by the governor of Vatican City, the German Embassy, and General Stahel, commander of the Roman presidio, which declares their extraterritorial character and the exemption of those premises. In other premises of the Holy See there has been posted a notice – in Italian and German – declaring it the property of the Holy See. This constitutes not so much a right of exemption as a moral safeguard.

In fact, this notice has been placed on the Coazzo holding belonging to the Propaganda. A group of German soldiers had entered a farmhouse with the intent of requisitioning pigs. They saw the notice and left. In religious houses a notice has been posted documenting the dependent character of those houses on the Holy See. It is said that if the Germans want to visit these places, they must first get the consent of the ecclesiastical authorities.

So far, this notice has sufficed to safeguard these houses. We were determined to assure the supply of milk to the 200 young people of Urban College. The milk comes from the Coazzo holding, property of the Propaganda. To avoid any danger, and especially that of the requisitioning of cows (as has happened in other holdings), we have transported seven milk cows to the courtyards and homes adjacent to Urban College, as well as recovering some 15 pigs and other animals, so that a good part of the necessary nourishment is assured for the students. We still hope that this abnormal situation will soon end.

26 OCTOBER 1943

Msgr. Gonzato [Giuseppe] tells me that at Ciampino Airport a mother accompanied by two little daughters had gone to collect some rags. The airport had been bombarded and many curtains had been ripped. She was seen by some German soldiers, with whom there were some Fascist soldiers. The Germans said to the Fascist soldiers: "Shoot that woman." And the Fascists manoeuvred a machine gun and with a hail of bullets killed the woman and mortally wounded a little girl of 12 years. The woman (aged 34) had four children ... What sadness! And it is even greater if it is true that this assassination (this crime cannot be defined otherwise) was carried out by Italians. These are the fruits of an education inspired by "Book and Musket."

26 OCTOBER 1943

This morning Prof. H. came to me. He said he had heard grave news from a German lady who has a contact with the German High Command and thought it opportune to communicate this *sub secreto* [in secret]. The Germans, before leaving, will blow up the gas works, the aqueducts, the bridges over the Tiber, and various buildings. They will leave Rome in a frightening state of ruin.

I responded that I do not believe these catastrophic reports. They swarm from people's obsessive fantasies. Sometimes they are put in circulation for fun. I see it this way: the Germans will do whatever they can that is to their advantage. Now, what advantage would they gain from this destruction? None. The newspapers controlled by the Germans have repeatedly declared and proclaimed that Rome is an open city.

Rome is a universal city; it is the holy city of the Pope, and whoever touches it, touches the world. I think that everything will be resolved without a catastrophe.

Later, Msgr. Monticone[59] told me that today an accord was signed in which Rome would be entrusted to the police of neutral nations. God willing that this news is true! But I find it hard to believe!

26 OCTOBER 1943

The proverb from Scripture has come true – against Hitler and Mussolini: *Lucerna impiorum extinguetur"* [Job 21:17; The lamp of the wicked shall be put out]. I am not talking about their inventions, I just observe the facts. Hitler wanted to weaken England. But instead of landing and striking the enemy at its heart, he has scattered himself all over Europe. And now, under Russian pressure, he must begin to withdraw troops from several fronts. I hope that he will have to withdraw them even from Italy. Mussolini should not have waged war. But if he really wanted or had to, he should not have massacred the army in the Alps and then in Albania and Greece, moving toward Egypt. The great strategists!

It seems that Germany is doing everything to stir up and increase the hatred against itself. They say that prisoners of war deported to Germany cannot easily write to their familes. Even in Rome, mothers and wives, desolate, have come to me to see if it might be possible to solicit some news of their loved ones made prisoner by Germany. The Vatican works miracles in that sense but cannot satisfy everybody.

My niece Maria writes: "Of Giovanni, prisoner in Germany, we have not yet heard any news. From day to day, we live always with the hope of receiving some, but a month has now passed. The only thing that can comfort us is that no prisoner has yet sent news from Germany."

Some say that the Germans are taking revenge by making the Italian people suffer – who are innocent. But day after day one feels the ferment and the will on the part of the Allies to strike down Germany and reduce it to a state in which it can no longer repeat numerous cruelties such as these.

Marvellous Work of the Holy Father Pius XII for Prisoners of War
In the Vatican many offices have been established for correspondence with the soldiers of various armies and with concentration camps. The

---

[59] Giuseppe Monticone, archivist of the Sacred Congregation of the *Propaganda Fide*.

work grows every day, and they have to find new places for the correspondence and for offices for the archives. Even the Vatican Museum has now been assigned to this immense work.

The polyglot Bishop Evreinoff[60] heads this imposing and pacific exercise. The Pope's representatives are mobilized around the world to do research on prisoners and disappeared persons, for the repatriation of prisoners, and to bring aid to the victims of war and other disasters. Vatican Radio lends an extremely precious hand for the diffusion and seeking out of news. The radio transmissions that began in June 1940 in the aftermath of the occupation of Belgium and France, with a few hundred listeners per week, have gradually extended to Australia, Egypt, England, India, Kenya, China, the Belgian Congo, Italian Africa, South Africa, etc. How many anxious hearts are lifted by the inexhaustible charity of the Pope.

The Cowardice of Mercenaries

Today, *Il Lavoro Fascista*[61] has the impudence to write: "COMMUNIST IDIOCIES. In some lower-income neighbourhoods, they continued to besmirch the walls with anti-Fascist graffiti. Human misery, proof of a chronic imbecility before the effulgent beauty of the Fascist Idea and of the mighty work produced by Mussolini for the renewal of Italy across all sectors."

It seems that they are not talking about Communists but simply about men who say "Away with the Germans!" A meeting of the pseudo Council of Little Republican Ministers has established extraordinary provincial tribunals that are empowered to impose extremely severe penalties against:

a) Fascists who have betrayed their oath of loyalty to the idea;

b) those who, after the coup d'état of 25 July 1943 – XXI – have in any way, with words, writing, or otherwise, denigrated Fascism and its traditions;

[60] Alessandro Evreinoff (1877–1959) was born in St Petersburg and consecrated as a bishop in 1936 in the Byzantine rite. During the Second World War he carried out responsibilities as consultant to the Sacred Congregation for the Eastern Church. In 1947 he was elevated to the position of archbishop of Pario.

[61] *Il Lavoro Fascista* was a review published in Rome from 1923 to 1943 by the Confederation of Syndicalist Corporations.

c) those who have in any way committed violence against Fascist persons and property, against those belonging to the organizations of Fascism, or against the things and symbols belonging to same ...

For the crimes referred to in art. 1(a), a penalty of death is imposed. For the crimes referred to in 1(b) and 1(c) is imposed a penalty of imprisonment from 5 to 30 years. The public accuser promotes the official penal action on the request of the head of the provincial organization of the Republican Fascist Party.

Prof. Giglioli, in speaking of a brother of his, told me with horror that according to these regulations, loyal people run the risk of execution – those who gave their support to Fascism for the good it had done but who, now that Italy is in the abyss, by fulfilling a duty contemplated in the Fascist laws had caused the meeting of the Grand Council of Fascism to take place to remedy the disastrous situation to which Mussolini had led Italy. The world reacted with disgust to the sentences of the Russian tribunals. Hitler suppressed his first collaborators. Now a frenzy of desperate men raise on the Italian front a new and malevolent spectre of death ... May God will that Italy does not stain itself with similar infamies!

28 OCTOBER 1943

I went out at night to see how Rome appeared on this anniversary of the march which the Fascist press was at pains to galvanize. It was drizzling. Rome had its usual aspect, serious and withdrawn, with a rare flag here and there in public places. At the Caffè Aragno I could hear voices like those of a demonstration. Drawing closer, I understood that they were shouting "Duce, Duce." It was a group of rowdy Fascists: big young men, an occasional young woman, and the common faces of the "unemployed patriots." Many of those, unemployed, without any resources, and with a propensity for violence, gave themselves over to Fascism – a Fascism that is in its death throes but dies slowly.

The demonstration could not have been more than 50 to 70 people. It was the epilogue of the "great Roman commemoration." They sang "Giovinezza" [Youth] and then dispersed toward Via del Tritone. The people looked at them with cold hostility. Some women fled, frightened. In the distance I heard some prolonged whistling. Beside the demonstrators passed two German tanks. That is the product and significance of today's Fascism. They insist on the treason of the King and Badoglio, and seem to have forgotten that Mussolini was mainly responsible for throwing Italy into the abyss. The King and Badoglio committed the recent wrong of that disgraceful and mendacious declaration, "The war continues." But now Badoglio is like a doctor who is called to the bedside of a desperate dying man. It is not the doctor's fault if the sick man dies.

Msgr. Monticone tells me that the pastor of Boves, in Piedmont, was charged with flushing out and delivering two English prisoners who were being hidden in the town. They threatened to torch the town and had begun their nefarious outrage. The pastor succeeded in finding and handing over the prisoners. The German soldiers then sprayed petrol on the pastor and burned him alive.[62]

Today Father Wang told me that at Mount Mario two farmers were executed because arms had been found in their homes. Then a ditch was dug on site and the cadavers were buried. The German soldiers, once their work was done, lit a cigarette and left …

Manzoni recalled the Longobards. But their descendants, in war, are not that dissimilar. Of late, Hitler and his followers have become bestially enraged against the Jews. Yet one cannot forget that, on the whole, the Germans are a great people. One cannot forget that Catholic Germans are admirable, by character and culture, and that German missionaries are not inferior to missionaries from any other nation.

I have known Italian soldiers in Italy and abroad, and I can say that they, the vast majority of them, are human. But it must yet be said, with bowed head, that some, in union with other delinquents, have stained themselves with horrendous cruelty. Today, the German people are, like the Italian people, victims of a terrible tyranny and of an adverse foreign policy that would like to keep a people of 80 million persons in chains. As for the rest, on the subject of barbarism, he who is without sin should cast the first stone. Even the so-called "gentle Latin blood" has committed these atrocities, which make one hang one's head, in shame.

The painter Efisio Oppo, vice-president of the Universal Exposition in the Ostiense quarter, tells me that the offices of the exposition have been

---

[62] In reality, the terrible events at Boves have much larger and darker dimensions than those narrated here. The Germans carried out the first mass executions of civilians since the beginning of the Resistance. The slaughter took place on 19 September 1943 and involved the barbarous assassination of 32 civilians.

vandalized. They had seen a deliberate targeting and barbaric pleasure in the destruction. There he met a German official whom he had known in Germany through study and art. The official was sad and mortified by the spectacle of that barbaric destruction. Even the Church of Sts Peter and Paul suffered some damage. A grenade had ripped open the cupola. From every corner I hear tell of raids, plunder, and armed harassment. Everybody awaits the coming of the Allies, even though they know they are foreigners; but they trust that the Allies will not commit many abuses, trampling on all the laws. Nobody has created more propaganda for the Allies than the German invaders themselves.

29 OCTOBER 1943

The external ruin of Italy is the consequence and mirror image of an interior disorientation; the soul is sick, confused, taken up in a kind of diffused frenzy. On the basis of certain dispositions that are called laws emanating from the self-styled Little Republican Government and on the declarations made in Rome last night by a hallucinating or delinquent assembly, the members of the Grand Council of Fascism should be executed. Why? Because they are accused of treason, having provoked in the night sitting of 25 July the fall of Mussolini. But they were not conspirators. They exercised a right and a duty. Mussolini had placed himself outside the law, casting Italy into the chasm of war without first having convoked and heard the Grand Council of Fascism. He had failed to recognize, in the most important and truly crucial moment of the new history of Italy, the high constitutional body that he himself had created. Having witnessed Italy adrift, the Grand Council requested to be convoked to see how to confront the situation. Naturally, the session resulted in a formidable indictment against the pseudo-strategist, full of defeats. But this is not treason, and it is not conspiracy: it is a legal act determined by an indispensable moral imperative. Now it is sad indeed that the many members of the Grand Council of Fascism must be executed. Some are already in the hands of the Fascist Little Republicans; others remain hidden. I firmly hope that this horrendous crime will not take place. Besides, we are talking about honourable men, in large part, who gave their entire support to Fascism until it degenerated, and they had the civic courage to oppose it, at least, before ultimate disaster. In Russia and Germany there have been killings that have the character of assassination. God willing that nothing similar will happen in Italy.

29 OCTOBER 1943

There is an insistent rumour that Rome will be declared a neutral city, with a zone of respect around it of 30 kilometres. Thus Rome will be attached to the sea. It would be governed by an international police force comprised of Italians but commanded by citizens of neutral nations. *Faxit Deus!* [May God make it so!]. One would be able to prepare on neutral ground for the peace conference.

29 OCTOBER 1943 [SIC]
30 OCTOBER 1943 [SIC]

Today the director of typography of the Island of Liri came to see me. He told me that he had buried underground the printed edition of my *Memories of China*. He says that the Germans had taken away the chains of the machines; they destroyed all the wool that was in the paper mill, valued in the millions. He added, "Nobody has generated more propaganda in favour of the Allies than the Germans have. They rob us of everything."

An official whom I knew at Fiume tells me that he was charged with leading an inquiry for A.R. He found that seven million lire of funds destined for welfare projects had been tampered with. Bocchini called him and told him to burn the report because Il Duce did not want any scandals. He added that he had to be careful because if he had refused, it would be prison for him.

Feast of All Saints

Rome has its usual aspect: an occasional tank and small groups of German soldiers maintain a cloud of sadness over the face of Rome. There always remains the tragedy of the officials, the functionaries, the Jews, and the young people who keep themselves hidden. There continues at the Propaganda the influx of men and women seeking help and counsel. This day reminds me of the Feast of All Saints of 1917 and the rout of Caporetto. Back then, the Italian spirit collected itself and got up; and on the Piave was erected an impenetrable wall of chests. In Padua, on All Souls in 1917, I met Ojetti and D'Adamo,[63] commissioner of civil

---

[63] Agostino D'Adamo was, to be exact, director of the General Secretariat for Civilian Affairs in the Italian Supreme Command during the Second World War. Costantini speaks about him in his book *Foglie Secche. Esperienze e memorie di un vecchio prete* (Rome: Tipografia artistica, 1948), 263, and refers to him with the title of "Commendatore."

affairs. "We shall return," everyone said. "With arms or for peace?" asked D'Adamo. "With arms." And we did return. Our victory on the Piave in June and October 1918 represented the key turning point of all the previous wartime events. On the Piave they prepared for a decisive victory, even for the Allies of the time. Then England, France, and America wanted to disavow at Versailles the merit and the rights of Italy. And thus they sowed the evil seed of this second and disgraced war. Even this time, with the fall of Fascism and with the armistice, a great blow was struck against Germany. But I fear that even this time the sacrifice of Italy will be lost. At Caporetto the weakness of the flesh gave way, but the spirit reawakened immediately. Today even the spirit has died. And Italians tear at one another. They speak of a future republic. It is certain that the King himself, stubborn and cynical, will be buried, overwhelmed by the rancour of the entire nation. But the dynasty? The hereditary prince, unhappily, is not of great character..

You will rise again, poor dear Italy; you will re-enter the current of your great history; but it will take several generations to recreate the conscience of Italians and forge a new character. Dishonour is especially hard to erase. Humility is required. We ruined ourselves and made ourselves a joke around the world with the megalomania of Mussolini and with the dogpack around him who knew nothing but to bark at, applaud, and exaggerate his deficiencies. Humility cannot be preached to a nation. But one can preach it to individuals; it is they who comprise the nation. To remake it, it is necessary to remake citizens. Humility, probity, work – in a word, "fear of God." No longer "Book and Musket," this aberration, this barbaric "Prussianism" has been transported onto gentle Latin soil, but it is necessary to urge the Christian re-education of children.

THE MOSCOW CONFERENCE   2 NOVEMBER 1943
The radio last night communicated the decisions of the conference held in Moscow by the representatives of America, England, and Russia. Even the China of Chiang Kai-shek signed onto those decisions. One of the conditions laid down for peace affected and profoundly saddened me: affairs concerning Italy will be discussed and regulated by a commission of which Greece and Yugoslavia are to be members. This is a supreme shame inflicted on poor Italy, the shame that as a nation it has never suffered! It has instead created Roman *aequitas* and announced the principles of *parcere victis*. We have been vanquished, and we know – *vae*

victis.[64] But this saying was not uttered by a Roman. Our enemies do not have the blood that runs in the veins of a people who are overwhelmed but most noble. About this wretched decision one can offer four considerations:

1 The enemies punish Italy without thinking that it itself is a victim. The guilty are Mussolini, the King, Badoglio, and the Senate. They – and not Italy – pursued or allowed to be pursued a reckless and criminal policy.
2 One detects in this decision disrespect and personal pique against Mussolini and Fascism. But this is undignified.
3 It is not really Greece and Yugoslavia that defeated Italy. Greece and Yugoslavia are flies on the driver; and besides, victory is not yet concluded. It would have sufficed, in any event, that the judges would sit at the tribunal table and not the little ushers.
4 If we begin like this, a super-Versailles is being prepared that will contain in itself the germs of a new revolt and a new war. We must aspire to justice, not vendetta and not personal rancour.

5 NOVEMBER 1943

I learned today from a very authoritative source that the project of making Rome a neutral city was well underway. But then it fell to pieces because of the opposition of Mussolini, who said of it that they should not entertain possible fantasies over a new state, that in some way it could have appeared as a type of resurrection of the dominion of the Popes, putting the Conciliation under discussion once again. To be sure, it would be a misfortune for the Church and for Italy to resuscitate the phantom of temporal dominion. But in the words of Mussolini one hears the rancid anticlericalism of the agitator of the Red Week at Ancona.[65]

---

[64] The two expressions mean, respectively, "to be indulgent with the defeated" and "woe to the vanquished."

[65] The Red Week [*Settimana rossa*] of Ancona refers to the month of May 1914, when, at the congress of the Socialist Party, Mussolini pressed his revolutionary line in contrast to the bourgeois/reformist wing of the same party. His intervention contributed to the announcement of strikes and popular insurrections, in which he did not participate personally but supported in his writings in *Avanti!* [Forward!], the party's daily paper, of which he was director.

The night of 5 November four bombs were dropped on Vatican City.[66] This has raised in everyone a sense of profound indignation. The newspapers raise shouts of horror and protest. Who committed this nefarious outrage? The Allies blame the Germans; the Germans blame the Allies. Who is to blame? *Is fecit cui prodest?*[67] It is a common opinion that it is about an anticlerical outburst and that one must look for the culprits in the hooliganism that slithers deep within Fascism. Many remember the insults of Farinacci against the Vatican.

This evening around 7 PM I saw in Piazza Venezia a group of people who were talking loudly, shouting and singing. "Who are they?" I asked a gentleman who, along with others, were contemplating this uproar. He replied, "They are Fascists who left the assembly that was convened today. I think they are making propaganda to promote membership." The mob circled around Piazza Venezia and then formed a column and headed toward the Corso. There were probably around 200–300 – blackshirts, graduates, city folk, young men, and the occasional young woman. They were waving Japanese and German flags, and perhaps even Italian ones. I could not distinguish them well because it was dark. They were going toward Corso Umberto, shouting "Duce, Duce." People watched them, cold and hostile. After lots of propagandas, lots of money spent, the membership drive had very limited success.

THE ROMAN PEOPLE RUSH TO ST PETER'S SQUARE

"Just as happened after the two aerial bombardments over Rome, the Roman population even this time – after the aerial bombardment of Vatican City – wanted to demonstrate its filial devotion to the Supreme Pontiff."

---

[66] On the aerial bombardment, see the note of Mons. Tardini and the subsequent positions taken, in *Le Saint Siège et la guerre mondiale, novembre 1942 – décembre 1943*, vol. 7 of *Actes et documents du Saint Siège relatifs à la seconde guerre mondiale* (Vatican City: Libreria editrice Vaticana, 1973), 688–707.

[67] This Latin expression, cited from memory, is found in Seneca's tragedy *Medea* at verses 500–1. Translated, it means "Who committed the crime is the person to whom it brings advantages."

10 NOVEMBER 1943

The lawyer Arpesani[68] of Milan tells me that up there, there is a whiff of the five days. Many Milanese have taken refuge in the mountains, and in the city there has been organized a kind of ancient Carboneria, which assists the irregular army. It is commanded by a general and officials.

18 NOVEMBER 1943

The civil war is getting more and more bitter. Yesterday at Verona the reconstruction program of Republican Fascist Italy was published. Fascism is transforming itself, repudiating the many errors of the past. The program invites Italians, especially the youth, to again go to war against the foreigner. But what game are they playing? There are two foreigners that have invaded poor Italy: the Germans and the Allies. Everybody, in desperation, wants the Allies to come, trusting they will be able to breathe the air of freedom a little more. And the Fascists would have to find the deluded, the fanatics, or the paid-off to find those with the courage to invite Italy to go to war under German command once again. Almost everybody is refusing, either going into hiding or taking to the mountains. We are also not without acts of terrorism committed by Germans and some Italians. Mussolini is nothing but a ghost at the gates of a cemetery.

23 NOVEMBER 1943

Last night around 8 PM a vast and distant bombardment could be heard. I went up to the terrace. In the direction of Ciampino Airport, you could see luminous rockets that in clusters lit up in the sky and slowly

---

[68] Giustino Arpesani (1896–1980), a lawyer, Italian politician, and diplomat, was a member of the Liberal Party from 1921 to 1947, when he left the party after being named an ambassador. He worked toward the political resurgence of the parties opposed to Fascism, which led to the crisis of 25 July 1943. He was the Liberal representative on the Committee for National Liberation for Northern Italy [Comitato di Liberazione Nazionale per l'Alta Italia; CLNA]. He participated in the Resistance and took part with Raffaele Cadorna, Riccardo Lombardi, and Achille Marazza in the group that met with Mussolini on 25 April 1945 to propose an agreement. He was under-secretary to the Presidency of the Council in the government led by Ferruccio Parri and in the first government led by Alcide De Gasperi, and was plenipotentiary ambassador of Italy in Argentina from 1947 to 1955, and then held the same position in Mexico.

descended. The bombardment continued with loud thuds. Rome was enveloped in darkness.

In Rome, a sad and disheartened spirit continues to prevail. The feeling of almost liking the Allies has gradually grown colder; this eternal and useless waiting and this curious strategy that has caused the Allies to land in the south of Italy to come to the north has elicited criticism and contempt. They say that Rommel and Kesselring[69] are laughing over it. In the meantime, in Rome the fear of manhunts, growing hardship, and a sense of fatigue persists. Young men, moreover, who have gone into hiding, suffer in the mountains as a result of the intemperate season and for the lack of food. At the front, German troops destroy everything, even the olive groves. The Germans swan around Rome as if they owned the place. And the Little Republican Fascists huddle around them like domesticated dogs.

On the eighteenth of this month the lawyer Suppiej,[70] the former national councillor, came to see me. He was beaten down. An honest

[69] Albert Kesselring (1888–1960), the German field marshal who directed the aerial bombardment of Poland and France in 1939–40. In 1942 he was sent to the coast of Sicily with the task of maintaining a connection with the African front commanded by Rommel. After 8 September 1943 he directed the retreat of German troops from the south to the north of Italy. He then positioned his troops at Cassino, stopping the advance of the Allies for an extended period. When Rome was liberated, he had to retreat slowly to the so-called Gothic Line. It was during this period that he shared responsibility for the massacre at the Fosse Ardeatine. In 1945 he took command of the Western Front in Germany, demonstrating ability in the attempt to save an increasingly critical situation. He was captured, tried, and condemned to death in 1947, but the penalty was commuted first to life imprisonment and then to 20 years' imprisonment, which was ultimately reduced to five years' imprisonment.

[70] Giorgio Suppiej (1897–1982), a Venetian lawyer, was head of the secretariat of the National Fascist Party for the province of Venice for about ten years and then assumed the responsibilities cited above. Marked with a strong Christian faith, he represented the Catholic-moderate wing in the heart of Fascism and defended Catholic Action against the aggression perpetrated by the squadrists in Venice. His life was in danger after his refusal to accept any position in the government of the Social Republic constituted by Mussolini. He found a hidden refuge in the home of Cardinal Massimi in Rome until the liberation of the capital from the Germans. He then resumed his profession of law, which he had suspended as a result of his other responsibilities.

soul, he had adhered to Fascism sincerely. He had been named vice-secretary. He closed his lawyer's office in Venice. He did not profiteer from Fascism. And now he finds himself thrown out onto the street. He said to me, "What to do? I do not intend to follow Mussolini." I replied, "There is nothing to do. Remain in the shadows because you did not stain yourself by plundering the finances of the state as many Fascists have done. Await new days with confidence. Ella is young and can still work." He replied, "They offered me the position of president of the X Company; I did not accept because the activity of the company would be reduced to paying salaries to me and the staff."

Speaking of Mussolini, I talked about the good he had done at the beginning, after which he lost himself in infatuation. According to Nietzsche's theory, he thought he was an infallible superman. In Germany they inebriated him, and he lost himself, leading the nation to perdition.

24 NOVEMBER 1943

The newspapers are publishing an article entitled "Liberty." They have the courage to talk about liberty, those who until only yesterday tyrannically suppressed it and who today are the shoeshine boys of the Germans.

After throwing the paper to the ground, M. says: "Clowns! They are like a bank manager who, after robbing the bank he has brought to bankruptcy, turns to the creditors and says, 'Give me your money; from now on I will be very honest!' Clowns!"

24 NOVEMBER 1943

Someone has sent to me a clandestine manifesto containing the following excerpt: "YOUNG MEN OF ROME, let us unite to put down the remnants of the Fascist mob, exponents of corruption and misery, who in these recent days, supported by the *Landsknecht* of Hitler, make a display of ridiculous arrogance, launching their most recent and most vile insult against the dignity of the Italian people.

YOUTH MOVEMENT FOR ITALIAN RECONSTRUCTION"

25 NOVEMBER 1943

There is talk of the Constituent Assembly that will be convoked in northern Italy at the end of December. It has been affirmed that it will not be a party meeting ... Poor Italy, how far she has fallen! They talk of the Constituent Assembly while almost half of Italy is invaded by the Allies and the other part, in the north, is dominated by the Germans! Rome, the Mother of Law, ashamedly covers her face – at the defeat in the war, at the chaos of the civil war, to which is now added this juridical "bluff," this solemn hypocrisy that surpasses the byzantinism of the decadent court of Constantinople. What kind of juridical value could a pseudo Constituent Assembly possibly have, convoked in such circumstances? The dishonour for which we have had to hide our faces to the world was not enough; they had to add this unprecedented juridical abuse. It is known that Mussolini has neither sense nor juridical education. But around him is there nobody who can make him understand this enormity? It is a Babel, not just of languages but also of ideas. In the meantime, it is true that the Fascists have disavowed the Fascist program.

FROM A LETTER OF ALCIDE DE GASPERI

27 NOVEMBER 1943

"Cordial thanks for the good wishes you forwarded from my home; I have to thank you also for the produce that you offered to my little ones. May the Lord bless and repay you." If the Christmas at Fiume was called the Christmas of blood, what will ours be called? The duration of this trial has made it extremely painful and the peregrinations in search of a quietude that cannot be found hardens the temper but exhausts the nerves.

29 NOVEMBER 1943

I am sad and worried for the turn that justice is taking in the so-called Italian Social Republic. When one substitutes law for arbitrary measures and an objective sense of justice for vendetta, one has fallen into the worst kind of barbarism. We are talking about a wartime tribunal in which the judges, apart from two or three lawyers, are squadrists and workers, without education or legal training. And these people have to judge men like Federzoni, De Stefani, etc., with the power to condemn them to death. At Ferrara they have killed 12 to 14 hostages – respectable and innocent people. They killed them in reprisal for the assassination of a fascist leader.[71] The bodies of the executed were – they say

---

[71] The Fascist leader was Igino Ghibellini, a *federale* of Ferrara, later assassinated by the Communists. As a reprisal, 11 people were killed on 15 November 1943 in front of the Estense Castle, located in the centre of the city.

– exposed in the piazza. Owing to the merciful intervention of Archbishop Bovelli,[72] they were then buried.

4 DECEMBER 1943

The heads of the nations coalesced against Japan – Churchill, Roosevelt, Chiang Kai-shek – held a conference in Cairo and published their program for the prosecution of the war. According to this plan, Japan must return all occupied territories, including Formosa, Korea, etc. But haven't they understood that Japan must survive? That it cannot remain suffocated on its old islands? That it must every year digest half a million men over and above the demographic increase? It would be good if Japan just renounces its domination of China by military means, because it has no right and because China cannot offer it space for its demographic excess, with China itself a country restricted by its own rising population. But why wasn't there at least an admission of the theoretical principle of the right to life? Why didn't they say that Japan can, *servatis servandis*, expand elsewhere? With these proposals, if they can win and dictate the peace, it will be a peace of reprisal. They speak of the collaboration of nations, but they understand this collaboration – as Smuts[73] has clearly said – to be a regime in which America, England, and Russia hold the levers of power. The situation has simply been reversed: Hitler said the same thing in relation to Europe. There is nothing different except the following, that the Allies have more respect for the law and reject the action against the Jews and other barbarous deeds. As for the rest, it's more or less the same thing. Poor humanity, overcome by egotism and by the *sacra auri fames*.[74] Words of justice and equitable peace are only a label to let contraband through.

DECEMBER 1943

A few days ago a rumour circulated that the police, with the consent and assistance of the German authorities, have raided Braschi Palace,

[72] Ruggero Bovelli (1875–1954), originally from the Diocese of Todi, was archbishop of Ferrara-Comacchio from 1929, after having served as bishop of Modigliana and then also of Faenza.

[73] Jan Christian Smuts (1870–1950), a philosopher, politician, and soldier who was twice prime minister of South Africa. He was against racial separation in his country. In 1941 he was made a field marshal in the British army.

[74] "Hunger for sacred gold."

arresting many Fascist leaders and uncovering a vast network of organized crime. They even talk of a room with instruments of torture. A notorious Fascist was the ringleader of these delinquents who, under the aegis of Fascism, oppressed the poor Roman population. It was revealed that many acts of brigandage and blackmail emanated from Braschi Palace. Popular fantasy of course creates legends. But the fact of the seizure at Braschi Palace supports them. Everybody has a sense of relief, and Count Giorgio Cini[75] said to me, "We have fallen so low. Fascism has degenerated to the point that we have to seek recourse to the intervention of the Germans."

6 DECEMBER 1943

On the 4th a group of three or four persons met one another in the Piazza di Spagna, across from the Spanish steps that lead up to Trinità dei Monti, exactly where the bus stops. A Fascist youth passed them, and it seems that someone in the group said something regarding his black shirt. The youth took out a revolver and shot one of the group, a young magistrate, who then collapsed. He was assisted and brought to a pharmacy, where he died on arrival.

Today, one newspaper names some Fascist delinquents who had built their nest at Braschi Palace. At the head of the list is the *federale* Bardi with the notorious Pollastrini.[76]

[75] Giorgio Cini (1918–49), an Italian entrepreneur, was the only son of Count Vittorio Cini and the actress Lyda Borelli. Giorgio obtained a degree in jurisprudence at the University of Padua in 1940, and the following year a degree in political science. After his studies, he dedicated himself to the family businesses. In June 1944 he obtained the liberation of his father from Dachau concentration camp, where he had been interned the year before. After negotiating with the Third Reich, Giorgio brought his father to Italy, escaping by plane. In June 1945, with the war concluded, he helped his father once again (his father had been a minister in the Fascist regime) to rebut the charges presented by the High Court of Justice for Sanctions against Fascism, succeeding in obtaining their dismissal. He died in an airplane accident in Cannes in 1949. In his memory, Vittorio dedicated the Giorgio Cini Foundation of Venice and a cultural institute in Ferrara to his son.

[76] This refers to the Fascist group in Rome responsible for torture and abuse of every kind, against which the police of Rome intervened with the support of the Germans. The group comprised 120 men and was called the Armed Guard of

6 DECEMBER 1943

The snail strategy of the Allies is advancing with difficulty against the winter line organized by the Germans. The Eighth Army is camped at Pescara; the Fifth at Cassino. They gain a kilometre or so a day. Destruction, slaughter, scorched earth. Some think that the Allies are not interested in the rapid resurgence of a viable Italy. "They are leaving us to cook in our own juice, according to the phrase attributed to Churchill. At Rome the Allies are awaited with a painful impatience to emerge from the terror of the Germans and the criminals camouflaged as Fascists. The tragedy of the families of soldiers, functionaries, and young men in hiding has dragged on for too long. For many, there are unemployment and hunger as well.

6 DECEMBER 1943

This evening I met the artist Laurenzio.[77] He had a purse. "See?" he said to me, raising the black bag. "I went to get some flour. I transform my sketches, the product of my hard work, into foodstuff. Oil is at 300 lire a litre, wine at 30 lire, flour at 40 lire a kilogram, etc. But it doesn't matter. I have to live. Besides, what will I do tomorrow with these bills of 1,000 lire? Best to spend them in the black market. I went to his studio. His printing press was covered with bags of beans and chickpeas. Among the sketches on a table, a carton of potatoes. On the ground, an open box with a few packages. "It's flour," he tells me, "and I am airing it out so it doesn't go bad." On a shelf is a little gas oven: "I cook as best I can, alone." The bell then rang. The painter warmly received a man; they went into a small room and left something in the corner.

VICTOR EMMANUEL III   6 DECEMBER 1943

Nobody wants to know about either him or his son Umberto. The Little Republicans of the north have already thrown monarchy and dynasty into the sea. The Italians of the south are less radical. It seems that they

---

Braschi Palace. It was commanded by Guglielmo Pollastrini, who was put in that position by the Roman *federale* Gino Bardi. The two men, along with another 54, were tried and convicted, respectively, to 28 and 22 years, six months. Bardi also had to pay monetary reparations for his crimes.

77 Laurenzio Laurenzi (1878–1946), an artist and graduate of the Accademia delle Belle Arti of Rome, created many works inspired especially by landscapes of the countryside, with a predilection for his home region of Assisi.

would accept a regency with the little six-year-old prince. It seems that this would be the best solution. The monarchy forms a stable base, a source of law, a guarantee against the agitation in which Italy would be thrown at every presidential election. Italy, united for nearly a century, does not yet have a solid and mature political conscience. This is proved by the fact that it allowed itself to be tyrannized by a dictatorship that lasted twenty years; and unfortunately, this is confirmed by the miserable political predicament in which Italy operates today. It is like a serpent writhing uselessly because it has had its spine cut in half. In any event, it seems that the King has to go. It is said that he has made himself deaf to this moral imperative.

Poor King! He is certainly a man of culture, of simple life, and of noble family sensibility, but he appears to have been a man bereft of high political principles and religious conscience. The skepticism and absence of any religious principle have rendered him a minor character, a character of little consequence who, entrenching himself behind the material scruple of constitutionality, nearly always did what governments wanted him to do, and ultimately what Mussolini wanted. It is said that once in a while he refused to sign the decrees proposed by Mussolini, but unfortunately he allowed the Italian constitution to be degraded, to which he had sworn to remain faithful. He conceded that the succession to the throne should have the sanction of the Grand Council of Fascism … He signed on to this war without consulting the Senate, the Council of the Crown, or anybody else. He did not determine whether Italy was capable of waging war, and he did not evaluate America's power. He was not equal to the task, and even though he did not want it, he permitted the crime – the true crime – of throwing the nation into the abyss of war, as if he did not need to answer for the life and well-being of the nation.

Once Mussolini fell, he should have abdicated, just as his ancestor Carlo Alberto did. He should have proclaimed his son King or establish a regency with his nephew. Instead, he allowed "The war continues" to be said, even against the Allies. After 25 July, Badoglio should have immediately initiated negotiations with the Allies. Even the Senate, terrorized and mute, has its own serious guilt. I am truly sorry to see this sad end for the King, whom I met various times in the last war. At that time, he was dressed in grey-green, simple, austere, in continual contact with senior commanders and the military hospitals. He could frequently be found at various posts along the front. I saw him one day sitting on a riverbank eating a frugal meal with tins of sardines and bread. His presence animated the armed forces without embarrassing the commanders or interfering with strategic plans. On the tomb of Victor Emmanuel III, could be written, as an epitaph, Shakespeare's words: "The evil that men do lives after them; the good is oft interréd with their bones" [*Julius Caesar*, act 3, scene 2].

7 DECEMBER 1943

The Moscow Conference, Cairo, Tehran … bombastic words, like the dry sound of a far-off thunderstorm that threatens hail and cyclones. Not words of humanity, of Christian sense. They want to destroy their enemies. If the Allies win in a way that allows them to dictate the peace of the world, there will be another terrible illusion.

Christ is ignored and practically disavowed; yet there is no other through whom we can hope to be restored. We understand this in Italy. Mussolini, agitated by his own dark demon, attempted to introduce into Italy a Prussian-type culture. He ruined the Latin spirit of our youths. We must reconstitute the Latin patrimony harmoniously, the *humanitas* and *aequitas* and, as a perfection of these great natural Roman virtues, the *sensus Christi*. Italy will be resurgent, on one condition – that it quenches its thirst at the pure source of its Romano-Christian tradition.

9 DECEMBER 1943

The bombing of Vatican City, beyond the unanimous condemnation of this insane act, has awakened in the entire world a kind of race to express to the Supreme Pontiff sentiments of devotion to his person and admiration for the work that he is carrying out to reduce the horrors of war. The *Osservatore Romano* refers to "huge quantities" of telegrams and letters sent to the Vatican, not just from cardinals and bishops, religious families, Catholic associations and institutes, but also from heads of state and of government, the diplomatic corps, universities, and scientific institutes … all signalling the homage not only of the non-belligerent nations, but also the belligerent states themselves.

The sculptor Canonica wrote me from Pietralla on 9 December 1943: "I beg you to give me some cigars, or a Toscano or a 'Roma'; preferably a Toscano, which here I am not able to have, and it is my only consolation. If you saw the villa, it would make you weep! I no longer even have my bed – it was requested and taken away."

THE VISIT OF COMMENDATORE BATTISELLA

11 DECEMBER 1943

He tells me that his nerves are shot, that he prays, but the war itself raises many religious problems for him which he does not know how to solve. He tells me that he had conversations with a scholar priest; but that these very conversations multiplied his doubts ... I replied, "When we turn to God, we have to bow our heads. We cannot penetrate the many mysteries that surround us. And how can we divine the mystery of mysteries: God? We speak of justice and want to see it realized within our brief lives, while God operates in eternity. Look, you take a mouthful of food. The food in your stomach transforms itself into blood, cells of flesh, bones, nerves, antibodies, lymph cells, etc. How do you explain all that? It is a mystery. Remember the words of Christ: "*Nisi efficiamini sicut parvuli ...*"[78] We have to make ourselves into children, to be small and humble, to see things with the eyes of the innocent, and God will reveal Himself more easily. Read the Gospel. Everything is there. And the Gospel goes for everybody, for the ignorant as much as for the learned, because it is the word that God has revealed to humanity." I gave him my recent book *Jesus Christ: The Way, the Truth, and the Life*. He left somewhat more serene.

THE VISIT OF DIPLOMAT X   12 DECEMBER 1943

We talked about the situation. At a certain point he said to me, "And you, who do you support?" I responded, "*De facto*, I recognize the authority in power, as I did when I found myself in China and governors of various factions succeeded each other. *De jure*, I have to recognized the government of the King. But frankly, I don't like either the government of the King or that of Mussolini. The King and Badoglio fled, provoking a disgraceful "Caporetto" throughout Italy. They declared (one does not know why) that the war would continue, and then they concluded an armistice.

I do not like the government of the so-called Italian Social Republic because it has no legal foundations. It is propped up by the German Army, which has made itself an object of total loathing. Also, Mussolini is the man who brought Italy to ruin, pushing it into the abyss, down from the heights to which he had elevated it. Who could have faith in a

---

[78] Mt. 18:3: "Unless you are converted and become as little children, you shall not enter the Kingdom of Heaven."

man who has failed so sadly? The recent crimes of Fascism (the disgraces of Braschi Palace, the killings in Ferrara and Florence) elicit pure horror. I am not for current governments or with the armies of Germany or the Allies, but for poor Italy. The armies – either one – are foreigners. The English and Americans present themselves today as liberators; but in the meantime they continue to blast Italy by their inhumane strategy. In the message that Mussolini broadcast yesterday on the occasion of the Tripartite Pact, we heard the same rhetorical bluff, but the next period contains, unfortunately, some painful truths: "The continued aerial attacks against large and small Italian cities, the great loss of innocent human lives, and the destruction of monuments that were witness to our creative force in the fields of the spirit will not succeed in subduing the Italian people but will spur hatred and tenacity."

15 DECEMBER 1943

The *Osservatore Romano* reports that "cases containing documents and volumes from the archives and library of the Badia of Montecassino have been taken to the Vatican to avoid exposing them to the consequences of fighting that is unfolding in this region. The cases, consigned on 8 December to Italian authorities by the German authorities, which provided transport from Montecassino to Rome, were entrusted to the Vatican Library, in whose custody they will remain." Other precious memorabilia and monuments coming from various cities have been sent for safekeeping to the Vatican.

THE INEXHAUSTIBLE CHARITY OF THE POPE

20 DECEMBER 1943

This year also the Holy Father has put conspicuous sums at the disposal of pontifical representatives for Christmas disbursements to those who have been most affected by the war. For prisoners in particular, the Pope has sent the following message: "To beloved prisoners of war and to those with them who, far from their dear ones, yearn for the Christmas joys of the domestic hearth, I impart with warm affection Our paternal benediction, with the fervid wish that the peace brought by Jesus Christ to all the oppressed will be ample recompense for their ills and a genuine wish for a renewed Christian prosperity."

P. Chang, a Chinese person, offered assistance to English prisoners and succeeded in escaping from L'Aquila. He came to see me.

A LETTER FROM SWITZERLAND   22 DECEMBER 1943

Exile is difficult, especially for the terrible thought of the sufferings and dangers faced by family members left behind (my family is almost all on that side); but I seek to put up with it in a dignified way, working and praying. My major effort is approaching the youth, who have an immense need of spiritual assistance; in the midst of great difficulties, we can succeed in doing something. May God help us! I dare to ask you, if you have the opportunity, to please relate my situation to the Holy Father, of whom I recall the suffering on his face the last time I saw him; in that expression was the presage of everything we were to suffer. How much do I seek in spirit to be close to you all! But I do not despair! The very immensity of evil that surpasses our imagination reveals the divine design through these terrible experiences. We will rise again. In the infinitesimally small circle of my powers, I set myself to preparing young people for this objective.

                                                            Francesco Carnelutti.

                                                            23 DECEMBER 1943

Ambassador X told me that Mussolini said, "Fascism has been reduced to a rump of *sans culottes*. But I have to rely on them because they are the only ones who remained loyal ..."

Poor Mussolini, he still believes in loyalty! If Providence condemns him to live, he will see what the loyalty of the *sans culottes* will be reduced to!

From the Social Republic arrives news of attempts and assassinations against Fascist leaders and reprisals against innocent victims of these crimes. Here in Rome, it is commonly thought that our worst enemies are self-styled Fascists who spy for and direct Germans in their raids. It is said that the Germans despise these cowards. Groups of hidden soldiers and functionaries resign themselves to giving themselves up to save their families from hunger.

Today an ordinance was released by the German authorities that obliges families by 31 December to declare all members in a census. They say that they are mounting this census to give work to the unemployed. The truth is the following: they want to know the names of the people in hiding, especially Jews and officials. To many families the spectre of hunger is threatened ... Here is the ordinance: "The census will serve as a basis for releasing ration cards that will not, however, be distributed to those who are not enumerated in the census. Those who do not respond to the call, those referred to in the second paragraph, and those – including family members – who aid contravenors either directly or indirectly will have their ration cards withdrawn, cancelled, and not returned."

Poor Rome, poor Italy. And there are Italians who put themselves at the service of the foreigner to impose this heavy yoke on the necks of their fellow nationals.

24 DECEMBER 1943

A sad Christmas Eve. There is a little more activity in the streets; but one sees that the nightmare of a precarious and dangerous situation weighs on people's spirits. The churches are not packed because there will not be many functions.

The Gestapo has returned to Rome. In the city there is a mute agitation and a growing malaise. The snail strategy of the Allies has disillusioned and upset everybody. They are fighting on the front from Ortona to Cassino without penetrating the formidable German lines. The soldiers and functionaries in hiding can no longer withstand it. Some place themselves cautiously in circulation; but rumours of Communist attempts, cruel repression, raids, and mass arrests create an atmosphere of tension, suspicion, and repressed anger. Colonel Scarpa, from Veneto, comes to see me sometimes; he announces himself with the name of Gennaro. Even the academic Piacentini was imprisoned for four days at Regina Coeli [a Roman prison]. There were raids and arrests at both Lombard and Russico colleges. At the Russico a young Jew died of fright.

Germany and the Allies wage their "own" war, and they do so at the cost of an Italy that is martyred, mutilated, and divided by two antagonistic governments who revile and fight each other. Never before has the bitter Dantean passage been more true than today:

Ah, servile Italy, grief's hostelry,
Ah, ship unpiloted in the storm's rage,
No mother of provinces but of harlotry![79]

---

[79] CC: *The Divine Comedy, Purgatory*, 6:78–80, trans. J. Ciardi.

CHRISTMAS 1943

Yesterday I was at the Vatican to offer the Pope greetings. I had the feeling of emerging from a tempestuous sea and being deposited on an island of salvation. The vision of a world at war was present in our spirits and weighed on our hearts, but we sought to lift ourselves above the earthly horizon, to the vision of God. The beautiful face of the Pope, thin and illuminated by an interior spirituality, was serene but sad. He delivered two addresses: one in response to the greetings of the cardinals and the other to the entire world.

CHRISTMAS 1943

The fourth Christmas during the war, a squalid Christmas, a Christmas full of the contrast between its Christian significance and reality. The weather is nice enough, but spirits are in anguish. It seems as if we are walking in the dark, with the danger of falling over into an abyss.

ROOSEVELT'S CHRISTMAS MESSAGE   26 DECEMBER 1943

Yesterday evening I listened to Roosevelt's Christmas message: prattle, prattle, prattle ... Not a concept of sincere humanity and justice. He says that he does not want to render the German people slaves. Thank you very much! But no human word for Japan. One feels the old "commercial" antagonism between America and Japan. It is said that they are waging war to give the world peace, if not a just peace, a durable one under the control of the Great Powers: America, England, Russia. They talk of liberty. But who believes them? We do not forget the promises of Wilson, a true exemplar of the pseudo-prophet of ingenuity and unsubstantiated doctrinairism. We do not forget, we cannot forget Versailles. We went in with half a million dead and with a shining victory; and we were kicked by these same gentlemen who today are promising seas and mountains, and who recently have been tough, cruel, and obtuse against our Italy. It asked for mercy, but that was rejected with the demand of unconditional surrender. Certainly, the Americans will help us because they have a generous spirit, especially the Christians, who feel deep in their hearts the irrepressible voice of Christ, charity, and brotherhood.

America and England have one excuse: that because of the King's foolishness and Mussolini's criminal infatuation, Italy declared war. We are vanquished and we endure our fate, but at least they could have left us the spiritual freedom not to believe in the passionate love of our enemies who have imposed an inhuman armistice.

VOICES FROM FRANCE   25 DECEMBER 1943

Yesterday evening the French spokesman on Radio London said, "Hitler gave the order to seize the Pope and bring him as a hostage to Germany. Kesselring had to execute the order. But the ambassador to the Holy See made the observation that this would cause the whole world to rise against Germany; and Germany is not strong enough to confront this new challenge ..."

ECHOES OF THE ADDRESS OF THE HOLY FATHER

27 DECEMBER 1943

The Christmas messages of the Holy Father Pius XII have had a vast and profound resonance of consensus and have given a measure of relief to oppressed spirits. There were no words of criticism, but rather a chorus of homage (naturally less from the "Fascist regime"). Everybody has noted the finesse with which the Holy Father alluded to the bombing of the Vatican. The radio of the pseudo Italian Republic, giving a summary of the message to the Sacred College referred to "solemn treaties" rather than "solemn treaty." But all have understood that the allusion was to Italy and represented a handful of troublemakers. Two points were particularly noted: the condemnation of the methods of war and the program of a prospective peace, not as an arithmetic result of measures of power but as a moral fact founded on respect for the rights of all people, great and small.

27 DECEMBER 1943

Speaking of the papal message, the former prefect Faccini said, "A magnificent address. In its first part it is pastoral, with a broad sociological vision. In its conclusion it is precise and political, illustrating those Christian principles that alone can offer the base on which to build a new order and peace."

THE THOUGHTS OF AN ARCHITECT   28 DECEMBER 1943

The architect Giovannoni[80] tells me: "Mussolini fell because he did not understand men." True. One can, however, complete the observation as

[80] Gustavo Giovannoni (1873–1947), an engineer, historian, and architectural critic, was one of the first promoters of the first Faculty of Architecture in Italy (in Rome) in which he held the professorship of Recovery and Restoration of Monuments. With Marcello Piacentini, he founded the review *Architettura e Arti decorative* in 1921.

follows: he did not understand them because he never evaluated the moral element. The architect told me that young students are absent minded, without a strong faith in whatever ideal. They are only interested in career ...

Mussolini, in his totalitarian vision of the state, said, "Everything for the State. Nothing outside or against the state ..." People applauded, and thus we have come to these days of shame, decay, and skepticism.

29 DECEMBER 1943

It seems that a second front is opening up. Perhaps they will attempt a landing on two regions of France, from the Mediterranean and the Atlantic. Corsica is full of "de Gaullists"[81] and the Azores seem also to figure in the strategic plan of the Allies. Stalin insists on the following point of view, that the Italian front matters too little to reduce the German pressure on Russia.

A MOTHER   30 DECEMBER 1943

Today's *Tribune*[82] contradicting assertions broadcast on foreign radio, says that "The 19 of the Grand Council – the traitors – will be judged and found guilty ..." They pronounce the verdict before the judgment. I still want to hope that Italy will be spared from such a shame and the men are saved, among whom there are truly honourable and innocent men. It is said that Ciano, who sought refuge at the German Embassy after 25 July, was transferred to Germany, to Munich. He realized quickly, however, that he was a prisoner. His wife Edda[83] worked hard

---

[81] The name derives from the French general and politician Charles de Gaulle (1890–1970), who while exiled in London during the German occupation of France in the Second World War exhorted the French to resist Nazism. He was the head of the provisional government of the republic from 1944 to 1946 and returned to active politics in 1958, when he succeeded in reforming the French constitution into its current form. He was president of the French Republic from 1959 to 1969.

[82] Roman daily published from 1883.

[83] Edda Mussolini (1910–95) was one of the five children of Benito Mussolini and Rachele Guidi. In 1930 she married Count Galeazzo Ciano, with whom she had three children: Fabrizio, Raimonda, and Marzio. A Germanophile, Edda always supported her father's policy regarding the Second World War, in contrast to her husband who was not convinced about the conflict. On 25 July 1943

to save him. But it is said that Hitler gave her to understand, brutally, "that she had to choose between her husband and her father." It is confirmed that De Vecchi leads a group of patriots in Piedmont; that Federzoni and Bottai have not been captured. De Bono is in prison.

There is someone whom the newspapers have never mentioned: "the widow Ciano."[84] From time to time I think of her because I see in her a mother who must suffer immensely. In the spring of this year she told me that she would like to see me. I went to see her. She spoke of spiritual things, of matters of conscience. She seemed to be a serene woman, though she was in mourning because of her recent widowhood. She was very proud of her son, and she enjoyed being a holder of the Order of the Most Holy Annunciation ... Poor Lady, how hard and dark these hours must be, in which she sees the whole shining world collapsing. But her son's life put in danger! Many friends have either abandoned her for fear of compromising themselves or have turned against her.

Ciano voted for the Grandi motion of non-confidence in Mussolini, a choice that cost him a death sentence after the trial at Verona in 1944. Edda had furious arguments with Il Duce in a vain attempt to save her husband, who was executed on 11 January 1944. She then fled to Switzerland from where she was extradited on the request of the Italian government that was established at war's end. She was sentenced to two years of confinement on the island of Lipari, but benefited from an amnesty after serving a year of her sentence. She was later reunited with her children.

[84] The mother of Giangaleazzo Ciano, Carolina, was widowed in 1939 on the death of her husband Costanzo, an admiral, president of the Chamber of Deputies and then of the Chamber of Fasci and Corporations.

The Year 1944

It is a squalid New Year's. Stores closed, public spaces deserted, people silent and sad, German carts and trucks on the road. These vehicles are camouflaged in a yellowish base with dark stripes; they call to mind the skin of certain serpents.

Senator Salata reminded me of the words that Senator Corbino[1] uttered many years ago in the Senate in speaking about scientific discoveries: "In substance, these discoveries are not good for humanity." Unfortunately prophetic words. If only a fraction of a percent of scientific endeavour were put into the service of medicine and human progress. But today it is one hundred percent harmful to life. Science is completely directed at the destruction of life.

At 5 PM General Pugliese's chauffeur told me that the general had been followed and then arrested this morning by the German police in the service of the SS and taken to the infamous building on Via Tasso, ante-chamber of torturous acts.

I later learned with joy that in the evening he managed to get released. After insistent questioning, the general had the good fortune that

---

[1] Mario Orso Corbino (1876–1937), less noted than his younger brothe Epicarpo, became a senator in 1920. He was part of the Liberal Democrati group and then of the Democratic Union.

afternoon of the intervention of the official in charge of that service. The official was passionate about naval shipbuilding and had been familiar in Germany with Pugliese's works on naval architecture. Thus, after an animated technical conversation, he was allowed to leave freely to collect documentation regarding his career record. Occasionally, the Germans show themselves to be more humane than certain Fascists. Their comportment toward the Holy See is correct, and it is becoming increasingly clear that the outrage of the bombing of the Vatican was due to the initiative of the Fascists.

2 JANUARY 1944

This evening, from the Pincio one could hear shellfire in the distance; at one point, a great crash went up from the Piazza del Popolo. Drawing closer to the parapet of the Pincio, in the company of Ambassador Cerruti, I saw in the vast Piazza del Popolo a column of around 50 tanks moving in the direction of the Corso, proceeding slowly and noisily, equipped with multiple wheels that were turning inside an iron track, which also turned moving the heavy machines forward. They appeared to me armoured monsters with long noses pointed in the air; they were long and thin, probably anti-tank guns. The Germans have given the name Tiger to this type of tank.

In the distance, through a cloudy sky, was the great image of the cupola of St Peter, giving a message of peace, of justice, of suprahuman stability over the homicidal fury and hurricane of death unleashed by men.

The ambassador related to me the following story when he was at Pincio a day or two ago – a story that he learned from two different and authentic sources. A woman and her little girl found themselves at the Pincio. A German official passed. He saw the little girl and said to the mother: "Would you permit me to give her a caress?" "Yes, of course!" replied the woman. The official then took a photograph from his wallet of a woman with five children and said, "This was my family. Do you see this girl? She is the spitting image of yours. They all died in a bombardment in Berlin. Would you permit me to kiss your girl?" "Yes, of course!" she replied. The official hugged the girl. He then gave her mother an envelope, with the following recommendation: "Keep this safely for the girl for when she is grown." The official then left. He disappeared amongst the alleyways, then threw himself on a bench and shot himself in the head with a revolver. The woman, on arriving home, opened the envelope. It contained 40,000 lire.

2 JANUARY 1944

The words of the Pope have not been heeded: but there are healthy seeds disseminated all over the world, and they serve at the least to create an attitude and an orientation of spirits.

5 JANUARY 1944

This evening at dusk I stopped to read one of the many posters that are continually placed on the walls. The tricolour design of one proclamation attracted me as much as its brevity. It exhorted Italians to unite with the Social Republic for the honour and future of Italy: "The future is not conquered except with the will. Garibaldi – from the Janiculum – rallies Italians," etc.

A little old man, just after reading the proclamation, looked around and then, winking, remarked under his breath, "Agreed. But a Republic without Germans at home and without Fascists."

6 JANUARY 1944

Epiphany. A cold and brisk day, but disturbed by the hovering ghosts of war and the dark drama of countless families whose members are in hiding, loath to follow the Republic of Mussolini. The drama is often made worse by the threat of hunger. The requirements of the statistics put many people on the cross, especially the few remaining Jews and many of the government's former officials and civil servants.

I went to celebrate the "Pontificale" at Urban College [Collegio Urbano]. An amazing function, a wonderful refuge for the spirit, a miracle of harmony in the wild disorder of the world! My altar servers were alumni representing eight nationalities, some of which were at war with the others. And yet the kiss of peace that they exchanged – indeed, I would say, more affectionate than usual. One feels more than ever the need to express, at least in front of altars, an affirmation of love and fraternity.

Senator Perez was moved. The literary figure Rossi[2] told me that as soon as circumstances permit, he will write an article on this

[2] The reference to the "literary figure," or *letterato* and the fact that his surname is "Rossi" leads to the conclusion that Costantini is referring to Vittorio Giovanni Rossi (1898–1978), an Italian writer who was a foreign correspondent for several papers. Among his works published at the time that Costantini was writing his diary were *Tropici* (Milan: Bompiani, 1934), *Via Degli Spagnoli*

extraordinary spectacle, and on this light, which is a reflection of the great light of Christ and the Vatican.

In the evening I went out briefly, wanting to see Piazza Navona, which during peacetime years was bursting with a festival atmosphere and a laughing garden of children rejoicing for the "Befana." Today, the piazza was deserted and dismal! Returning along Corso Umberto, I saw a column of many German tanks; in the first shadows of evening they seemed to be antediluvian monsters. With the clamour of iron, the tanks moved along toward Via Del Mare. To Ostia? Rumour has it that the Germans are thinking of compressing the front by retreating to the Po River. That rumour seems logical, all the more so since the Germans can retreat honourably.

An Echo of Distant Trouble

Around the year 593, Rome was threatened by the Longobards. Gregory the Great called a consistory. The great saint and Pope, like his predecessor St Leo the Great, who in 452 stopped Attila on the Mincio, left the walls of the city one day, approached the enemy encampment, and met with Agilulfo on the steps of the Church of St Peter. The Pope pleaded and threatened, and Agilulfo bowed in the majestic presence of the great Vicar of Christ. This murky description lives again in our own day as the new Longobards roam, with their *tigers*, around Rome.

In the struggles over the centuries, the voice of the Church has always been the same: it is the voice of innocence oppressed, of trampled rights. It has varied in form down the ages but been constant in its substance. Strong in its own suffering and in the suffering of others, the Church perpetually offers people the opportunity to look into themselves and understand the terrible vanity of evil. Pius XII has the same heart and same courage as his predecessors to defend Rome. He also is worthy to be called, along with St Gregory, "*Dei Consul.*"[3]

(Milan: Bompiani, 1936); *Oceano* (Milan: Bompiani, 1938); and *Pelle D'Uomo* (Milan: Bompiani, 1943). In fact, Rossi knew Costantini and sent him a letter of thanks on 27 May 1942 for agreeing to confirm his son (which can be found in Constantini's letters in the *Epistolario* found in ASCDP, Celso Costantini Collection).

[3] "Consul of God."

8 JANUARY 1944

I saw Count Volpi. He is at his own place but is under surveillance. He has become old and is very sad. He is also very embittered by the thought that so many friends and the Venetian contingent have abandoned him – for whom he procured work and other benefits.

Anfuso,[4] ambassador in Berlin, has come to Italy; and here he opened our eyes. He visited Mussolini but found only the shadow of Il Duce; Kesselring told him that the Germans are nauseated by the Fascist contingent, especially of the criminal element who seek refuge and impunity in Fascism.

I understand that Frugoni[5] has been summoned by Mussolini. It is said that he found him in a state of extreme intellectual and physical deterioration.

12 JANUARY 1944

Around Rome for a few days a rumour has again been circulating that the Germans are preparing to leave, and a few signs may confirm this

[4] Philip Anfuso (1901–63), an Italian politician and diplomat, was initially the German correspondent for the dailies *La Nazione* and *La Stampa*. He participated as a journalist in the Fiume expedition of D'Annunzio. He joined the diplomatic corps in 1925 and occupied various positions abroad. In 1938 he became chief of staff of Minister Giangaleazzo Ciano, his longtime friend. In 1942 he was sent to the legation in Budapest and in 1943 joined the Italian Social Republic, becoming ambassador in Berlin. He was implicated in ordering the assassination of the brothers Nello and Carlo Rosselli and was condemned to death in absentia in Rome in 1945 by the High Court of Justice for Sanctions against Fascism. After the war he sought refuge in France, where he was arrested and detained for two years, whence he fled to Spain. In Italy he was pardoned by decision of the Court of Appeal of Perugia in 1949. He returned to Italy in 1950, joined a far-right organization, the Italian Social Movement [Movimento Sociale Italiano (MSI)], and in 1953 he was elected member of the Chamber of Deputies and then re-elected in two successive legislatures. Filippo Anfuso left an important published memoir entitled *Roma-Berlino-Salò, 1936–1945)*, published in 1950, in addition to a series of books, articles, and writings of a biographical, historical and political nature.

[5] Likely Cesare Frugoni (1881–1978), Italian medical pathologist, professor of medical pathology in Florence, and then of clinical pathology in Padua and finally in Rome (1931–51).

rumour. But a high German official of the s s denied the rumour, saying that the Germans have now strongly reinforced the front in the narrowest part of Italy. "Certainly, we will leave Rome," the official concluded, "but not now. When we leave we will leave Rome without causing damage or destruction. Rome must, however, guard itself against the Communists."

Clerici, whom the Fascists named the chief of police after Senise, was arrested some time ago and brought to a jail in Belluno. He died, and the police explain his death as follows. In prison he dabbled in ironsmith work. By accident, a box of dynamite was mixed with coal. He threw the coal on the fire and the dynamite exploded, killing him.

England has protested against Spain about the Falangists who are fighting against Russia. This may constitute a pretext for landing in Spain.

Many await the internal collapse of Germany; they tell me that even the people cannot endure it any longer, while the Nazi theories head toward bankruptcy.

12 JANUARY 1944

There is a subterranean ferment wherein diverse currents encounter each other (Communism, Christian democracy, liberalism, etc.). The ferment has a common interest: a revolt against Fascism and in part against the King, and the desire for peace and liberty. We impatiently await the arrival of the Allies so they can drive the Germans out and guarantee tolerable forms of living; but there is little sympathy for them. The devastation that continues to be created in the cities are fresh wounds to the hearts of Italians. One thing, however, is notable and comforting: in the midst of the messiness of ideas and tendencies there is no manifestation of an anti-religious or anti-clerical current. The same workers, nearly all of whom call themselves socialists or Communists, seem immune to the anticlerical "virus." There is even a group who call themselves Catholic Communists. This attitude of respect toward religion is due principally to the action and words of the Pope. The people, including the upper classes, love the Pope and look to him as the only spirit of true charity and consolation amidst so much furious hatred and destruction. This attitude is also due to the full pastoral sensibility of the bishops and clergy. But we must not delude ourselves. The vast movement of ferment will explode in diverse directions as soon as the Allies reach Rome and establish a regime of liberty. And Communism can take on dangerous attitudes. I urge that at that moment Catholics be present, that they be prepared and active. The political and social program, as doctrine, is already established. But it needs to become a fact. The three things therefore seem to be a primordial and urgent necessity:

1 Create a leadership group with a recognized leader;
2 Establish newspapers.
3 Give this leadership group the necessary freedom of movement, especially regarding the possibility of agreement with other parties.

12 JANUARY 1944

Commendatore Cirmeni, inspector of the Interior Ministry, told my brother that many young people in the ministry would like to rally around a representative of the Christian Democratic Party. The name of the Hon. De Gasperi, who was head of the Italian People's Party [Partito Popolare Italiano] in the Chamber of Deputies and enjoys solid prestige for his probity, his social conscience, and also because of the personal price he has paid. It seems that many are thinking of a future situation based on the following social foundations: nationalization of the great industries and reduction of the great landed properties.

The Devil and Holy Water

On 12 April 1919 the Communist organ *L'Ordine Nuovo* published an article that was not without interest: "Religion must be abolished. To the Cardinals, Bishops, Pastors and Priests we will give some good hoes and files and send them to work and produce goods in the fields and in the workshops; let us confiscate the immense treasures of the Church and distribute them to the proletariat!" Thus wrote Giovanni Roveda,[6] who in the *piazze* also added: "The convents, the churches,

---

[6] Giovanni Roveda (1894–1962), a unionist and Italian politician, was secretary general of the Federation of Metal Workers [Federazione Impiegati Operai Metallurgici (FIOM)], a member of the national leadership of the Italian Communist Party, which he helped found, and a senator of the republic. In 1928 he was sentenced, by a special tribunal, to 20 years and 4 months in prison for his anti-Fascist activity. He was freed under an amnesty and sent to the border. He moved back to Rome after 25 July 1943 to prepare the General Italian Confederation of Labour [Confederazione Generale Italiana del Lavoro (CGIL)]. After 8 September of the same year, he took refuge in the Pontifical Lombardese Seminary in the capital. Arrested in December 1943 and transferred to a prison in

the monasteries can house hundreds of thousands of poor people and proletarians." In 1943 the same Roveda, touched by grace, found asylum in a convent which Christian charity opened to him, but only after he was baptized."[7]

THE VERONA TRIAL   18 JANUARY 1944

The Verona trial is a tragic and horrendous mockery of justice. The members of the Grand Council of Fascism enforced – unfortunately, too late – one of their laws. It dealt with stopping poor Italy's rush to the abyss. They were accused of treason, and their case was submitted to a special court which gives no guarantee of competency or impartiality. Some rumours are being spread about this horrible trial. One feels a sense of horror and abhorrence for the sentence handed down in Verona on 10 January and the execution on 11 January of those charged. The jurors revealed the unreasonableness of being part of a partisan court, with no guarantee of impartiality. Everyone agrees that this massacre greatly damages the Fascist movement. People say, "If the leaders, the founders, the most important representatives of Fascism are killing each other, accusing each other of treason, who can we believe in now?" A person said to me, "Either Mussolini was aware of and agreed to the massacre or he was kept in the dark of everything and his voice wasn't heard. In the first case, he comes off as a murderer; in the second, he shows himself as nothing but a puppet in Hitler's hands." The common opinion is that Hitler wanted to get revenge against Ciano and was planning to teach a lesson to the German and Italian Fascist party officials ... They say that the convicted were forced to sign a petition for reprieve. However, three hours later (specifically at 7:20 PM on 11 January) they were shot. Either their petition was not forwarded or their pardon was denied. Ciano's demeanour was dignified and Christian. He was an example of strength and faith to the others. He knew some prayers and said them in order to help his companions in misfortune. He had been brought up well, and the comfort of his faith brightened his last tragic hours.

Among those condemned to death in the Verona trial were three former ambassadors to the Holy See: De Vecchi, Alfieri, and Ciano. It

---

Verona, he was liberated by a group of partisans. He was elected the first post-liberation mayor of Turin.

[7] CC: *La Tribuna*, 18 January 1944.

is believed that if there had been time to take a breath between the sentencing and the execution, the Holy Father would have intervened to ask for a pardon. One of the judges was killed by a bomb. Even the public prosecutor was marked for an attack.

20 JANUARY 1944

Don Pancino[8] of the Concordia Diocese went to see Mussolini. He says that he is physically exhausted. Mussolini maintains that he had

[8] Giusto Pancino (1907–1981) was born in Portogruaro in the Diocese of Concordia. As a young boy he followed his family to Milan, where it relocated for work. During that period he had the chance to meet Benito Mussolini's family, specifically Edda, who was more or less the same age. He entered the Order of Friars Minor [the Capuchins] and took his solemn vows in 1930 in Milan. He was ordained as a presbyter by Cardinal Schuster in 1932 and acted as a teacher in Saiano [near Brescia] until 1936. He was called to arms as a military chaplain in 1940 and sent to the Greek-Albanian border and in 1941 to the Mediterranean, where he served as an assistant in a field hospital. During this period of service he had an opportunity to see Mussolini again – who visited the aforementioned hospital on 6 March 1941 – as well as Edda Mussolini, who was a Red Cross nurse for more than a month in the same hospital.

For this reason, what is written in *Le Saint Siège et la guerre mondiale*, vol. 11 of *Actes et documents du Saint Siège relatifs à la seconde guerre mondiale* (Vatican City: Libreria Editrice Vaticana, 1981), on page 123, is not correct. It states that Pancino was "prêtre du diocèse de Belluno, alors curé dans environs de Cortina d'Ampezzo, ancien aumônier militaire, il avait connu en Albanie la comtesse Ciano..." Having returned from the front, Pancino was based in the Diocese of Concordia, where in October 1941 he was already acting as the temporary spiritual adviser/administrator for Erto – he would become parish priest there in December 1942. In 1946 he was put in charge of the Vivaro parish and in 1973 became the parish priest of Murlis. Regarding Pancino, on the same – as well as the following – page of the volume quoted above, Domenico Tardini, who was secretary of the Congregation for Extraordinary Ecclesiastical Affairs, notes: "This priest, Don Giusto Pancino, was sent to Rome on 2 February 1944 to meet with the secretary of state in Mussolini's offices. They wanted to know Edda Mussolini's address in Switzerland because they wanted to send him there to tell Edda that Mussolini had no responsibility in the death of Galeazzo Ciano – the Germans were the ones to blame." A full account of the relationship between no direct hand in the killing of Ciano.[9] He added that he is always closely watched.

GALEAZZO CIANO'S LETTER TO HIS MOTHER

VERONA, 10 JANUARY 1944

My adored mother,

I would never have thought it possible to cause you such great pain, I who in life always tried to do everything that I could to make you happy. But if this is God's will, I must lower my head and resignedly accept my fate regarding this most difficult ordeal that has been forced on you. Once again – as you have always been – you must be strong, because there are three children who will need your love, three little ones who are entering life in the midst of this dreadful sadness. And there is Edda, who is good, sincere, and generous. She loves you very much. Together, you will have to rebuild the family hearth and, thanks to you both, the family will still carry on and find its tomorrow.

I prepare myself for my departure with a serene mind and heart. I am aware that I have always carried out my responsibilities, and today, if the justice system of man is faulty, that of God and that of time will carry out their noble deed to right this wrong. If I am given the chance to be in the presence of our great Holy Father, in front of him I will have nothing for which to reproach myself.

My adored mother, I ask of you one favour. Be strong. Try to withstand this blow from fate. Make sure that Ciccino, Dindina, and Marzio see in you a bit of me, as you will see Maria and me in them. A kiss for you Mummy, with all my heart and I ask for you to be blessed.

Yours always, Galeazzo

Pancino, Il Duce, and his daughter Edda regarding Ciano's death was written by Mons. Tardini and can be found in the same volume on pages 162–4. On pages 264–5 of that volume we can also find Edda Mussolini's answer to her father, as told to Pancino when he saw her in Switzerland: "Tell him that I feel sorry for him and to flee or go kill himself!"

[9] CC: Countess Carolina Ciano, Galeazzo's mother, told me that on 18 August 1946 Mussolini signed his death sentence. She showed me the letter that her son wrote to her from prison that I quote here.

The Last Hours of the Convicted
[Letter to Countess Ciano from Mons. Chiot,[10] who attended the convicted men in Verona]:

Verona, 18 February 1944
Countess, I have in my heart the stressful days of waiting, the very sad night, down here, after the conviction and death of your dearest. He carried on by preparing himself for his last hour with a greater sense of his faith. The same night of his conviction he asked me to listen to his confession, and in his cell he received Holy Communion with edifying piety. As he did, so did his companions in misfortune.

At 9 PM they were receiving the Eucharist in communion with the Lord. They expressed their desire to stay together on that last night. From 9 PM to 9 AM we conversed calmly, talking of things other than recent events, highlighting only memories and love of family and uplifting spiritual matters. Spiritually we already were all beyond earthly issues. When the Angelus sounded from the convent nearby at 6 in the morning, officer De Bono jumped to his feet and said, "Lads, let us give a final farewell on earth to the Madonna whom we will see in Heaven." We recited the Angelus together. As the hour came upon us, I accompanied them to the place of their execution. The count's last words were ones of faith and hope. He thought of you and his family, and said to me, "If you see my children, tell them never to hate, to love everyone; and that I am dying in the love of God and without any resentment toward anyone." The kiss of the cross sealed his lips.

I put his body in a double casket of zinc and spruce so that in the cemetery where he was buried, it will keep until he will be sent to his loved ones. I placed a crucifix and rosary beads between his hands, and I surrounded his body with violets to represent the love of his family. You can pray for him with complete faith in his eternal salvation. Countess, may the Lord illuminate your maternal tears with the same faith that shone from the count's soul, which was made pure by accepting his death in the hands of the Lord.

With my respects,

your obedient Don Chiot.

---

[10] Giuseppe Chiot, a monsignor of the San Luca parish in Verona and chaplain in the Scalzi prison. By virtue of the latter role, he attended Galeazzo Ciano and the other members of the Grand Council of Fascism during their imprisonment and execution.

On Galeazzo Ciano

It is not my intention to put forward a judgment of Ciano as a politician. I am lacking facts. I will only give my impressions of him as a person. He was a brilliantly intelligent man and basically a good person. But having been put beside Mussolini, he could not do anything else but serve as the executor of his orders. Nor, on certain occasions, did he lack sufficient expertise. But he did not prove himself a man of noble character. Had he been such a man, he would have resigned rather than sharing the responsibility and playing for both teams in the game of war. He became lost in his own ambition! His role in the war in Albania and in Greece is a sinister one. I have to mention the friendly rapport I had with Galeazzo Ciano in China. He was always considerate when it came to our missionaries, and he showed a great sense of responsibility in his duties. In 1933 when I left China, quite ill, Ciano offered me the kindest assistance in Shanghai. He always openly professed his Catholic faith, even though his private life at times clashed with the strict Catholic discipline. *Requiescat in pace*!

22 JANUARY 1944

The radio has spread rumours of the landing of the Allies on the Tyrrhenian coast, it seems between Minturno and Anzio. The news made many happy, giving them a sense of relief and expectancy, though they say that the landing was supposed to take place farther north. All have their hearts turned toward new events and forecast the withdrawal of the Germans. But some speak in a hushed voice and only with those they trust.

Tonight I saw many trucks full of different troops going by in the direction of the sea. The vehicles were commandeered haphazardly at 1:00 in the afternoon. During the night there was constant noise from the passing troops. There were German sentries posted on the bridges over the Tiber.

22 JANUARY 1944

Over the hinterland of the Montecassino front were dropped little pieces of paper with the following proclamation: "All supplies, provisions, livestock, flour, potatoes, etc., belonging to the Italian people will be confiscated by the troops for their own use. In the event that the reserves of provisions and livestock – including donkeys and horses – cannot be transported behind the lines, they will be destroyed. Hiding places will be burned in good time. As soon as this document is read, it must be destroyed. Signed, Müller."

Is this document authentic? One would have difficulty believing it if one wasn't familiar with the way Germans give orders. A German soldier, a Catholic, said that the Germans will not carry out completely their orders to destroy. They themselves feel disgust for this criminal act. He added that in the Bishop's Palace in Gaeta he was forced to smash – with sorrow – the bishop's radio with the butt of his rifle.

THE LANDING OF THE ALLIES AT ANZIO   23 JANUARY 1944

Rome is reliving one of the tragic moments of its thousand-year-old history. Around its hills, the weapons and battles assure that past events repeat themselves. With the landing of the Allies at Anzio, we feel ourselves barricaded by the pain and fear that Rome will also be swept into the vortex of war. This is a stupid crime. Why didn't the Allies think of landing at Livorno, perhaps even at La Spezia? Why bring war to the gates of Rome? Even from a strategic viewpoint, the landing at Anzio seems to be a glaring error. If the landing had been attempted farther north, the German Army would have been forced to retreat in order to avoid being attacked from the rear. There are those who think that in this foolish act there is a bit of Protestant influence.[11]

I went out at 6 PM. Rome was half-deserted, though partly because of a fine and cold drizzly fog. Tanks full of soldiers speeding toward the Appian Way; tanks loaded with crates and sacks departing toward Via Flaminia. People were looking at the scene in a hostile way whilst secretly nourishing the hope of the coming liberation from the Germans. When I returned home to the Propaganda, I heard three loud shots in the distance.

LEAFLETS DISTRIBUTED BY TWO OPPOSING FRONTS

From the Allies: "Sabotage the Germans!"

RAILWAY WORKERS! TRANSPORTATION WORKERS! FARMERS! REMEMBER! The Germans while retreating will liberally plant mines. They will place them along the streets, in the fields, in houses, and in both predictable and unexpected places. These mines are a danger to you and your children and are an obstacle to the liberating troops who are advancing. For your safety and to hasten the day of our arrival, carefully

[11] CC: This is also the thought of Marshal E. Caviglia, expressed in his *Diario*, April 1925 – March 1945 (Rome: Gherardo Casini Editore, 1952), 498.

note and remember the position, type, and size of the mines that the Germans have placed in the areas around you. Also try to obtain information regarding the buildings around which the Germans have left mines. *Do not arouse the German soldiers' suspicion by asking too many questions or by following them. You will be able to gather a lot of important information while you are out and about minding your own business.*

WARNING: While our troops are advancing, make contact with our vanguard patrols. But before giving them any information, make sure that they are Allied soldiers and not German soldiers wearing different uniforms. With the information you can provide us, our sappers can readily destroy and render useless the enemy mines. It is enough for them to know the places where they have been placed and, if possible, their size and type. By doing this, you will save your families from further danger, your homes from destruction, and you will hasten the advance of your own soldiers who today are fighting alongside the Americans and English for the liberation of Italy.

OBSERVE CAREFULLY, REMEMBER WITH ACCURACY, TELL US IMMEDIATELY.

From the German Front

MY ITALIAN BROTHER! A blow to the back of the head is waiting for you too! The English and Americans are traitorously handing over southern Italy to Bolshevism! At this precise moment, the prosecutor of the Soviet Union WYSCINSKI has arrived in southern Italy. What does this mean? It means MASS EXECUTION!

THOUSANDS of innocent victims killed! The bodies of THOUSANDS of miserable Italians, men, women, children, thrown into mass graves!

Remember the red massacres in Spain, Latvia, Lithuania, Estonia, and Poland. Now this ill-fated wave of blood and tears wants to flood your country too! This is not speculation! *The first lists of Italians killed in Istria and in Dalmatia are documented proof of this terrible reality!* Their names cry out for revenge …

For the Reconstruction

I was given the 23 January edition of the underground newspaper *Il Popolo*. I am going to write out this passage: "The essential issue is whether the new regime that we will have to put into power, once the liberation of the country is achieved, will be a true democratic state in which *de facto* sovereignty is assigned not to one person or one class, but (as in England and America) administered by a representative system to all members of the community."

24 JANUARY 1944

Yesterday evening – Sunday – at dusk, an airplane was flying around over Vatican City. From the roar of its engine we were sure it was an Italian plane. Around 6:30 PM the pilot dropped two bombs which fell not far from the walls of Vatican City on the side of Via Aurelia. One of them demolished a house and killed a woman. We think that the pilot was aiming at the group of houses inside Vatican City where the foreign ministers are housed. The airplane then fell to the ground in flames in Villa Pamphili. But since it was already late and the curfew imposed, no one was able to see the plane and the pilot or pilots. During the night every piece was cleared away. Left at the crash site were only a few metal fragments. Father Bonardi picked up a piece of zinc from it. This second and stupid attack, for which everyone is blaming the Italian Fascists, has given rise to a feeling of universal indignation.

25 JANUARY 1944

Yesterday evening, a little before 7 PM, I had just returned to the Propaganda when I heard a loud explosion, like a bomb falling not far from where I was. Today I learned that in Via F. Crispi, between Capo le Case and the Tritone, a hand grenade had been thrown at a German truck, which was left quite damaged.

The afternoon newspapers are publishing this new order: "Reckless groups, supported by the enemy, have once again carried out two attacks on houses and German army vehicles. Since these acts of sabotage took place between 5 PM and 7 PM, it has been decided that from today, the curfew will begin at 5 PM and continue until 6 AM.

26 JANUARY 1944

I went out at 4 PM to see what the city looked like. It was a dreary sight, with its closed stores, people silently hurrying along the streets toward their homes, German tanks in every direction, and motorcycles – also German – noisily darting around. There is anxiety in people's hearts and minds, but it is mixed with hopefulness, and there is also a repressed impatience for the arrival of the Allies. Today a woman said to me, "I am not fond of the Allies. My heart aches when I think of them as victorious in Rome, but we can no longer stand this nightmare in which the Germans keep us. So many people in hiding, anxious, their own lives in danger, eagerly cry out for their 'liberators.' And they are true patriots."

In Via F. Crispi there are small groups of people. A guard told me that the Germans had shot at a young man, who then fell to the ground, wounded, and was taken to hospital. In the tunnel under the Quirinale are pitiable groups of evacuees and disaster victims: children sitting on little benches or curled up or stretched out on the ground, all looking like bundles of rags, their faces dominated with sad and blank expressions. Some children, pale and barefoot, stick their trembling hands out to passers-by. Scattered here and there were small fires and people seated around them, as if in a daze. There was no sadder sight than a young man who was unwrapping and then drying in front of the fire the bandages of his baby. He said to me, "We are evacuees. Help us."

In the midst of so much misery I noticed three mothers, all calm, who were breastfeeding their babies. They were sad and silent, but there was also something sacred and august in their lowered eyes, which were directed at the little creatures who were so unaware of what was going on while receiving an act of love. This act raised the image of those mothers to symbols of goodness in the midst of the abominable tragedy of war, a war started by the foolishness of a few men.

Along Corso Umberto there are German tanks going the wrong way; those heading for the Piazza Venezia are full of soldiers. A long procession of German tanks passed by, dragging behind them large guns covered in foliage, a spectacle of great humiliation for Rome. They were going, obviously, toward the sea to face the advance of the Allies.

26 JANUARY 1944

The newspapers in Rome, published with the prompting and aid of the so-called Social Republic, continue to talk about the "honour of Italy," the "salvation of Italy," the "betrayal by the King and Badoglio," etc., as if all of Italy's misfortunes should be blamed on the King and Badoglio; as if Mussolini was not at fault or was not responsible for the ill fortune that has befallen Italy. It is an enormous as well as grave error of judgment – the impudence of the press is revolting.

The truth of the matter is this: Hitler wanted to put into practice the theories of Nietzsche, the philosopher – who later died insane. Unfortunately, Mussolini was caught up in a similar megalomania.

28 JANUARY 1944

It has been a dark day, full of fear and spent waiting anxiously. The war has arrived in Castelli Romani. They say that these people are evacuees and that the Villa Pontificia at Castel Gandolfo is full of refugees. Even Urban College's villa has opened its doors to the injured.

The son of the pharmacist of the Sant'Andrea delle Fratte's parish, a three-year-old who is ill, is in Ariccia.[12] His parents are anxiously trying to bring him to Rome. Father Moretti called on me to see if Urban College, which has always been associated with the villa at Castel Gandolfo, can transport the child during one of its trips. However, the college's bursar tells me that the trips have been suspended and that, in the college in Rome, wine distribution has been done away with because the cantinas are at Castel Gandolfo.

This evening I went out around 4 PM. There were stores closing, trucks full of evacuees going in the direction of Via Flaminia, small groups of people – silent, cautious, worried. At Santa Maria del Popolo a young mother with two children begged me to hear her confession. I said to her, "I am not from this church. Go into the sacristy and call for a priest." She replied, "I have been there and I didn't find anyone. I am an evacuee and I have to get back, with these two children, to the home of an acquaintance before 5 PM. I listened to her confession.

I passed by Corso Umberto; it was full of the noisy comings and goings of tanks, trucks, and cars that were crossing in every direction. They are the overflow of the approaching war. But how sad it was to see in old Via Flaminia, at the foot of the Campidoglio, the Germans parading past as if they owned the city! What a change from so many years ago when the victorious armadas were returning after defeating the Germans!

A question keeps coming back to me and causes a pang in my heart: Why did the Allies bring the war so close to Rome? Why didn't they land farther north? There is widespread concern about provisions. The Germans have confiscated all means of transportation; the roads in the areas around Rome are clogged with all the troops passing through them. They say that the new governor of Rome is a remarkable and able person, possessing a lot of experience from when he was in Naples. He is actively doing his best to find the means of transportation. He also made an appeal to the Vatican and received a great deal of help from it.

---

[12] A municipality in the province of Rome.

Without doubt, a very dark and threatening problem within the crisis in Rome is the one of provisions. Heaven help us if there is no food! They are also talking about Communists, of armed patriots! I think they represent a lesser danger than that of not having food. May God help us!

29 JANUARY 1944

The Vatican has granted to the governor of Rome a large number of trucks for provisions. Excellent.

The Generosity of the Pope

I feel the need to note here the enormous act of charity carried out by the Pope. He possesses something not short of miraculous. I have no intention of giving a summary of all the numerous spiritual and material provisions generated by the Supreme Pontiff. Later on, someone will probably recount everything in minute detail.

Where the storm of exterminating hatred has raged or where other disasters have struck, there passes through a love that rebuilds: the Pope's spiritual and material aid, and an air of serene peace. "How many times," said the Holy Father during his 1943 Christmas message, "how many times have We had to repeat with a racked heart, the exclamation of the Divine Master: *Misereor super turbam?*[13] The Pontificia Opera di Assistenza's [Vatican Relief] aid to children and other needy groups merits a special mention. I must also mention the aid given to the evacuees who took refuge in Rome and in the Villa Pontificia at Castel Gandolfo, the asylum offered to many Jews and other people risking deportation to Germany, the assistance that was sent to prisoners of war, internees, and so on.

When the Vatican Archives are opened and people read about these dark times, they will see the variform and unlimited acts of charity offered by Pius XII. They make an interesting comparison to those carried out by Gregory the Great in the seventh century, in times that were equally turbulent. What is less known, but is also so very important, is the Holy Father's involvement in saving from execution many people who ran up against the harshness of military law.

[13] The biblical quotation can be found in Mk. 8:2 and means "I have compassion on the multitude."

29 JANUARY 1944

Yesterday the conference for various political parties opened in Bari. What we have heard until now is not very comforting. It seems that they have returned to the old arguments about words. Lots of words said against the King, Badoglio's Fascism. But it is not enough to be in agreement on a negative platform. A broad vision is needed, one that will rebuild civil life and also be precise and true to life.

Italy is climbing Mount Calvary, but it has not yet reached the summit. Eloquent doctrinarism serves no purpose; what is needed are simple and sincere intentions for practical hard work. This is not the time to give vent to old grudges, let alone personal vendettas. It is so sad to see Zaniboni,[14] Mussolini's assailant, called to be president of the conference. The collapse of every moral direction, a controversial aberration in very bad taste, and producing a very dangerous result. Is this how they intend to rebuild our poor Italy, by glorifying a crime?

They are making the same stupid error, the same error as when in Italy they erected laudatory plaques and monuments to Oberdan.[15] If we want to work toward rebuilding poor Italy, we must place Christian morality at the base of the new building, otherwise they will be building on sand.[16]

[14] Tito Zaniboni (1883–1961), an Italian politician, was a member of the Chamber of the Socialist Party in 1919. The target of many attacks by the Black-shirts [squadriste; Fascist paramilitary squads], he convinced himself that the only way to oppose Fascism was to kill Mussolini. After Matteotti's murder, with the collaboration of General Capello, he organized an attempt on Mussolini's life. This attempt was thwarted on 4 November 1925 only moments before it was to take place. In 1927 he was sentenced to 30 years in prison; on 8 September 1943 he was released and once again took up his political activities. In 1945 he founded the Democratic Socialist Union [Unione Democratica Socialista], which later merged with the Italian Democratic Socialist Party [Partito Socialista Democratico Italiano].

[15] Guglielmo Oberdan (1858–82) was born in Trieste, a city which at the time was part of the Austro-Hungarian Empire and became a representative of Italian irredentism. He organized an assassination attempt on Emperor Franz Joseph during one of his visits to Trieste, and for this he was executed in December 1882.

[16] CC: Livy, *History of Rome*, I, book 4, chap. 9. The Latin text says: "*Ex certamine factionum ortum, quae fuerunt eruntque pluribus populis exitio quam bella externa, quam fames morbive.*"

30 JANUARY 1944

Today's edition of *L'Avvenire d'Italia*, whilst commenting on the murder of Bologna's federal secretary Facchini,[17] used words both Christian and humane: "Terrorism does not resolve crises, it only exacerbates them and can produce only one result – that of feeding the frenzy of hate and causing cutthroat reactions like vendetta and reprisal."

Let us ask God, for the blood that thus far has been shed, that Italians will again feel like and see themselves as brothers. This reconciliation between our citizens is the most urgent of all matters, for it will allow Italy to rise again.

31 JANUARY 1944

Around 11 o'clock the radio broadcast the warning to open all windows because there was to be a large explosion. We opened wide the windows in the Propaganda offices and in the private residences. The explosion took place a little after 1:00 PM, but it was fairly far away and not very loud.

Last night two German soldiers were killed; they were guards on the Ponte Risorgimento over the Tiber. In the morning – perhaps as a reprisal or simply because of the needs of the war – the Germans rounded up a large number of adolescents, taking them from the streets (Via Merulana, Via Nazionale, Piazza Vittorio Emanuele, etc.) The young people, loaded onto trucks, were taken to the Macao Barracks. They were trying to send notes to their families. Father Michotte[18] told me that as he was passing in front of the Macao Barracks he saw, crammed together inside, the young people who had been taken, and outside he saw about a hundred people (fathers, mothers, siblings) who were looking for information about their family members.

[17] Eugenio Facchini (1912–44), an Italian politician, was a member of the Italian Social Republic [Repubblica Sociale Italiana] and was appointed its federal party secretary in Bologna. On 26 January 1944 he was killed, shot in the back by a commando from the emerging resistance movement.

[18] Raimondo Michotte, who was Belgian, was also the vice-president/director of Public Prosecutions for the Paris Foreign Mission Society, which had been founded in 1660 and approved in 1664. The society's efforts were directed at the education of native clergy, to support the preservation and propagation of the faith, as well as the conversion of indigenous peoples.

I went out around 4 PM. Closed stores, only a few people on the streets, the dark appearance of the city, but nothing new. Wherever one looked, passing here and there were grey cars, with darker serpentine stripes on them, and yellowish-coloured trucks full of soldiers. A long line of trucks on the Corso going toward Via dell'Impero were camouflaged with olive branches. What a striking contrast!

In the tunnel under the Quirinale, there were groups of refugees warming themselves around small fires. The tunnel was thick with smoke. I ran into Count Zara on Via Nazionale, looking haggard and almost in tears. He had escaped from Velletri with his wife and daughter, walking all the way from Velletri to Rome. He had spent the night in a cave with other refugees; among them was a group of nuns. He told me that Velletri has been partly destroyed and is completely in the hands of the Germans.

The afternoon newspapers publish the speech that Mussolini gave on the twenty-eighth regarding the meeting of the officials of the pseudo republic ... His words explain the proposal to defend Rome by using the foolish and wicked "scorched-earth policy." May it be God's will that at least the city is saved, in spite of the Allies' plan ... But there is fear that is both widespread and pessimistic. I want to hope that the storm will pass while clearing outside of Rome. The Pope keeps watch.

I FEBRUARY 1944

We heard the faraway boom of shellfire around Villa Borghese. On top of the pounding thunder, there were some resounding explosions. It was like hearing an echo of the [Giulian] Carso, when they used to start big operations.

I went to visit Vittorio Cini's daughters at Assumption College. Outside were many German and Italian trucks. The caretaker showed me the iron gate full of holes: "Last night – and we don't know why – they shot at it with a machine gun."

An Illegal Leaflet from the Communists

WE WANT TO EAT.

ROMAN WOMEN, the regular looting carried out by the Germans in the city and the countryside has left us hungry. We have no bread, no pasta; they no longer distribute oil or lard; there is no meat and there aren't even any vegetables. You are waiting in vain to be able to buy the meagre rations. You will have nothing unless you demand it. As they are aware that in a few days they will have to leave the city, the

Nazis/Fascists will not allow anything to reach the people if you do not make yourselves heard …

ROMAN WOMEN, save yourselves, your men, and your children from the horrors of hunger. As a mob, go to the municipal delegations and demand the distribution of groceries. Stop the Germans from pillaging what little is left in our warehouses. Take over their trucks that transport food and seize their contents. By doing this you will save your family from hunger, you will greatly assist in the city's fight to overcome Nazi-Fascist domination, and you will have the gratitude of your children and your nation. Let's get the Nazis who are starving us out of Italy.

1 February 1944, THE COMMUNISTS

3 FEBRUARY 1944

Nothing special or new. Rome shows the sad face of war: German tanks passing in all directions, a few groups of blackshirts with the air of arrogance and carelessness. There are a few people on the streets who look indifferent or hostile and cautiously stay silent or speak in hushed tones. The tracks from the *Tigers* that passed through are left on the Corso's asphalt. The sound of shellfire is heard by no one. However, there is the feeling that the war is coming closer. Rome is closed off to the south by a wall of iron and fire.

Little news about the war. From the news bulletins, we gather that the clashes with the enemy armies are terrible and that the Germans are showing extraordinary skill in opposition. They announced, however, that the English and Americans broke through the ring of fire north of Cassino. If the breach gets wider and the Allied troops can go ahead, the German army will find itself in difficulty in the Gariglione Valley and will have to retreat. Everyone anxiously waits for news, but that feeling is mixed with a certain amount of disappointment: no one believed that the Germans would fight back with such tenacity.

The Roman castles have been severely bombed. In Albano, 16 Poor Clare nuns perished, buried alive under the rubble. What a pity! Yesterday in Rome two Fascists were murdered.

REFORMS TO THE RUSSIAN CONSTITUTION

3 FEBRUARY 1944

The 3 February edition of *Il Giornale d'Italia* states: "The Supreme Soviet unanimously decided to make radical changes to the constitution of the Soviet Union. They approved motions that would allow the Soviet

Union's constituent republics to have direct diplomatic relations with foreign powers and to train their own armies, which will then form the backbone of the Red Armada."

This is a very clever move and will have great importance for the future. Stalin seems to be the most far-sighted man of all the heads of state. By promising autonomy to the small countries he gives the illusion of freedom and opens the doors for them. Of necessity, these countries will have to lean on the larger countries: Stalin then offers a helping hand. The Russian troops are already at the border of Estonia. What will Estonia do? What will Finland do? The lure of joining Russia is too enticing.

With regard to religious issues, they should respect its autonomy. But we cannot have faith that this will happen. In addition, under this system, Stalin will try to gather a certain number of votes in the League of Nations, a number even higher than that of England.

5 FEBRUARY 1944

Today I saw Count Giorgio Cini; he was returning from Germany where he had gone to visit his father. He told me that his father is a mere shadow of himself, a skeleton dressed in skin. He had been interned in a concentration camp in Bavaria[19] and was kept in an underground prison. In his cell he saw an Italian general die from privation. Then Senator Cini was taken out of prison and now has been interned, but in less unpleasant surroundings. Poor Cini! A man who used his immense wealth to do good, who gave his services to Mussolini for free, who managed the work on the Universal Exposition without getting a salary or compensation, and who honestly, while he was the minister of communications, had the courage to turn against Mussolini by asking to know the status of the war in order to be a more knowledgeable collaborator. This man then found himself sentenced without a trial and put in a situation where he could die from privation!

What a nice reward that Mussolini set aside for a few honourable men who served him without robbing the state. Now, over Vittorio Cini's head he hangs the threat of a trial which, if it in fact takes place, could lead him to execution.

Vittorio Cini told his son that the only comfort he has is his clear conscience and his religion. He spoke to his son in front of the Gestapo. He did not utter my last name, but he simply remembered with affection

---

[19] He is referring to the Dachau concentration camp.

his friend Celso. He advised his son to do work that brought about some good. His son asked me how he can make some donations: "Sometimes I think about cursing our wealth because it brought about these results. I want to at least use this money to come to the aid of those who are destitute."

I advised him on different ways to give to charity. When we parted, he headed toward Via xx Settembre to visit Count Volpi, who is still confined to his home.

Senator Cini wrote me, in pencil, a short but noble letter, from which I quote this passage: "It has sustained me and it sustains me in these difficult times, the Faith that you helped to nourish. It is also for this that I am so very grateful to you. I have with me the *Imitazione di Cristo*[20] that you gave me. Every day I read a few chapters from it."

Giorgio Cini has shown a filial love that is alive with intelligence, affection, and courage, a love that is superior to any form of praise and cannot be fully appreciated unless you are someone who is familiar with the vicissitudes and risks that he has happily overcome.

5 FEBRUARY 1944

In Rome there has been an uncommon coming and going of Red Cross ambulances.

The Allies have not yet been successful in breaking through the circle of iron and fire that surrounds Rome to the west and south. Everyone is pointing out Alexander's[21] slow and weak strategy, finding fault with the

[20]   The literary work *De Imitatione Christi* [The Imitation of Christ] (Venice: P. Loslein, 1483) was translated into Italian with the title *Imitazione di Cristo*. Ascetic in nature, it is attributed to a shortlist of authors, specifically Thomas à Kempis and/or Jean Gerson. After the Bible, it is the most popular piece of Christian literature.

[21]   Harold Rupert Leofric George Alexander (1891–1969), a British general, was appointed commander-in-chief of all the troops in North Africa in 1943 and then of the Allied forces that landed in Italy. On 8 September 1943 he was present at the signing of the armistice between Italy and the Allies, which was signed on the British battleship *Nelson* by Badoglio and Eisenhower. In 1944 he was promoted to Field Marshal and was entrusted with the responsibility of Supreme Allied Command in Italy and the Mediterranean, in addition to the mission for the landing in the south of France. In 1946 he was appointed governor general of Canada. From 1952 to 1954 he was minister of defence for the United Kingdom.

thoughtless landing so close to Rome. In the meantime, the bombing of Italian cities continues; it's as if they fall on the living body of an unfortunate mother with many lives.

URBANIA, 5 FEBRUARY 1944

The 5 February 1944 edition of *Il Giornale d'Italia* writes: "On 27 January last, squadrons of enemy bombers chose as a target this quiet town in the Marches and dropped their deadly devices on a built-up area, right at the moment when the inhabitants were coming out of church after the Mass at noon. Because the streets were so crowded with people, the English-American bombers caused a massacre. Out of Urbania's population of 4,000, more than 650 were left dead from the explosions in the streets or were killed under the rubble of their collapsed homes."

We hope that the news is somewhat of an exaggeration, but even if the figure was reduced, the event produces a feeling of horror and abhorrence for these "sportsmen" of death." If they are looking for military targets, let them proceed with caution and believe that it is a horrendous crime to kill so many innocent people whom they claim to be liberating. Why gun down people on the streets? Did they want to hit soldiers or did they want instead to spread terror or just practise a "sport" with the lure – on top of all this – of winning some award? So many monuments, so many churches have been destroyed or damaged. The job done by the ancient Vandals seems as nothing when compared to this. This destruction of the noblest examples of civilization will weigh heavily on these men in the course of history.

6 FEBRUARY 1944

This morning I was at the Urban College, where I conducted Mass for the university professors in Rome. There were about 50 of them, among whom were some members of the Italian Academy. I explained the Gospel of the day, the first Sunday of Septuagesima, as well as its missionary role. "This college," I said, "was founded by Urban VIII three centuries ago. And while all things age with time, this instead grows young again. It is the divine secret of the energy of the Church."

I reminded the professors of their other responsibility, that of cooperating in the rebuilding of our nation. This rebuilding must begin by educating the young. For this reason, their profession is being raised to the level of apostleship, one that is both religious and civil.

Then I visited the schools of the *ateneo* [university].[22] In the courtyard there were groups of men and women evacuees from the Propaganda Ministry's property in Castel Romano. The large classrooms had been transformed into dormitories, with mattresses and bags on the floor. Here and there were some old pieces of furniture brought from Castel Romano and in some corners there were piles of potatoes and wheat. In the college's isolated courtyards were cars and vehicles and the tracks of the cows that had been found to provide milk, as well as little mountains of hay. Even our college has taken on a warlike appearance.

8 FEBRUARY 1944

Words heard in passing along the street: "I'm telling you that the Russians didn't bomb the city." These words then prompted: "But is that really true?" The answer: "It is quite true. Those who live without Christ respect the cities. It is Christ himself who attacks them. But we will settle the score with Christ."

The person speaking was clearly a Communist. However, he had not read the newspapers that yesterday told of the Russians who bombed Finland.

In the city there is the movement of camouflaged trucks covered with wire mesh and foliage. They were going in the direction of the coast. In Spanish Square there were five Red Cross ambulances.

A POLICE RAID ON SAINT PAUL'S MONASTERY

8 FEBRUARY 1944

The 7–8 February edition of *L'Osservatore Romano* reports: "During the night, between 3 and 4 February, armed guards calling themselves units of the state police, under the command of Pietro Caruso,[23] – whose

---

[22] This is a reference to the Pontificio Ateneo Urbano de Propaganda Fide, for which Costantini served as chancellor. The *ateneo*, which was made up of the Faculties of Theology and Philosophy and the Missiological Institute, is now known as the Pontificia Università Urbaniana and has grown in size, with a greater number of faculties, including one in Canonical Law.

[23] Pietro Caruso (1899–1944), a member of the National Fascist Party since 1921, participated in the March on Rome of 28 October 1928. He served in the port militia of Trieste until 1944, when he became, for a short time, *questore* [police chief] in Verona. This was during the period when members of the Grand Council of Fascism were sentenced by a special court and then executed. During

appointment as *questore* of Rome was announced in the papers a few days ago – violently entered the buildings of the Patriarchal Basilica of Saint Paul, violating the rights of the extraterritorial status that was established in the formal treaties. After they were advised of the incident, Vatican officials immediately went to Saint Paul, found Mr Caruso and his armed guards, and made a formal protest. The Holy See publicly repeated its strong disapproval of the incident."

Many politicians – among them Bonomi, De Gasperi, Nenni, and others – had taken refuge on the premises of the Roman Seminary of St John Lateran. However, after the events at Saint Paul's[24] they no longer felt safe and spread out looking for other shelter.

THE HON. DE GASPERI COMES TO THE PROPAGANDA

8 FEBRUARY 1944

Yesterday evening, around 5 o'clock, the Hon. De Gasperi's wife came to see me. Extremely worried, she told me: "My husband had to leave the Roman Seminary, where he had found shelter with other people. You said that you would be willing to help him in times of danger." I answered, "Yes, I did." She continued, "He is in the bar down there. I beg you to take him in here for tonight and for a few days, until he can find something."

De Gasperi came up, pale but calm. He told me of the treatment he had received in the Lateran Seminary, which was truly Christian in nature.

I was happy to offer him a place to stay overnight in the midst of such turbulent times. He is a personal friend of mine and is not sought by the

---

the first days of February in 1944 he assumed the role of *questore* of Rome. Following the attack in Via Rasella he was asked to draw up a list of prisoners to be executed. While the English and Americans were preparing to enter Rome in June 1944, Caruso tried to escape to the north in his own car. Having been injured in an accident during his trip, he was admitted to hospital in Viterbo, where he was arrested by the partisans. He had his trial in Rome in September 1944 and was sentenced to death by a firing squad – a sentence carried out on the twenty-second day of the same month.

[24] For information regarding the measures taken by the Vatican after the raids in the buildings of Saint Paul's Outside the Walls Basilica and the connecting abbey, see *Le Saint Siège et la guerre mondiale*, vol. 11 of *Actes et documents du Saint Siège relatifs à la seconde guerre mondiale* (Vatican City: Libreria Editrice Vaticana, 1981), 108–22.

police, nor does he have to do compulsory military service. He is an official of the Vatican, but he is also considered an opponent of Fascism to be feared.

He is a very noble example of both a Christian and a scholar; he has already served as a member of parliament in Austria and then in Italy. Now, after Don Sturzo's departure from Italy, he is secretary of the Italian People's Party. He is a man who has tempered suffering with steadiness of character and has served time in an iniquitous prison for the crime of thinking freely and not prostituting himself to Mussolini.

THE COLLAPSE OF THE VILLA AT URBAN COLLEGE
AT CASTEL GANDOLFO   10 FEBRUARY 1944

This morning, at 9:45, I found myself in the Sistine Chapel waiting to attend the Funeral Mass in *die anniversaria* for the late Pius XI. During the ceremony we could hear the faroff rumble of shellfire and explosions of bombs that made the windows shake. After the funeral rite, a celebrant told me that Cardinal Fumasoni Biondi wanted to speak to me. I went out and met him outside the chapel where he was waiting for me. His expression was both serious and sad. He told me that a short time before there had been an air raid on Castel Gandolfo, and the villa at the Propaganda had been hit.

I felt a pain in my heart, thinking also of the thousands of evacuees who had found shelter in the villa.

11 FEBRUARY 1944

This morning I left for Castel Gandolfo, along with the college's vice-rector, Mons. Borgna.[25] The cardinal greeted me in the following way: "May the Guardian Angel protect you!" Along the road we came across trucks and vehicles full of refugees, sitting on piles of mattresses, bundles, kitchen utensils, etc. Many women held their children tenderly to the breast. Other refugees were walking alongside. Everyone was heading in the direction of Rome. Behind some horse-drawn carts, one or two sheep were tied. The faces of the refugees were very stunned and sad.

Ciampino Airport seemed to be completely destroyed, with the carcasses of a few gutted huge airplanes; in the light of day, their shells gave the impression of being the ribs of some kind of huge antediluvian beast. Upon entering Albano we saw houses and trees ripped open; the street

25 Pompeo Borgna was a monsignor in the Diocese of Civita Castellana.

was completely ravaged. Albano seemed uninhabited and very seriously hit; it looked almost like a deserted street in Pompei. On the way up to Castello we saw some smashed trucks left by the sides of the road.

Part of the Urban College villa was gone; the rest caved in and destroyed. All the buildings above the refectory and around the ancient cloister that had preceded it were in pieces, and the surrounding area was covered in huge piles of rubble. A few perimeter walls were still standing, but they were damaged and shaky. Hanging from a wall were twisted iron beams whose opposite ends were buried in the rubble. The firemen, who came from Rome, were working to shift the rubble and recover the bodies buried underneath.

In the refectory yesterday morning, at the time of the air raid, a great number of evacuees had gathered – most of them women and children – for the apportionment of milk. The American four-engine planes suddenly appeared and dropped a hail of bombs that crushed everything. Up to this morning, 110 dead bodies had been extracted from the rubble, in addition to the wounded. They say there are many other victims buried under the rubble. The newspapers estimate that 500 people have been killed.

While the firemen shifted the debris, I saw a bent hand sticking out from the rubble; it was encrusted with black-coloured dust, and on it there was a wedding ring. Slowly they removed the pieces of cement and bricks that were covering that poor woman. The hand remained in the air as supplication for her life. When the poor body was freed from the rubble, there appeared underneath a pile of dark crushed rags. From that pile they extracted a small purse, which was given to a priest, who removed a food-ration card from it. An outburst of tears made us turn and look at a man who was beating his head with his fists. The card showed that the poor victim was his wife.

Many bodies were brought to a nearby church that had not been hit by the bombs. What a sight! There were many women, pitifully covered, with their feet and legs stretched out; they looked as if they had been paralyzed in a spasmodic twist. Here and there on the ground were spots of blood. I said a De profundis.[26] Then I went from the church into the college, going down a small staircase that I had used many times with Cardinal Fumasoni Biondi and the students of the college. In the hallway, from the stairs that go to the refectory, were two long rows of dead

---

[26] The reference is to Ps. 129, which is recited during the liturgy for the dead.

bodies, covered with old dusty clothes. I saw beside a body the bare foot of a little boy, cleanly cut off at the ankle. "We don't know who it belongs to," said a Jesuit who was looking after the recovery of those poor bodies. There was a pile of rags higher and bigger than the others. A man pulled back the blanket and underneath was a woman who was clutching her son to her chest...

The cafés and such around the college, toward the villa's park, were still standing, but all were damaged, with windows off their hinges. The courtyard had been destroyed by huge bombs on which were leaning huge trees that had been knocked down. The park was completely destroyed, its trees all felled. I saw against a wall, beside Lourdes' Cave, some makeshift huts. Some women came out of them eating pasta made from boiled flour. I took a look at the adjoining Villa Pontificia, formerly Villa Barberini; it looked like a gypsy camp. I went into the parish and left the generous donation received from Count Cini with the parish priest. I also gave the Jesuit 5,000 lire for the Poor Clare nuns, who had previously lost 17 members; two others were left dead by this last bombing. The survivors went to Rome with nothing.

I saw the papal villa full of evacuees, who were waiting for the soup that was offered by His Holiness Pius XII. So, in the midst of the horror of these murders rises the light of charity. I say "murders," because this attack is to be defined as murder. Even though there were some Germans near the villa, there is no justification for it. But there are many German battalions throughout the countryside! They could have gone after them, since they knew full well that by dropping bombs on Castel Gandolfo they would have most likely struck shelter areas and the papal villa.

These airmen strike me as unhappy soldiers, for they cannot apologize for the necessities of war. But they will not stop the Germans by taking such ferocious action against Castel Gandolfo. Such a great victory do these airmen add to Alexander's pathetic failures! They don't even realize that they are writing the pages of a sad story, an abominable story that will remain even when the war is over.

12 FEBRUARY 1944

The newspapers are highlighting the Germans' strength against the Allies' bridgehead at Anzio, as well as the attempts to break through to Cassino – which the Allies are doing without success. They say that the undertaking has now passed to the Germans.

This evening I saw many *Tigers* [tanks] and trucks pass by along the Corso. One truck was full of hoes and pickaxes. They were going toward the front. "These guys know how to wage war," said Professor G., an ex-marine official, "a lot more than the Allies do!"

13 FEBRUARY 1944

This morning the English radio station said that Castel Gandolfo is now part of the war operations zone ... This confirmation is an attempt to come up with an alibi for the atrocious and stupid massacre perpetrated by the Allies on 10 February at the villa of Urban College. However, it could also be a warning to justify future attacks.

There are the Castelli Romani and many other places held by the Germans in their own defence. The Allies have every chance of having their bravery bring them great success. It is not necessary to violently attack areas that were declared and are recognized as areas of immunity ...

Once again, from the depths of our hearts rises the bitter question: "Why did the Allies bring the war right to the doors of Rome?"

The Tower of Babel

Seeing from a distance the huge buildings of the Universal Exposition, half of them finished and half still awaiting completion – huge and tragic symbols of a faded dream – brings to mind the story of the Tower of Babel. Having had the responsibility of looking after the Church of the Holy Apostles Peter and Paul, I had regular contact with the general administrator of the exposition, Senator Vittorio Cini, as well as with Foschini, the architect, and others in charge of the organization of the exposition. I attended a stately meeting in the Campidoglio. Mussolini spoke about the exposition as the "Olympiad of Civilizations"... There was something harsh in Mussolini's tone of voice, and it had sounded very defiant. The exposition buildings now look something like the remains of the Tower of Babel. The Word of Life is still represented by the Church of the Holy Apostles Peter and Paul. The Church will preserve its doctrine and will live, because it relies not on man but on God.

SUNDAY, 13 FEBRUARY 1944

Last night, around 9 o'clock, the sky was full of the sinister and widespread rumble of planes. One wave came after another wave. The flashes from the rockets lit up the sky toward Saint John Lateran. All of a sudden we heard the thunder of an explosion of bombs not so far away.

Today we learned that some of the bombs fell between Piazza Vittorio Emanuele and the Oppian Hill, hitting a clinic and causing more deaths. Apparently, a German plane was hit by an Allied fighter plane, and as it fell to the ground it released its bombs. The newspapers reported the episode without attributing what happened to the Allies.

This evening on the Corso there was a lot of coming and going of German trucks and Red Cross ambulances.

THE PONTIFICAL COUNCIL OF THE CONGREGATION
FOR THE EVANGELIZATION OF PEOPLES   14 FEBRUARY 1944
Today the Pontifical Council of the Congregation for the Evangelization of Peoples convened. The oblations poured in more than they usually do. We have overcome many difficulties regarding the shipping of aid to Catholic missions.

A few million lire that we were not able to send overseas have been used to purchase industrial "stocks." By doing this we hope to save at least part of our capital.

While the world is devastated by war and poisoned by hate, the missions offer a display of incredible charity. Many missionaries are internees, others have been killed, and some – although they remain at their posts – have no freedom of movement. But they are all to be admired for their courage and their great charity. Everyone hopes – in the words of Saint Paul – against hope, and they wait impatiently to resume their work that was interrupted.

We at the Propaganda Ministry are in contact with the apostolic delegates via telegram. Correspondence by letter is either blocked or greatly delayed. However, thanks to Vatican City, an oasis diplomatically immune to the turmoil of war, we have so far been able to give out timely instructions.

15 FEBRUARY 1944
On the night of the 14th instant a bomb fell on Professor Polidoro's clinic in Via Mecenate. The professor, who served as director of the clinic, was killed. There are also other victims.

Last night around 8 o'clock we heard a resounding explosion far from us. Today's *Il Messaggero* says that a bomb fell on the Villa Bianca clinic, killing Professor De Maria.

The popular limericks that were bitter jabs at Fascism and the Fascists are no longer passed around. Tragedy takes the place of comedy.

15 FEBRUARY 1944

The newspapers are now blaming the Allies for the bombs that fell on Rome over the last few nights. They say that today they dropped bombs on the Trastevere area and beyond, leaving more victims. The influx of *Tigers*, other tanks, trucks, flamethrowers, and so on continues, and all are directed at somewhere south of Rome. Toward the Anzio bridgehead there must be a massive amount of heavy artillery, which must be very difficult to break through.

16 FEBRUARY 1944

During the night and at the break of dawn, a large number of planes flew over Rome. The radio said that the Allies have made a lot of flights over northern Italy in order to strike, they say, railway junctions. My heart aches when I think of the human casualties and the damage that must have been done to the monuments, especially the Romanesque monuments in Emilia and Ferrara.

THE DESTRUCTION OF THE ABBEY OF MONTECASSINO
17 FEBRUARY 1944

Don Gaetano Fornari, the prior of Montecassino,[27] came to the Propaganda offices and assured me that there were neither German soldiers nor munitions in the monastery. There were only some Benedictines with the abbot[28] and many evacuees from Cassino. For this reason we are dealing with a truly useless and inexcusable attack, perpetrated coldly

[27] Father Gaetano Fornari used to live in Sant'Anselmo Monastery in Rome, and for this reason it was not difficult for him to get to Propaganda Fide to meet Mons. Costantini two days after the destruction of the well-known Abbey of Montecassino.

[28] The Abbot of Montecassino (1909–45) was Gregorio Diamare (1865–1945), a member of the Benedictine Congregation of Cassino. In 1928 he became bishop of Costanza d'Arabia, having been made head of a *nullius dioeceseos* [belonging to no diocese] abbey with ecclesiastical jurisdiction over a portion of the clergy and the people of God. In September 1943 he sent almost all of his monks to Rome because he feared that the monastery would be bombed. He remained there with a few other clergy. Diamare won the gold

and thoughtlessly against religion, history, art, and humanity. The prior's solemn assertion was confirmed by the following statement that was widely distributed throughout Rome:

> Statement: Don Nicola Clemente, administrator of the Abbey of Montecassino, and Don Francesco Falconio, bishop's delegate for the administrative office of the Diocese of Montecassino, having survived the bombing on 15 February in which the whole abbey was destroyed, "state" that inside the monastery and around its perimeter there were neither German defensive fieldworks nor troops or military vehicles of any kind.   Rome, 16 February 1944.

21 FEBRUARY 1944

The tanks continue to come and go in Rome, accompanied by some Red Cross ambulances. We can tell that the conflict is getting closer to Rome, and at night especially it lets its grim voice be heard with the sound of airplanes, shellfire, or bomb explosions.

Today I met with Ambassador X, from a neutral country. He told me that Rome needs to be saved. Moral and sentimental pretexts are not enough; a technical accord is necessary, with a specific plan that can place Rome outside the conflict ... They are good ideas, but are they practicable? Certainly, the Holy See will do everything possible to save Rome.

People are repeating the following comment more and more: "If the Allies wanted to show Rome some respect, why didn't they think of landing farther north, on the Tyrrhenian coast?"

A CONVERSATION WITH MONS. MONTINI

25 FEBRUARY 1944

He told me that the Holy See will keep its distance from international conflicts and national political parties. It will value and encourage all that is good and that contributes to alleviating the people's pain and that facilitates the coming of peace. However, it will not take the side of any particular political faction.

The negative impression and bitter disappointment surrounding American military strategy will be long-lasting. Many people feel that

---

medal for civil valour for his extensive charity work and his guidance and aid during the years 1943 and 1944.

America lost a good match and in doing so put into clear view the military efficacy of the Germans and their superiority in the art of war.

26 FEBRUARY 1944

The *Tribuna* reports that the former British minister Hore-Belisha[29] gave an address to parliament in response to Churchill's speech, making particular reference to Poland: "No one holds great affection for the Germans, but to propose a similar removal of a large number of Germans is tantamount to wanting to create a new irredentism ... There are only two possibilities for the development of British politics: one is to support a political federation and the other is to support an economic federation."

To move people from one place to another, as if they were flocks of sheep, is a new form of calculated barbarism, more inhuman than the barbarism of the past. What about the promises made in the Atlantic Charter? Is this the way he honours his own signature?

The notion of a confederation of European nations roughly like that of the United States makes one's heart swell; the war would introduce some benefits.

26 FEBRUARY 1944

Don Pancino, from the Diocese of Concordia, is passing through Rome. He saw Mussolini. He says that he is distressed. He also saw Mons. Chiot, who attended to the condemned men in Verona. Don Pancino says that Mons. Chiot told Mussolini about the convicted men's demeanour. Mussolini was deeply impressed and said that death seems horrible from a distance, but seen up close – in the light of Faith – it is much less frightening. He was astonished to hear how those men knew how to be uplifted by the comfort of Faith.

In the horror of that dark night of worry, when everything began to fade (wealth, fame, and the honours of the past, our nearest and dearest),

[29] Leslie Hore-Belisha (1895–1957), a British politician and member of the Conservative Party, was minister of transport, 1934–37, and then secretary of state for war, 1937–40. After the sanctions placed by the League of Nations because of Fascist Italy's attacks in Ethiopia, he took steps toward the rapprochement of the governments of Great Britain and Italy. In 1945 he became minister of national insurance in the cabinet led by Churchill.

one thing remained: Faith. The tragic walk of those about to die toward their execution was illuminated by a higher light.

28 FEBRUARY 1944

Badoglio, who has a hideous lack of moral sense, entrusted Zaniboni with the task of purification.

1 MARCH 1944

The underground newspaper *Il Segno*, the mouthpiece of Catholic officials, got through to me.

A BOMB AT URBAN COLLEGE ON THE JANICULUM

2 MARCH 1944

Last night, toward 8 o'clock, I was proofreading the book *Dio Nascosto*[30] when I jumped because of the explosion of some bombs that fell on the city. I didn't move, being already used to the many sounds of war, but in the house I heard heated conversation. After dinner – around 9 o'clock – Cardinal Fumasoni Biondi called me to tell me that a bomb had fallen near the nuns' residence at Urban College.[31] There was damage to the building, but there were no victims. At that hour the nuns and students were in church.

This morning I went with the cardinal to inspect the damage. The students were dispersed throughout the courtyard and were speaking with an unusual liveliness. The bomb had fallen close to the nuns' residence and made an opening in the wall and a deep hole. The whole wing of the building is damaged.

Beyond the boundary of the college is the vegetable garden of the Augustinian Fathers. Father Casamassa[32] stood on the edge of a wide

[30] The book was published as: C. Costantini, *Dio Nascosto. Splendori di fede e d'arte nella Santa Eucaristia* (Rome: Tuminelli editore, 1944); it is 544 pages long, plus a bibliography and chapter index in Roman numerals.

[31] The secretary of state of the Holy See's reconstruction of the air raid that took place on the evening of 1 March on the Janiculum can be found in *Le Saint Siège et la guerre mondiale*, vol. 11 of *Actes et documents du Saint Siège relatifs à la seconde guerre mondiale* (Vatican City: Libreria Editrice Vaticana, 1981), 193–4.

[32] Antonio Casamassa, a prelate of the Augustinian Hermits and a well-known patrologist for whom a street was named in Rome, had many different

hole that had been made by another bomb, and he told us that a priest had been wounded. He added, "This is the third attack on the Vatican. Is it perhaps a *triplex ammonitio?*" From the square, looking toward Via delle Fornaci, we saw the breached corner of a building. We were told that near Saint Peter's oratory a man was killed and that a piece of a bomb had gone through a window in the Palazzo del Sant'Ufficio, passing between Cardinal Marchetti-Selvaggiani and Mons. Traglia[33] while they were having dinner.

The *Tribuna* blames the attack on the Allies but no one believes it. In the court of common opinion, the offence was committed by the Fascists, with the tacit complicity of the German troops. It seems that the bombs were directed at Vatican Radio and were meant for the ambassadors taking shelter in the Vatican. In any case, it was a stupid criminal act against the Vatican.

2 MARCH 1944

The Hon. Longinotti said to me, "I attended a meeting with friends that I hadn't seen in a while because they keep themselves out of sight. They had all lost weight."

The war rages on, and it looks as if the Allies are going to be thrown back into the sea.

In Rome we continue to have glimpses of the next front. People who were waiting for the so-called liberators are discouraged, sad, and have bitter feelings toward those "arrogant soldiers" who are – they say – especially capable of organizing senseless destruction like that of Montecassino. The inclination to like them has been transformed into a feeling of spiteful disappointment. Nevertheless, people are waiting for the Allies to get them out of this tragedy of life and away from the difficulties they are having in getting supplies. "At least," they say, "when

---

assignments: adviser for the Pontifical Commission for Bible Studies, honorary member of the Roman Pontifical Academy of St Thomas Aquinas, censor for the Roman Pontifical Academy of Archaeology, apostolic examiner of the clergy of Rome, and professor of patristics in the Faculty of Theology of the Pontifical Lateran University. He wrote many books, among them *Patrologia*, vol. 1, parts 1–2 (Rome: Tipografia Cuggiani, 1938 and 1939).

[33] Luigi Traglia (1895–1977), titular archbishop of Caesarea in Palestine, 1936–60, and vice-regent of Rome, became the Pope's vicar for the Diocese of the Roman Pontiff in 1960, when he was also made a cardinal.

the others come, we will be able to sleep safely in our homes." The severe judgment and resentment to the Allies is also caused by the news from northern Italy. I myself have received letters from my family; letters in which they speak of the horror of the attacks and the victims of the Allied airplanes in the impoverished villages that are scattered throughout the countryside where there is no military objective (Teglio Veneto, Concordia, Cordovado, Carbona, Sussulins, etc.). Are the Allies going to devote themselves to this horrible sport? Do they want to terrorize people? They are doing nothing but spread hate and disesteem.

4 MARCH 1944

Yesterday, around 11 PM the sky was full of the grim noise of airplanes. There were about a hundred of them. Suddenly in the distance we heard the loud and low sound of the bombs exploding. The Propaganda's windows shook. We found out later that the planes had bombed Ostiense Station, at the same time striking some houses and producing more victims (they say that so far 40 dead bodies have been pulled out of the rubble, and there is a large number of wounded). Even in the Aurelio district, near the Vatican, an incendiary bomb fell on the small residence of the Pius Mothers and set it ablaze.

4 MARCH 1944

The Hon. De Gasperi is going to be a welcome guest of mine for about fifteen days. His kind and learned behaviour, delicate sense of discretion, as well as his disposition – so considerate, averse to demands – mean that his company is both pleasant and desired. His presence is further sought after because at the table there is an exchange of ideas on the political situation or on religious issues. De Gasperi has never let himself be moved by petty emotions! His noble character is further refined by his Christian sense.

However, fearing that some indiscretion or hasty decision by the Germans might upset a peaceful cohabitation, I came to an agreement (with the highest ecclesiastical authorities[34] and Dom Albareda,[35] the

34 The use of the plural "authorities" refers directly to the Pope and his secretary of state.

35 Anselmo Maria Albareda, a Spanish Benedictine, held different posts. He was prefect of the Vatican Apostolic Library, for which Cardinal Giovanni Mercati held the title of librarian of the Holy Roman Church. He was also

prefect of the Vatican Library) to make De Gasperi's stay at the Propaganda official, which in fact does reflect the truth. I therefore wrote Dom Albareda the following letter:

Prot[ocol]. n. 345/44   4 March 1944
As you are aware, the Hon. De Gasperi, the secretary of the Apostolic Library, is preparing a translation of the book *Vatikan, Bild der Weltkirche*.

During the course of his work, he has discovered that it would be advantageous for him to update and find supporting documentation for various chapters of the book by using the precious resources that are kept here in the Propaganda Archives. This is the reason, therefore, that De Gasperi is consulting and studying these documents and manuscripts.

The publication of the aforementioned volume is quite urgent, because it provides a scientific explanation of missiological concepts conveyed by the Holy Father Pius XII in his first encyclical, *Summi Pontificatus*. It would therefore be extremely useful, for further study and for greater ease in carrying out research, if the Hon. De Gasperi was transferred here to the Archives of this congregation for a short while. Also worthy of consideration is the hour at which the library is closed to the public; such a temporal constraint would cause him difficulty in accommodating his requests.[36]

Father Albareda sent me the following answer:

Vatican Apostolic Library 81/P The Prefect   8 March 1944
In reply to your important letter dated 4 March, n. 345/44, I take care in notifying you that, also by order of His Eminence, the Most Reverend Cardinal

---

adviser to the Sacred Congregation of Rites, Section 3 (for the historical causes of the Servants of God and the revision of liturgical volumes), in addition to being a member of the Permanent Commission for the Protection of Historic and Artistic Monuments of the Holy See and Pontifical Academy supernumerary.

[36] Alcide De Gasperi, although released from prison in the summer of 1928, was under constant surveillance. He submitted an application in the autumn of the same year to be hired at the Vatican Library as a supernumerary. His acceptance came on 3 April 1929, about two months after the drawing up of the Lateran Pacts. He was promoted to secretary of the same library on 15 January 1939. This resulted in a notable rise in salary; in the past, his salary had been reduced to such a degree that it put him financially in dire straits when it came to personal and familial necessities.

Librarian of the SCR, that the secretary of the Apostolic Library, Alcide De Gasperi, will be transferred to the archives of the Holy Congregation de Propaganda Fide, for the time necessary to complete the work that Your Most Reverend Excellency has anticipated, which without a doubt will be well received by His Holiness Pius XII, who is very interested in missiological studies.

Anselmo M. Albareda, m. b., Prefect.

I gave the Hon. De Gasperi some old tattered books that dealt with indigenous members of the clergy. He brought the pages translated from the German book that I had loaned him quite some time ago, and he once again began to work on his translation. I gave him the rough copies of two books that my brother and I are in the course of publishing, and in this way we had an authentic, honest, and adequate alibi in case someone launched an inquiry. He also most diligently revised the pages of the book I am editing: *Il Divino Consolatore*.[37]

7 MARCH 1944

Today at the Propaganda there was a meeting of a Plenary Congregation with the participation of five cardinals. One minute before 10 o'clock we heard the ominous sound of the siren. The cardinals lifted their heads – halting for a moment their discussion – then began looking around as if they were asking themselves what was happening. But no one said a word, and they quickly got back to their discussion about the Propaganda's business. Later we again heard the widespread noise of airplanes, followed by the dull, thundering explosions of distant bombs that made the Propaganda's window panes shake.

Our talks continued until all topics were exhausted. Then the cardinals stood in the waiting room while waiting for the all-clear signal. "We, too, have become accustomed to the bombs," said Cardinal Marmaggi,[38] who lives in the Trastevere area.

[37] The volume was published two years later with the following bibliographic information: C. Costantini, *Il divino consolatore. Il senso della vita e della morte* (Rome: Editrice Danesi, 1946).

[38] Francesco Marmaggi (1870–1949), appointed titular archbishop of Adrianopoli in 1920, was made cardinal of Saint Cecily in 1935. He was the prefect of the Holy Congregation of the Council. Currently, the duties of this ministry are, for the most part, within the jurisdiction of the Congregation for the Clergy.

In the evening we learned that the attack had struck, in particular, the Ostiense district and Monteverde, unfortunately, resulting in great damage and many victims. May God free us from this horrible and stupid war! Everyone is feeling sadness, disgust, and exasperation at both the Germans and the Allies, who have massacred Italy in order to attack Germany. They destroyed the Abbey of Montecassino for no military advantage. Not even the ruins were occupied. People are saying, "What fools they are!"

9 MARCH 1944

From the meetings that I often have *horis subcessivis* with politicians, I believe I have determined the following:

Secret Political Activity
There exists a Committee for National Liberation [CLN], which is made up of different political parties. These parties are:

1 The Liberal Party (the old Cavourian party);
2 The Christian Democratic Party (made up of members of the old People's Party and young people from Catholic Action. It bases its platform on the social principles preached by the Church and on adherence to pontifical guidelines);
3 The Labour Democratic Party (old radicals who, however, state that they have renounced anticlericalism);
4 The Socialist Party;
5 The Communist Party;
6 The Action Party (which follows Mazzini's ideology and has accepted several Masons).

These parties, which are linked together all over Italy within the Liberation Committee, are anti-German, anti-Fascist, anti-Badoglian, and lean toward the creation of a coalition government. Their opinions often differ, however, regarding methods of combat, and it is believed that in a short while they will have to clear up the matter. The Christian Democrats act as moderators. Beyond the Liberation Committee there are other small groups, like the Catholic Communists, the Social Christians, those from the National Centre, and some others of various democratic gradations, more or less in favour of Badoglio.

Political Trends of the Christian Democratic Party
In the Christian Democratic Party the youth wing, with large representation, has rather advanced ideas; another group, which is more moderate, is made up of magistrates or officials; the centre of the party is made up of labour organizers for workers and farmers, ex-members of parliament and intellectuals.

Sporadic Periodicals (of necessity, underground)
1 The Christian Democratic Party publishes *Il Popolo*.
2 The group made up mainly of Catholic magistrates publishes *Il Segno*.
3 The democratic youth group publishes *La Punta*.
4 The Social Christians publish *L'Azione*.
5 The Liberal Party publishes *Il Risorgimento Liberale*.
6 The Labour Democratic Party publishes *La Democrazia del Lavoro*.
7 The Socialist Party publishes *L'Avanti!*.
8 The Communist Party publishes *L'Unità*.
9 The Action Party publishes *L'Italia Libera*.

Various Political Trends
Regarding the institutional regime, the political trends can be roughly reduced to three:

1 monarchists (the abdication of the King to Prince Umberto or to his younger nephews, with regency);
2 republicans (the immediate declaration of a republic);
3 constitutionalists (acceptance of the monarchy now, but subject to Victor Emmanuel III's abdication, while referring to the constitution [Constituent Assembly]; it would convene at the end of the war, then decide on the type of regime).

The Christian Democrats adhere to the third trend; it is also supported by all the moderate parties of the anti-Fascist coalition.

Social Content
The political currents can also be reduced to three:

1 the Extremist or Communist;

2 the Socialist, which distinguishes itself from the Communist current because of religious reasons, and which holds a more moderate view of the nationalization of property and favours a national concept;

3 the Moderate, which allows the division of major properties and includes the workers in industrial profit sharing, but allows managerial autonomy and the free flow of capital.

In the Christian Democrat group there are two trends: the more moderate one of the elderly members and the more radical one of the youth and the workers.

The Partisans

Groups of young people, having avoided being drafted by Graziani, went into hiding and many took refuge in the mountains, together with other patriots against the Germans and Mussolini's pseudo republic. They live a very hard life; they are constantly exposed to the gravest of dangers, and with help from the Allies who drop supplies from their planes, they organize guerrilla warfare. It is a shame that among the partisans – who are inspired by absolute patriotism – some thugs have snuck in and, under the guise of patriotism, carry out acts of cruelty, retaliation, and theft. History repeats itself: with Garibaldi and with D'Annunzio in Fiume it was the same thing!

10 MARCH 1944

Yesterday, around 11 o'clock, there was another huge raid by American planes. They struck the Littorio airfield and the neighbourhoods of Tiburtino and Piazza Bologna. I was at the Grande Albergo, near the Baths of Diocletian, and the anti-aircraft fire and the bombs ominously shook the windows. They say there are 200 dead.

I had been called to give the last sacraments to Senator Salata. He had suffered a brain haemorrhage. I found him very close to death. But I think he recognized me and understood what I was saying. He died around 6 PM. Providence saved him the pain of seeing the recent decline of Italy, with the probable loss of those "unredeemed" territories for which Salata fought so hard.

While returning to the Propaganda I came across two trucks full of bags, bundles, household belongings, and on top of these piles of destitution were men, women, children, all dazed. It was a sight that caused tremendous pain through the streets of Rome, which were being crossed by German soldiers in trucks or cars, soldiers with an air of indifference and sometimes of disdain.

In these last few days, due to the damage inflicted on the aqueducts, many areas were without water, and the women and children lined up near some fountains that still could offer the very precious resource. At the Moses Fountain beside Via xx Settembre, I saw a real swarm of people around the basins; young people had climbed up the lions' backs and stuck hoses in the lions' mouths. All to be seen and heard was the bustle and clamour and the moving of flasks, buckets, pots, watering cans to draw water. The scene was lively and bustling; it really matched the one that was carved by G.B. Della Porta on the fountain's panel. Moses' gesture, the work of Prospero da Brescia, looks as if he wants to impose a bit of order in the midst of that uproarious bustling.

Last night around 6 PM, the nuns came home slightly fearful because they had seen people running toward Via Tomacelli. This morning we learned that a squad of Fascists had been passing through there and someone had thrown grenades into the middle of the squad. Five dead and about twenty wounded.

11 MARCH 1944

A diplomat who had accompanied Mussolini to Berlin was beside him when at Verona Station, D'Annunzio came to say hello to him. He told me that D'Annunzio said to Mussolini three times, in a loud voice: "Don't trust the Hun."

A SPECIAL AND ADMIRABLE AUDIENCE
IN ST PETER'S SQUARE   12 MARCH 1944

What a special and marvellous audience in St Peter's Square. The Holy Father Pius XII had a wonderful idea when he decided to gather the refugees, evacuees, and the people of Rome in Saint Peter's Square, today being the sixth anniversary of his coronation. He had also found out, as he himself told me, how to overcome the not so minor objections that were made for reasons of safety. Everything went well, without the smallest incident. The rain that day cleared. The square was a living thrill. Between the Pope, dressed in a simple white robe, and the people, a sharing of affection and thoughts was quickly established. His speech was excellent.

Everyone was hanging on the Holy Father's words. Many eyes were wet with tears. A woman next to me, with a baby in her arms, cried silently and kissed her child and then kissed it again. It occurred to me that the child must be a war orphan. Then the Holy Father, uplifted by a wide world view, spoke these brave and holy words: "If any city anywhere in the world is struck by an air war that respects neither law nor restraint – in itself a terrible act of accusation against the cruelty of similar methods of fighting – how can We believe that someone would ever dare to transform Rome ... into a battlefield, a theatre of war, and in so doing perpetrate an act that is just as militarily inglorious and abominable in the eyes of God and of humanity, conscious of the highest and most intangible moral and spiritual values?"[39]

The crowd, which carried on its applause throughout the speech, left the square unwillingly, for it was there that they were able to breathe air that was both pure and comforting before returning to the heavy, dark air of the city.

14 MARCH 1944

Even today, around 11 o'clock, there was a massive raid carried out by Allied airplanes. Huge amounts of damage to the areas of Tiburtino, Prenestino, and Nomentano. Many are dead. Even Virginio Gayda, former director of *Il Giornale d'Italia*, was buried and killed under the rubble of his own home. He lived in an isolated area. Some time ago he had asked me if I believed that the Allies, coming to Rome, would want to prosecute him for his fierce articles against England. I answered while at the same time reassuring him. On the table against which the journalist was crushed was my illustrated book, *Gesù Cristo Via, Verità e Vita*.

This evening there was an unusual traffic of trucks and Red Cross ambulances. Two big signs were hung on the walls. One of them showed the spectre of death rising above a city in flames, and it says "Here come the liberators!" In the other, a black soldier is grabbing a girl (the image is taken from The *Rape of the Sabine Women* by Giambologna). On the poster is the caption: "The liberty ... of the liberators."

15 MARCH 1944

During the 14 March air raid seven nuns were crushed to death. A bomb fell near a fountain where there was a group of women. They say that one was decapitated and thrown onto the tramlines.

[39] Pius XII's speech, here partially quoted, can be found in its entirety in AAS 36 (*Bollettino Ufficiale della Santa Sede*, 1944), 97–100.

18 MARCH 1944

This morning there was also the grim and far-reaching noise of Allied planes over the Roman sky; a sound that disappeared toward the outskirts of the city, where a number of loud explosions were heard. A large strike is going on at Cassino and Nettuno; so far, nothing decisive has happened. Rome more than ever is invaded by the passage – in the wrong direction – of trucks, cars, Red Cross ambulances. The demeanour of Rome's inhabitants is serious and almost indifferent. Their mental attitude has changed greatly. They await the arrival of the Allies without any positive feelings toward them; in fact, they wait with conscious loathing because of the massacre of innocent people on the outskirts of Rome. Everyone holds a concise and severe opinion of them: "The Americans and English are powerful when it comes to machines, but they don't seem to have brilliant or extensive strategic ideas like those of the Russians. Theirs is a short-range strategic outlook. After the strange decision to land at Taranto to ... conquer Italy by slipping through mountain ravines, they repeated that little trick by landing at Nettuno instead of Follonica or Livorno, or even better, La Spezia. There is nothing great about them."

Someone says that the *piccolo fante italiano* [humble Italian infantryman] would have had a more nimble spirit. And so the Allies brought the war to Rome. They had respect for Athens and Cairo, but they weren't able to respect Rome enough. If the Germans had had a bit of diplomacy, a bit of respect for personal freedom, they would have made themselves – if not liked, at least tolerated, as the Allies will be. But the German way – nighttime raids on homes, pillaging, etc. – makes people hate them.

This evening, passing through the streets, I ran into a group of evacuees: women, men, children clinging to their mothers' skirts. The adults were laden with bundles, wearing clothes that show their destitution and their unexpected escape. A few women, standing on a street corner, a child at the breast, wait for alms but do not ask for them. On one of the small lawns at the base of Victor Emmanuel's monument there was a woman kneeling, bent over the ground looking for some good leaves to eat. The black market rages on. People fear hunger. The Holy Father is doing everything possible to supply provisions.

Il Giornale d'Italia reports that in the vicinity of Rome, the Allies machine-gunned a Vatican truck, killing the driver and wounding the mechanic. Yet the papal colours are clearly visible on Vatican trucks.

DE VALERA'S[40] PASSIONATE WORDS
FOR THE SAFETY OF ROME   23 MARCH 1944
Words of sympathy, protest, and love for both the Holy Father and the
city of Rome have come from all over the world, especially after the
damage caused to the Vatican by the bombs that fell on 2 March. We
will publish de Valera's[41] very noble message (he is the head of the Irish
government).

BOMBS ON VIA RASELLA   23 MARCH 1944
Today, the anniversary of the founding of the Fasci, was a day – at least
until the early evening – that seemed to be passing without disturbance.
At 4:30 I was saying the breviary when I heard the singing of a squad of
German soldiers that was crossing Spanish Square, heading for Via dei
Due Macelli. A few moments later we heard in the distance a loud explosion. I went down and saw people all over the square turning here and
there and running around utterly frightened. At the entrance of Via dei
Due Macelli a small crowd was looking curiously toward the intersection of Via dei Due Macelli and Via del Tritone. At the bottom of the
street there was some activity that involved soldiers, police officers, and
trucks. Some PAI [Police of Italian Africa] agents were coming toward
Spanish Square and were ordering its doors to be closed. A Fascist
grasped and shook a revolver while shouting threatening words.

They say that some bombs had been dropped on a squad of German
soldiers from a house in Via Rasella, killing some of them and wounding

[40] Eamon de Valera (1882–1975), an Irish politician, was sentenced to death
for having participated in the Easter Rising of 1916, but the following year he
was pardoned. As president of the irredentist organization Sinn Féin, which
means "we ourselves," he was again put in prison but was able to escape to the
United States, from where he directed the revolutionary government. He founded
an extremist republican party of opposition called Fianna Fáil that won the 1932
election and brought him the role of prime minister. His government distinguished
itself for breaking away from the United Kingdom, a decision shared by the
majority of the Irish people. From 1938 on, their relationship improved. During
the Second World War he kept his country neutral. He held the office of prime
minister until 1948 and again in 1951–54, and 1957. He was elected president of
Ireland in 1959, an office he held until 1973, when he retired from political life.
[41] Costantini is referring to de Valera's speech – here omitted – from the
23 March 1944 edition of *L'Avvenire d'Italia*.

others. Real fear spread among the people. I got back to the Propaganda, where some frightened women had also taken shelter. We closed the main door. Later on, Spanish Square seemed almost deserted and more peaceful.

I went out and went to the Piazza del Popolo. There was nothing extraordinary going on there except for passing trucks with soldiers and armed PAI militiamen, and some small groups of people. Going down the Corso, I arrived in front of Palazzo Chigi. I ran into a lot of trucks all going in different directions, full of soldiers and armed militiamen. I also ran into a group of German soldiers who, in a threatening manner, grasped and shook their revolvers.

At the entrance of Via del Tritone there were people looking curious and speaking softly, looking toward Piazza Barberini. At the intersection of Via dei Due Macelli there were trucks, armoured cars, and soldiers. All of a sudden we heard the ominous chatter of a machine gun. The ways out of the streets toward Tritone were guarded by soldiers. In front of San Claudio's Church there was an armed squad from the PAI. They said that German soldiers had surrounded the house from which the bombs were thrown. Because blood calls for more blood! O Lord, have pity on us!

THE FOSSE ARDEATINE MASSACRE   24 MARCH 1944
In retaliation for the soldiers killed in Via Rasella, the German Command ordered the execution of 335 Italians, taken at random from the prisons. They were killed at the Ardeatine Caves with the standard shot in the back of the head. They were not given the Last Sacraments, but among those taken was the good Father Don Pietro Pappagallo.[42] It is to be believed that he suggested to those about to die that they raise their thoughts to God, and he absolved them. This horrendous murder – that cannot be justified with any excuse – has generated in everyone a feeling of horror and deep hatred toward the Germans.

                                                  3 APRIL 1944
After the statement with which German Command announced the demilitarization of Rome, we see fewer Germans in the city though still

[42] Pietro Pappagallo, a presbyter, was in jail because he was caught participating in the Roman resistance against the Nazi-Fascists. His work, together with that of Don Giuseppe Morosini, was highlighted in the renowned Roberto Rossellini film *Roma città aperta* [Rome Open City].

encounter some empty trucks, some cars with officials, and Red Cross ambulances – but no one sees tanks anymore.

They say that this type of truce was of great concern to the Holy Father and that, in fact, he tried to make it more definite with a bilateral accord, which until now, however, has not been made.

People are tired, apathetic, and distressed about the reduction of the bread ration. Black market prices go up every day.

There is moral depression and bitter disappointment about the Allies' failure on the Cassino front.

The horror for the massacre of 335 hostages lingers on. The Communists, from the mouth of Ercoli (Togliatti), who have returned from Russia, are proposing to be part of the government by deferring the issue of the monarchy. A bold and skilful move that confuses everyone. They obviously are striving to take over the armed forces.

3 APRIL 1944

The black market runs rampant: they don't even have the usual concern about its activity. At Tor di Nona the market is openly thriving. I'm jotting down some items and their price per kilogram:

Pork	L350
Beans	L150
Flour	L110
Bread	L40
Lettuce	L40
Eggs (each)	L12
Wine (per litre)	L25
Oil (per litre)	L400
Shoes (per pair)	L1,600
An artichoke	L15
Broccoli or cauliflower	L55

A PAPAL FLEET FOR ROME'S PROVISIONS[43]   8 APRIL 1944

[Here, the cardinal cites a newspaper article that is not reprinted here.] Last night the newspaper *Tribuna*, carrying an article on Easter 1944, was confiscated.

[43] Costantini transcribes an article that appeared in the 8 April 1944 edition of the *Tribuna* entitled *Le navi battenti bandiera dello Stato della Città del Vaticano avrebbero come scalo di Roma il porto di Fiumicino.*

EASTER, 9 APRIL 1944

What a sad Easter! There appears on the face of every soul the image of their homeland not only defeated but disunited, disintegrated. Hunger appears in Rome as a sinister shadow. Office workers have squandered all their savings and they are on the streets with no money. The evacuees, especially women with babies at the breast, standing still on the sidewalk, are transformed into something desolate on this holiday, which is usually so happy and gay because of its comforting religious and humane significance, as well as because of the natural world that reawakens and blossoms again.

Everyone is again anticipating being freed from this tragic waiting, but the Allies are confined to Montecassino and Anzio. We often hear distant shellfire. Last night I saw Count Volpi. He is no longer the man he was. After his imprisonment and later confinement in his palace, he has aged. He has lost his brilliant ability to resolve problems quickly, as well as his quickness of insight. Even his legs seem to be unsteady. He was very sad, thinking of what he had done for Mussolini's government, in particular resolving the debts from the other war in America and Britain, and look how he was repaid!

He was also embittered by how his own Venice has disowned him! He told me that the church in Marghera to which he gave 2 million lire to have built was hit and possibly destroyed by American planes. He showed me, with visible satisfaction, a lovely letter from Cardinal Piazza,[44] patriarch of Venice. Even when all your friends drift away, the Church always remains a faithful friend.

[44] Adeodato Giovanni Piazza (1884–1957), a prelate from the order of the Barefoot Carmelites – which he served as general secretary (1923–29) – was in 1930 appointed archbishop of Benevento, a diocese that he served until 1935, when he was promoted to patriarch of Venice. He was made cardinal presbyter in 1937. During the Second World War he did his utmost to have Venice declared an open city so that it would have sufficient foodstuff. He stood out for his work assisting young people. Immediately after the war, along with the bishop of Trieste, Mons. Antonio Santin, he denounced the barbaric acts that were committed by the Communist Yugoslavs in Julian Venice, Istria, and Dalmatia. Pius XII called him to Rome in 1948 to serve as secretary of the Sacred Consistorial Congregation, presided over by the Pontiff himself, and in so doing promoted him to the order of cardinal bishops.

298 The Secrets of a Vatican Cardinal

Today at the Propaganda there was a meeting for doctors, university professors, and private tradespeople that Mons. Ruffini[45] had arranged at Easter Communion with a series of sermons in our chapel. There were many people at the meeting, which was one of great significance: science, which at one time seemed to be the enemy of Faith, has once again taken its place on a physical – not metaphysical – level. Faith illuminates the spirit, raising it to be able to see the greatest visions of life, of the universe, and of God.

MONTECASSINO: A SENSELESS AND USELESS ACT

Lisbon, 12. In an article[46] discussing the destruction of the famous Montecassino Abbey by the British-American air force, the British Catholic weekly *Fedman* poses the following question to the British government: What result did the Allies obtain with the destruction of a historic monument like the Abbey of Montecassino? Are there still people who hold the belief that the German artillery was positioned in the monastery and that, to the Germans, the cloister served as a more useful observation point than its rubble? Wouldn't it have been more sensible to recognize that it was not the monastery but the mountain that was useful to the Germans and that with the vandalistic destruction of the abbey, the Allies obtained no positive results, since they left the mountain untouched and, furthermore, left it in the hands of the Germans? The article asks that the issue be discussed in the House of

---

[45] Ernesto Ruffini (1888–1967) was based in the Diocese of Mantova but moved to Rome as a professor of theology at the Pontifical Roman Major Seminary at St John Lateran's Basilica. He became a substitute book censor for the Holy Congregation of the Holy Office, adviser to the Pontifical Biblical Commission, and then secretary to the Sacred Congregation of Seminaries and Universities. He was appointed archbishop of Palermo in October 1945 and made cardinal in 1946. In Sicily he favoured political unity among the Catholic electorate and put into action an anti-Communist mobilization. In his honour, they built a neighbourhood called Villaggio Ruffini, which served to provide decent housing to families living in very poor areas. At the Second Vatican Council he took a very conservative doctrinal position, together with Cardinals Alfredo Ottaviani and Giuseppe Siri.

[46] The article is from the 13 April 1944 edition of *Il Piccolo*.

Commons and that the British government give its assurance that in future such actions will not be repeated. "The criminal destruction of the Abbey," concluded the Catholic weekly, "will remain as a senseless and useless act."

DON GIUSEPPE MOROSINI   12 APRIL 1944

On Monday of Holy Week, 3 April 1944, Don Giuseppe Morosini[47] was killed by a firing squad. In the days before his death he had been a source of great edification for his fellow prisoners (each night the prayers of the rosary resonated through the vaults of the third wing of the Regina Coeli prison). On the day of his execution he asked to be allowed to celebrate Holy Mass; he was assisted by the vice-regent of Rome, His Excellency Monsignor Traglia.

They say that Don Morosini, while on his way to the execution site, before the order to fire was given, wanted to give his blessing to the soldiers of the firing squad – and the first tears shed in his memory were those that appeared in the eyes of his executioners.

[47] Giuseppe Morosini (1913–1944), a member of the Congregation of the Mission, was ordained a presbyter in 1937 by the vice-regent of the Diocese of Rome, Mons. Luigi Traglia. He was a military chaplain in 1941 in the Fiume area in Istria. He moved to Rome in 1943 and dedicated himself to helping young evacuees in the areas hit by the war in the Della Vittoria district. On 8 September he joined, as a spiritual assistant, the Roman resistance against the Nazi-Fascists. However, he also worked toward procuring weapons and provisions of fresh supplies, getting in contact with La banda Fulvi, a group under Giuseppe Cordero Lanza di Montezemolo. From an official in the Wehrmacht, he obtained the German forces' plans for the Cassino front, but he was arrested by the Gestapo on 4 January 1944, having been accused by a paid informer, Dante Bruna. Subjected to torture in the Regina Coeli prison because he would not reveal the names of his accomplices, not only did he not give in but he tried to shoulder all responsibility for every one of the movement's offences. In spite of the pressure applied by the Holy See, he was shot at Forte Bravetta on 3 April 1944. He was accompanied to the place of execution by Mons. Luigi Traglia. He received many posthumous awards, among them the Gold Medal of Military Valour on 15 February 1945, a square dedicated in his name in the Roman district of Della Vittoria, and a commemorative stamp issued in 1997.

12 APRIL 1944

The Hon. X sent me this note: "The usual source (a typist for the Fascists) informed me that in all probability the planned action against the Urbano would take place tonight. I don't know of course if the news is very reliable, but I thought it important to warn you."

At the same time the rector of Urban College[48] came to me somewhat alarmed by the same rumour. We decided to go to the central police station. There I found the second-in-command, a man who made a good impression on me; he was serious, kind, and deferential. He said that he was not aware of any such plans. In answer, I explained to him that as we had advised the authorities, the responsibility now fell on him. I also underlined the international nature of the college and its particular legal position.

13 APRIL 1944

Within the Christian Democratic Party there are many technical committees that study their administrative and organizational problems while also keeping in touch with the ICAS[49] and other organs of Catholic Action. They think that right now the ideal way to face Communism is to gather into one or two volumes "documents and objective studies on Communism" (their principles, procedures, politics, and economics). A collection of material such as this could then direct and prompt popular propaganda.

Preliminary talks with Socialists and Communists are ongoing; these talks concern the future framework of the union organization of public law. The condition enforcing the utmost respect for the religious and political beliefs of workers has already been accepted.

[48] Urban College [Collegio Urbano de Propaganda Fide] takes its name from its founder, Pope Urban VIII, who established it with the bull *Immortalis Dei* on 1 August 1627. In 1944 the rector of the ecclesiastical university college, connected to the Pontificio Ateneo Urbano de Propaganda, founded by the same pontiff, was Mons. Domenico Brizi.

[49] The acronym ICAS stands for Istituto Cattolico Attività Sociali, which was one of the only papal union organizations that survived during Fascism. In order to guarantee its survival, ICAS had to undergo a type of "confessionalization," which it used as a shield when dealing with the government led by Mussolini, and also had to agree to substantial collaboration with the regime.

The Christian Democrats propose always to keep in mind and defend the encyclical's statements about Communism,[50] but they believe that in reality they will be forced to come to an agreement with the Communists, at least at the beginning, in order to be able to work together in the government. This doesn't seem to be difficult because on 10 April in Naples, Ercoli-Togliatti gave a speech "guaranteeing that the Communists will respect Catholic beliefs and that they have the highest respect for the Church." But can we trust the Communists' statements?

The Action Party of young liberals is revealing more and more its anti-clerical stance. A recent booklet, published under the name of Francesco Marchi,[51] *Il Partito d'Azione nei suoi metodi e nei suoi fini*, foreshadows on page 20 and on the following pages a campaign against "the past substantial assistance granted [by the Church] to Fascist despotism" as well as against the Concordat. It seems that some of the few moderate members intend to leave the party.

13 APRIL 1944

Beautiful days, thanks to the weather and the season, but also empty, colourless, uncertain, full of anxiety when it comes to people's state of mind.

The tragic reality of people hiding to escape capture, enlistment, or the commandeering of labour becomes even more distressing and frightening. People who live on the "black market" are quickly using up their savings. Poverty is spreading; it is visible on the streets with the women and children evacuees who ask for alms, and it is hidden in those who, having lived in civilized conditions, are now becoming beggars, this perhaps being the greater of the two torments. Old officials, having fired their maids, line up in front of food stores.

14 APRIL 1944

There haven't been any incidents at Urban College. I found out that a group of Roman Fascists had asked police headquarters to carry out the

[50] The encyclical mentioned here is that of Pius XI, issued on 19 March 1937 and entitled *Divini Redemptoris*.

[51] The real last name of the author, who was of Sardinian origin, was Fancello. Marchi was his mother's last name, but he also used the pseudonym Brundu. The volume quoted was published by the Società Anonima Poligrafica Italiana of Rome in 1944.

planned raid. The answer was that "Rome's Fascists remain free to do what they think, but on their own responsibility." The intervention of police headquarters probably spoiled their plans, and the raid has been averted, at least for the time being.

THE MURDER OF GIOVANNI GENTILE   18 APRIL 1944
The murder of poor Gentile,[52] carried out yesterday in Florence, fills me with horror, and it disgraces the faction that committed such an act. Poor Gentile! I was on very cordial terms with him. When announcing a series of lectures at the Istituto per il Medio ed Estremo Oriente, Gentile said many kind words about me. However, and above all, he paid homage to the Catholic Church by using words that could have come from the mouth of a prelate. He was, I think, a soul trapped in internal anguish. They assured me that he used to pray. It wasn't so long ago that he was invited to an audience with the Holy Father Pius XII.[53]

[52] Giovanni Gentile (1875–1944), an Italian philosopher of Sicilian origin, a representative of right-wing Hegelian idealism, was one of the major exponents of national culture in the first half of the twentieth century. In 1903 he helped found Benedetto Croce's magazine *La Critica*. In 1920 he founded *Il Giornale critico della filosofia italiana,* a publication he managed until 1943. He became a professor of philosophy at the University of Palermo in 1906, at the Scuola Normale di Pisa in 1914, and finally at the University of Rome. He took up Fascism in 1922 when he was appointed senator. He became minister of education in the government led by Mussolini, 1922–25, and in this role he brought about an extensive scholastic reform that bears his name. Afterwards he took over the running of the *Grande Enciclopedia Italiana* (Treccani) as well as the Scuola Normale di Pisa. After the armistice 8 September 1943, in collaboration with the Republic of Salò, he accepted the position of president of the Italian Academy – a choice that cost him his life. On 15 April 1944 he was killed by the Political Action Group [Gruppo di Azione Patriottica (GAP)]. He authored many theoretical publications and different kinds of cultural writings in which he often brought into focus the relationship between philosophy and religion. His last literary work, published in 1943, is entitled *La mia religione* (Florence: Sansoni, 1943)

[53] Costantini quotes from the 17–18 April 1944 edition of *L'Osservatore Romano* where, regarding the murder of Professor Gentile, he refers to "these proud and holy words."

AN UNDERGROUND MANIFESTO   19 APRIL 1944

I was secretly delivered a flyer with the following manifesto:

ITALIANS! We are in a time of great turmoil for our nation. What we do now will be able to have a decisive effect for many, many years to come in the history of our homeland.

In the north, a foreigner who introduced himself as one of the Allies has indisputably behaved like an enemy ... In the south, the English, French, Italian, and American armies advance. From this there is some hope, but also danger ... a menace ... There is the "Communist" menace ...

We therefore have to defend ourselves against the aberrations of the Fascist-Republicans and against an anti-Catholic and anti-national show of democracy.

The CENTRO POLITICO ITALIANO has published an IMPLEMENTA-TION PLAN. Ask for it, study it, join, and as a result, act. Long live Italy! Praise the Lord!

THE ORGANIZING COMMITTEE OF THE CENTRO
POLITICO ITALIANO

THE BRAVE LETTER OF 17 BISHOPS FROM THE VENETO[54]

20 APRIL 1944

Crimes against human life are being committed more frequently, as never before, so much so that we must think of this as a hidden civil and fratricidal war that could spin frighteningly out of control. The bishops, who are worried by this situation, feel it is their responsibility to remind their followers that to be a brutal killer, to traitorously kill another man, is an act that goes against the Commandment "Thou shalt not kill," as well as against the code of all civilized people. One is equally deemed a murderer – except in the case of self-defence – if one cuts short a human life because of vendetta, reprisal, or free enterprise (whether personal or pertaining to a political party).

Another cause of deep unhappiness and lack of courage is linked to the forced removal or deportation of people, those who are unaware of the fate to which they are heading.

Finally, the clergy of the Tre-Venezie, who deeply share the anguish of their sons and daughters, send to all those who are suffering physically and spiritually – particularly those in cities and countries tortured by

54 "Veneto" refers to today's Triveneto (Tri-Venetian) area and the Fiume area in Istria.

disastrous and lethal raids and by other aspects of war – a paternal word of comfort, of blessing, and of a Christian invitation to offer their martyrdom in exchange for the salvation of souls, of their homeland, and of humanity. Venice, 20 April 1944[55]

FIRST COMMUNION WITH THE EVACUEES 23 APRIL 1944

In the first days of the month of December in 1943, a group of farmers from Castelforte had looked for shelter on a farm near Monteverde Nuovo that had. been abandoned by airmen following the events of 8 September. In the huge hangars that were recently built – though without windows or doors – the poor ill-fated individuals had settled near a perimeter wall. They had nothing but a few blankets, taken during the hurried escape from their homes. They slept on the bare ground.

As soon as they heard about these poor people, a group of charitable people began an operation to provide them with aid. Since it was impossible to get beds for them, they were given some mattresses for those who really needed them and, for all of them, some straw. In the meantime, the number of the poor people grew. They came from Cassino, Ostia, and Acilia; there were whole families, with many children. They took advantage of the large buildings and settled into their improvised lodgings. Many were without food-ration cards and were in serious condition. Having gone to see the meritorious Circle of St Peter, the helpers were able to obtain supplies: 300 bowls of soup to be picked up in Via della Lungaretta. Given the great distance between the circle's kitchens and the place where the evacuees had settled, it was necessary to provide transport for the soup. This was accomplished by a group of young university students and graduates who gladly took it upon themselves to carry out the job, which was neither easy nor light. Every day, after the visit to each of the evacuee groups, we said the rosary and gave a short sermon. Each Sunday, in a structure in Casermette, which was respectably transformed into a chapel, we held Holy Mass. They were supplied with clothes and medicine; doctors who usually attend the poor, as well as necessary disinfection facilities, were provided for them. Since a large group of children were at the age of First Communion, we decided to

---

[55] Following the date are the signatures of the bishops or, for the vacant sees, those of vicars capitular, as well as the signature of the vicar general of Concordia, which was a *sede impedita* diocese looked after by an apostolic administrator because of Bishop Luigi Paulini's illness.

prepare them appropriately. The date of the ceremony was set for Good Shepherd Sunday, 23 April 1944. We decided to take the boys for a short retreat to the San Cosimato Institute and the girls to the Sisters of the Blessed Angelina.[56] And to prepare the evacuees with the Easter precept, we organized a sermon in the Casermette, which was attended by all the evacuees.

While the feverish preparations were underway and a feeling of happiness was in everyone's heart, something happened that threatened to upset all the plans. On the morning of 22 April, while those poor people were sleeping curled up on the floor, a group of Metropolitani [urban police] entered the Casermette, waking everyone and ordering them to gather their things because they were supposed to be transferred elsewhere. It was a horrible moment. The boys and girls were far from their parents on a retreat; we didn't know where those unfortunates would be taken, and the danger of perhaps a very long separation turned their hearts upside down. Very loud screams and sobs resonated throughout the structures, thus getting the attention of those who lived in the neighbouring houses. A phone call was made to the priest who was directing the aid mission in an attempt to save the poor group. The priests from nearby churches were made aware of the situation, and they hurried over and began to take action near the police agents. The immediate reaction was that the parish priest of Trasfigurazione was arrested because he was protesting too loudly. With the intervention of Mons. Ercole, he later obtained his freedom.

Meanwhile, the priest who was helping the evacuees phoned police headquarters describing the severity of the measures and explaining the situation. The authorities realized the delicacy of the situation and the consequences of acting hastily, so they allowed the evacuees to return to the Casermette.

In the evening, while continuing the preparations for the Easter precept, the priest directed his words to the evacuees and began to tell the story of the storm on the lake. When he reminded them of the apostles'

[56] The female religious institution *di diritto pontificio* is that of Blessed Angelina of Montegiove. It was founded in Foligno in 1385, and in 1903 it obtained exemption from the Council of Trent regulations. It was approved by the Holy See on 27 February 1923 and was aggregated with the Order of Friars Minor Capuchin.

cries, "*Domine, salva nos, perimus*,"[57] all those present, reliving the painful horror of the events that morning, burst into tears.

On the morning of the twenty-third, everyone beheld the complete transformation of the large empty room that served as a chapel. The walls and floor were decorated with rugs, damasks, white flowers, and green branches. In the background was the altar, covered by an elegant canopy and adorned with candelabras and with flowers around the picture of the Sacred Heart of Jesus. The ceremony was presided over by His Excellency Mons. Casaroli,[58] the archbishop of Gaeta, who also was a refugee. The children, all in new clothes from head to toe, didn't look at all like the poor of the day before – like evacuees. After the Mass, the children had a good breakfast, and at noon all the evacuees were gathered together in a large room that had been set up as a refectory. On its tables were steaming plates of pasta. Meat was served to all, as well as sufficient amounts of bread, and then a dessert was handed out. This hospitality was made possible by the charity of the Holy Father who, moved by the letter of one of the little girls who received First Communion, had sent 50 kilograms of pasta, 10 kilograms of peas, potato flour, jam, and bread. There were about 300 people who ate in the large room. A little girl expressed the gratitude of all the evacuees to the Holy Father. At the end of the lunch, the whole group of evacuees raised their voices, loudly expressing their feelings of devotion and gratitude to the Supreme Pontiff.

Having eaten their meal, these unfortunate people returned to their bunks, and after putting together their meagre possessions, laden with bundles they began to walk toward a more secure shelter, far from the threat of deportation.

24 APRIL 1944

From the many signs, it seems that the beginning of the famous "second front" – which for so long and in so many voices has been shouted from the rooftops – is imminent. So they would also put Anzio into operation. In Rome our long wait, which has already left us disillusioned and tired, has now become a source of nervousness. The situation appears serious

---

[57] Mt. 8:25. The phrase, translated in English, means "Lord, save us: we perish!"

[58] Dionigio Casaroli (1989–1966), who originally came from the Bologna Diocese, was archbishop of Gaeta, 1926–66.

because of the precariousness of future provisions. Although there are ration cards, there is little flour, no oil, and no lard.

In the last few days some bakers' shops have been stormed. People have been begging at the doors of the Vatican. On the walls I see written, "We want bread!"

Yesterday and today the crisis was resolved by obtaining supplies from different organizations. And tomorrow? German Command seems very worried. The Vatican is making admirable efforts to contribute toward the provisions in spite of the machine-gun fire that has struck Vatican convoys many times.

Last night a poor woman, Brussa from Ovoledo [Udine, now in the province of Pordenone], who for many years had been working in Rome, was waiting for me at the door of the Propaganda. She was the phantom of hunger and could not even stand up because in Grottaferrata her leg had been pierced by a bomb fragment. She begged me to find a job in the Vatican for her son, who was also there and seemed emaciated. A job in exchange only for bread. I said, "I will give him the ration of bread listed on the food-allotment card, but it is not enough to live on!"

25 APRIL 1944

The sad story of the people in hiding has become even sadder. They have been talking about a list of 3,000 men (senators, diplomats, university professors, officials, academics, officers, etc.) who should be deported to northern Italy. Many are in hiding or have moved. Some came to the Propaganda to see if it was possible to find refuge.

Days ago in Quadraro,[59] during the night the Germans made a raid on all the powerful men and deported them – no one knows where – and put them to work. We've gone back to slavery. They don't respect the fundamental rights of life.

27 APRIL 1944

The battle front is calm. Even the sky over Rome smiles serenely; in the last few days it has not been crossed by airplanes. The price of food is astronomical; a flask of oil is 1,500 lire; a kilo of coffee 5,000 lire.

---

[59] Quadraro is an urban area in the Tuscolano district of Rome, between Via Tuscolana and Via Casilina after Porta Furba.

Tonight, around 6 PM, I left the Propaganda and I saw near Piazza Mignanelli a bus full of people that had been stopped. At its corners were four policemen. People were walking around it, looking at it with curiosity. They were doing a round-up of young people and men to take them off to work … This evening many families will be waiting for their loved ones – a husband, a father, a son – and he will not arrive, nor will he have been able to send any news … This is Hitler's new civilization!

I was shown the homily that Cardinal Piazza, patriarch of Venice, gave on Easter Day, which was later published as a booklet. It is an excellent pastoral document, full of Christian feeling and courage, and delivered while Venice is still under the German heel:

The Resurrection of the Nation
We await the resurrection of this Italy, the turmoil overcome in this massive conflict. Italy, its territory divided, also its spirit; its sons and monuments humiliated and tortured, made into a desert and a cemetery where the gusts of the infernal storm have passed and will pass.

"How is the gold become dim! How is the most fine gold changed! The stones of the sanctuary are poured out at the top of every street" [Lam 4:1]. Alas, today the lamentations of Jeremiah have become for us a burning reality. Still, we do not want to give up hope. More than the reserves of kindness and volitional energy of our people, more than the bravery of the servicemen and the destiny of war, we who believe trust in He who has given our country the privilege of the Apostolic See and the primacy of Faith, which in the span of twenty centuries has withstood heresy and schisms. The mission to spread throughout the world a civility that is genuinely Christian is not yet finished. Now, in the crucible of the most bitter of purifications, Italy prepares herself for future responsibilities. But only one thing is important: that she remain Catholic – the type of true Catholicism that leans on the unfaltering stone of the Roman Pontificate. A different Italy would be destined to vanish in the wreckage of all of its religious and civil values.

For this reason, we wish for a resurrected nation with its territory and population in total unity, absolutely free of any foreign domination, in a position to decide its own fate and its own future. But above all, a nation free from every outlandish influence that goes against its religious and cultural traditions. We prepare for its resurrection within our souls, and it is precisely here that the Church – faithful to its divine mandate, without political trespassing that in other times was disapproved of by its same prosecutors – will offer its collaboration, the only type of collaboration that adapts to both the nature of the Church and the true good of the nation.

Mane nobiscum, quoniam advesperascit[60]
There was no evening more dark and desolate than this world's tragic evening; no night that proceeded in a manner denser and threatening, with more bolts of lightning and so full of distress. Therefore, O Lord, stay with us. We can see you, a shadow of light in the haze of these times, a victim among victims in daily Eucharistic immolation, and our comforting spiritual nourishment.

Mane nobiscum, Domine. Stay here, protect our lives and our homes, our helpless frailties and our sacred innocence, our broken hearts and our souls full of bitterness. Here, among the survivors and the victims, in the hospitals and in the cemeteries, on the desecrated ground of the nation, among the rubble and the broken crosses, wherever you have placed the seal of your faith, where you come while preparing for the dawn of the resurrection. Because even in cemeteries and in the ruins of civilization, even on the battle-fields and fields of slavery, even in mangled bodies and wounded souls, even throughout the nation and in the destiny of humanity resonates, O Christ, your word of hope and salvation. O Christ, repeat your cry of love and victory: "I am the resurrection and the life."[61]

28 APRIL 1944

After a few days of calm, also due to bad weather, this morning we again heard the noisy rumble of bombs on the outskirts of Rome.

From Treviso has come some very sad news about the poor city's destruction by the Allies.[62] They say there are more than 10,000 dead ...

The state of mind of the Italians regarding the Americans and English is growing more bitter. These massacres of innocent people, like the useless destruction of Montecassino, have no justification in the explanations of the war. In fact, there is no relationship between the horrendous massacres and the alleged military advantages. There are many other places they could hit without massacres and without the destruction of famous monuments.

---

[60] The passage from Lk. 24:29 means "Stay with us, because it is toward evening."

[61] The passage can be found in Jn. 11:25.

[62] The dreadful bombing of Treviso occurred on Good Friday, 7 April 1944.

THE ANGLICANS AND THE ORTHODOX AGAINST ROME[63]

29 APRIL 1944

[Article extracts omitted here]

4 MAY 1944

The raging anti-aircraft strikes continue over the coastal areas (Genoa, La Spezia, Livorno, and etc.). One's mind is full of terror when one sees our beautiful and dear cities in ruins.

And all of this because after Mussolini fell they said, "The war continues." The machine-gun fire directed at the Vatican convoy that was bringing food to Rome – which was denounced by L'Osservatore Romano with crushing accuracy – provoked deeply felt contempt. We hope that these atrocious instruments of war represent the final epilogue of a tragic situation that has dragged on now for too long and could boil over into a revolt at any moment.

In Rome we fear that from one moment to the next there will not be any food. We also know that underground agitation is being carried on by antisocial groups.

Today the Belgian missionary M. told me that in his country a deep resentment has developed toward the Allies because they spread ruin without any regard for human life. "They are," he says, "for the most part, pagans for whom nothing exists except pleasure and money. They have no Christian sensibility."

Yesterday in Viale Flaminio there was a crowd of people carrying empty suitcases: women and men, who from their appearance seemed to be farmers. They were waiting for a makeshift vehicle to set off back along Via Flaminia. It is the organization of the "black market" that brings various items and food into the city, selling them at extraordinary prices. The villagers return to their homes with new supplies.

11 MAY 1944

It's been heard from various sources that during the meeting Mussolini had with Hitler – about 15 days ago – the Führer told him that he was forced to shorten the Italian front, pulling back troops on the pre-established La Spezia–Rimini line. Mussolini was absolutely against this,

---

[63] Here, Costantini quoted some sections of an article taken from Il Giornale d'Italia, 29 April 1944.

and one can understand why. By losing Rome and central Italy, what would be left of his republic?

So Hitler told him that to accommodate his wish, he would need 300,000 troops and 400,000 workers. Mussolini promised to deliver them. From this came the conscription of new social classes and the round-up of workers that has occasionally been happening in Rome.

The overseas radio services continue to talk about an imminent invasion of Europe by the Allies. But the public is tired, discouraged, and saddened because of the continual air raids. Many distinguished people (senators, academics, diplomats, university professors, high officials, officers, etc.) live with great anxiety and try to hide because they are talking about deportation lists in northern Italy.

Rome is truly living in a tragic time under the dreadful threat of hunger. Prices have gone through the roof. Poverty spreads. Often on the sidewalks we run unto emaciated women in rags, with a child at their breasts and with other little ones around them; they ask for nothing but look at us with a sad and dazed expression. People show themselves to be generous and merciful.

Every night at the Piazzale Flaminio a colourful crowd gathers. Apart from those who operate the black market, there are others who go in search of food for themselves. A woman said to me, "We have children at home crying, 'We are hungry.'"

14 MAY 1944

Mons. Montini phones me, his voice shaking with emotion because the Hon. Longinotti was killed in a car crash. Poor Longinotti! Yesterday he had breakfast with me and was calm and very happy to be seeing his old friend De Gasperi again. The two former members of parliament talked at length about the situation, so full of darkness, but both of them reaffirmed their unwavering faith in the resurgence of poor Italy, long, tiring, and faraway, but certain.

The news of Longinotti's death left us dismayed; De Gasperi burst into tears. The car he was driving back to Vico was crushed by a German military truck at a turn near Ronciglione. Longinotti's two children were also left seriously injured.

My poor dear friend! We used to get together fairly often and talk about the past, about the battle of thought and action for the Christian social movement. He had such a high awareness of good and evil, he was honest and cultured, an exemplary Christian and father. If he detested certain trends of Fascism, he never lowered himself to vulgar accusations, since he recognized the little good that Mussolini had done in the past. Longinotti was a gentleman. A noble man of strength in Catholic Action has disappeared.

The Government at Bari
A printed letter from Dott. A[ntonio] De Rossi was delivered to me. I will extract only a few sentences for your information:

> Dear friend,
> Finally, after months of busy negotiations, Badoglio has managed to form a "government," that is, to put together a jumble of... gentlemen of all colours and ages who are to endorse, with their signature at the bottom of all decrees, Moscow's orders. Yes, Moscow's orders, since the Communists are widely represented in the most important ministries, and Stalin will not miss the opportunity to let them feel the power of his will through the puppets, more or less aware that they represent him in Bari.
>
> The English and Americans, who have a lot to apologize for because of their inconvenient associate, have meanwhile left him control over Italy and the red divisions that will land in Bari and be the vanguards of terror. Thus concludes the first part of the betrayal, coldly plotted by the King and savagely carried out by his marshal ...
>
> Signed: Antonio De Rossi

SFORZA REPLACES ZANIBONI AS HIGH COMMISSIONER
FOR THE ANTI-FASCIST PURGE   16 MAY 1944
"In the invaded country of Italy the persecution of the Fascists continues and gets better ... Count Sforza[64] is appointed high commissioner of the

---

[64] Carlo Sforza (1872–1952), an Italian diplomat and politician, descendant of a secondary branch of the noble Milanese Sforza family, was invited to represent the Italian government in various offices, specifically in China (1911–15), in Serbia (1916–18), and finally in Constantinople. In 1919 he became a senator, following his position as under-secretary of foreign affairs in the first government led by Nitti. The next year he became minister of foreign affairs in the fifth government led by Giolitti. He negotiated and underwrote the Treaty of Rapallo in 1920. He returned to his career in diplomacy in 1922 but resigned as ambassador to France due to clashes with the Fascist stance. He continued his fight from the benches of the opposition in the Senate. There, on 3 January 1925, he was one of three senators who exposed Mussolini's responsibility for the

commission for the anti-Fascist purge, while Tito Zaniboni suspends his duties and is appointed high commissioner for war refugees."[65]

On 11 May the Allies' offensive resumed in Cassino. Today they announced that they have broken through a good stretch of the front. The Germans are retreating, but they think they will organize their defence on the Frosinone line. They say that the Allies will make a landing on the Tyrrhenian or Adriatic coast. Rome waits.

The nervousness grows because of the raids to round up workers and the alleged list of important people who would be sent up north.

Prices are always rising. On street corners, women and young girls offer baskets of eggs, each egg costs 15 lire; oil is 1,500 lire per litre. The radio announced that the Government of Naples set the price of wheat at 1,000 lire for 100 kilograms.

---

homicide of Giacomo Mateotti. From 1927 on he lived in exile, in France, England, Switzerland, and finally the United States, where he founded the Mazzini Society, together with Salvemini, Tarchiani, and Ciancia. In October 1943 he came back to Italy after passing through London, where he met Winston Churchill. Churchill, going against Sforza's beliefs, intended to favour the permanency of the monarchy in Italy. Sforza's contrary position impeded him, following an English veto, from being appointed minister of foreign affairs in the second government led by Badoglio. He became minister without portfolio in the government presided over by Bonomi, and from 13 May to 27 December 1944 he served as commissioner of the High Court of Justice for Sanctions against Fascism. In 1945 he was elected president of the National Council [Consulta Nazionale], a position he held until 1946, when he entered the Constituent Assembly [Assemblea Costituente]. Afterwards he became senator for life and a supporter of the Italian Republican Party [Partito Repubblicano Italiano], although as an independent. With the rise of Alcide De Gasperi's government, Sforza became minister of foreign affairs, 1947–51. In this capacity he underwrote the Treaties of Paris (1947) relating to the Second World War, promised Italy's adhesion to the Marshall Plan (1948), and Italy's entry as a member of the Council of Europe and of NATO (1949). In 1951 he signed the Frenchman Robert Schuman's plan for Italy's entry as one of the six countries in the European Coal and Steel Committee (ECSC). In May 1948 he was a candidate for president of the Italian Republic. However, Luigi Einaudi was elected. He wrote various books about his political and diplomatic activities. A short time before he died he received the last sacraments from Mons. Celso Costantini.

[65] CC: *Il Giornale d'Italia*, 16 May 1944.

In the city you often see men and women carrying heavy suitcases, stopping from time to time to place them on the ground and wipe their foreheads. We also see women with bags that have cabbage or artichoke leaves sticking out of them.

22 MAY 1944

On the twelfth of this month the offensive on the Garigliano front was launched. The Allies attacked the so-called Gustav Line and now they opened more than one breach in the Hitler Line [*sic*!]. Today the radio announces that the Allies have made their way through to Terracini. I think the Germans will retreat. The Allied troops in Anzio are still not moving, but it seems that from one moment to the next they will begin to go on the offensive on the German flank that runs along the Appian Way and Via Casilina.

Rome, from its outward appearance, is calm and almost indifferent. But if you speak with anyone here, you will notice right away a particular nervousness and their impatient wait for the Allies – they wait for their arrival so that the nightmare of insecurity and hunger will end. Today, diplomat S. said to me, "When leaving the house, one is not sure of coming back." In Anagni the Germans made the inhabitants come out of their homes, then divided the men from the women and led the able-bodied men away.

They continue to speak about people being tortured. We also know that executions are happening frequently. Mons. Nasalli Rocca,[66] who carries out admirable acts of charity for the prisoners, told me that two women and one young girl were waiting to be executed. They were later saved because of the Holy Father's intervention.

Unfortunately, some Italians are behaving even worse than the Germans. Badoglio's residence was ransacked. However, the Germans had respected the room where all his wife's remembrances were located. An Eritrean marshal was on guard there. The Fascists ransacked even that room. In addition to this, there is the abominable swarm of anonymous letters from informants. They say that it makes even the Germans feel sick.

The influx of sorrowful, frightened, and needy people continues; we do what little we can. They have confirmed that the bombing of the Vatican is the work of the Fascists.

---

[66] Mario Nasalli Rocca di Corneliano, a secret chamberlain *partecipanti*, looked after the wardrobe of the papal family, of which he was a member.

The Germans have put up signs to set up a circle that closes off the centre of the city. The signs say, "*Instadt Ringstadt.*"

24 MAY 1944

Yesterday in the afternoon, from Villa Borghese we heard continual shellfire directed toward the sea. Even at the Propaganda we heard, for the whole evening until midnight, the faraway pounding of heavy artillery. We can tell that there is a lot of heated activity.

In Villa Borghese women and children search for branches and wood, cutting sticks even from the hedges. Two boys carried off pieces of a table from the bandstand. Yesterday, near the Palazzo di Giustizia, I saw an elderly man and a boy who were ripping the bark off plane trees. They pull out the wooden parts of public benches. There is no gas, and the poor help themselves as they can.

25 MAY 1944

This morning there was a rumour going around that the German ss, helped by Italians, had burst into some homes during the night. They invaded the homes to take north – as hostages – important men holding various offices or those with other titles (academics, officials, professors, etc.). There was a list of names. Some people think that the Little Republicans want to deprive Rome of its distinguished men so that they don't work with Badoglio's government. X saw the list.

Poor Italy, how it has declined! Two admirals have been sentenced to death – Mascherpa[67] and Campioni[68] – because "they obeyed their

---

[67] Luigi Mascherpa (1893–1944), Italian admiral, who took part in the First World War as an aviator and distinguished himself in the bombing of Durrës, and for this reason was awarded the Silver Medal. He was involved in the military campaigns in Albania and Ethiopia. In 1941 he was promoted to captain of a vessel and in 1942 became the governing delegate for the islands of Leros and Astypalaia in the Aegean Sea. After 8 September he organized an untiring resistance against the Germans. He was captured, tried by a special Fascist tribunal in Parma, and sentenced to death. The execution took place on 24 May. Before his execution, he urged the soldiers of the firing squad to think of the good of the nation. He was posthumously decorated with the Gold Medal of Valour.

[68] Inigo Campioni (1878–1944) was commander of the Italian fleet until 9 December 1940, holding the rank of admiral. Having handled a battle over-cautiously, he was relieved of his duties and ended up carrying out other tasks within the navy. In 1939 he was appointed senator and following this became

superiors." Their condemnation is their badge of honour. This is murder, not an act of justice.[69]

Mons. Stanghetti, Commander Marini, Maestro Di Gennaro, and the lawyer Merlino came to see me as a committee. They brought to my attention the names of all the employees and their sad condition while begging that the bursar of the Urban College give them some financial assistance. We will do what we can.

Average prices of some foodstuffs:

Eggs	L18–201
Oil	L1000 per litre
Butter	L700 per kg
Suga	L500 per kg
Salt	L400 per kg
Flour	L200 per kg
Wine	L50 per litre
Fava beans	L20 per kg
Onions	L50 per kg

29 MAY 1944

There has been continual gunfire coming from the Anzio area. This evening the pounding sounds were filled with distant explosions, but they were very intense. While passing through Via dell'Impero I saw six Red Cross ambulances that were coming from the front, full of painful human cargo. There were three other ambulances, which were empty and going toward the sea.

The small lawns that surround the archaeological monuments and many parts of Villa Borghese have been tilled and transformed into war gardens. The wheat is already turning golden. May it be God's will that

---

governor of the Dodecanese Islands, which at the time were Italian possessions. He refused to collaborate with the Fascist government after 8 September 1943. For this reason he was tried by a special tribunal in Parma and executed for high treason, together with Luigi Mascherpa. Before his execution he too urged the soldiers in charge of the execution to think of the good of the nation. He was posthumously decorated with the Gold Medal of Valour.

[69] CC: In my book *Il Divino Consolatore. Il senso della vita e della morte* (Rome: Editore Danesi, 1946), on page 164 there is the description of their heroic death.

the Roman countryside can soon yield bread in this crucial time between the old harvest, which has almost all been consumed, and the new one. The supplies coming from outside the city have been stopped almost entirely because of the continual bombing. I've heard confirmation of the sad fact that the Germans, in certain places, scythed the wheat to give it to the horses. They are doing everything to make themselves hated.

Tonight I brought a French loaf to Mrs Librarian X. She was moved when she accepted it and thanked me profusely.

The Great Speech of the Holy Father

The second of June 1944 was the name day of His Holiness Pius XII. Responding to the good wishes of the Sacred College, he directed his thoughts to the problem of defending Rome and attaining peace.[70]

3 JUNE 1944

Hours of anxiety-filled and nervous waiting is disguised, however, by the usual air of outward indifference. The Allies have arrived near Velletri and Valmontone, cutting off the withdrawal of a group of divisions that were in the Liri Valley. These groups will have to fall back toward the Abruzzi. From Anzio, the Allies arrived near the hills of the Castelli Romani. The Germans are defending themselves with their usual skill – made up of science, experience, and the brave nature of their character. Theodoric watches them from the mausoleum in Ravenna, but he is worried because he knows that it will not be enough to assassinate Odoacre in order to finish the war.

From Anzio, a radio station is giving instructions to Romans and to the patriots in the groups that are in hiding. It is startling to hear the list of Nazi and Fascist spies that they have identified in Rome. First names, last names, physical descriptions, addresses, their activities. They urge Romans to remain calm. The sound of the guns has got closer to Rome; you hear more distinctly, and at more frequent intervals, the fury and the nearness of the war. From time to time the noise from planes, exploding anti-aircraft guns, and bombs fill the sky and make the windows of homes rattle.

This evening I noticed the usual traffic of trucks, cars, and Red Cross ambulances. I also saw three *Tigers* going through the Corso toward Via

[70] Pius XII's allocution on this occasion is printed in its entirety in AAS 36 (*Bollettino Ufficiale della Santa Sede*, 1944), 166–75.

Flaminia. I think they are signs of the Germans' departure. They say that certain Fascist commands and organizations have also left. Rumour has it that the Liberation Committee is getting ready to greet the Allies and that General Bencivenga[71] will assume command of the city during the interval between the departing troops and those who are arriving. The Germans have deported some young girls north. Why? Very negative rumours are circulating. Many believe that the Allies will arrive in Rome in the first days of next week. I hope that everything is carried out without confusion.

I arranged to pick up what has been printed of my book *Dio Nascosto* because Tipografia Tumminelli is not far from Via Casilini and I wouldn't want it struck by a bomb. The book is printed at night.

3 JUNE 1944

On the exterior, Rome has its usual appearance: calm and almost indifferent. But in people's hearts there is a nervous and impatient eagerness. Luckily the patriots received the order to stay put and await further instructions.

THE EXODUS OF THE GERMANS FROM ROME   4 JUNE 1944

Last night [3–4 June] a flood of tanks and retreating Germans were on the Corso going toward Via Flaminia. At 10 PM, I felt a light tremor and the lamp on the table squeaked. I thought it was an earthquake. But after this there immediately followed a terrible explosion; some distant munitions depot must have exploded. From time to time we heard other explosions, perhaps mines that were set off. They say that the Allies are spreading out from the Alban Hills. Perhaps they will be here tonight, or even this evening. Meanwhile, we take comfort from watching the passage of the Germans retreating and seeing everything calm.

---

[71] Roberto Bencivenga (1872–1949), a general and Italian politician and citizen of Rome, was awarded the Gold Medal in the First World War and followed this by taking up his political career by openly criticizing Fascism. For this reason he was removed from the army and sentenced to internment. As a partisan he became the president of the Italian armistice military mission and held the role of civil and military commander of Rome during its liberation from the Germans. For this reason, he set up office in the Campidoglio on 5 June 1944. A member of the Constituent Assembly, he then became a lifelong senator. He wrote various books, among them *Saggio critico sulla nostra guerra*, published for the first time in 1930 in Udine.

At 4 PM I went out to visit Contessa Cini [Lyda Borelli], who was taking shelter at the Palazzo del Sant'Ufficio. With me was Father Joseph Wang, from China. The city's appearance seems almost normal: groups of women, men, and children at their doors and looking out of their windows in a curious but calm manner. Every now and again there were shots from anti-aircraft guns, with people looking up at the sky to see if they could make out airplanes. Along the streets there were few people; they stayed at their windows looking curious but calm. Along the Corso, German trucks were passing, going toward Via Flaminia. In many places there were caravans of trams, empty and stopped on their tracks. The people gathered on the sidewalk observing the German trucks with a look of ill-concealed satisfaction.

The sun blazes. I arrive at the Tiber and see that the bridges are being watched by a picket of German soldiers. There are other soldiers near the bridges, on foot, armed; others with their arms down on the ground. I can pass over Ponte Umberto. Along the right side of the Tiber, from Palazzo di Giustizia to the entrance of Via della Conciliazione, there is a line of trucks under the trees and many soldiers lying on the grass without shirts, with long hair and beards, some barefoot, others in a deep sleep in unthinkable poses. It is a scene of misery, of decay, of pain, sustained by a secret discipline. Over Ponte Vittorio there is the continual transit of trucks, *Tigers*, Red Cross ambulances, and even wagons pulled by horses and filled with clothes, arms, boxes, etc. It is retreat, it is defeat, but it is not Caporetto.

The explosions from anti-aircraft fire and the faraway ominous croak of machine guns continue. On the faces of the Germans there is a proud and composed sadness. They have been defeated, but they fought like lions. On a tiny lawn near Castel Sant'Angelo, a truck covered with foliage looks like an enormous bush.

From the window of the Palazzo del Sant'Ufficio where Countess Cini is, you could see German soldiers parading by on foot, looking taciturn and sad. They were going toward Via Aurelia. "Poor people," said the countess. "They too have mothers, wives, children who are far away. I have sympathy for them. They too are victims of the political barbarism of their leaders."

I was returning toward Spanish Square, but they didn't let me go over Ponte Vittorio Emanuele. I was able to pass over the bridge at Castel Sant'Angelo.

They say that Mussolini called Kesselring on the phone to get news of Rome. Annoyed, Kesselring said to his secretary, "Tell him I'm not here. You sort it out." X tells me: "Last night a high German official went to dinner and came back to the Excelsior drunk. He offered a drink to some PAI [Police of Italian Africa] agents and yelled, "Long live Lenin, long live Churchill." An official thought he should say, "Long live the Führer." The general yelled back: "To hell with the Führer!"

Rome has started breathing. It is safe. It is free. Probably tomorrow the Allies will be here. We hope that everything will come about without confusion, without destruction. Blessed be God! The speech that the Pope delivered took place at an opportune moment. All those present interpreted certain statements to their own advantage. The Pope spoke the truth, the eternal truth. If Rome is saved, we will owe it to the Pope.

I feel my heart lift, as if a weight has been removed from it. I think again of the Germans entering Rome last year on 12 September, running around ostentatiously all over town with tanks, as if they were celebrating a victory. They looked at us with haughty pride. At the time, my heart ached while remembering that these Germans were entering through the same Via Flaminia and through the Corso – following the path that their ancestors took yoked to the carts of the victorious Romans ... But tonight the Germans are leaving, escaping, through Via Flaminia and Via Aurelia. Their faces are hard, rough, stamped with the internal torment of their defeat. They again pass through fatal Rome, defeated, humiliated, no longer feared. People have a dignified demeanour: they watch them, hostile yet calm.

THE ALLIES ARE ARRIVING   THE NIGHT OF 4 JUNE 1944
Toward 9 PM we heard a strange noise in Piazza di Spagna. We ran to the windows: the noises got louder and we could discern a lively clapping of hands. I went down to the Salone delle Congregazioni and looked out of the window onto Spanish Square. In the shadows of late dusk I saw groups of people applauding. But suddenly a German armoured car appeared, and it fired shots with a machine gun. Then the armoured car disappeared.

Right behind were lines of Allied trucks going through Via Due Macelli in the direction of Spanish Square. People at their windows applauded, clapping their hands. Other people on the sidewalks were celebrating the newcomers' arrival. There was not much light, and we could make out only the dark bodies of the tanks. One thing was certain, though: the Allies were in Rome. It was our liberation!

5 JUNE 1944

This morning convoys of American tanks passed through Via Due Macelli; people at their windows, people on the street all applauded. The soldiers waved back laughing. In many tanks were bunches of flowers thrown from the windows. The houses were quickly displaying flags, and the streets and squares filled with festive people noisily cheering.

At 11 o'clock I took a walk along the Corso, slowly arriving at Piazza Venezia. A flood of people had overflowed onto the Corso, flanking the tanks that were going toward Piazza del Popolo. There were frequent bursts of applause. The soldiers, with their chiselled blondish Anglo-Saxon faces, were laughing with kindness, and waved. The Romans' joy, excitement, and enthusiasm are indescribable. It seemed, in that moment, that all ill feeling had been forgotten.

Now we understand how precious a gift freedom is, the certitude of life. Mussolini hadn't understood this – he believed himself a god! What a difference from the "forced" demonstrations at Piazza Venezia! Today souls were quivering, the pure human soul that wants, yes, order and discipline, but also wants the amount of freedom that is part of human dignity.

Mussolini stupidly kept antagonizing his dissidents; he tightened the brakes on his tyrannical machine until those brakes snapped and the machine exploded, burying Fascism at the same time.

A parade of automobiles full of policemen is going through the Corso; loud applause bursts out from everywhere. I went past an old Garibaldino wearing a red shirt; two young men were carrying him on their shoulders. He was weeping with emotion. I passed a truck with a picture of the Pope on it and a sign that said "Long live the Roman Pope." Everyone was waving and applauding. A truck full of Communists appeared, with a red flag and red scarves and waistcoats. They were singing "Bandiera Rossa." When the truck with the Pope's picture passed by, even they gave a salute by raising their closed fists. A man said to Mons. Joliet,[72] "The miracle has happened. The Pope has saved Rome."

---

[72] Oscar Joliet, representing Belgium, a member of the the Superior General Council of the Pontifical Society for the Propagation of the Faith and of the International Secretariat for the Missionary Union of the Clergy. He was also

This morning as I was going out, two women were looking in the door. They kissed my ring and said, "Today they closed the novena to the Madonna of Divine Love and today we are free." On the walls they are starting to hang posters and signs. In the flood of people, often in their midst are trucks full of partisans; some of them have come from the front, others from their hiding places. They wave flags, laugh, sing, and people applaud. The men who were in hiding had let their beards grow; now they reappear clean-shaven and beaming.

They say that General Bencivenga is in control of maintaining order. There is surely the feeling that discipline exists. Soon, however, the city will be under Allied command.

The Roman People in St Peter's

Rome has poured into St Peter's even without well-timed preparation. They had said that the Pope would greet them. Rome would like to thank He who, like Leo the Great and Gregory the Great, presented himself as the *Consul Dei* e *Defensor Urbis*!

I left the house around 4 PM. Like rivulets that flow into the sea, there were lively groups of people directing themselves toward Saint Peter's Square. Little by little as I approached the square, the stream grew thicker and the square already seemed to be teeming with people. Along the Tiber, under the shade of the trees where yesterday the Germans were lying dispirited, there were many American trucks stopped and full of smiling soldiers. There also were many trucks in Saint Peter's Square.

Mons. Kass[73] invited me to come up to the terrace above the left colonnade, Bernini's colonnade. The square offered an impressive sight, full of noisy people, full of different colours from the flags of different associations. I also saw the Communists' flag. A sublime sight, even more beautiful because it was spontaneous and inspired only by ideal

---

rector of the Belgian College in Rome, in Via del Quirinale 26, and apostolic *protonotary ad instar*.

73 Ludovico Kaas, the bursar and secretary of the Sacred Congregation of the Reverend Basilica of St Peter and the president of the Vatican Mosaic Studio belonging to the same dicastery, was part – as was Costantini – of the staff at the Papal Chapel, and he was one of the few apostolic protonotaries participating. Finally, he was an adviser to the Institute for the Works of Religion [Istituto per le Opere di Religione (IOR)].

motives. The passage of the troops – yesterday the Germans, today the Allies – and the overturning of governments – yesterday Fascist, today anti-Fascist – show the caducity of human things. Amidst this overwhelming wave there is one thing that is stable, eternal, and always the same: the Church.

The Pope appeared at 6 PM on the dot. The crowd burst into uncontrollable applause. Then at every pause in his short, profound, clear, and wonderful speech was the resumption of applause. At a certain point, to one of the Pope's questions, the crowd answered with a prolonged "yes."

When I was about to leave, I found myself among the throng: an indescribable crowd of people. But on everyone's face, in everyone's voice, was immense joy.

Yesterday evening American tanks, agile and light, went by ... This evening genuine mountains of steel will go by.

6 JUNE 1944

The newspapers are beginning to be published. My notes become more infrequent. An air of relief, of celebration and joy continues. Rome is still covered in flags. By day and night there are new hordes of tanks and soldiers going toward Porta del Popolo. We understand that they are following the Germans. Where will they find them? Where will a new line of resistance be established? No one knows anything. There is no electricity, and the radios and electric bells don't work. Not bad. We are happy just the same.

Something interesting is happening now. All those people who were in hiding and for nine months lived a life of anxiety and fear – Jews, anti-Fascists, sought-after officials to be deported up north, officers and soldiers who hadn't answered Mussolini's call and didn't show up before 25 May, notable people whose names were written on a special proscription list – all of these people have now returned to the world, with brighter faces beaming with happiness. Many of them have shaved off the beard they let grow during their period of hiding. However, on their faces remain the traces of suffering and sometimes hunger. Rome is full of young people.

Now another type of phenomenon is taking place: the Fascists are trying to hide. What will happen to Federzoni, Bottai, and De Stefani, who were sentenced to death by the Fascist tribunal in Verona? Their lives have surely been saved, but it seems that the new government wants to arrest them. It has already arrested some iniquitous Fascists and national advisers such as Giglioli and Calza Bini.[74] My brother [the archbishop Giovanni] will see to their release.

6 JUNE 1944

The Hon. Alcide De Gasperi, who for exactly four months [6 February to 6 June] had been in hiding at my residence, has left the Propaganda. May God help him and help the new government in the arduous task that is waiting for them. The Hon. De Gasperi leaves us with the dearest memories because of his uncomplicated, pleasant, and educational company. His kind and unobtrusive nature awarded us the comfort both of his good friendship and of his gift for conversation – since he is an expert on political events and particularly learned when it comes to social issues. He is a humanist in the finest sense of the word and has a character that is honest and rational. I had told him that he shouldn't meet with politicians at the Propaganda. For this reason he went out sometimes, taking all possible precautionary measures.

In truth, this applies also to the Germans. I have to confess that I never had any problems with anyone.

Today, the Hon. De Gasperi has again begun – in complete freedom – to establish contact with the men of the National Liberation Committee. He will certainly pursue what is best for the nation and for the Church. For me, it is a personal satisfaction to have helped a man so worthy, a man who tomorrow will provide an important service with the honesty and impressive platform of the Christian Democrats, for whom he acts as secretary.

The people of Rome once again hurry to Saint Peter's Square to thank the Pope.[75]

[74] Alberto Calza Bini (1881–1957), a Fine Arts professor and an Italian politician, taught in various Italian universities. He was dean of the Faculty of Architecture in Naples and president of the National Institute of City Planning. He was elected a member of the cabinet in 1929, re-elected in 1934, and made a senator in February 1943. From 1939 on he was part of the Chamber of Fasci and Corporations. The High Court of Justice for Sanctions against Fascism ordered the end of his senatorial term, and the sentence was upheld by the Court of Cassation.

[75] CC: *L'Osservatore Romano*, 6 June 1944.

6 JUNE 1944

In everyone there is a great sense of relief; it seems as if one can breathe more freely. The serenity of these magnificent June days seems connected to the joy of the liberation, to peace, and to our spirits now at rest, recently awakened from the nightmare of uncertainty and persecution. To understand this feeling of rebirth, one must keep in mind the anguish of the recent past and especially of the last few days.

Father Wang tells me that he saw three dead bodies along the Tiber, at Ponte Margherita. The body of an American, guarded by his colleagues and two bodies of Germans, left abandoned. Someone had stolen their shoes and it was sad to see the feet of those poor dead men.

Many officers who, during the terror, had gone into hiding and run from serious danger, turned up at the Allies' military headquarters. However, they were greeted very coldly and sent back home. The Allies don't trust the Italian Army: the greatest offence to a nation. They don't respect it because it didn't know how to withstand the German invasion of Rome, not even with a well-organized attempt. An Allied officer, Taylor,[76] went down to Rome to organize the defence of the city with Badoglio – but he left disillusioned and annoyed. Fascism had poisoned the national structure while spreading dissolution in the army.

[76] Maxwell Davenport Taylor (1901–87), an American general, had been posted at the American Embassy in Tokyo from 1935 to 1939. During the Second World War he found himself in North Africa, in Sicily, and in the advance toward Rome. He was in charge of a secret mission in the capital, where he was to meet with the Badoglio government. From 6 June 1944 onward he was in Normandy to support the landing of the Allies. At the end of the war he was appointed superintendent of West Point, where he remained until 1949, when he became chief-of-staff of the American troops in Europe and subsequently commander of the US forces in West Berlin. In 1953 he was sent to Korea, and in 1955 he assumed command of all the American and United Nations forces in the Far East. In 1958 he became chief-of-staff of the United States Army, but the following year he resigned from his duties because of differences of opinion with President Eisenhower. In 1961 President Kennedy called him to the White House as his military representative, then made him chairman of the Joint Chiefs of Staff. Two years later, he was appointed ambassador in Saigon, where he favoured the expansion of the conflict between South and North Vietnam. In 1965 he returned to the United States and became chairman of the president's Foreign Intelligence Advisory Board.

I used to like to write a few notes to remember the occurrences in those dark and tragic hours and had been warned not to write the names of people in full. I had hidden many documents and my own pieces of writing inside Propaganda's archive, scattering the material in large old registers of past accounts or between the pages of books in storage. I will soon retrieve this material and try to reorganize it. However, some pages will remain lost among those registers.

7 JUNE 1944

An attack of that old arthritis in my knee makes it difficult for me to walk. Despite this, yesterday evening I couldn't resist going for a short walk, albeit very slowly: Via Due Macelli, Via del Tritone, Corso, Via Condotti. The face of the city is beaming. All of Rome is on the streets or hanging out of windows with the tricolour flying right beside them. It's obvious that no one has gone to work. They want to enjoy this moment of freedom and show each other their feelings of joy. In the cheerful hustle and bustle in the streets there is something new to see: lots of young people – who in the last few months had disappeared from sight.

You also see some new faces, faces with goatees and moustaches – they are men who kept themselves hidden and had changed their facial features.

The walls have been covered in brightly coloured posters. The National Liberation Committee heroically worked in the "catacombs." Some paid for their boldness with their lives. As soon as the German forces collapsed, General Bencivenga took over the management of the city and by doing so guaranteed its order. This was a source of immense comfort to us, especially when we remember how the city was left neglected after the King and Badoglio's escape.

General Umberto Pugliese came to see me. He was beaming. However, he is worried about his sister and other Jewish relatives in San Remo who have probably been deported to Poland.[77] Unfortunately, I think they probably died from torture, hunger, or hardship. Colonel Scarpa from Fossalta di Portogruaro also came to see me. In the previous months he had been hiding in Rome with false documents.

The American soldiers are fraternizing with the public. They take children onto the trucks, hand out candy. Unfortunately, they also fraternize with many young girls – taking them around in their trucks, laughing.

[77] The infamous concentration camp Auschwitz is in Poland.

On a distressing note, however, in all of the joyous fervour, there are still a lot of things missing. The streets are full of discarded paper and other litter. Water and sanitation facilities, electricity, and the gas supply are either problematic or non-existent. As we don't have electricity, we cannot listen to the radio. However, all the newspapers are published regularly, except for the *Tribuna* and *L'Avvenire d'Italia*. There are also some new newspapers, some that have been revived, like the Christian Democrats' *Il Popolo*, after being in hibernation for twenty years. It seems like a miracle.

Last night they announced a landing in France. Today it has been confirmed with some very good news. A breach has been opened in the German wall. Nazism is collapsing. Some Nazis had thought of replacing the Gospel with the book *Mein Kampf*.[78] *Gurges gurgitem vocat cum fragore cataractarum* [Ps. 41:8].[79]

8 JUNE 1944

Today Mr Siè, the Chinese minister at the Holy See, came to see me. He was beaming. "Finally," he told me, "I can leave the Vatican." Taking his place will be the Japanese ambassador. Minister Siè spoke about the strength and moral greatness of the Church, reminding me also that like the memory of Confucius, it is still alive in China after 250 years. It is not brute strength that counts but the strength of an idea.

He mentioned Mei-ti, a philosopher who flourished in China in the fifth century BC. Later I went to research a fantastic piece of writing on war that I will transcribe because it is current and contains a striking truth:

Chapters kien-nai: *What the Chinese philosopher used to say*. To remedy the sad situation of the Empire, it is necessary – as all good doctors do – to go to the root of evil. Now, this root of all current evils is that men no longer love one another. Each of them places his own interests above all else, in spite of

[78] The book *Mein Kampf* [*My Battle*] was written by Adolf Hitler and published by Max Amann in 1925. After the first edition, many others followed, since the volume had very wide distribution as it was considered the "catechism" of German youth. It contains Hitler's political thoughts and the platform of his National Socialist German Workers Party.

[79] The passage means "Abyss calls upon abyss with the voice of your floodgate."

the interests of others. For the love of one's own principality, one tries to ruin the principalities of others. For the love of one's family, one tries to harm other families. For the love of oneself, a father works against his sons and the sons plot against their father.

Yes, all evil comes from the exclusive love of oneself, from selfishness. Each good would come, for individuals and for the state, from the charity of all, from the reciprocal respect of every person's titles and rights. Consider the affairs of others as you would your own; help others with kindness to obtain their favour, and the world will suddenly be transformed. All evil arises from the distinction between you and me, between mine and yours. From here stems all quarrels and all wars. Stop being too selfish; become altruistic; give your uncommon good to the common good, and everything will change in front of you ... A man who takes other people's harvests, chickens, pigs, or horses either by force or by false pretenses is called a thief or a bandit by everyone. Do we have to use these insults more with him who takes over – either by force or by false pretenses – the domain of someone else?

He who has killed a man is a killer once; he who has killed ten men, is a killer ten times over. Whoever kills 100 men is a killer 100 times over. So the conqueror prince is a killer for as many times as the men he made perish. Nevertheless, far too often, this arch-killer is admired and finds admirers. What a perversion of moral sense.[80]

9 JUNE 1944

At 6 PM I went out for a quick walk through the city. The lust for life and the joyful air of recent days continues. Piazza Venezia was full of tanks, soldiers, and people. Children were climbing on the tanks, putting the soldiers' helmets on their heads. The soldiers, patient and kind, were laughing. They don't seem like soldiers at a battle front; instead, they seem cheerful and relaxed.

However, there are two false notes: too many young girls on the trucks and here and there a few drunk American soldiers. In Piazza Venezia bundles of barbed wire mark a restricted area – the square in front of the General Insurance Building. The Allied Military Command is in that building.

What a scene of striking contrast to the former mobilized rallies in which it was compulsory to call Il Duce to his balcony. This man has now graciously agreed to show his face, strutting about as if he were a

---

[80] CC: Kien-nai-fei-koung.

Homeric hero or a Roman emperor. After losing Rome, he declared three days of mourning; the farce becomes a tragedy.

I went to the Church of Santi Apostoli. Upon leaving it, I came upon in the portico a little old woman holding a baby that was a few months old. The old woman, dishevelled and wearing rags, was the image of hunger. She asked me for alms in a timid and demure manner. I invited her to follow me to the Propaganda, promising her some pieces of bread. Along the way she told me she was from Formia. She had lost her husband in Tripoli, and then her only child was killed by a torpedo. He had left behind a pregnant wife. Five months ago the baby was born; however, the mother was crushed under their house's rubble. She and the baby saved themselves behind a barrel. She went on: "Now we are all alone in the world and we don't even have a food-ration card. They put me up in a room, and for everything else, I get by on charity. I am never without that."

The baby was crying because he was hungry. Passing in front of a bar I entered and bought four pastries: six lire for each one. The baby put one in his mouth, but he began to cry because it was hard. "He is cutting his teeth," said the old woman. I managed to help this poor woman, as well as a few of the poor, thanks to a sum of money from some benefactors for which I had asked.

THE PILGRIM POPE AT SAINT IGNATIUS' CHURCH

11 JUNE 1944

"To join together with his beloved people, and as proof of his endless love, on Sunday, 11 June 1944, the Holy Father, the august Pilgrim, will go to the Church of St Ignatius to worship the prodigious image of the Madonna of Divine Love. There, as he presides over prayers thanking God for keeping Rome safe and prayers begging the Lord's divine mercy for the most urgent necessities, he will stress to the faithful the observance – which is not only essential but beneficial – of the Law of God."[81]

Badoglio has finally gone away. He had enough intelligence to understand the void he was creating around himself. He is the man who said, "The war continues." He is, politically speaking, a failure – as always happens with generals who attempt to be politicians. Another example of this is that scoundrel Graziani.

---

[81] *Discorsi e Radiomessaggi di Sua Santità Pio XII*, vol. 6 (Milan: Società Editrice "Vita e Pensiero," 1945), 35. The whole speech is on pages 35–40.

The King didn't know when it would have been the right time to abdicate, thus creating a *fait accompli* with the succession of the new king. Instead, today Umberto is the Lieutenant,[82] and the issue of either monarchy or republic remains open and will be discussed ...

The Government of the National Liberation Committee

De Gasperi as general secretary. Wonderful! The government has been formed with the men from the National Liberation Committee. The Lieutenant gave the blessing of legitimacy to the new government. Italian and foreign authorities have come to visit the Pope, a magnificent tribute to the Universal Shepherd and not to the Prince. The papacy, because it is without old secular rule and also because it was represented by great pontiffs, has greatly risen.

The Pope is the most helpless and poorest king on earth, thus naturally the most powerful of all. May there be a tribute to those thinkers who, as prophets, suffer to defend Christian ideas against those of worn-out political leaders.

There continues to be a huge flow of American, English, French, and New Zealand troops coming into Rome, with some black-skinned men from America or the Sudan or Mauritania, and some from Annam. I hate to see the parade of tanks and guns on the Corso. I wouldn't like them to attract enemy bombs being eventually dropped on Rome.

The evacuees depart for their homes. We no longer – or rarely – see mothers begging.

SIXTEEN COFFINS AT THE CHURCH OF JESUS   11 JUNE 1944
This conflict between the human desire for revenge and the generous act of forgiveness – this need to surpass hate with love – I felt in the strongest way ever when I attended the funeral on 11 June 1944 in Rome for

[82] Umberto II of Savoy (1904–83), the son of Victor Emmanuel III and Queen Elena, married Princess Maria José, daughter of Albert, King of Belgium, in 1930. In September 1943, after the armistice, he followed his father and the government led by Badoglio to the south of Italy, abandoning Rome and leaving it in the hands of the Germans. He was appointed Lieutenant of the Kingdom of Italy on 5 June 1944, following the decisions made by the National Liberation Committee regarding the King. He ascended to the throne with the abdication of Victor Emmanuel III on 9 May 1946. After the referendum on 2 June 1946, which proved unfavourable for the monarchy, he went into exile.

the 14 patriots who were perfunctorily killed on 4 June at La Storta, not far from Rome. The 14 coffins were lined up in the transept of the Church of Jesus. There were also two other coffins of fallen soldiers. A row of flags, representing all parties, acted as wings around the coffins. A huge crowd of people, sad and silent, jammed onto the church's flight of steps and filled the large nave. In the church an austere silence reigned and a feeling of horror and dismay. The crowd closest to the coffins stood on tiptoe to make out the alignment of the coffins.

Holy Mass was celebrated, and the dead were given absolution. We all felt as if we had been transported outside this ephemeral world and placed in front of the face of God, crying out for mercy, eternal light, and peace for the souls of those victims. The cross dominated the scene. Christ – from the cross – was opening his arms in that perfect embrace with which he embraced mankind, which was redeemed by his blood. Then we remembered his great words: "Father, forgive them, for they know not what they do."[83]

The heart would ask for revenge, compensation and justice. Yes, justice must re-establish order. But we must be hard on ourselves by compressing our feelings of personal resentment. Christ is not against justice, but he is against the personal desire for revenge. So the martyrs and the saints forgave, beginning with Saint Stephen, the first martyr. So many of the condemned forgave before being sent to their execution. And like them, endless other victims of this abominable war, in their final hours, in a sublime overtaking of human nature, knew how to forgive. This is what is necessary for us, necessary for our nation: to ask God to forgive our faults while promising in turn to forgive those who have wounded us. Dante translates the very noble appeal of the *Pater Noster* this way:

Even as we forgive all who have done
Us injury, may You, benevolent,
Forgive, and do not judge us by our worth
    [*The Divine Comedy, Purgatory*, 11:16–18].

Forgiveness is necessary for the nation; the nation has to begin its life again, bandaging and healing with love all its many wounds. Italy has gone through other dark times because of the hate that made men

[83] The Bible passage can be found in Lk. 23:34.

ferocious … "whom one same wall and one same moat enclose" [*The Divine Comedy, Purgatory*, 6:84].

At the time, Saint Francis and Saint Catherine of Siena, the sweet protectors of Italy, preached love, forgiveness, and peace. "*Pax et bonum*" was Saint Francis's greeting.

Oh mothers, oh wives, the disarming of evil spirits and application of restorative and healing virtue must begin with you, you who have the very noble privilege of pity, you who are the blessed and incomparable sowers of love.

16 JUNE 1944

Rome continues to teem with American, French, and English soldiers, as well as others. But they are here as visitors; they are not armed. We observe *de facto* respect for the open city. We also see bands of black troops. The liveliness of the people and the traffic of cars are great. There is an air of joy on everyone's face.

Spreading underneath, however, is a certain uncomfortableness about the scarcity of food: small amounts of vegetables, no meat, no fruit, and little milk. People live on their ration cards and the black market, with some private help from soldiers. We look with faith to the future, because we are already harvesting wheat, and the lines of communication have been repaired; and also because we think that the Allies will furnish Rome with the things that are necessary. Rome trembles when the city sees the shadow of hunger. It has been saved, and we must remember the precious and kind help given by the Vatican.

The lire of the occupation begin to circulate; it is another inflationary puff of air that will turn Italy upside down.

The walls are plastered with posters showing violence against Mussolini and the King. Yesterday, at the entrance of Piazza Venezia, I saw a sign on which was written: "Death to Mussolini." On another, someone had written: "Long life to Don Sturzo." Who would ever have thought of something like this, of such a reversal of positions?

Another reversal: Prince Doria Pamphili, who was ferociously persecuted by the Fascists, is mayor of Rome. Upon taking office he said some very noble words. People freely repeat his Roman phrase: *Volemose bene.*

16 JUNE 1944

They say that Mussolini proclaimed that for Ferragosto [holiday celebrated on 15 August] he will come to free Rome at the head of half a million men ... This type of bragging makes us laugh. He is like an actor, made up like an emperor, who has taken his role too seriously. He really believed that all those cowardly people in his circle loved and adored him. They were wearing nothing but masks – and his crown was nothing but painted cardboard.

Yesterday, French soldiers were parading through Via dell'Impero. With Maramaldo's act[84] Mussolini had stabbed France when it was already lying face down, and in doing so he had aroused a wave of outrage against Italy. The French now fight with the Allies, not exactly for our benefit. However, we hope that Italians will go and fight in France and contribute to the erasure of Mussolini's offence.

Rome is still full of American, Canadian, French, Indian, Moroccan, and Senegalese soldiers, as well as others. There is such a fervour, so much coming and going – an indescribable liveliness. On the main streets you can still see flags. People carry on cherishing the festive atmosphere, as if they had come out of a quarantine of isolation and fear. The problem regarding provisions has still not been resolved, but there are not too many complaints, and we know that the authorities and the Vatican are working hard to obtain food. In the meantime, the harvesting of the wheat is in full swing.

I am taking note of four things:

1 The soldiers, crouched on trucks, standing near them, sitting on the sidewalk, or stretched out in the small gardens are enjoying a happy period of idleness. They seem to be glowing with health and always have a smile on their faces. We see a lot of bottles passed around; the young boys and, unfortunately, the young girls, fraternize with them.

2 The Romans have put together a small business. Swarming around the soldiers, who are stopped usually near the monument to Victor

---

[84] Fabrizio Maramaldo was a historical figure, a Calabrian captain of fortune, a condottiere who led the imperial troops to conquer Asti in 1526. He participated in the sack of Rome in 1527 and in the siege of Volterra in 1530, a city defended by the captain of the Florentine army, Francesco Ferrucci. In the latter mission, Maramaldo was defeated. He faced Ferrucci again in Gaviniana, and it seems that although Ferrucci was already mortally wounded, Maramaldo struck him one last time to finish him off. This incident has led to the saying, "You kill a dying man." In the figurative sense, the term *maramaldo* connotes a vile man who keeps attacking the defeated.

Emmanuel or along Via della Conciliazione, they sell guides, maps, postcards, medals, rosary beads, souvenirs of Rome, etc.

3 The soldiers are enjoying running around Rome, but hardly any of them stop to look at the monuments. In the area around the Roman Forum and Trajan's Forum I've seen only the odd few soldiers with a guidebook, standing in contemplation of the monuments. Everyone, however, even the Moroccan Mohammedans, go to see Saint Peter's.

4 Young spry boys, with smiling and flashing eyes, are acting as shoe-shiners and are making a ton of money from the soldiers. They are identified with the nickname *sciùscià*. I watched a young lad who was shining the shoes of a black American sitting on the steps of the Campidoglio.

A SOLEMN AUDIENCE WITH PONTIFICAL
MISSIONARY WORKS[85]   24 JUNE 1944

Today the Holy Father received the Pontifical Missionary Works.[86] We recognized in Him, in His expression of paternal goodness and His comforting words, the Ultimate Shepherd who repeats the sigh of Christ: "And other sheep I have, which are not of this fold: them also I must bring, and they shall hear my voice; and there shall be one fold, *and* one shepherd."[87]

In the darkness of hate and discord that covers the world, this divine ray of love and call for unity calmly rises up in the Vatican ... We were deeply moved.

26 JUNE 1944

Yesterday evening, Sunday, the former minister Guido Jung came to me and told me that he would like to have an audience with the Holy Father to pay tribute to him and to thank him for the vast amounts of charity given to the Jews. Jung is a convert and truly has a profound sense of what it means to be a Christian. However, his baptism has not caused him to renounce his legitimate blood ties. I phoned Monsignor Arborio

[85] Pius XII's speech on the occasion of the audience with those who worked for Pontifical Missionary Works is printed in full in AAS 36 (*Bollettino Ufficiale della Santa Sede*, 1944), 207–11.

[86] The event is also quoted by Costantini in his book *Ultime Foglie. Ricordi e pensieri.* (Rome: Unione missionaria del clero in Italia, 1954), 283–8.

[87] This passage can be found in Jn. 10:16.

Mella,[88] His Holiness's chief chamberlain, who told me that the audiences have already been booked but Jung could join another group and he would have him enter a room alone so that he could say a few words to the Holy Father. He added that he would supply Jung with a ticket. So it was done.

Jung came back to see me, his face full of excitement and joy. He said to me, "I had the exact feeling about the divinity of the Church. I had come out from the turmoil of this world and I found myself face to face with a soul, a soul who alone represents the eternal principles of justice and charity. In the Pope, one truly feels the spirit of Christ. He is a living miracle. I thanked him for the aid he gave to the Jews; I brought him the feelings of a battalion of Palestinians who admired and were moved by the Pope's work. He is the saviour of Rome. One needs only to have passed through the ruins of other cities to understand and appreciate Rome's privileged destiny ..."

27 JUNE 1944

Yesterday, Colonel Scarpa from Fossalta di Portogruaro came to see me. After the liberation of Rome, he had gone to see the Allied military authorities. He was expecting a better welcome. He would have liked to go back to his position in the army and devote his work to the liberation of the country. This is the desire of many Italians, who feel the humiliation of having a quasi-absent Italy while it is being liberated by foreigners, some of whom are black. Today *L'Unità*[89] [the Communist newspaper] reports: "The direct and real participation of Italy in the war for liberation is still very insufficient; we are not talking about the real possibility of our own autonomous war effort but about the will of the Italian people to fight."

[88] Alberto Arborio-Mella di Sant'Elia belonged to a noble Sardinian family. He was the chief chamberlain and butler of His Holiness, president of the Heraldic Commission for the Papal Court and chaplain for the Noble Guards of the Papal States. He was the governor of the conclave that led to the election of Pius XII. Because of a serious illness, he resigned from his duties as chief chamberlain in 1946.

[89] *L'Unità*, founded in 1924 by Antonio Gramsci, was suppressed by the Fascists in 1926. Its publication was carried on underground at irregular intervals, until June 1944, when its editions began to come out again in the capital and served as the official mouthpiece of the Italian Communist Party until 1991.

The truth – the painful truth – is that the Allies have no respect for the Italian Army which, on 8 September, crumbled like a paper castle. Nor do they trust the army. They think that for three years the Italian Army fought against the Allies. Colonel Scarpa adds another explanation: "They don't want us as part of the Allies because we are the defeated and are left to their discretion. If they accept us as co-belligerents, this could create a precedent that would allow Italians to claim a seat at the peace table next to the victors."

1 JULY 1944

The Axis radio service said that the Germans respected Rome as an open city by transferring military command to outside Rome. The Allies, on the other hand, set up their military offices inside the city. For this reason, the Axis reserved the right to bomb Rome. Let's hope that the Holy Father, who has already saved Rome, saves it also from this threat by persuading the Allies to move their offices away from Rome.

Inflation continues. We keep receiving newly minted bills from the Bank of Italy, and the American currency is being widely distributed. Black market prices have been raised to dizzying heights. Wine was sold for 3,500 lire for 100 litres and, in the taverns, for 100 lire per litre. Fruit goes for 70 lire per kilogram.

10 JULY 1944

Last night Countess Cini, who was very angry, told me this story: "There was a great reception at Villa Valadier that was hosted by foreign officials. They had invited the daughters of families who were part of good Roman society, as well as many aristocratic ladies. The condition of entry to the reception was that "the young ladies must *not* be accompanied by their parents or the wives by their husbands." It is a disgrace, it is roguery committed by invaders who lack manners. If no one had accepted their invitation, it would have served them right. Of course, many respectable people did not make themselves available for this type of humiliation."

Poor Italy, above all else it must suffer this vileness. Its soul, which was ever rich in character, has been battered in these twenty years of slavery.

A WONDERFUL INITIATIVE BY THE ROMAN NOBILITY

12 JULY 1944

A charitable initiative has been put forth by the noble families of Rome in response to the paternal appeals of the Supreme Pontiff and in aid of the many evacuees and the needy. For those who every day ask the Vicar of Jesus Christ for help, these families were able to gather a substantial sum of money with their spontaneous fundraising.

This sum of money – more than a million lire – was presented to His Holiness during a brief audience that took place on 11 July 1944 in the Hall of the Throne, where representatives from the donor families were waiting. The reception was intimate and simple, as planned. The spokesperson of the group, His Highness the Most Eminent Prince Don Lodovico Chigi Albani della Rovere,[90] wanted to add some words of devout homage whilst placing the generous offering in the august hands of His Holiness. The Holy Father – himself an attestation of divine kindness – responded by putting together some words that entered into the hearts of those present.

27 JULY 1944

Today, General Umberto Pugliese came to see me. He told me that everyone has abandoned the King. He added, "What is worse, he has been abandoned by God. He was never overly religious; more than a skeptic, he is a cynic. When, because of the racial laws I had been rejected by society, I felt the pain of being deprived even of my civil life – but my soul was full of my sense of God. He was my great consoler."

THE CRIMES OF MOROCCANS   28 JULY 1944

Some very sad news of the brutal conduct of some Moroccans who were fighting in the liberated territories. This evening's *L'Osservatore Romano* writes: "Under this headline in its 27 July edition, the newspaper *La*

[90] Lodovico Chigi Albani della Rovere (1866–1951), a descendant of one of the most important and influential families of the Roman nobility, married in 1893 Anna Aldobrandini, with whom he had two children. Following the death of his wife in 1898, he decided to embrace the religious life and entered the Sovereign Military Order of Malta, following its vows of chastity, poverty, and obedience, but he continued to live in Chigi Palace. In 1914 he succeeded his father as Prince of the Holy Roman Empire. In 1931 he became the 76th Prince and Sovereign of the Order of Malta. His reign had to endure persecution from the Nazi regime in Germany as well as in its occupied territories. There was further harassment against the order by the Communist regimes. During the Second World War he was the head of a huge operation that aimed to alleviate the suffering caused by the war and to give aid to the refugees.

Ricostruzione[91] reported the news, published by other papers, of tragic violent acts again being carried out by Moroccan soldiers. These were against some women who boarded a train at Ciampino. On the tracks about 25 kilometres from Rome, they discovered the body of a dead woman as well as four women and a baby in very serious condition. The baby and one woman died at St John's Hospital, where they had been taken, together with the other unfortunate victims, one of whom now lies dying. *La Ricostruzione* affirms its certainty that 'those who committed these crimes will be prosecuted, however possible, by Allied Command, and the punishment will be severe.'"

5 AUGUST 1944

This evening I was passing through Via Borgognona. An American or English soldier was seated at the base of a column with his elbows on his knees and his head in his hands, and he was throwing up. Two men then passed by, and one said, "The Germans took all of our pigs away. Then these other ones turned up."

6 AUGUST 1944

The so-called purification rages on. Of course it is necessary to lash out at those responsible for the ruin and dishonour into which poor Italy has fallen. Furthermore, it is necessary to lash out at those responsible in high places. However, it seems to me that things are becoming a bit excessive; that is, it is almost like Fascism in reverse, and they are prosecuting, in the name of freedom, the so-called thought crimes.

Today the newspapers announced that Professors Pende[92] and Cecchelli,[93] along with many others, have been suspended from their jobs. Others have in fact been let go. Pende and Cecchelli may have made the mistake of saying something against the Jews. But is this all it

[91] The newspaper *La Ricostruzione* was published in 1943 by the Fronte Unico della Libertà.

[92] Nicola Pende (1880–1970), an Italian endocrinologist and professor at the University of Rome, conducted research on the relationship between endocrine activity and constitution, from which he derived the concept of the "biotype." His name is connected with the *Pende Syndrome*, which is characterized by a rise in systolic pressure and a lowering of diastolic pressure.

[93] Carlo Cecchelli, a professor of Christian archeology at the University of Rome, was among the professors who expressed approval of the racial laws.

takes to ostracize two remarkable men who are a credit to the university? This is the Fascist way of doing things – that is, punishing people for their thoughts. Where will this measure end?

The 6 August edition of *Il Risorgimento Liberale*[94] writes: "There is a great need for us to discuss things amongst ourselves, also because after twenty years of Fascist journalism we have got out of the habit of doing it. However, to discuss things in a productive way, we have first to try and understand what in our reasoning our adversary opposes. Then, even from their opening statements, we have to avoid suffocating that voice with screams and threats."

In the same edition Benedetto Croce[95], writes: "It goes without saying that it is necessary, first and foremost, to resist the impulse – which many have – for revenge, because revenge is made up of something that is altogether evil and stupid, and damages he who carries it out much more than he who endures it. The goal that we need to propose, even in this task that awaits us, lies solely in doing what we can and what we must to recognize and contribute to – in proportion to our strengths – the creation of a better world, or at least one better than the one before."

THE PURIFICATION RAGES ON   8 AUGUST 1944
Today *Il Risorgimento Nazionale* published a long letter from Count Sforza. He has divided the senators into six groups: the first five would

[94] *Il Risorgimento Liberale* was a Roman newspaper, the mouthpiece of the Italian Liberal Party [Partito Liberale Italiano], run by Mario Pannunzio (1910–68), who was an Italian journalist and politician as well as the founder of the Radical Party [Partito Radicale]. The newspaper began publication on the day of the liberation of Rome. It supports a liberal position with secular and agnostic overtones.

[95] Benedetto Croce (1866–1952), an Italian philosopher, historian, and critic, studied Marxist thought as well as that of G.B. Vico. In 1903, with Giovanni Gentile, he founded the philosophy journal *La Critica*. In 1910 he was appointed senator and was minister of education from 1920 to 1921, when he prepared a sweeping reform of the education system, which at the time was not implemented. He was initially supportive of Mussolini but from 1925 on, he became openly anti-Fascist. He was a minister without portfolio in Badoglio's government (April–June 1944) and was president of the Liberal Party until 1948. The Crocian system of philosophy is outlined in four volumes that comprise *La Filosofia dello Spirito* (Milan: Adelphi, 1993). He also authored numerous other publications.

have to endure judgment by the purification committee. The senators in the sixth group – about 170 of them – were declared worthy to stay in the Senate. To me, it seems quite a depressing document and juridically unfair (that is, going against *equitas*). Many senators were in favour of the Fascist government, but that was a legitimate government – and what was legitimate yesterday cannot become illegitimate today. There is no retroactivity in penal law. They know that the Senate has its High Court of Justice, which could have been set up – if so desired – by senators free of the blemish of Fascism. If they believed it possible to subvert the Statute, according to which senators are appointed for life, it would have been more reasonable to dissolve the Senate, which *in corpore* failed in its duties. Now they are setting up hundreds of single trials. In these trials, what will come into play are many influential factors, a spirit of revenge and, God forbid, monetary corruption.

But it was up to Sforza himself to carry out the thankless task of reporting for expulsion many excellent, worthy, or at least harmless men, while he – when Mussolini wanted him to lose his seat in the Senate – was saved by Federzoni, who made the case that one cannot change the Statute of the Kingdom.[96] It seems to me that all of this disgraces Italy and contributes to the spreading of discord at a time when it is of vital importance to work toward harmony and reconstruction.

An interview with Count Sforza that was published in *L'Avanti* on 24 September caused me great pain. What is more impartial, nobler, and more humane than the Pope's vision, which hopes for the collaboration of all people who are capable and honest, even if they are in different political camps? It is the far-seeing vision of a father who is both loving and watchful.

13 AUGUST 1944

Today I met Senator Balbino Giuliano, the former minister of education[97] in Villa Borghese. I said to him, "I was sorry to have seen your name among those of the senators whom they would like to 'purify.'"

---

[96] CC: Count Sforza had also finished the purification process when he presented himself as a candidate for president of the republic.

[97] Balbino Giuliano (1879–1958), an Italian politician and university professor, taught moral philosophy and the history of philosophy in different universities, later becoming dean of the Faculty of Arts and Philosophy at the University of Rome (1935–40). When it came to politics, he adhered to the National Fascist

He replied, "It is of no great importance to me, as long as Italy can rise again after these incredible and painful ordeals. Pain can bring about a beneficial uprising." Then I added: "Yes, we all hope for that. Pain can make you return to your senses. Jesus says that a woman, when she gives birth, cries out because of the pain; but then she is happy because a man is born into the world."

15 AUGUST 1944

Colonel Poletti, the governor of Rome,[98] is going away. Bon voyage. His memory will hold little significance for us. Rome is left in poverty. There are foodstuffs in Naples and in southern Italy, but they don't know how to – or they didn't want to – organize their transport.

I approached him, pleading the case of the Institute of Roman Studies and asking for electric light for the Propaganda. I was left quite unsatisfied. As for the rest, it was bad luck that offered Rome a man of Italian origin who, from what they say, abandoned the Catholic faith to become a Baptist.

In the evening, they announced the successful landing of the Allies at Toulon. They are also talking about Nice. If the landing happened at Nice, from there the Allies could reach Cuneo. So the Germans in southern France and those in Italy should withdraw in haste. May it be God's will!

Party and was elected a member of parliament both in 1924 and in 1929. He was appointed minister of national education of the Mussolini government from 1929 to 1932, after having been under-secretary of the same government. He was made a senator in 1934. At the collapse of the Fascist regime he was deferred to the High Court of Justice for Sanctions against Fascism, but he benefited from Togliatti's amnesty. Afterwards he retired to private life.

[98] Charles Poletti (1903–2002), born in Vermont, was an officer in the United States Army during the Second World War. He had been vice-governor of the State of New York (1939–42), and then its governor. He left office in 1943 to join the army with the rank of colonel. He prepared the landing of the Allies in Sicily, supported by his connections with the mafia, in particular with Vito Genovese. He became military governor in Palermo during the military administration of the Seventh Army, and with the advance of the Allies toward northern Italy, he carried out the same role first in Naples, then in Rome, and finally in Milan. He was a Protestant and was known for his hostile feelings toward the Catholic Church.

On 16 August 1931 Giuseppe Donati,[99] expatriate, had died in Paris. We were friends, and each time we met he let me get to know his beautiful soul better, nourished by the strong sense of his religion, enriched by a bright intellect and vast knowledge. He was a noble martyr of freedom. This is how Guido Gonella remembers him in *Il Popolo*, the paper that had been founded by Donati: "From 1925 to 1930 he lived in exile in Paris. Once a journalist, he became a bookshop sales clerk and then it seems a waiter. No amount of humiliation was able to crush his spirit, which was so strong that it was even able to support his unstable health. After having taught in Malta for a brief period, he returned to the French capital where there was a slow agony waiting for him. Finally, on 16 August 1931, came the restful sleep of death."[100]

22 AUGUST 1944

The news of the death of Cardinal Maglione arrived unexpectedly. From what we understand, his heart wasn't able to withstand the medication for his arthritis.[101] What a dear, sweet soul! He was a modest man, pious, friendly, a man of acute and balanced judgment. Of course, he was one of the most distinguished members of the Sacred College.

[99] Giuseppe Donati (1889–1931) had his cultural and political upbringing in Faenza, where his family settled. He earned a degree in sociology in Florence and began to collaborate with various periodicals, among them Gaetano Salvemini's *L'Unità*. A Catholic irredentist, he fought as a volunteer during the First World War. He was wounded and awarded a Silver Medal for his bravery. After the war, he joined the Italian People's Party [Partito Popolare Italiano], which was founded by Don Luigi Sturzo. In 1923 he became the managing editor of the newspaper belonging to the same party, *Il Popolo*. He openly sided against Fascism and implicated the highest members of the regime in the Matteotti murder. For this reason he had to leave Italy. He escaped to France, where he was forced to take makeshift jobs in order to live.

[100] cc: *Il Popolo*, 15 August 1944.

[101] Cardinal Maglione, who was ill and then admitted to the American hospital in Naples, wanted to leave the hospital on 12 August 1944 and go to his house in Casoria, where he eventually died. These and other details can be found in *Le Saint Siège et la guerre mondiale*, vol. 11 of *Actes et documents du Saint Siège relatifs à la seconde guerre mondiale* (Vatican City: Libreria Editrice Vaticana, 1981), 502.

After his sudden death I grieve for both him and the friendship he extended to me. I grieve for the Church, to which he gave his devoted and sagacious spirit while admirably serving the Holy Father. We have lost him in one of the most bitter moments of this tumultuous era as it is ravaged by war. The void he left is immense, and we do not know how it can be filled.

I remember the cordial and sincere hospitality that Cardinal Maglione offered me in Paris. When I was appointed secretary of the Propaganda, he sent me a telegram from Paris with these words: "*Deo gratias!*"

In Via Veneto I saw a young boy, a *sciùscià* [shoeshiner], who was kneeling on the ground with a shoeshiner's block. He was counting a handful of change. "How much did you earn today?" I asked him. "Up until now, 70 lire," he answered, "but these are not my day's earnings; this is what I earned in half an hour."

23 AUGUST 1944

We are fighting to have electric light.

How many formalities there are! We were granted permission five days ago and still we haven't seen any light. A trifling and oppressive bureaucracy is jamming up life in Rome. Yesterday and today I strongly urged that the Franciscans and the Oblates of Mary be allowed to transport provisions that belong to them to Rome.

A sense of disappointment is confusedly emerging. Some people are starting to say, "Who will liberate us from the liberators?"

In Propaganda's hallways there is the smell of a grocer's shop. They are collecting groceries; they come from the Vatican and the *Convivenza* and will be distributed to the employees. Yesterday they handed out dried salt-cured cod.

With the help of Father Wang and Don V. Mazza, I tried to locate the pages that I had hidden among the books and old registers in Propaganda's archives. I don't remember all of my pieces and their specific hiding places. However, I recovered a large part of my notes.

29 AUGUST 1944

Churchill's message was a good one. Finally, it seems they understand that Fascism is one thing and Italy is another. Finally, it seems they welcome the Italians' desire to participate in the liberation movement. There are also signs that German troops are withdrawing from the Gothic Line[102] and hopefully from all of Italy.

The attempt on de Gaulle's[103] life is a very sad crime, and it shows that the "desperate" Fascists and Nazis are "stubborn."

Scenes in Rome that are becoming even more painful to watch:

1 the "young ladies" – the girls – who shamelessly become friendly with the soldiers;
2 the young shoeshine boys, who offer their services in front of the monuments of the ancient empire;
3 many young children, haggard and sickly, who go through Rome shirtless and barefoot;
4 the women, whom we see clothed in makeshift fabric made of varied patches and different colours.

SURSUM CORDA   I SEPTEMBER 1944

I quote here, with deep feeling, some noble thoughts from the message that the Holy Father Pius XII delivered to the world today, the fifth anniversary of the beginning of the war.[104] They are words of life that point out the way – the only way – to render fruitful the sacrifice of the fallen and the pain shared by all Italians: "An ancient world lies in the midst of ruins. To see it rise up as soon as possible, healthy, juridically better organized, more in harmony with the needs of human nature – this is the thing for which tortured nations yearn …"

---

[102] The Gothic Line or Gothic Front was the dividing line of defence that extended from the Adriatic (Rimini) to the Tyrrhenian (Massa) across the Apennines. It was drawn by the Germans during the Second World War to block the advance of the Allies who, during 1944, had already liberated southern and central Italy from Nazi occupation and from the Fascist regime.

[103] During his life, Charles de Gaulle was the target of many attempts on his life; there were at least 30, all of them thwarted, and in each case, without any causing him injury.

[104] Pius XII's radio message on the fifth anniversary of the outbreak of war is transcribed in its entirety in AAS 36 (*Bollettino Ufficiale della Santa Sede*, 1944), 249–58.

6 SEPTEMBER 1944

Today Selva,[105] a sculptor and former academic, and the former senator Leicht[106] came to see me. Yesterday Oristano, the philosopher and former academic, was here. Today these learned men find themselves on the street. Leicht, who was referred to the purification committee, was relieved of his teaching duties at the university and is not yet eligible for a pension. Oristano, who had already given up teaching at a university in opposition to the Gentile Reform, takes in nothing else but a minimal pension, a bit more than a thousand lire per month. Selva has no commissioned sculptures to create as his commission to sculpt a Pietà for the church in Rome's train station was suspended. These respectable people are now forced to sell family heirlooms, clothing, and utensils so that they don't die of hunger. Selva said to me, "I had to sell even my typewriter. You need to live and especially you need to think of your family."

This type of destitution that strikes many men, who deserve and are used to an honest way of life, is one of the saddest consequences of this period and this uncivilized and unjust purification. While farmers and retailers of groceries are filling their pockets with 1,000-lira notes, they are suffering hunger in silence. They cannot change professions, nor do they dare ask for charity. Oristano and Leicht asked me if I could give them a few teaching hours at Urban College. This is not going to be possible. The tragedy of the intellectuals and many employees becomes more serious.

[105] Attilio Selva (1888–1970), a sculptor originally from Trieste, where he created a monument dedicated to Oberdan, received his training at Leonardo Bistolfi's school. He moved to Rome in 1907 and set up his studio at Villa Strohl-Fern, but he did not object to going overseas, to Egypt and to Libya in order to create his works on site.

[106] Pier Silverio Leicht (1874–1956), an Italian politician and professor of the history of law, taught in various Italian universities and became dean of the Faculty of Law, first in Modena, then in Bologna, and finally in Rome. A member of parliament sitting on the benches of the National Fascist Party in 1924 and 1929, he was under-secretary of education, 1928–29, in one of the governments led by Mussolini. He was appointed senator in 1934, an office he lost after the Second World War because of his referment to the High Court of Justice for Sanctions against Fascism. He authored numerous publications, some of which concern the region of Friuli.

9 SEPTEMBER 1944

General Castellano,[107] who is negotiating the armistice with the Allies, came to see me. He told me something very important. He was able to include a section that lays down how the Allies will handle Italy. This will be negotiated because of the aid that will be brought to the war for liberation. He added that if the army had not taken part in that pitiful performance on 8 and 9 of September, in which it tried to run away, our two nations who are fighting a common enemy would have already formed an alliance.

A GREETING TO THE POLISH SOLDIERS   15 SEPTEMBER 1944

During the usual general audience in the Sala delle Beatificazioni there were present, among many others, 200 Polish soldiers and Bishop Gawlina, chaplain general of the Polish Army,[108] as well as Ambassador Papée.[109] The Holy Father directed some touching remarks to them. I will quote some of his thoughts here: "However may it be of comfort to you, know that Our hearts have bled over the destruction of your great capital, Warsaw. Within its walls has taken place one of the most painful – and most heroic – tragedies in the history of your nation."[110]

15 SEPTEMBER 1944

Today the *Voce Repubblicana*[111] published this very sad news:

[107] Giuseppe Castellano (1893–1977), an Italian general, who was promoted to that rank for his merits in the First World War, had a leading role in the negotiations with the Allies after the fall of Mussolini in July 1943. In August 1943, in a non-official capacity, he met with the Allies in Lisbon and directed the ongoing talks that led to the armistice in September of the same year.

[108] Joseph Gawlina (1892–1964), the chaplain general for the Polish Army, was the bishop of Mariamme from 1933 on; he was promoted to Archbishop of Madito in 1952.

[109] Casimir Papée, Poland's ambassador to the Holy See.

[110] *Discorsi e Radiomessaggi di Sua Santità Pio XII*, vol. 6 (Vatican City: Tipologia Poliglotta Vaticana, 1951), 135. The complete speech is on pages 133–6.

[111] The Italian newspaper *Voce Repubblicana* was founded in Rome in 1921 as the official mouthpiece of the Italian Republican Party. It was suppressed by the Fascist regime in 1925 and began underground publication in 1943; then, in 1945 it was legally allowed to publish. Publishing was suspended from 1978 to 1981.

A correspondent from the UNN reports that on 16 August the Germans publicly hanged three youths in the main square in Rimini. The "crime" they were charged with was escaping from a forced-labour detail for the Germans. Their bodies were left hanging in the square for 48 hours as "an example" for the other citizens.

In the main areas of the city these killings were quite a common occurrence ... On many occasions women were no longer able to tolerate such atrocities, and there were many demonstrations all over the city. One day in Imola more than 700 women gathered together in the streets shouting in protest. The Fascists had been ordered to fire shots to restore order.

They were careful not to shoot toward the sky. They shot instead with the intention to kill, and among the women taken down during the first round of fire was one woman who had seven children.

If it is true – as we unfortunately believe it to be – that some Italians shot at a crowd of defenceless Italian women, we feel not only great distress but also humiliation! Never in the history of Italy has there been such a crime, such an act of such base cowardice and ferocity. I would like to hope that all of this isn't true or that it is an exaggeration of the facts. These wretched Italians have been subjected to moral and civil corruption from the Fascists and the German soldiers, and this type of perversion has lowered them to the level of the most barbaric of people. They have left an indelible mark on the face of the nation. I lower my head. As a man, as a Christian, and as an Italian I am humiliated because I would never have imagined that Italy – even in this time of terrible crisis – was capable of lowering itself to such an abyss of iniquity. How was all of this possible? They used to tell fantastic stories about the gentle, stable, and kind temperament of the Italians. Now even this cliché has been destroyed.

ITALO BALBO   17 SEPTEMBER 1944

Today *Il Popolo* published an excerpt from an old letter that reads like a sinister warrant, which in part refers to the person responsible for the murder of Don Minzoni. The letter was directed to Lieutenant Beltrami, a political trustee. It states: "If they insist on staying and thus as a consequence bring about moral uneasiness, it will be necessary to berate them without going too far, but regularly until they decide. Go ahead and show this letter to the prefect, to whom you will say, on my behalf, that I have sufficient grounds to justify my demand not to have similar villains in the city and its environs. The police will do well to harass them by taking them into custody at least once a week. It will be a good thing if the prefect makes the king's prosecutor understand that in the event of beatings (which should be done effectively), they need not bother with trials. You will read this part of the letter to the Federal Council. If I write this letter from Rome it is a sign that I know what I am talking about. Your Italo."

However, it needs to be said that Balbo seemed to be repentant. When I had the opportunity to approach him in Tripoli and Rome, he gave me the impression of a man who had detached himself from the past and was busy with new and good resolutions.

AN ABOMINABLE CRIME   19 SEPTEMBER 1944

My pen shakes in my hand as I jot down some notes about the abominable crime that took place yesterday at the foot of the Palazzo di Giustizia. Mr Carretta,[112] a vice-warden at the Regina Coeli jail, who was supposed to be a witness at the Caruso trial, was lynched in such a way that it goes beyond any gruesome imagination. He was thrown dying and bleeding into the Tiber and tried to swim to shore. Some men in boats came near him and struck him on the head each time he emerged from the water until he died. The body was then dragged to the Regina Coeli jail and hung on the gates with his head hanging down.

---

[112] Donato Carretta, whom Costantini describes as the vice-warden of the Regina Coeli jail in Rome during the German occupation, in fact was warden of the jail at the time. He was at the Palazzo di Giustizia at 9 AM on 18 September 1944, waiting to testify at the trial of Pietro Caruso, who had been head of the Questore [police force] of Rome until the Allies arrived. Caruso, together with Buffarini Guidi, had made a list of 50 names that were requested by Kappler in order to complete a list of Italians to massacre at the Fosse Ardeatine. For months he treated with ferocity the anti-Fascists who had been captured by the police. The crowd pushed its way through to the courtroom to witness his assured conviction. As a way to calm the frenzied crowd, the trial was postponed. At that point the crowd, which was in control of the situation, lashed out at Carretta. Caretta had, among other things, helped the Resistance during the occupation and helped Pertini and Saragat escape from Regina Coeli. He became a scapegoat, unjustly pointed out and accused by a woman who said he was the murderer of her son. This spark caused the explosion that led to his lynching, as retold by Costantini.

A crime such as this has diffused a sense of horror, shame, and humiliation in everyone. We have sunk to the level of animals. How do we explain this abominable and stupid murder? It is not enough to justify it as one of those sudden uprisings in which the members of a crowd lose their sense of personal responsibility. How could this uprising take place among a nation of people who are usually peaceful and calm?

It seems that it goes back to three main causes:

1 an exasperated despair due to the slowness with which they carry out the punishment of the guilty, made worse by the continual news of the victims at the Fosse Ardeatine;
2 hunger, poverty, unemployment, the shortage of electricity, coal, wood, etc;
3 a more remote yet profound cause: a habit of violence and the practice of taking the law into one's own hands, which began with and was glorified by Fascism.

This crime, even though it took place in a time of so-called freedom, absolutely bears – perhaps unknowingly – the mark of the Fascist way of doing things.

THE DISPLACED MADONNA   23 SEPTEMBER 1944

Like the ancients who when forced to flee from their sites took their Penates[113] with them, the people of Velletri brought to Rome the very old painting of the Virgin of the Graces – the venerated protector of devout people on the run. The people of Velletri, before taking the holy picture home, wanted to bring it to the home of the Supreme Shepherd as an act of piety and as a way of thanking the Holy Father for the aid he had given to Velletri. Directing his words toward the refugees he said, "Gazing upon you here today, beloved sons and daughters, it is dear to Us the thought that herself, the Very Holy Virgin of the Graces,

---

[113] The Penates are ancient Roman deities, protectors of both family and home. Their name derives from the word *penus*, which means the entirety of provisions set aside for domestic consumption. Each family had its own Penates, which were different from the Lares, who were the ancestors of the same family as they belonged to Olympus and were chosen as their protectors. Their domestic place of worship was in the atrium of their home where the flame of their hearth burned, a flame sacred to them and to Vesta.

patron saint of your city and of the Velletri Diocese, inspired you to reunite here around her before leading her back to her centuries-old abode."[114]

5 OCTOBER 1944

The writer Maria X, who is Russian and a serious and well-educated person, came to see me today. She said to me, "They are spreading a lot of propaganda in favour of Communism, saying that it has changed its approach, that it no longer persecutes religion, etc. Don't believe it: Communism remains as it always was, basically and necessarily anti-Christian. A Russian officer who just returned from Russia tells me that the anti-Christian sentiment is always the same; they are only trying to trick the West."

Today I was reading in the breviary "*Gloria eius quasi stercus et vermis est*,"[115] and I thought about the so-called Salò Republic.

A few days ago, at Castel Gandolfo, I stopped along the street near two diggers. They were digging in the ground to expose a water main that had been destroyed by bombs. It struck twelve noon. The two diggers stuck their shovels into the loose ground and sat down on a little side wall. From a small paper packet they took out a bit of grey bread and some fruit. "You see," one of them said to me, "how can we work on this little piece of bread? If I eat it now there will be nothing left for us for this evening. And we are hungry. Damn those people who have reduced us to these conditions!"

There was a threatening glare that flashed in the eyes of the worker. I thought, here is Bolshevik propaganda. Tomorrow these workers, and many, many others will be Communists – not so much because of the Communist platform, but as an act of rebellion against this savage civilization that during the life of one man has caused four wars.

9 OCTOBER 1944

What a battle for electric light. I was able to get it given to the Propaganda, but I was not able to obtain it for Urban College. There is a shortage of

---

[114] *Discorsi e Radiomessaggi di Sua Santità Pio XII*, vol. 6 (Vatican City: Tipologia Poliglotta Vaticana, 1951), 143–4. The complete speech is on pages 140–5.

[115] The passage, translated from Latin means "His glory will turn into dung and worms."

electric light for the Romans, but there is a dazzling display of it for the military, the cinemas, the clubs, etc.

Behind Rome's outward appearance, abject poverty spreads through certain strata. They say that there have been some cases of people who died of hunger. At the Propaganda we hear "jeremiads" of desperation! By contrast, those who mess around with the black market have loads of 1,000-lira bills – devalued bills – but bills that come in handy all the same.

9 OCTOBER 1944

With the taking of Rimini, we were hoping that the military fieldwork of the so-called Gothic Line would have been taken down. I was planning to go see my family in October; I haven't had any news from them since May, except for the general news of the crimes committed by the Germans.

No one understands Hitler's strategy, which orders the German troops to continue to seize Italian territory as well as that of Yugoslavia, Greece, Poland, etc., while German territory has begun to be invaded. However, in these last few days there are signs that the Germans are withdrawing from Liguria, Piedmont, and Lombardy. The Fascists will have to cover the retreat and then they will be disarmed.

28 OCTOBER 1944

The intellectuals who cannot work with the black market or exercise other professions are suffering from hunger. Today the writer Arturo Lancellotti[116] showed up at my door. He is a shadow of his former self. He says that he doesn't know how he is going to carry on.

Count C., a former important employee with the Ministry of the Interior, wrote to my brother and told him that his family lives on soup made from inexpensive ingredients. At the Propaganda we are trying to obtain groceries from the college [of the Propaganda *Fide*]. There are piles of foodstuff in the hallways.

---

[116] Arturo Lancellotti, a member of a noble Roman family, was a writer of historical and anecdotal works published between 1919 and 1962. Among his works is *Il Beato Giuseppe Sarto (Pio X)*, published in 1951. He was also a contributor to various magazines and an art critic, mainly dealing with the Biennale of Venice.

1 NOVEMBER 1944

I went to visit Mons. Bartolomasi to express not only my solidarity but also my opposition to the vulgar attacks made on him by some newspapers. He doesn't give great importance to these rude statements because his conscience is clear, since he served the Church and not Mussolini.

Speaking about the poor King he said, "Mons. Masera[117] was the court chaplain. When he was made bishop of Biella, he went to the King. They said to him, 'Try to stay afloat.' Masera answered, 'Our boat is reliable and solid. Your Highness should try to keep his boat from capsizing.'"

Prophetic words, as now the King's boat has rotting wood and soon it will fall apart. The Church, on the other hand, is more steadfast than ever.

Daniele Varé,[118] a diplomat and an unscrupulous man, said to me, "Everyone loses this war, even those who win it. Only one person doesn't lose; on the contrary, he profits immensely: the Pope."

4 NOVEMBER 1944

Prince Umberto of Savoy, the King's lieutenant, had someone tell me that he would be happy to see me. Today I went to see him. I had a cordial conversation with him for an hour. In answer to one of my subtle questions, he said that he hoped to receive his consort but that France had made things difficult for the planned trip.[119] "I hope," he added, "that

[117] Giovanni Andrea Masera (1867–1926) was vicar general and then bishop of Ivrea from 1906 until 1912, when he was transferred to the auxiliary office of the Diocese of Sabina.

[118] Daniele Varé (1880–1957), a diplomat and writer, was minister for Italy in Luxembourg (1926–27), China (1927–31), and finally Denmark (1931–32). In the largest country of Asia he was well acquainted with Celso Costantini, who was there as an apostolic delegate. In 1928 he signed a treaty of friendship and trade between Italy and the Chinese Republic that replaced the one signed in 1860. Among his books is *Diplomatico sorridente*, published in 1941.

[119] Maria José of Belgium (1906–2001), Princess of Piedmont, the wife of Crown Prince Umberto of Savoy (the Lieutenant of the Kingdom and later King of Italy). She was considered politically the most distant from Fascism among the members of the House of Savoy, not only for her political initiatives, which were undertaken from 1941 when she put herself in contact with anti-Fascist representatives, but also for her personal opinions about Benito Mussolini and the key people in his Fascist regime, even before its collapse. On 6 August 1943

later on she will be able to come. I am worried about my two sisters who are in Germany [the Princess of Hesse[120] and Yolanda[121]] and also for

---

the King, who had not spoken to Maria José for two years, sent for her and ordered her to cease all contact with the anti-Fascist opposition immediately. Her relationship with her husband was also in crisis. On 8 September 1943 she was in Sarre, in the Aosta Valley, and it was there that she heard on the radio news of the armistice. She then escaped to Switzerland. She embarked on a very difficult return trip to Italy in February 1945 while Germany was surrendering to the Allied siege. She was greeted by the partisans, who escorted her to Racconigi. She waited there until the end of June, when an airplane was sent to take her to Rome, where Umberto, after not seeing her for two years, was waiting for her.

[120] Matilda of Savoy (1902–44), the second daughter of King Victor Emmanuel III and Queen Elena of Montenegro. In 1925 she married Philip, Landgrave of Hesse (1896–1980); the marriage produced four children: Moritz, Heinrich, Otto, and Elisabeth. In September 1943, before the signing of the armistice treaty with the Allies, and while the King, Queen, their son Umberto, and government leader Badoglio escaped to southern Italy, she left for Sofia to assist her sister Joanna, whose husband Boris III was dying. Matilda found out about the armistice in Bulgaria and, not caring about the chance she would be taking, wanted to return to Rome. She reached Rome on 22 September 1943 and went to the Vatican to see her children, who were there under the care of Mons. Giovanni Battista Montini, the future Pope Paul VI. The following day she was urgently called to German Command. However, it was a trap. She was arrested and deported to the Buchenwald concentration camp, where she was locked up under a false name in shed no. 15. In August 1944 the English and Americans bombed the concentration camp, and as a result, Matilda suffered serious burns and contusions all over her body which, as they were not attended to, caused her death on 28 August 1944. Her body, thanks to the camp's Bohemian presbyter Father Tyl, was not cremated but was placed in a wooden coffin and buried in a communal grave with the number 262. This number allowed them to find the body, which is now buried in the cemetery for the Princes of Hesse in Kronberg Castle in Taunus.

[121] Yolanda Margaret of Savoy (1901–86), the eldest daughter of King Victor Emmanuel III and Queen Elena of Montenegro. In 1923 she married Giorgio Carlo Calvi (1887–1977), Count of Bergolo and an Italian general. The marriage produced five children. A town in the province of Ferrara is named after her.

my sister who is in Bulgaria."[122] Then he told me that he had visited different areas of Lazio and felt great compassion for the destruction and the conditions in which the poor unfortunate people as well as the priests find themselves. "In certain places," he said, "people were upset because they didn't have Mass. I don't mean to interfere in something that is the responsibility of the bishops. However, make them aware of this painful fact because, if they can, they can remedy the situation."

Then we spoke at length about the Catholic missions. He seemed to enjoy the conversation. The Prince made a good impression on me; he seems balanced in his judgments, intelligent and learned. It is a shame that he put himself in jeopardy as the commander of the army against France and then, having escaped to the south, against the Allies.

Afterwards I saw Mons. Bartolomasi. He said to me, "Either monarchy or anarchy."

19 NOVEMBER 1944

I went to lunch with Ambassador Cerruti. He told me: "The impression that foreigners have of Rome is a great one, thanks to Ancient

---

[122] Joanna of Savoy (1907–2000), the fourth daughter of King Victor Emmanuel III and Queen Elena of Montenegro. She became ill with typhus and swore that if she recovered, she would become a devotee of Saint Francis as Franciscan Tertiary, which later did occur. In 1939 in Assisi, in a Catholic ceremony, she married King Boris III, the Czar of Bulgaria, who was Orthodox. Together they had two children: Marie Louise and Simeon II of Bulgaria. Joanna, who became Queen of Bulgaria, was very popular with her subjects. Together with her husband she assisted the Bulgarian Jews, even by helping them escape to Argentina to protect them from the growing suppression carried out by the Germans who, in 1941, were allies of Bulgaria. On 28 August 1943 King Boris died after being in the throes of death for days; rumours circulated that his death was probably caused by the Nazis. In 1946, after a referendum influenced by the Soviets who led the country, the Bulgarian monarchy was abolished. Along with her two children, Joanna was forced into exile. She spent an initial period in Egypt with her parents, then from 1950 lived in Spain, and finally went to Portugal to be with her brother Umberto II of Savoy. After the fall of the Communist regime, Joanna returned to Bulgaria in 1993 and was welcomed with great enthusiasm for the 50th anniversary of the death of her husband Boris. She died in Estoril, Portugal, on 26 February 2000, but she wished to be buried in the cemetery in Assisi, in accordance with her great devotion to Saint Francis.

Rome and Papal Rome. The austere majesty of the Vatican wins them over. The Pope, with his sweetness and his proficiency in many languages, with his noble and informed words, leaves them enchanted and enthusiastic. However, an officer in a private conversation said to me, "The Vatican is too Italian. The Church is universal, and we do not find an adequate representation of people from other nations in the Holy See."

22 NOVEMBER 1944

It is popular opinion that the government is doing what it can but that the Allies are really the ones in charge. The good feelings toward the Allies are noticeably in decline because living conditions are harsh and difficult. People have also formed the opinion that the Allies are not worried about freeing Italy but are fighting to keep the German soldiers busy and far from Germany. In the meantime, northern Italy is going through an ordeal of unspeakable terror and punishment.

There is also a sense of uneasiness because the government is practising Fascism in reverse; that is, it is showing no mercy to the Fascists of yesterday simply because they were well-known Fascists. No one is working toward reconciliation, unity, or peaceful justice. The Fascists took away the Jews' right to exercise a profession; now former Fascist professors are being fired for mere "thought crimes," and many lawyers are being deprived of the power to practise their profession.

The Pope had once said some noble words: "Take heed of some honest and competent men, even if they served in another party." With our current government's methods, which don't dare touch the important people who are responsible for Italy's ruin or the generals who deserted their posts and left Rome at the mercy of the enemy, they are not preparing for Italy's resurgence. Justice and a more Christian direction – not vendettas – are necessary for Italy's rebirth.

In the meantime, America and England look down on us. How could we expect them to judge us more leniently if they didn't find an army here, and if they hadn't seen the King, the government, and the generals run away frightened, deserting us?

The Italian soldiers are demoralized. However, we have to sympathize with them. They left to fight a war against the Allies, and now they have to turn against Germany. They no longer have any faith in the governments that condemn them and carry on with illogical, inhumane, and unjust wars.

The cost of living rises appallingly. A pair of shoes, made of fabric, costs 3,000 lire; those made of leather, 5,000 lire.

We are looking for a stoker to light the furnaces, at least in the morning and evening. One asked for 300 lire per day: 9,000 lire per month. A Jew, a member of the Assicurazioni Generali, said that he conducted a study of the lira's value: 100 lire are worth a lira and a half.

10 DECEMBER 1944

On 8 December they observed the solemnity of the Immaculate Conception around the monument in Piazza di Spagna with a special show of devotion (floral offerings, songs, and a procession). I received the mayor of Rome, Prince Doria,[123] whose wife left a very beautiful bouquet of flowers.

It had been mentioned that people could make donations for the refugees in the form either of money or clothes. They collected almost 100,000 lire and a large number of packages of clothing. These were brought to the Propaganda. The caretaker who opened them told me that almost all of them contained "black shirts and black Fascist uniforms."[124]

14 DECEMBER 1944

The year is drawing to a close in a gloomy haze. Northern Italy is still under the heel of the Germans, with the atrocious depravity of civil war. Days ago the radio station in Milan ironically said that the Allies had had success at Faenza. They had advanced 200 metres.

---

[123] Filippo Andrea Doria Pamphili (1886–1958), prince of the homonymous noble Roman family, carried out the role of first mayor of Rome after the liberation from the Nazis and Fascists, from 10 June 1944 to 10 November 1946.

[124] The intention of those offering, by way of their pseudo-donation, was to free themselves from the awkward symbols that recalled their adherence to Fascism. The hand-woven coarse woollen fabric was made by a particular manufacturing process that dates back to very ancient times (this fabric probably was used for the Ancient Roman soldiers' clothes), and it was used during the Fascist period. Its framework was woven and its typical black colour was obtained through dyeing. The special quality of this fabric, which was obtained by selecting the longest fluff during the carding process, consists of it undergoing – after weaving – a process of milling that causes felting, which renders the fabric coarse, strong, and waterproof.

In Rome it seems that all efforts toward reconstruction are reduced to two things: the establishment of the political parties and the purification. They don't believe that the parties are for Italy, but rather that Italy is for the parties. The government's crisis, after a pitiful skirmish that lasted 18 days, was resolved with an amalgam of the various parties. Extremely decadent Byzantinism.

The other thing that stands out is the purification; that is, the manhunt. They do it in the name of freedom. Count Sforza, who had taken charge of the thankless task of purification and who appeared as a spiteful and vindictive man by creating special tribunals even for senators, has been struck by the ostracism of the English and abruptly ousted by the new ministry.

A sense of uneasiness and simmering revolt is spreading. Instead of rebuilding the social structure with a standard of high, civil, and Christian tolerance while trying to get "all" honourable men to come to an agreement in order to restore a normal life, they sow new seeds of dissolution.

Today, while I was in an audience with the Holy Father, I mentioned this crisis whilst also mentioning the words that His Holiness had used during his speech on the fifth anniversary of the beginning of the ongoing war. The Pope was saddened by this show of moral wretchedness.

This evening I met Professor Carnelutti and General Bencivenga at the Grand Hotel. They, too, deplore this moral illness and think that it may be necessary to organize a committee that has the courage to introduce a degree of moderation. Attack the thieves, yes, and the dishonest, the profiteers, and those responsible for the destruction; but leave many honest people alone, even if they served not so much Fascism but Fascist Italy. We must not forget that the Fascist government was a legitimate government. What was legitimate yesterday cannot become illegitimate today. Above all, we have to try and enlighten the young. Men of 30 or 35 years of age were moulded by Fascism; they know no other political or social theory. We must treat them with love and lenience.

I ran into the former senator Gasperini,[125] who had been president of the Court of Auditors. He told me that he had sold his overcoat to get by. It is the tragedy of many former officials.

[125] Gino Gasperini (1885–1961), a Roman, an administrative magistrate, a state adviser in 1924, and a first-class prefect in 1926, was president of the Court of Auditors from 18 December 1928 to 3 September 1944. He was appointed

The lira continues to lose value every today: today 100 lire are not worth more than one lira. Fish costs 300 or 350 lire per kilogram. In Concordia, before the war of 1914–18, I used to buy it for 130 lire. A cabbage costs 50 lire; I used to buy it for 20 cents; an egg costs 35 lire; I used to sell those I gathered through the church for 11 cents. Today in Via della Croce I saw a broom seller who was shouting, "One broom for 20 empty bottles!" They make exchanges in kind.

Banditry rages on. Apart from local criminals, some American gangsters have arrived. Automobile theft is frequent. Often, at night, they strip passers-by of their clothing. A woman was stripped of her clothes in Via Condotti! A few nights ago a doctor, after leaving the Holy Spirit hospital, came upon some clothing thieves. They stripped him and left him in his underpants. At first glance, the nuns thought he was crazy. He was put to bed and then his family was called; the following day they brought him some other clothes.

I should go to Tivoli, but I have a particular fear of thieves and have not yet decided to make a move.

CHRISTMAS MESSAGE   24 DECEMBER 1944
Addressing the Sacred College, the Roman Prelate,[126] and the world,[127] the Holy Father's Christmas message was, as always, a masterpiece of pastoral concern, theology, and social or political science. The Pope is an architect who builds the perfect cathedral under whose vault humanity will finally be able to take shelter and rest.

THE HOLY FATHER AT THE GREGORIAN UNIVERSITY
                                                   25 DECEMBER 1944
On Christmas morning the Supreme Pontiff wanted the children of the refugee families who are visiting Rome to receive a gift. Therefore

---

senator in 1934 and lost that position with the sentence that became final in the Supreme Court on 8 July 1948 after being referred in 1944 to the High Court of Justice for Sanctions against Fascism.

[126] The above-mentioned speech of Pius XII to the Sacred College of Cardinals and the bishops and prelates of the Roman Curia on Christmas Eve 1944 is printed in its entirety in AAS 37 (*Bollettino Ufficiale della Santa Sede*, 1945), 5–10.

[127] The above-mentioned Christmas radio message by Pius XII has been transcribed in its entirety in AAS 37 (*Bollettino Ufficiale della Santa Sede*, 1945), 10–23.

the Pontificia Commissione di Assistenza [Vatican Relief] distributed 12,000 packages of clothes, fruit, and candy in every area of the city. Two thousand children were later assembled in the great hall of the Pontifical Gregorian University so that they could have a charitable remembrance of a noble Christian holiday from the hands of the Vicar of Jesus Christ himself.

The wonderful and moving scene called to mind the divine image of Jesus Christ, who advised his Apostles: "*Sinite parvulos venire ad me*" [Mk. 10:14].[128]

---

[128] The passage means "Suffer the little children to come unto me, and forbid them not."

The Year 1945

The Allies are not getting along well. Stalin[1] has formally recognized the revolutionary government of Poland that was established in Dublin.

[1] Joseph Stalin (1879–1953) is the pseudonym of the Georgian politican Josif Vissarionovic Dzugasvili. He was able to gain a unique cultural education thanks to the support of his priest, who let him into the seminary even though he quickly gave up the idea of becoming a clergyman. At age 20, Stalin was discharged from the institute that was to prepare him for the presbyterate, within whose confines he had set up a Marxist-inspired group. From that point on he personified the type of revolutionary that was theorized by Lenin, whom he met in 1905. He organized strikes and working-class demonstrations, for which he received several sentences. In 1912 he was able to escape to Vienna, where he wrote *Marxism and the National Question*. After he returned to Russia in 1913, he was deported to Siberia. However, he was able to come back after the revolution in February 1917, when he and others, while waiting for Lenin's arrival, assumed control of both the Bolshevik Party and the newspaper *Pravda*. Alongside these men, he built himself a solid position of power, which allowed him to defeat rivals such as Trotsky. In 1922 he became general secretary of the Communist Party of the Soviet Union (CPSU). However, his actual rise to power occurred after Lenin's death in 1924. From the following year on, he upheld the theory of "socialism in one country," and by centralizing control in his own hands he dedicated himself to the internal transformation of Russia in both a beaurocratic and repressive way. The so-called purges began in 1936 and carried on until 1940, when all the energies of the Russian people were directed toward the war against Nazi Germany.

Roosevelt and Churchill, however, recognize the old Polish government in London. The rift between them continues to widen.

3 JANUARY 1945

Tonight I met with Professor Paribeni; yesterday I saw Professor Giovannoni. Both of them were Italian scholars; now they are left impoverished. Their emaciated faces and white beards reveal how much during these times they have suffered both morally and financially. Professor Giovannoni said that he supports himself by selling his books...

What misery! Good, honest people who were once a credit to Italy now have been exiled and are starving to death. By going over the list of professors who were appointed, you can see that some of them managed to get into the assembly, thanks to the Fascists! But they shouldn't destroy the Academia!

After the signing of the Molotov-Ribbentrop Pact on 23 August 1939, he divided up Poland with the Germans and then proceeded with the annexation of Estonia, Latvia, and Lithuania and initiated hostilities against Finland (1940). The following war against the countries of the Fascist-Nazi Axis (1941–45) brought with it huge losses (it was calculated there were 12 million Russian soldiers killed), but it obtained important results: the blocking of the Nazi attack, the occupancy of Berlin, and victory. Being very clear and decisive in his postwar settlements, he was a supporter of the division of Germany.

From 1945 on, Stalin concentrated on two fronts: the internal reconstruction of Russia and hostility to the West, which was made even more evident by Soviet experimentation with the atomic bomb in 1949 and the creation of an Eastern coalition which, according to his plans, was also to be made up of Korea and Mao's China, along with the satellite states in Europe and Asia. They were the "cold war" years in which the Communist Party was markedly monolithic, both inside and outside the Russian borders, under the undisputed rule of the dictator. He supplied military and financial aid to North Korea, which was at war with South Korea (1950–53), the latter backed by the United States, and he also financially supported various Communist parties in different countries all over the world. Stalin died on 5 March 1953; he was embalmed, and after a stately funeral his coffin was interred in Lenin's mausoleum in Moscow. During the "de-Stalinization" process set into motion by his successor Nikita Khruschev, Stalin's coffin was removed from Lenin's tomb.

The purification movement rages on. Thank goodness Count Sforza
has gone away. Even Caronia,[2] an excellent professor who was made
to suffer under Fascism, was turned in to the purifying committee with
110 other university professors.

Duchess Trigona's maid tells me that they pay 900 lire for a kilo of
sugar and 850 lire for a kilo of butter.

24 JANUARY 1945

"We shall continue to operate on the Italian donkey at both ends, with
a carrot and a stick." The cruel echo of Churchill's harsh words against
Italy continues to resound. I think that England is operating on an
incorrect point of view. It needs to treat Italy as a friend not as a foe.
After the armistice, which was imposed with both hostility and severity,
England continued to behave like Italy's enemy. Italy's defeat represents
another episode in its painful history, but she is alive and will live on;
her geographical position, which cannot be changed, asks to be considered friendly territory. And if it is not? Italy will turn the other way. It is
not enough to win with weapons; a spiritual victory is what is needed.

The Russians advance *magnis itineribus*.[3] It seems that we are inching
toward the end of this horrendous tragedy, and I hope the German
wolves and the wolves of Mussolini's republic are getting ready to flee or
to return to their lairs.

24 JANUARY 1945

The Hon. Luigi Gasparotto[4] came to see me. I met him in the other
war: a proud and sincere soul. A patriot who accepted the negative

[2] The person mentioned only by his last name seems to be Giuseppe Caronia
(1884–1977), a professor of medicine who protected Jews during the Second
World War. After the war, he became a member of the Constituent Assembly of
Italy and then a member of parliament representing the Christian Democrats.

[3] The Latin expression means "by forced march."

[4] Luigi Gasparotto (1873–1954), originally from Sacile, which at the time
was part of the province of Udine but now belongs to the province of Pordenone, was a lawyer and Italian politician. He was elected a member of parliament in 1913 and later fought in the First World War. In 1921, as minister of
war, he introduced the rites for the Unknown Soldier, whose religious ceremony
was presided over by Bishop Celso Costantini in Aquileia on 4 November 1921.
Gasparotto retired from politics in 1926 because of his aversion to Fascism, but

consequences of his actions, he was ostracized by the Fascists and now has been called to work with the government. He is minister of the Air Force and president of the Veterans' Association. He told me that his son, who was taken by the Germans, was put in prison. The judge apparently said, "We like him and we will pardon him, because he is a worthy enemy." Instead, he was tortured and slaughtered. Gasparotto, although proud of his son's sacrifice, could not repress his sobs. He told me that a month before the war started, the Pope had written to Mussolini begging him not to go to war.

THE PROVINCIAL GOVERNMENT OF ROME
VISITS THE HOLY FATHER   25 JANUARY 1945
As expressed by the municipal government of Rome in July last year,[5] the provincial delegation, in its entirety, wants to make known to the Supreme Pontiff the deep gratitude felt by the people of this region. His varied and untiring acts of charity, while sensitively easing so much suffering, are in themselves a support and serve as an example for additional necessary provisions and eventual reconstruction.[6]

26 JANUARY 1945

The news of the severe armistice has not yet been released. One can – and at times one must – punish a nation, but the punishment cannot go beyond a certain limit and cannot last longer than a certain period.

---

he became politically active again toward the end of the Second World War as one of the founders, in 1944, of the Labour Democratic Party [Partito Democratico del Lavoro]. A member of the Constituent Assembly and a minister in different governments led by De Gasperi, he was elected president of the Senate following the resignation of Giuseppe Paratore on 24 March 1953. However, the following day he declined the position. In 1945 he published the book *Diario di un deputato. Cinquant'anni di vita politica* (Milan: Dall'Oglio, 1945).

5 The audience with Pius XII and the representatives of the city of Rome took place on 12 July 1944 as described in *Le Saint Siège et la guerre mondiale*, vol. 11 of *Actes et documents du Saint Siège relatifs à la seconde guerre mondiale* (Vatican City: Libreria Editrice Vaticana, 1981), 451–2. Transcribed in the same volume, on pages 682–4, is the Pope's speech to the municipal government of Rome.

6 This speech given by the Pope is transcribed in *Discorsi e Radiomessaggi di Sua Santità Pio XII*, vol. 6 (Vatican City: Tipologia Poliglotta Vaticana, 1948), 291–3.

The Hon. A. De Stefani is being hidden by Monsignor Carinci[7] in the Palazzo delle Congregazioni in Trastevere. He has let his beard grow thick. On one visit he expressed the desire that the Holy Father would agree to persuading the Allies to publish a direct order to pacify the Italians. They would order that all those who freely and actively collaborated with the Germans after 8 September 1943 are to undergo the purifying process.

If the Allies welcomed such a suggestion – which essentially reflects the opinion as well as the warning expressed by the Holy Father in his message delivered on the anniversary of the beginning of the war – it would immediately achieve two impressive results:

1 It will rebuild the spiritual unity that is necessary for the reconstruction of Italy.
2 It will put up a barrier against the threatening and rising tide of Communism.

I answered, "The Pope has done and will do all that *et ultra*, but he is not always listened to."

Today, Father Tacchi-Venturi[8] came to my residence. He deplores the vindictive and fractious spirit in which the purification has been carried out. He says that following this purification, an amnesty will be necessary to harmoniously repair Italians' torn souls. In addition, he deplores that people condemn outright everything that Mussolini did, when some

---

7 Alfonso Carinci (1862–1963) was the secretary of the Sacred Congregation of Rites [Sacra Congregazione dei Riti] and adviser to the largest number of pontifical ministries, among them the Sacred Congregation of the Council [Sacra Congregazione del Concilio]. He used to live in Rome at Piazza San Callisto, 16. He became the titular archbishop of Seleucia of Isauria and was appointed on 15 December 1945.

8 Pietro Tacchi-Venturi (1861–1956), a Jesuit and Italian historian, was the general secretary (1914–18) of the Society of Jesus and authoritative collaborator of the magazine *La Civiltà Cattolica*. A great intermediary who promoted the "Conciliation" between Italy and the Holy See, both before and after it came into effect in the Concordat of 1929, he often held official positions in the office of the Pontifical Secretary of State of the Holy See in the Italian government during the Fascist regime.

of his projects remain, such as the Conciliation.[9] Without Mussolini and without Pius XI, who also had a dictator-like character, the Lateran Pacts would not have been signed.

6 FEBRUARY 1945

A suckling pig costs 10,000 lire; a tire for an automobile wheel 50,000 lire; a shirt 3,300 lire; a box of matches 35 lire. We bought a donkey for the Propaganda property: 30,000 lire!

THE YALTA CONFERENCE   12 FEBRUARY 1945

The "Big Three" [Roosevelt, Churchill, and Stalin] didn't say one word about Italy. The Italian public feels bitter disappointment. The Big Three don't realize that to resolve all the peace problems favourably, they no longer have to "look to the past" but also know how to "look to the future."

Italy will carry on, and it will need to make amends with its 45 million people who, because of their geographical location, their ability to work, and also because of Italy's history, will have considerable influence on Europe's stability.[10]

---

[9] The term "Conciliation" refers to the historic accord between the Holy See and Italy, with the signing, on 11 February 1929, of the Lateran Pacts (whose name was taken from the Lateran Palace where they were underwritten by Benito Mussolini, as head of the Italian government, and Cardinal Pietro Gasparri, as Pius XI's secretary of state). They were called pacts because they consisted mostly of legal acts. First listed was the treaty that resolved the "Roman issue," which was a consequence of the annexation of the Pontifical state to the kingdom of Italy in 1870, and also restored the full sovereignty and independence of the Pope in the new state of Vatican City. Secondly, it dealt with the Concordat between Italy and the Holy See regarding the matter of the so-called "mixed subjects" and the legal stipulations of the Church in Italy. Finally, the pacts were spread out over four addenda, all integral parts of the treaty, the most relevant being concerned with the financial agreement that cancelled, with compensation, the Holy See's credit in Italy. Pius XI wanted the pacts to be linked to one another in such a way that they proved unbreakable, because while the treaty favoured the Italian state, the Concordat awarded the greatest benefits to the Holy See.

[10] CC: *Gli accordi di Ialta (Crimea)* [The Yalta Pacts (Crimea)]. On 3 February 1945, Roosevelt, Churchill, and Stalin met at Yalta. Documentation of the pact was made public on 12 February.

In the meantime, the feeling of hatred toward the Allies is growing stronger. I wouldn't want us to start having in Italy revolts similar to those in Greece.[11] The suffering and humiliation should have ended, and should end once and for all, and we should acknowledge the ability to be free.

17 FEBRUARY 1945

In a message broadcast yesterday to the people of southern Italy, General Clark,[12] commander of the Allied Forces in Italy, warned people to stay away from industrial sites and communication lines because in the next few days Allied planes will increase *en masse* the bombing of these locations. This, as General Clark explained, is to block a possible withdrawal of the Germans from northern Italy, which could be ordered by German High Command.

Wonderful! We used to say the Allies landed in Italy to free us. Instead, they spread, *in corpore vili*, ruin and more ruin to strike at Germany. Today they declare that they will continue to rage on ferociously in northern Italy to prevent the Germans from leaving.

A Tragic Case of Premature Delinquency
Who are the very young criminals who slaughtered Professor Salto?
The killers of Professor Salto of Siena are in the hands of the authorities. The three killers committed their crime (crimes, there was more than one, for they are also responsible for car thefts) with cold cynicism. After they had killed Professor Salto and taken his car, they went

[11] The reference to Greece alludes to the internal situation that developed after the landing of the Allies in 1944, when the partisans had already freed large areas of the country. A conflict arose after the withdrawal of the Axis forces. On one side was the monarchy and the regular army, and on the other side the Communist Party and the partisan gangs, who assembled a people's republican government. The major crisis, which took the form of a civil war, continued for a few years after the end of the Second World War.
[12] Mark Wayne Clark (1896–1984), an American general, led the American forces that had been sent to Britain and then went on to direct the Allied military operations that freed Italy in 1944 and 1945. They seized Rome on 4 June 1944. After the war, he was the head of the American forces in the Far East and then, in 1952–53, of the United Nations' special forces in Korea.

to Naples, where they sold the Aprilia and then returned to Rome, confident of their impunity.

It is the Fascist youth, who were educated by the book *Libro e moschetto* and are thrilled by the psychosis of war!

POOR POLAND   19 FEBRUARY 1945

The Big Three – at the conference in the Crimea – confirmed the dismantling of Poland. The War had begun in order to defend Poland, and in England a Polish government was recognized. Now we are tearing up the Atlantic Charter, and a legitimate government has been thrown into the sea. *Mundus totus in maligno positus est* [1 Jn. 5:19].[13] Nothing but violence prevails, and it is trying to write another chapter by placing the new Europe on top of the cooled magma of a volcano.

                                                      21 FEBRUARY 1945

De Gaulle refused to accept Roosevelt's invitation to meet him in Africa. Roosevelt got the American newspapers to say that de Gaulle's refusal was a great disappointment to him. But the senior commander's act has been met with great approval; there is dignity, pride, and French glory – a lesson that the Big Three deserve. They said they went to war to free people from dictatorships and to give them back their freedom; but then, by stepping on the Atlantic Charter, they rearranged Poland's borders without taking into consideration the legitimate government that was based in England. And they discussed the vital interests and future of France without having acknowledged de Gaulle's wish to participate in the Yalta Conference. The first lesson does them good. And others will follow. One cannot humiliate a nation with impunity.

On the eighteenth, at the partisan celebrations in Piazza del Popolo, when Russia was mentioned there was a lively cheer of approval, whereas when the Allies were mentioned the crowd fell silent. If the Allies do not change their ways in dealing with Italy, something very serious will be set into motion, something that will exceed de Gaulle's actions.

[13] This Latin phrase can be translated as "The whole world is seated in wickedness."

23 FEBRUARY 1945

Today I was visited by the Hon. Guarnieri, the former minister of foreign exchange and commerce.[14] He said to me, "If we don't act as soon as possible, the lira will crash. Today 100 lire are worth one lira. The government should tell the Allies: 'Either you help us save the lira or you accept all responsibility for leading Italy into bankruptcy. This way, we put the government in your hands and you take all responsibility for it.'"

23 FEBRUARY 1945

A few days ago on the Pincio[15] I read something written underneath the bust of Eugene of Savoy on its pedestal: *Va' morì ammazzato* [Go and kill yourself]. Beneath this, someone had written: "He has already been killed."

Last night on the side of the crypt belonging to Saint John of the Florentines, I saw written in large letters: "Long live the King." Two workers passed by and one of them gave it a sinister look and muttered, "That writing should be covered with ..." The King has shown himself to be a man of incredible stubbornness and lacking in understanding. If he had abdicated after Mussolini's arrest, the monarchy and the House of Savoy would have been saved. Instead, he said, "The war will continue!"

[14] Felice Guarnieri (1882–1955), an Italian economist, together with Beneduce and Azzolini, led the political economy of the Fascist regime, mainly during the period immediately before the Second World War. He had a leading role in Italy's adaptation of the new reality of international commerce during the crisis in the thirties and created a new structure for state monetary funding that focused on and was designed around national goals. For this purpose, in 1935 he was brought in as under-secretary for exchange and commerce; then in 1937 he was promoted to minister of foreign exchange and commerce. He changed a generous and liberalistic structure into one that was typically Fascist: protective, autarchical, and corporative. However, it did not disregard overseas commerce.

[15] This bust can be found among the more than 200 busts that line the famous walk that leads to Pincio Hill in Rome. The aforementioned sculpture depicts Prince Eugene of Savoy (1663–1736), a general in the Austrian Imperial Army.

REVOLTING MORAL WRETCHEDNESS   23 FEBRUARY 1945

"When Claretta, Miriam,[16] Francesco Saverio, and Donna Petacci – taken by surprise on 25 July at their house in Meina – were transferred to the prison in Novara, the authorities found a surprise. In their bags and in the young people's clothing they found 43 letters from Mussolini to his female companion, two letters from the girl to her lover, and one from Il Duce to Miriam, along with other documents."

As I was reading this news, which was printed in the 21 February edition of *Il Risorgimento Liberale*, a sick feeling began to build in the depths of my soul. A man who brought Italy into an abyss and watched it thrash about in agony, amid so much blood, destruction, pain, and unending misery, found the time to amuse himself with an adulteress. I will quote another passage from this disgusting document: "How tired I am of everyone and everything! Traitors, I have only traitors around me; and tomorrow morning you are coming to reclaim your place in Palazzo Venezia beside me. I will be waiting for you."

26 FEBRUARY 1945

Professor Severi,[17] member of the Pontifical Academy and already a member of the Italian Academy, came to see me. He had been ordered to report to the purifying commission, as were Professor Giuseppe Tucci and many others. He was very angry. When he was sent overseas to give lectures, he had never made himself open to Fascist propaganda. The new government, instead of raking up the past, should prepare for the future.

I think that Severi worked on building Italy's cultural prestige. I told him that only the Pope is seeing clearly. I read him the words of his speech that was delivered on 1 September 1944: "Is it perhaps desirable

[16] Miriam di San Servolo Petacci, whose real name was Maria, was the daughter of Francesco Saverio Petacci and Giuseppina Persichetti, and therefore the sister of Claretta. She was an actress, known by the name of Miriam Day.

[17] Francesco Severi (1879–1961), a member of the Pontifical Academy since 5 April 1940, was a professor of advanced geometry at the Istituto Nazionale di Alta Matematica, which he founded and ran within the Università La Sapienza of Roma; he was rector of the university 1923–25. His scientific research is documented in more than 400 publications. He tells the story of his life in his autobiography *Dalla scienza alla fede* (Assisi: Edizioni Pro Civitate Christiana, 1959), written in 1959 after he converted to Catholicism.

that people who are honest, upright, experienced, frank, and free of the stains of crime or true deviation – even if in the past they had found themselves with a foot in a different political camp – should contribute to the common good and thus aid in levelling the obstacles to peace?

Professor Severi left our meeting feeling proud and also consoled.

2 MARCH 1945

Churchill gave a speech in the British parliament and our hearts opened a bit to let in hope. He understood that Fascism is one thing and Italy is another. For the good of all, for both the victors and the vanquished, may God hasten the arrival of peace, that peace which has been so long awaited. We are tired of chatter; we want facts.

On 27 February I found myself having lunch in the Cerruti home with Senator Bergamini[18] and the Hon. Mr Boeri.[19] These two men act as the general secretary of the purifying committee. I spoke to them with great frankness, explaining the noble ideas that the Holy Father expressed regarding the delicate problem of the political parties and the purification. I told him that from the start it was a huge mistake to nominate Zaniboni, the man who had ordered the attack on Mussolini, as head of the purifying committee. Badoglio showed himself to be lacking in the most basic moral sensibilities. Another error committed by Count Sforza was the creation of special tribunals for senators, thus copying the Fascist way of doing things, while the Senate has its own High Court of Justice. As a result, great unrest became widespread. I told him that he has to think about the rebirth of Italy, for which honest and competent men are needed. It is necessary to strike back at the thieves and at those who are to be held responsible, but Italy also needs the expertise of honest men, even if they fought for other political parties, as the Pope states.

[18] Alberto Bergamini (1871–1962), an Italian journalist and politician, who founded and ran *Il Giornale d'Italia* from 1901 to 1923. He was appointed a senator and after the Second World War was part of the Constituent Assembly. From 1956 to 1962 he was president of the National Federation of the Italian Press.

[19] Giovanni Boeri (1883–1957), a lawyer and member of the National Liberation Committee, was secretary of the High Court of Justice for Sanctions against Fascism, having been appointed by the president of the Council of Ministers [prime minister] Ivanoe Bonomi. He was also the president of a subcommittee of the Constituent Assembly.

We need to prepare for what the future holds. It was an enormous legal mistake to give retroactive validity to the Penal Laws. Saint Paul says *"ubi non est lex, neque praevaricatio"* [Rom. 4:15; Where there is no law, neither is there transgression].

The Hon. Mr Boeri said that he will come to see me.

THE AGENDA OF THE CHRISTIAN DEMOCRATS

3 MARCH 1945

The leadership of the Christian Democrat Party had a meeting last night that was chaired by Vice-secretary Scelba.[20] It was attended by the other members of the leadership committee: Fuschini,[21] Gonella,[22]

[20] Mario Scelba (1901–91), an Italian politician who like Don Luigi Sturzo – his close associate – was from Caltagirone. During the twenty-year Fascist period he became friends with Alcide De Gasperi. As one of the most prominent representatives of the Christian Democrats, in 1943 he helped draft the first policy document for the party. He was minister of the interior for several governments that were led by De Gasperi 1947–53, and it was during these years that he became famous for being fiercely anti-Communist. In fact, with the 1948 elections in sight, he took steps to expel personnel with questionable loyalty from the police force in order to stifle the beginning of any possible attempt at a civil war. Scelba became prime minister (1954–55) and then again minister of the interior in the third government led by Amintore Fanfani (1960–62). In 1966 he was elected President of the National Council of his party, and three years later he accepted the presidency of the European parliament.

[21] Giuseppe Fuschini (1883–1949), a journalist from Ravenna, was active in social labour disputes, but with the rise of Fascism he retired to private life and worked as a lawyer. He was one of the founders of the Christian Democrats, from whose ranks he was elected to the Constituent Assembly in 1946 and to the Chamber of Deputies, in which he served as vice-president in 1948.

[22] Guido Gonella (1905–82), an Italian journalist and politician, was a professor of philosophy of law at the University of Bari and the University of Pavia. During the twenty-year Fascist reign he was active in FUCI, the Italian Catholic Federation of University Students, having been appointed by Mons. Giovanni Battista Montini (the future Paul VI). He contributed to *L'Osservatore Romano* as editor of the successful column "Acta diurna." In 1939 he was arrested by the Fascists and shortly afterwards was released, thanks to the intervention of the Holy See; however, he had to give up his university career. From 1946 on, acting as its managing editor, he attempted to breathe life into the daily *Il Popolo*, the

Piccioni,[23] Restagno,[24] and Spataro.[25] Absent, with justification, were De Gasperi, Gava[26] and Grandi.[27] At the meeting the following

---

official publication of the Christian Democrats. From 1946 to 1951 he served many terms as minister of education. From 1953 to 1973 he was elected no less than nine times as minister of justice. He was the first president of the College of Journalists, created by law no. 69 in 1963.

[23] Attilio Piccioni (1892–1976), an Italian politician, was one of the founders of the Christian Democrats. He was elected many times as minister of foreign affairs and vice-president of the Council of Ministers in the fifth, seventh, and eighth De Gasperi governments. His political career was greatly damaged by his son Piero's alleged involvement (for which he was later cleared) in the murder of Wilma Montesi, a case that was closely followed nationwide.

[24] Pier Carlo Restagno (1898–1966), an accountant originally from Turin, became a member of the Italian People's Party in 1920 and managed Catholic Action in his diocese. He was the editor of the newspaper *Il Momento*, and when Fascism fell he participated in the founding of the Christian Democrats and then served as their national administrative secretary, 1944–53. Acting as under-secretary to the minister of public works in the third De Gasperi government, he was elected both to the Constituent Assembly (in 1946) and the Senate (in 1948). He was also elected mayor of Cassino in 1949 and of the town of Sora in 1961.

[25] Giuseppe Spataro (1897–1979), an Italian politician, was one of the founders of the Christian Democrats and its publication *Il Popolo*. He emerged into Italian politics from FUCI, the Italian Catholic Federation of University Students, for which he served as president, 1920–22. After the collapse of the Fascist regime, he was a part of the National Liberation Committee, with Alcide De Gasperi and Giovanni Gronchi. He acted as president of RAI [Radio Audizioni Italiane], 1946–51. In successive governments he was in charge of the following ministries: Public Works, Transport, Shipping, the Interior, Post and Telecommunications.

[26] Silvio Gava (1901–99), an Italian politician and one of the founders of the Christian Democrats, was a minister (Justice, Treasury, Industry) for no less than 13 times between 1948 and 1975.

[27] Achille Grandi (1883–1946), a politician and Catholic unionist, was a member of parliament for the Italian People's Party (1919–26) and was in the Constituent Assembly (1946). He was the founder and president of the Italian Christian Workers Association (ACLI), and was co-founder of the Italian General Confederation of Labour (GCIL).

people spoke: Andreotti,[28] Campilli,[29] Cassiani,[30] Cingolani,[31] Gronchi,[32]

[28] Giulio Andreotti, born in 1919, an Italian politician, author, and journalist, was one of the main representatives of the Christian Democrats and was at the centre of Italy's political scene during the second half of the twentieth century. During the Second World War he was president of FUCI, 1942–44. Serving as secretary to De Gasperi, he was active in the Constituent Assembly, and in 1948 he was elected to the Chamber of Deputies. Since 1991, he has been a senator for life. In his political career he served seven times as the head of the government, eight times as minister of defence, five times as minister of foreign affairs, three times as minister of state investment, twice as minister of finance and the budget, and was once minister of the treasury and also minister of the interior.

[29] Pietro Campilli (1891–1974), an Italian politician, served in FUCI before the beginning of the Fascist regime as well as in the Italian People's Party with Don Luigi Sturzo. During Mussolini's leadership he was active as an entrepreneur. He took part in the creation of the Christian Democrats and in 1946 was a member of the Constituent Assembly. Two years later he was elected to the Chamber of Deputies. Within the governments led by De Gasperi, he served as minister of foreign trade, finance, the treasury, transport, industry, and trade. From 1953 to 1958 he was the minister of la Cassa per il Mezzogiorno [Fund for the South]. He was president of the National Council for Economics and Labour (CNEL) from 1959 to 1970.

[30] Gennaro Cassiani (1903–78), an Italian politician and lawyer, began to organize the Christian Democrats in Calabria in 1942. He was one of the founders of the party at the national level. He became under-secretary in a number of ministries, then served twice as minister of post and telecommunications and three times as minister of the merchant marine.

[31] Mario Cingolani (1883–1971), a teacher and Italian politician, was a member of parliament (1921–26) and under-secretary for the two Facta governments. Elected to the Constituent Assembly through his ties with the Christian Democrats, he became a *senatore di diritto* (senator for life) in 1948. He served as minister of the air force (1946–47) and minister of defence (1947).

[32] Giovanni Gronchi (1887–1978), an Italian politician and one of the founders of the Italian People's Party with Don Luigi Sturzo, became under-secretary of industry in the first government led by Mussolini. Later, during Fascism, he left the public eye and became an entrepreneur in the commercial and industrial sectors. He returned to politics after 8 September 1943 and became minister of industry in the second and third Bonomi governments and in De Gasperi's first government. In 1946 he took part in the Constituent

Jacini,[33] Mattarella,[34] Rodinò,[35] Scoca,[36] Segni,[37] and Tupini.[38]

Assembly and in 1948 was elected president of the Chamber of Deputies. From 1955 to 1962 he held the office of the third president of the Italian Republic. He therefore was later appointed senator for life.

[33] Stefano Jacini (1882–1952), a representative of the Christian Democrats, was made minister of war in 1945; he became a member of the Constituent Assembly in 1946 and a senator in 1948.

[34] Bernardo Mattarella (1905–71), an Italian politician, originally from Palermo, was one of the founders of the Christian Democrats, for which he became vice-secretary. He acted as an under-secretary in two of the governments led by Bonomi and he was elected to the Constituent Assembly in 1946 and to the Chamber of Deputies in 1948. He was a minister many times between 1953 and 1966 in the following offices: Post and Telecommunications, the Merchant Marine, Foreign Trade, Forestry and Agriculture.

[35] Giulio Rodinò (1875–1946), a lawyer and politician with the Italian People's Party, was minister of war in 1920 and minister of justice in 1921–22. After his digression into Fascism, he returned to political life in the ranks of the Christian Democrats and became vice-president of the Council of Ministers in the second Bonomi government (1944–45).

[36] Salvatore Scoca (1894–1962), a magistrate and Italian politician, was the under-secretary of the Treasury (1944–45) and of Finance (1946–47). He was elected by the Christian Democrats to the Constituent Assembly in 1946 and to the Chamber of Deputies in 1948 and 1953. In 1958 he became attorney general of Italy.

[37] Antonio Segni (1891–1972), a university professor and Italian politician, taught in the Faculty of Law at the University of Perugia as well as the University of Sassari, where he served as rector, 1946–51. He had joined the Italian People's Party founded by Don Sturzo and then withdrew from the political sphere during Fascism. He returned to politics in 1942. He was one of the founders of the Christian Democrats. Elected to the Constituent Assembly in 1946, he first became minister of agriculture in various governments led by De Gasperi and then was named minister of education in the seventh government led by De Gasperi, as well as in the one led by Giuseppe Pella. He was twice prime minister (1955–57 and 1959–60). He became president of the Italian Republic in 1962, a position he had to leave in 1964 because of ill health.

[38] Umberto Tupini (1889–1973), an Italian politician, was elected to the Constituent Assembly in 1946 by the Christian Democrats. He later became vice-president of the assembly and entered the Senate in 1948. He also served as

Gonella reported on the numerous studies that had been carried out and the subsequent conclusions reached by the party's foreign policy commission. In many meetings, he discussed the analysis of the problematic relationship between Italy and Yugoslavia, in particular the issue of the border shared by the two countries, while reminding those present of the firm guidelines that had been announced by the Ministry of Foreign Affairs during the ministers' meeting on 17 April.

AUDIENCE IN PIAZZA SAN PIETRO. HARSH WARNINGS
ISSUED BY THE HOLY FATHER   18 MARCH 1945
The Holy Father, anxiously awaiting peace, spoke today to the people of Rome from the central balcony on the front façade of the Vatican. Prince Lancellotti and I had gone up to the terrace above the right-hand colonnade. From there one could see the flood of people filling the square.

The Inspiring Architect of the moral world, wanting to hasten the declaration of a truce, the peace that has been so eagerly awaited, warned the crowd of the dangers of immoral behaviour. He said, "May none of you be among those who have fallen into this great calamity, those in the human family who see nothing but a propitious opportunity to grow rich dishonestly, taking advantage of the neediness and misery of their brothers by indefinitely raising prices in order to secure scandalous profits for themselves."

The Pope raised his voice while denouncing the danger of nationalism: "There remains no other path to salvation than the one that leads us to renounce definitively the idolatry of absolute nationalism, the pride of lineage and bloodlines, the lust for hegemony in land ownership. It is this path that will resolutely turn us toward the spirit of true brotherhood, which was founded in the faith of the Divine Father of all men."[39]

When the thunderous applause of the crowd died down, I said to a diplomat, "At least there is one man in the world who speaks the truth, just one man." The diplomat replied, "You are right."

---

the mayor of Rome (1958–60). He was appointed minister of various departments, among which were Justice, Public Works, Tourism, and Performing Arts.

[39] The excerpt of Pius XII's speech that was quoted above can be found in its entirety in AAS 37 (*Bollettino Ufficiale della Santa Sede*, 1945), 111–15. The passage containing the two quotations can be found on pages 112 and 113, respectively.

The Magnificent Act of a Bishop
On the evening of 17 March 1945 in Piazza Campitello in Belluno, four
partisans were hanged. Since the four victims had been forbidden any
priest to administer the last rites, Mons. Bortignon[40] himself burst
through the military ranks as they were preparing to carry out the hangings. He laid down his cape with dignity at the feet of the men about
to die, forced the hangman to give him a ladder, mounted the scaffold
in order to administer the extreme unction to the partisans, and gave
them the kiss of faith, of family, and of country. It was rightly pointed
out that this act was the most meaningful and distinct of the whole
resistance movement.[41]

20 MARCH 1945

Yesterday I met Countess Giuliana Rota, Pietro Badoglio's son's wife.
She was pale, and beneath a weak smile she concealed deep sadness. She
has not heard anything either about her husband, taken prisoner by
the Germans, or her father, Senator Francesco Rota, who is in Friuli. She
told me that her uncle Ludovico committed suicide in Florence. He could
not withstand an attack of neurasthenia that was made worse by the
present tragic circumstances.

It is sad, however, to think that a life he had lived only for himself
should end so tragically, since he had been given so much intelligence
and good qualities. Many believe that after this war, the figure of the
"signore" should no longer be an option, for the signore, living only for
himself, knows nothing but how to live off the revenue from the work
of others.

22 MARCH 1945

We have been talking about the official meetings for peace. Our souls
open themselves to hope. Considering the progress made by the Allies
and the Russians, we have faith in the coming collapse of the German
army and of Nazism. *Faxit Deus!*

---

[40] Girolamo Bartolomeo Bortignon (1905–92), a Capuchin, became titular
bishop of Lidda on 4 April 1944 and apostolic administrator of Belluno and
Feltre (two cities joined together in one diocese by Bortignon). He was appointed
bishop on 9 September 1945, and in April 1949 was assigned to the Diocese of
Padua, a position he held for 32 years.
[41] CC: Please see the 18 July 1953 edition of *Il Quotidiano*.

From home, there is fairly good but general news. At this point we hope there will be no other disturbances in northern Italy and that our dear cities will be safe from further destruction. The Allies have shown a lack of consideration for every city except Venice. It will be better if the Germans have to lay down their arms for the internal defeat of Germany.

There is a widespread sense of distrust in the government. This group cannot lead by means of *métayage*; that is, by attempting to obtain a consensus among all the parties with regard to important appointments and posts as well as serious state business.

The fury to "purify" continues to rage on. Strike down those who are guilty, yes, but allow those who are honest and competent to live, even if they were Fascists. Didn't we say we wanted to establish an order of freedom? Mussolini's escape, which for many seems to be only trickery, as well as Roatta's escape discredits the idea of public power. At the bottom of our hearts remains a feeling of skepticism and a type of bitter resentment toward the government, because so many of us have the feeling that the structuring of the government is insecure and false.

Many people have been attacked. But so many others ask themselves, "Why don't they attack the leaders? Why don't they bring to justice the important people who are responsible?" And who are more responsible than the generals who abandoned Rome with unprecedented and shameful desertion? Who are more responsible than those people who let Mussolini escape? With so many atrocities, he created a civil revolution in northern Italy, with horrifying acts that will make putting our souls at peace very difficult once our soil has been liberated.

In Calabria there was a bloody Communist revolt involving the killing of a very respectable parish priest and other innocent people. There is a lot of talk about the Communists. But it is more correct to refer to them as low-lifes, scoundrels who once called themselves Fascists and now call themselves Communists, who have no other goals than to carry out revenge, steal, raid, etc.

23 MARCH 1945

Professor Leicht, the former senator who at the time of the Lateran Treaty was the under-secretary of the Ministry of Education, told me, "Mussolini sees the Lateran Pacts simply as a political event that, while increasing the party's prestige, established trust in Fascism and closed the rift between Italy and the Holy See."

A MOVING REMEMBRANCE IN ROME OF THE MARTYRS
OF THE FOSSE ARDEATINE MASSACRE   25 MARCH 1945
I transcribe here, from the *Risorgimento Liberale* of 25 March 1945, a
description of the painful incident that took place at Santa Maria degli
Angeli during the commemoration of the fallen at the Fosse Ardeatine:

> An evocative and touching ceremony took place yesterday at 10:30 at Santa
> Maria degli Angeli. At the initiative of the prime minister, a Mass for the souls
> of the dead for those 335 martyrs was celebrated. An hour before the begin-
> ning of the Mass, a crowd of those invited had already filled the Michelangelesque
> temple. At 10:00, as the Lieutenant [Umberto of Savoy] entered the church,
> the military ordinary H. E. Mons. Carlo Ferrero[42] of Cavallerleone, assisted by
> the military chaplains Chiardini and Fannabo – who are survivors of the
> Caulonia massacre – began the celebration of Holy Mass.
>
> But the first very sweet notes of Sgambati's music didn't even have time to
> spread throughout the high vaults of the basilica when an incident disturbed
> the austere solemnity of the mass. A young woman from the crowd, carrying a
> small child with its arms around her neck, moved toward the Lieutenant and,
> with a loud and clamorous voice, violently addressed him. Those present tried
> to guide her gently away from him, but the woman, shaken and sobbing, with
> her nerves on edge because of her desperation, continued to shout her hate.

It seems to me that the demonstration against Lieutenant Umberto of
Savoy is truly pitiable. How do we explain this incident? We explain it
with such resentment for the King who, along with Mussolini, is most
responsible for the war and its consequences.

This is one of many symptoms that reveal the rising discontent with
the government. The King and Badoglio didn't understand that on
25 July a fictitious world, dictatorial and hated, collapsed and the Axis
was finally broken. They didn't understand that those who were most
responsible should have known when to retire.

---

[42] Carlo Alberto Ferrero of Cavallerleone (1903–69) became the titular archbishop of Trebisonda on 28 October 1944. He was a military ordinary in Italy
and an adviser, together with Celso Costantini, of the Congregation of the Oriental Churches. He left the direction of the military ordinariate in 1953 to accept
the position of prelate of the Sovereign Military Order of Malta.

The European Federation

A United States of Europe is not a utopia. It represents the only civil and Christian solution.

The Persecution in the Ukraine

The Pontifical Colleges of Rome have welcomed many clerics from the nations that fell under Russian domination. There are also three Ukrainian clerics. There the persecution of the Catholic Church gets more and more fierce.

Roosevelt

On 12 April 1945 Roosevelt was struck dead by a cerebral hemorrhage. He disappeared into the glowing phosphorescent light of a victorious battle. But it is known that even certain reptiles can produce phosphorescent light. Roosevelt let himself be ensnared into the coils of the Russian reptile. With the Atlantic Charter he had flaunted the notion of liberty and the principles of fair-mindedness by stating the four freedoms: freedom of speech, freedom of worship, freedom from want, freedom from fear.

But then he signed the agreements in Teheran [1 December 1943] and Yalta [3 February 1945] that predicted absolute imperialism by the victorious over the defeated. In addition, it seems necessary to note that, for Roosevelt, peace had been obtained with difficulty, as had happened with Wilson. We hope that his successor, Truman,[43] freshly appointed and free of compromise, asserts the idea of justifiable peace.

[43] Harry Spencer Truman (1884–1972), a North American politician and a Democratic senator since 1934, was president of the United States 1945–53. He had been elected vice-president in 1944. After Roosevelt's death on 12 April 1945, he assumed the presidency. He was elected president of the United States in 1948 but declined to run for a second term. In foreign politics he resolved a post-war accord at the Potsdam Conference (17 July to 2 August 1945), the principles for which had already been outlined at Yalta, and he made the decision to drop two atomic bombs on Japan. One bomb was dropped 6 August on Hiroshima and the other on the ninth of the same month on Nagasaki. In addition, he looked after the development of the so-called Truman Doctrine in order to prevent the Communist forces from getting the upper hand, especially in Western Europe. This would be carried out by means of economic intervention with the Marshall Plan, put forward by his secretary of state, as well as by military measures among which was the establishment of NATO in 1949.

Italy is still, in practice, under the control of the Allies. But Truman and Churchill will also have to understand that a Sovietized Europe would be a terribly passive victory. Italy will be able to assume the role of an element of balance.

In Italy, Roosevelt is remembered as the "champion of idealism"; but we have the right to ask if his idealism lives up to the facts before us. Only facts count. It is said that the road to hell is paved with good intentions.

FATA TRAHUNT   15 APRIL 1945
Germany's fate is sealed. He who lives by the sword shall die by the sword.[44] Mussolini has gone to his maker. Dante's tercet, verses 49–51 from the eighth Canto of Hell, comes to mind; it applies perfectly to those who were so infatuated with pride that they caused this horrible war:

> How many now hold themselves mighty kings
> Who here like swine shall wallow in the mire,
> Leaving behind them horrible dispraise!

18 APRIL 1945
An ambassador, watchful of politics, said to me: "Fascism has given rise to a new approach. Once a single political party, there are now five that procure favours for themselves. And since there are five instead of one, things are not going well."

18 APRIL 1945
A large military action to free northern Italy has begun. From 11 to 12 April the sky over Rome was full of the grim noise of airplanes loaded with bombs to spread ruin and death throughout our land.

The pain in my heart is inexpressible.

19 APRIL 1945
There is an explanation for the Allies' treatment of Italy, why they humiliate her and continually contribute to the ruin of her financial situation while multiplying the destruction and threatening to rob her of her old colonies and amputate Istria from her territory. Many observe that

---

44 This was said by Christ in Mt. 26:52.

England has no desire for Italy to raise her head. The more she remains spiritually and materially exhausted, the more England secures for itself command of the Mediterranean ... All of this is so sad, but it is what politics is all about. And the Atlantic Charter?

27 APRIL 1945

Great days. Italy, exhausted by Fascism and humiliated by the Allies, is raising her head. Cardinal Boetto[45] and the partisans have won German surrender in Genoa. They are negotiating surrender in Milan. Northern Italy is rebelling and is freeing itself from the enemy and redeeming itself in front of the tough Allies.

When all is said and done, the Allies are arriving. There is some humour in these wonderful heroic deeds. The Allied landing in Salerno was to "free" Italy, but the north will free itself, without leaving the trail of ruin that is characteristic of the Allies' passage through Italy.

There has been talk of a *cordon sanitaire* between the north and the south. The Allies have made the mistake – with the flood of Am-lire[46] – of sinking state finances lower than the Germans did in the north. It is distressing that a mayor, who carries a great and proud name, believed that it was necessary to give a gold medal, in the Campidoglio, to Poletti. *Et erat videre miseriam.*[47]

But northern Italy will save itself. One might think that this will more or less please the Allies, but it will please us even more. They excluded us

---

45 Pietro Boetto (1871–1946), a Jesuit, a provincial superior of Rome (1928), assistant to the general superior of Italy (1930), adviser to the Holy Congregation for the Religious (1931), and made a cardinal (1935). In 1938 he was granted episcopal ordination and was named archbishop of Genoa. He was well known for his anti-Fascist stance and protected many Jews from Nazi-Fascist persecution.

46 The "Am-lira" (Allied military currency) was the currency of occupied Italy that was put into circulation in July 1943 when the Allies landed in Sicily. It circulated until 1946, when the Am-lira began to be used together with Italian notes. The Am-lira ceased to be legal tender on 3 June 1950. Its value, calculated in relation to the US dollar, was 100 Am-lires to one US dollar.

47 The biblical passage quoted above is found in 2 Ma. 6:9 and means "Then was misery to be seen."

from the San Francisco Conference,[48] at which the Negus [Ethiopia], Greece, Yugoslavia, and others sat together. But Italy looks at San Francisco with the pride of its noble history and with the knowledge that San Francisco cannot stop history.

27 APRIL 1945

Tonight on the radio they announced that Mussolini, Pavolini, Farinacci, and Buffarini were captured ... Graziani gave himself up. They are nothing but a pack of wolves who, for their boundless vanity and greed for power, committed the horrendous crime of throwing Italy into the arms of civil war. The Hon. Bonomi addressed the northern Italians with a good message. But it was too cautious. Small and spiteful men will move on, but nations will remain. The Romans, with their great tenet *debellare superbos ... parcere victis*,[49] were much nobler than the Allies.

VIXERUNT
                                                                29 APRIL 1945

Mussolini and his *gerarchi*, along with Claretta Petacci, have been shot. When Cicero announced the death of Catiline and his relatives, he said to the Roman Forum, "*Vixerunt!*"[50] They lived; they live no longer; they hope no longer. A world of tyranny, immorality, and supreme authority has disappeared and is buried with Mussolini and his followers. One can and must also remember the good things that Mussolini did over these

---

[48] The San Francisco Conference was held in the United States between April and June 1945 with the participation of at least fifty Allied countries, those that defeated the Axis. The conference set up the act of foundation of the United Nations, whose statute was approved on 26 June of the same year. Among those who signed the act was Poland, after being freed by the Germans, but Italy was excluded from the conference because it was considered a defeated power. The political-military summit also defined the strategy to be followed in the final defeat of Germany and its subsequent organization after the war.

[49] The meaning of the Latin passage is "Spare the conquered ... hold down the proud."

[50] The famous phrase, quoted by Plutarch in *Parallel Lives: The Life of Cicero*, was delivered by Marcus Tullius Cicero, consul of Rome in 63 BC, when he announced to the Senate that the conspirators (Lentulus, Cethegus, and others), along with Catiline, who wanted to overthrow the republic, had been brought to justice. Actually, in contradiction to Costantini's recounting of the event, Catiline was not killed at the same time as the others.

twenty years. However, upon freeing himself from Hitler, he was unmasked and was revealed to be a maniac and criminal who turned his back on his motherland. So much innocent blood was spilled by his mob; many horrific crimes were committed under his ill-fated rule. The head of the Italian Social Republic was swept away under the ruins of this fake structure that was held up by the Germans!

Vixerunt! They no longer make attempts on the life of poor Italy, crushed into surrender. They say that the bodies were displayed in Milan and that people pass in front of them reflecting feelings of disgust and horror and satisfaction for justice done. All those innocent hostages, shot and hanged by the Germans – or by the *brigate nere* – have been avenged!

But the violence toward the dead is exceptionally deplorable! The rage of the people knows no limits. When a man, when an enemy has died, he enters a sacred domain in which men cannot themselves dispense God's judgment. The light of freedom in the north is now covered by a blanket of darkness. Even the hurried way they shot them brings dishonour. Clara Petacci was also killed. Why?

The news of Mussolini's death will facilitate the liberation of the Veneto region.

With this news that carries with it the solemnity of history, there is also a note of humour. The partisans are the real liberators of Milan and of the Veneto region, of Piedmont, and of Liguria. In front of the eyes of the world, they are the ones who restored freedom to northern Italy; they are the ones who put to an end a war of ransom. The bishops, who served as intermediaries between the Germans and the victors, have carried out a wonderful mission of salvation and peace. The fact that the Allies are going to the north is just routine. The damage has been done. And the Milanese can look the Allies in the face with that pride and dignity that reveals a new Italy, even if the Allies pretend to ignore it.

This morning, there was a large demonstration in the Piazza dei Santi Apostoli; big speeches were given by the representatives of the parties whose mouths were constantly forming the word "nation." What a farce! That "poor" nation – standing there in that square – is the same one that went to Piazza Venezia only a few metres away, to call Il Duce out onto his balcony.

And they were speaking of democracy, yet they fly the red flag while Stalin is a dictator just like Hitler and Mussolini. As a matter of fact, he is far worse than those two. "Poor" nation indeed! Only one person spoke honestly about democracy: the Pope.

It is, then, a pitiful show – the one put on by the government formed by those parties, each of which thinks of its own party instead of thinking of Italy. They look for votes. Instead of unifying Italy, they look to divide it for their own benefit. We hope that the northern wind will sweep away this black fog. After this, Italy will rise again with its true face, one that is tear-stained but also proud and determined.

30 APRIL 1945

At yesterday's – Sunday's – Holy Mass, the reading from the Gospel was "The prince of this world is already judged" [Jn. 16:11]. They say that Hitler – the Antichrist – was crushed by Germany's catastrophe. But we will be in deep trouble if with a dictatorship a new Fascism rises: Communism!

3 MAY 1945

Last night on the radio, news was spread that the truce had been signed by the German forces and the Allies. There were the first real feelings of joy. This stupid war has finally come to an end; there will be no more killing, they will no longer bomb our cities. But the joy does not fill our hearts, for we feel defeated and humiliated. There are foreigners in our midst who impose laws. No one from the government is taking part in these negotiations. The person who is really in charge of Italy is Admiral Stone.[51]

There are three things that weigh on our hearts and diminish our gratitude toward the Allies:

1 We are not in attendance at the San Francisco Conference, where it seems that everything being discussed concerns the future destiny of Italy.

2 Destruction is spread throughout Italy, and this destruction has not always been justifiable. Montecassino, San Lorenzo Outside the Walls, Castel Gondolfo's Villa at Urban College, and many other monuments

[51] Ellery Wheeler Stone (1894–1981), an American admiral, born in California, stationed in Europe in the Second World War. He was sent to Italy as chief of staff in 1943. From 1944 to 1946 he was president of the ACC [Allied Control Council]. From 1947 on, he was the head of International Telephone and Telegraph Corporation in the United States, a company for which he had worked before the Second World War.

suffered terrible and pointless damage, and it throws a negative light on the American airmen, so ignorant and hateful of Italian culture.

3 The financial crisis of the regions that have been liberated will only get worse, given the widespread diffusion of the Am-lira. The financial situation of already liberated Italy is worse than that of northern Italy.

The so-called liberators were, in all of this, less cautious than the Germans. It is now necessary to be silent. But the coldness that Italians feel for the Allies is irreparable and will not go away.

Yesterday on the radio I heard that the cities of Trieste and Gorizia, as well as the Venezia Giulia region extending as far as Isonzo, had been occupied by Tito's soldiers. This caused a deep wound to our hearts. Trieste is part of Italy! Only the hinterland belongs to the Slavs. We cannot face the fact that Trieste is being occupied by Yugoslavia. And the Atlantic Charter?

Today we heard that the Allies will enter Trieste. This is a heavy weight off our hearts.

5 MAY 1945

At the beginning of his electoral campaign Churchill said, "I must tell you that a socialist policy is abhorrent to the British ideas of freedom. Although it is now put forward in the main by people who have a good grounding in the liberalism and radicalism of the early part of this century, there can be no doubt that socialism is inseparably interwoven with totalitarianism and the abject worship of the state."

Fine words. But, in the meantime, *he is Stalin's partner.*

7 MAY 1945

The newspapers are saying that all of Germany has surrendered. The war, therefore, is over. I am reading now the noble words of Christ in the Gospel: "You shall be sorrowful, but your sorrow shall be turned into joy. A woman, when she is in labour, hath sorrow, because her hour is come; but when she has brought forth the child, she remembereth no more the anguish, for joy that a man is born into the world" [Jn. 16:33].

This peace has come after such a painful, long, and bloody birth. But then, instead of thinking about the pain of the past, we are happy because peace has been born. It is still an infant and cannot stand up or walk, but it will grow and grow stronger.

This peace is the victory of Christ over the Antichrist – Hitler. Christ has once again conquered the world, and in the brightest and most striking way. We must strengthen our hearts with faith.

However, there is a dark shadow still cast over the bloody skies of Europe: the threat of yet another Antichrist – atheist Communism. But it will not prevail. It is distressing and bewildering to see the joining of the democratic states of America and England with that other dictator, Stalin. We are witnessing a colossal absurdity. Will the red tide bring freedom or tyranny? Will we replace the Nazi regime with the Soviet one? Providence will keep watch over us. It will not be hurried.

The secondary causes get upset, become tangled and confused, but the primary cause guides them. Be sure of this: "*Ego vici mundum.*" The Nazi and Fascist regimes have fallen. If Communism doesn't transform itself into a regime of democratic freedom, it too is doomed. "*Princeps huius mundi jam iudicatus est*" [Jn. 16:11].[52] We read this in the same chapter in which they speak of a painful birth.

7 MAY 1945

At 6 PM I went out. Suddenly I heard the scream of sirens. People began to stand still. Out of habitual instinct, they began to look up at the sky, and then everyone was so delighted because the siren was to announce peace. Some unusual flags appeared in windows, and suddenly the bells of Rome filled the clear sky with their cheerful sound. But the news of peace didn't produce the type of joy, the demonstration of collective happiness that perhaps people were expecting.

And that is completely natural. The pain of war still presses on our hearts; misery torments the spirit, especially the spirit of intellectuals. Many await the return of prisoners. And, above all, the peace is not at present completely ours, completely real – Rome is still full of Allied soldiers.

As for friendship, we cannot forget that they are foreigners and that by waging war on the Germans in Italy they destroyed our cities and ruined our economy with the influx of the Am-lira. Nor can we forget that Italy, even though it was able to hold its head high for the bravery of the partisans, is still chained to the ungrateful conditions of the armistice.

---

[52] The passage in English is "The prince of this world is already judged."

I ran into Sacks, a lawyer from Fiume.[53] He was very worried. He said to me, "A victorious Russia represents for Europe a danger that is equal to if not greater than that one of a victorious Germany."

THE HOLY FATHER'S MESSAGE FOR PEACE   9 MAY 1945

At 12:00 today, 9 May, His Holiness Pius XII addressed his followers with a short message to commemorate the end of the hostilities in Europe and to invite both government and citizens to begin the real effort of reconstruction:

In spirit, kneeling before the graves, before the ravaged ravines red with blood, where rest the mortal remains of those who fell victim to battles and inhuman massacres, to famine or to poverty, we will commend them to our prayers, especially when we celebrate the Holy Sacrifice, the merciful love of Jesus Christ, their Saviour and Judge ...

The war has left a vast amount of chaotic material and moral ruin – more than ever experienced by the human race in the course of all its history. Now everything centres on rebuilding the world. As the primary material of this rebuilding, we long to see, after such a long wait, the prompt and fast return – circumstances permitting – of our prisoners, internees, soldiers, and civilians to their homes, to their wives, to their children, and to their noble work for peace ...

The war has sowed dissension, distrust, and hate everywhere. If, then, the world wants to restore peace it will be necessary to banish lies and resentment, and in the various countries to replace them with truth and charity.

May the Lord feel it worthy to awaken this new spirit, His spirit, in the people and particularly in the hearts of those who have been entrusted with finding the solution to ensure future peace![54]

The war that waged war has ended, but the human spirit has not been disarmed, and the cold war begins. The Holy Father did not forget to repeatedly bring to the attention of all men of goodwill more realistic, human, Christian ideas to give to the world at last a calmer and deeper breath of peace.

[53] He is probably referring to a lawyer from Fiume, Baron Niel Sacks di Gric.

[54] Pius XII's radio message is transcribed in its entirety in AAS 37 (*Bollettino Ufficiale della Santa Sede*, 1945), 129–31.

There are two Italys, one totally different from the other. There is the Italy of the King and Mussolini and the Italy that liberated itself. But the Allies continue to treat Italy as if it were still the one that belongs to the King and Mussolini, all the while admiring the wonderful spirit of the northern Italians. Is it blindness, an evil temperament? I hope, though, that they realize that it will not be good even for them to throw Italy into the arms of Communism.

A LETTER FROM SAN VITO AL TAGLIAMENTO   IO MAY 1945
It's been almost two years since we said goodbye in Rome. Two years in which first we worried about you and then, after your liberation, when you – for a longer period of time – worried about us.

We have in fact lived 18 months of perpetual distress. We have lived under the threat of internment, the threat of prison for accusations of patriotism, and under the danger of the bombings from the other side; and we lived with the idea that the war would bring itself to our last corner of Italy and reduce us to another Rimini. In fact, for six months the Germans have built small fortresses along our bank to the right of the Tagliamento in order to give themselves a strong line of defence. Thank God everything has suddenly fallen apart.

There was no fighting here, except for a small section inside San Vito. The dead number about ten; there is not a lot of damage. We are in a period of settlement that is difficult, yes, but not painful; it is carried out in freedom, not servitude.

However, not everyone reached that point. The bombings in San Vito last winter left about a dozen victims, and unfortunately among them were some people who are dear to you. The raid on 25 February struck Casa Bottos. The exceptional Mrs Bottos and her oldest son were killed; he was killed instantly and she died shortly thereafter. They were among the few left in the house. The day before, Celso and the children had been taken to Bagnarola. Otherwise there would have been even more deaths.

Giovanni Tullio

14 MAY 1945
Tonight, H.E. Mons. Margotti, archbishop of Gorizia, came to see me.[55] He had been sentenced to death but the sentence had been reduced to

---

[55] Carlo Margotti (1891–1951), a member of the clergy in Bologna and in 1930 already titular archbishop of Mesembria and an apostolic delegate in

expulsion from the land occupied by the Yugoslavians, who are now attempting a strong and barbaric repression of the territory leading to Isonzo and Judrio – all the while saying they are setting their sights on the Tagliamento. Monsignor Margotti has endured his persecution with a truly apostolic spirit.

The newspapers published Churchill's speech in which he states: "On the continent of Europe we have yet to make sure that the simple and honourable purposes for which we entered the war are not brushed aside or overlooked in the months following our success, and that the words 'freedom,' 'democracy,' and 'liberation' are not distorted from their true meaning as we have understood them ..."

Such beautiful words. Will they live up to the facts? We would very much like to know. But we remain skeptical. Everyone was feeling uneasy about the lie that made everyone talk about democracy while Stalin was setting up a totalitarian dictatorship no less harsh or hard or absolute than Hitler's. Churchill signed the Atlantic Charter and then he tore it to pieces and threw it in the Atlantic's turbulent waters. How can we believe in his new, tear-filled words?

15 MAY 1945

Today we learned that the Allies gave some sort of ultimatum to Tito.[56]

Turkey. He was transferred to the residential seat in Gorizia on 14 June 1938. The first Italian archbishop in the Goritian Church, he was imprisoned and then faced expulsion by the occupying Yugoslavian troops. He was later able to return to his diocese which, however, had been reduced by two-thirds, given the newly established borders. In his diocese, he again began to guide the faithful in their post-war religious life. His relationship with Celso Costantini was documented in the *Epistolario*, now published in Pighin's volume *Il ritratto segreto del Cardinale Celso Costantini in 10.000 lettere dal 1892 al 1958* (Venice: Marcianum Press, 2012).

[56] Tito, the nickname of Josip Broz (1892–1980), a Yugoslavian politician who fought in the Red army after the October Revolution and returned to his homeland in 1920. He dedicated himself to the activities of the Yugoslav Communist Party (YCP), a cause that cost him six years in prison. At the end of his prison term he took refuge in Moscow and then in Paris. Having become the secretary of his party, he secretly returned to Yugoslavia to prepare new senior members, whom he needed for the armed partisan battle against the Germans and Italians, who in 1941 had invaded his country. In 1943 Tito was named

21 MAY 1945

Some men who came from Milan say that a Communist wind is blowing there. But no one is giving credit to the stories. Castelli, the engineer, tells me there is no need to be scared; time will sort everything out.

The government is in the midst of a full-blown crisis. Many ministers are in the north. Everyone thinks only of his own party. We are beginning to feel the uneasiness felt during 1919–20, and are hoping for a government that governs.

The conditions of the armistice have not been published but they are still in force. At least the Allies were not able to put in a provision to neutralize Italy's geographical set-up again and reduce its demographic power.

The Allies are not forgetting the stupid and criminal statement made by the King and Badoglio: "The war continues."

Food Prices Are Continually on the Rise

An egg	L 50
Chickens	L 2,000
Flour	L 100 per kg
Meat	Has no price
Bread	L 15 per kg
Milk	L 10 per litre

---

marshal of the Council of National Liberation of Yugoslavia. With the support of the Allies, he liberated Belgrade in 1944, and the following year he became president of the government of a new federal republican state, supported by the Socialist regime. In 1948 he broke off his alliance with Stalin because he wanted to lay claim to his own autonomous regime. When it came to Italy, there was a lot of friction because of his expansionist goals, which were both territorial and ideological in nature, as well as his attempts to take control of Trieste. In 1953 he was elected president of the republic, an office he held for life. On the international stage, he was a major character in the group of non-Allied countries, the Allied countries being those in the two factions led by Russia and the United States, respectively. He prepared for his difficult succession by having at his side, during the last years of his life, a collective presidency, but after his death it was not able to stop the break-up of various ethnoreligious entities that were held together by Tito's dictatorial regime.

CHRISTIAN PEACE   31 MAY 1945[57]

Jesus Christ gave to his Apostles proof of his love: "Peace I leave with you; my peace I give you. I do not give to you as the world gives" [Jn. 14:27]. We are witnesses, like the popes whom we ourselves have met; they repeat exactly this commandment of peace. We remember how Benedict XV's phrase "the useless massacre" was misinterpreted when he hoped for a peace created from honourable compromises in his attempt to discourage peace created from revenge. This confusion came to an end at Versailles while preparing for the turmoil of this recent war.

Pius XII, who became Supreme Pontiff on 2 March 1939, saw – with great awareness – the hurricane that became the Second World War as it

---

57 Costantini quotes from an issue of *Il Popolo* published on 31 May 1945, which describes the return to a life of normality at the end of the month dedicated to the Madonna: "We were returning home late one night and ran into a darkening crowd of people with banners and torches, a crowd enveloped by a mysterious and solemn chanting, stopping at every street corner to express praise at the small well-lit newsstands. Paper lanterns and tapestries were hanging from the windows decorated with flowers, and a certain air – cosy and old – filled the whole neighbourhood. It is the parish that lives on during the warm Sunday evenings in the midst of all of humanity's turmoil, the parish that gathers itself together and isolates itself in its Christian dream. Parish life, where men unite not in the name of personal interest but in the name of true feelings and with a desire to give eternal value to their daily existence; and it is everything that they are able to lose themselves in the wonder of lights and hymns, in this standing around, this pilgrimage, from one newsstand to another, in serene liturgical tradition. The whole working-class neighbourhood is following the priest, who begins the chorus with a clear and high voice. Then the procession goes into the church with a festive chime that spreads through the streets, which had once again become silent, while the lights of the statues of the Madonna on the newsstands burn brightly among the flowers and, in the night, together form one single bright point of light. We finally return to lost memories of our adolescence, to faraway faded images on obstacle-laden roads, and that light is still the call and comfort for the tired and sad wayfarer. He again finds himself together with others who, like him, passing in front of the Madonna with the flowers, find that the mood brightens and they leave behind the burdens of the day. And in this silence the peacefulness of human relationships is interrupted, and the individual begins a social relationship. Only in front of the newsstands does he feel surrounded by so many voices, and he becomes the centre of the world."

began to gather over humanity, and he did all that was in his power to prevent it or to soften its terrible consequences.

SAINT EUGENE'S DAY   2 JUNE 1945
This morning, while responding to the Sacred College of Cardinals' wishes, the Holy Father showed us the secure path to peace.[58]

DEFENSOR CIVITATIS   2 JUNE 1945
On the afternoon of 2 June 1945 I attended at the Collegio Romano [the Jesuit college in Rome] a solemn meeting convened to thank the Supreme Pontiff, Defensor Civitatis. Both the Hon. Vittorio Emanuele Orlando and Minister Soleri[59] spoke.

                                                     10 JUNE 1945
The young Romans who belong to Catholic Action wanted to commemorate the first anniversary of the liberation and safety of Rome by going to the Vatican and offering the Supreme Pontiff, Defensor Civitatis, a loving and grateful tribute, marching with their flags from the Chiesa Nuova to the Vatican. His Holiness Pius XII addressed the congregation with a moving speech.[60]

[58] Pius XII's allocution mentioned by Costantini can be found in its entirety in AAS 37 (Bollettino Ufficiale della Santa Sede, 1945), 159–68.

[59] Marcello Soleri (1882–1945), an Italian politician of liberal faith, was the mayor of Cuneo in 1912 and a member of parliament at the end of the First World War. He became minister of finance in 1921 in the government led by Bonomi and the following year was minister of war in the Facta cabinet. In the latter office, he did his best to declare a state of siege for Rome that would have stopped the Fasisct march on the city, but the King did not support the measure that was proposed to him. Withdrawing from political life during Mussolini's regime, Soleri in 1944 was nominated minister of the Treasury in the government of Ivanoe Bonomi, and he was again elected to that office in 1945 in the following government led by Ferruccio Parri. In 1944 he was also president of the National Alpine Association (ANA).

[60] Pius XII's speech given on this occasion is reprinted in its entirety in Discorsi e Radiomessaggi di Sua Santità Pio XII, vol. 7 (Milan: Società Editrice "Vita e Pensiero," 1946), 83–93. The quotation can be found on pages 85–7.

10 JUNE 1945

At my residence today arrived Professor Giuliano Balbino,[61] a former senator and minister of education. He confessed this to me: "The crisis of philosophical thought, especially of idealism, to which I had adhered, has led me back to the Catholic faith. There is a breakdown, a failure of all ideologies. We are disillusioned by this so-called civilization that has brought ruin to everything: to thought and to real life. Under the ruins remains a vital Christian seed, and I think that the world is preparing for a Christian rebirth.

[Balbino reported] that his wife ran into Giuseppe Bottai's wife, who said that her husband was quite taken with the appeal of religious studies, in which he finds comfort and hope.

THE NEFARIOUS PURIFICATION   10 JUNE 1945

Francesco Tullio,[62] an upright citizen and worthy senator since 1939, was arrested "at home" in Aquileia about 10 days ago because of his senatorial status. They wrote to me with urgency: "He is still at home. Situation unclear. Praying that H.E. Celso Costantini, who knows him well and is familiar with his history, will plead his case to the necessary

[61] Giuliano Balbino (1879–1958), a philosopher, Italian politician, and university professor, taught in the universities of Florence, Bologna, and Rome. At the University of Rome he was head of the Faculty of Arts and Philosphy, 1935–40. A member of parliament for the National Fascist Party in 1924 and 1929, he was made a senator in 1934. He was minister of national education, 1929–32. During his ministerial appointment, he forced all university professors to swear loyalty to Fascism; it was done by all but 12 professors. When Mussolini's regime collapsed, he was charged by the High Court of Justice for Sanctions against Fascism, but he was not sentenced because he profited from the plea of amnesty that was asked for by Togliatti.

[62] Francesco Tullio (1877–1969), a native of San Vito al Tagliamento, an industrialist and important landowner, graduated from the Faculty of Law in Bologna and was elected to the Chamber of Deputies, as a member of the National Fascist Party in 1924, 1929, and 1934. He was made a senator in 1939, the year he became president of the Fascist Confederation of Agriculture. Charged by the High Court of Justice for Sanctions against Fascism, he lost his senatorial seat following a sentence handed down by the Supreme Court, which became final in 1948.

authorities. The news has not come out here, so it is necessary that it remains confidential."[63]

Naturally, I will do whatever I can to see that justice is done.

10 JUNE 1945

I learn with great sadness that Riccardo Gigante was shot in Castua.[64] Poor Gigante! A true patriot, a bit of an idealist, but free from the stain of exploitation which so many others carry. His son is in prison because he belonged to the 10th Assault Vehicle Flotilla. And his wife and Riccardo's faithful sister Gigetta, where are they?

10 JUNE 1945

The Hon. Giuliano Balbino tells me that Princess Josè had said this to him in the past: "I do not want to seem excessively prudish and I don't want to busy myself with Mussolini's private life, but it must be said that a man, when he gets to Mussolini's level, has responsibilities that are of a public nature. His private life is no longer private; it takes on a public dimension."

Excellent! Mussolini and D'Annunzio considered themselves above the law, and they lived a life in which they chose to satisfy all the instincts of their animal-like sensuality. And in history they will remain, as men, two pathetic figures.

11 JUNE 1945

This unhappy period of governmental crisis continues, and it seems that it will never end. It is all about a government that has been in agony for 50 years; and it seems like a gathering of men who are too attached to their parties. We are repeating a situation like that from which Fascism arose.

And the purifying continues, under a legal system that is completely wrong.

---

[63] From Celso Costantini's *Epistolario*, kept in the ASDCP, we can gather that a letter, dated 11 June 1945 was written by the archbishop of Udine, H.E. Mons. Giuseppe Nogara, and sent to Costantini. He was asked to intervene and approach the appropriate authorities in order to obtain a positive solution for the case; this urgent request came from the wife of the arrested senator Francesco Tullio.

[64] Castua is a city in Istria that is part of the Quarnerino-Liburnica area, a small village of Roman origin and therefore one of the oldest villages in the region. Today it is a municipality belonging to the city of Fiume in Croatia.

While I was speaking today with the son of the Hon. V.E. Orlando, I said that the heads of the Communist and Socialist parties seem like dictators, as if they had a huge following in this country. It's all about influence peddling. After the abuses of power carried out by some of Tito's partisans and the foul deeds committed by some Italian partisans, many clandestine soldiers would no longer like to call themselves patriots instead of partisans. The good partisans surrendered their arms, and the others defy and trample every law. It seems that they are nothing but Fascists in disguise.

These people, the instability, and the Byzantinism of the parties that don't know how to create a government 50 days after the north's liberation discredit us in the eyes of foreigners. An error of the parties is the desire for revenge; it is the complete lack of a sense of self-restraint.

20 JUNE 1945

Finally, after two months of hard-working development, we have a government. It is a supergovernment; on the contrary, it is a thick soup made up of all the ingredients from the six parties … *Pertutiunt montes et nascetur ridiculus mus.*[65]

Everything was done, not with qualified men but with partisans, who are not serving Italy but their own parties. One day Mussolini said, "One general wins a battle; ten generals will lose it." And he was right. People are uninterested and lacking faith.

A LETTER FROM RAPALLO

SAN MICHELE DI PAGANA, 23 JUNE 1945

We were left unharmed by the events of the war, which grazed us without causing damage, as well as by the events that involved accusations and political revenge – they tried to strike us down, but they weren't able. The fault of me and my son was not wanting to cooperate with the Germans and the Neofascists.

This has all passed now, but – up here at least – we navigate through a sea of uncertainties and obstacles, a treacherous sea on which floats, sadly, the wreckage of past disasters and confusion, as well as the inevitable debris of opportunism, status seeking, and cheating that accompanies every instance of political and social chaos.

[65] The passage translated in English means "The mountains give birth and a ridiculous mouse will be born."

However, I will not lose heart, nor have I yet lost heart. To tell the truth, there is proof of plain common sense, humanity, and honesty. But how much amorality there is and how many immoralities in all of this! Italy will have to touch the bottom of the abyss before it begins its moral and spiritual recovery.

O. Rizzini[66]

MENACING CLOUDS   30 JUNE 1945

If you turn your eyes to the horizon, you will not see the bright sun of real peace but a bank of menacing clouds. From 25 April to 26 June in San Francisco, California, the much-discussed and very important United Nations Conference on International Organization took place. Fifty-two nations took part in the conference, including Ethiopia, Costa Rica, Cuba, Guatemala, Haiti, Liberia, etc. But Italy and Germany were excluded.

They are repeating the same mistake and the same injustice that caused the League of Nations to rise up as a coalition of victorious countries to keep Germany in its servitude.

These nations, which attempt to give an appearance of legitimacy and a guarantee to the *beati possidentes*, don't think that even those who have been defeated have the right to live well. For this reason the charters are destined to become, sooner or later, *chiffons de papier*,[67] into which the Atlantic Charter has now been reduced.

The Far East is in flames. Russia, with its satellites, has arrived in the Adriatic, trying to take possession of the port of Fiume. The lie of democracy and freedom has been shamelessly denied by the alliance with Russia, by its aggressiveness, and the uncivilized banditry of many Communists and other scoundrels who in Italy masquerade as partisans.

A sense of distrust weighs on the Italian people. The government is weak, divided, and incapable of restoring order and lawfulness. While there is unemployment, hunger, and the tragedy of the homeless, the parties in the government are busying themselves with *métayage*, promising the *métiers* a greater share for their products. It should be said that in

---

[66] The letter was sent by Oreste Rizzini. It was delivered to Celso Costantini by Roberto Einaudi, an engineer and son of Luigi, senator, govenor of the Bank of Italy, and second president of the Republic of Italy (1948–55), as can be found in his *Epistolario*.

[67] The French idiom, translated in English, means "pieces of scrap paper."

Italy the *métiers* make up the least unfortunate class. So many of them have tons of money, and they suffered the least during the war.

Byzantinism, bad faith, the race for power, the agitation of the parties – a display of unending wretchedness. In the meantime, the Communist hurricane wildly advances; from the steppes of Siberia it has already arrived at the Baltic Sea, Berlin, and the Adriatic. What has England gained?

A LETTER FROM PORDENONE 7 JULY 1945

... Here, life is trying slowly to get back to normal, but the horizon is not at all calm. The food situation in Pordenone is difficult, and all of the authorities' efforts are not enough to satisfy urgent needs, especially those of the working class. The mountainous areas have suffered severely during the past winter. The new bishop, H.E. Monsignor Vittorio D'Alessi,[68] has been the merciful Samaritan for every needy person. He has carried out heroic acts of courage, charity, Italianess.

The local residents worship him, and everyone pays tribute to his work and his fearless spirit. He has been, without exception, up to the task at hand and worthy of being appointed bishop.

The whole town of Barcis was burned by the Germans in retaliation and, unfortunately, not only by the Germans. Mezzomonte suffered the same fate, as well as a hamlet of Andreis.

The toll of blood paid by the patriots for Italy's cause has been high. The political internees in Germany are now slowly returning to their homeland – the captured soldiers, the oppressed workers. They bear the signs of unheard-of suffering on their exhausted bodies, on their torn clothes; and in their eyes you can see moral exhaustion, the anguish from the lengthy period of martyrdom. Poor souls! I believe that nowhere in the world have people suffered so much! You will hear, Your Excellency, everything that those who have returned home are going to tell!

[68] Vittorio D'Alessi (1884–1949), originally from the Diocese of Treviso, was appointed titular bishop of Lyrbe on 5 April 1944 as well as apostolic administrator pro tempore of Concordia Diocese, of which he became resident bishop on 10 October 1945 after the death of his predecessor Luigi Paulini on 24 February 1945. D'Alessi's meritorious work, at times almost heroic, to protect his faithful from the very serious dangers of war and to help people and the local residents who were struck by the cataclysm of war has been documented in B.F. Pighin, *Il Seminario di Concordia-Pordenone. La crescita fino al concilio Vaticano II (1920–1962)* (Pordenone: Seminario diocesano, 2005), 447–52; 468–87.

A priest sent by the bishop is greeting the members of your diocese at the organizational centres, first in Bolzano and presently in Pescatina [Verona]. Vehicles come daily to take them back to their homes.

Don Gioacchino Muccin, archpriest of Pordenone[69]

General Dunlop's Harsh Warning after the Schio Massacre
Brigadier General Dunlop[70] visited Schio after the horrific massacre of about 40 prisoners that was carried out by a group of partisans in the prison there.[71] While speaking at a meeting of the members of the National Liberation Committee and various civilian authorities, he remarked, "I came here today on a regrettable mission. For a year and a half I have worked for the good of Italy, in Sardinia, in the south, in Latium, and in Umbria. I know that my work and my friendship as a

[69] Gioacchino Muccin (1899–1991), a native of San Giovanni di Casarsa [Pordenone], called to arms in 1917, was ordained presbyter in 1923. He taught in the seminary of the Diocese of Concordia-Pordenone, with an appointment in the parish of San Marco in Pordenone, and also was an episcopal delegate for Catholic Action. He had an important role in Pordenone during the Second World War as he aided the needy and prevented further bloodshed during the German occupation. He was appointed bishop of Feltre and of Belluno (two dioceses that were united, thanks to his management of them as bishop), and was ordained by Archbishop Giovanni Costantini in 1949. He was very active in the enforcement of the provisions made by the Second Vatican Council until 1 September 1975, when he reached the age of retirement. His remains rest, according to his request, among those of the victims of Vajont (1963) in the cemetery in Fortogna [Belluno].

[70] John Kininmont Dunlop (1892–1974), a brigadier general of the United States Army, was head of the Allied Commission in Sardinia in 1943, of Latium and Umbria in 1944, of southern Italy in the same year, and of the Veneto region in 1945. Afterwards he was sent to Hamburg, Germany, until 1947.

[71] The perpetrators of the massacre were later identified as Ruggero Maltauro, who was brought back from Yugoslavia, where he had taken refuge along with the remaining fugitives: Gaetano Canova, Aldo Santacaterina, Valentino Bortoloso, Renzo Franceschini, and Antonio Fochesato. The last three men were sentenced to death, while the rest received life sentences. Two other accomplices were sentenced to 24 years, and a third received a 12-year sentence. Nevertheless, the penal sanctions were much less severely applied, thanks to the benefits of the law that were conceded to the guilty.

soldier is both appreciated and acknowledged. It is my duty to tell you that never before have I ever held the name of Italy in such low esteem. It is necessary that all of you, all Italians, look reality in the face. You ask for Italy to be accepted as an ally and a friend of the United States of America and Great Britain. I am telling you openly that you cannot earn friendship while these types of contemptible acts are being committed ..."[72]

18 JULY 1945

This morning I met an old woman who, from Piazza di Spagna, was leading two chickens back to grassland. She was taking them back with two strings tied to their legs. She led them to that little meadow that extends beyond the Fontana della Barcaccia.

Even here, in the Propaganda offices, the unmelodic voices of a few chicken resonate. And in the morning we hear, here and there, the crowing of some roosters rising up from the terraces of surrounding buildings. The effects of war. Now, during the best time of year for eggs, they cost 25 lire each; but people pay even 40 lire.

The Big Three

"The Big Three will meet at Potsdam, and Western Europe awaits their judgment. This continent, which was the centre of the world and for many centuries laid down the law in the world, now waits – passive and powerless – for others to decide its fate. From the Russian border to the Atlantic there is an immense political vacuum. Without a doubt, this void was created by the war. But it remains; and it will remain for a long time."[73]

From the vast tragedy of the war rises, like a ghost in a macabre dance of the past, the cruel joke of these conferences. Someone said that war had been waged for freedom, for democracy, because each nation would freely be able to decide its own destiny, etc. And then three men divide – "as they wish" – nations; they outline new borders, order mass deportation, etc. Two representatives of democracy support the train of the supreme pontiff, Stalin, the dictator who surpasses even Hitler.

All that is left for us to do is to address God with the same worry of the ancient psalmist: "Many calves have surrounded me. Fat bulls have

---

[72] CC: *Il Popolo*, 13 July 1945.
[73] CC: *Il Risorgimento Liberale*, 18 July 1945.

besieged me. They have opened their mouths against me ... But thou, O Lord, remove not thy help to a distance from me; look toward my defence" [Ps. 21:13–14; 20].

The Face of Death

A very eminent scholar, who seemed far from the Catholic faith, is phoning me, asking me to send a prayer to God because his mother is dying. His voice disappeared into trembling sobs. Even this man, who is facing the mystery of death, has found Christianity once again; he understands that only within Christianity do life and death make sense and there is comfort.

The widow of Ila Bacci, in whose home I found temporary and warm hospitality when I was the apostolic administrator of Fiume, came to visit me. How very sad! Fiume in the hands of the Communists, with its port handed over to Russia. Stalin is, therefore, in the Adriatic. What a defeat for Italy, but also what a mockery of her ally England.

Senator Gigante shot dead, Icilio Bacci[74] dying in prison, Iti Bacci just getting out of prison, Host-Venturi[75] gone into hiding, Doctor Blasich strangled in his bed – what a downfall, what disaster! Poor Fiume!

---

[74] Icilio Bacci (1879–1945), a politician from Fiume in Istria and a team manager, joined the National Fascist Party and was appointed senator in 1934. He was the commissioner of the Italian National Olympic Committee (1930–31). He was charged by the High Court of Justice for Sanctions against Fascism in 1944. On 29 March 1946 he was judged under the sentence "no grounds to proced because the accused is missing." In fact, convinced that he had done nothing wrong during Mussolini's regime, he decided not to leave his city, in which he was later arrested by the Yugoslav police and transferred to the prison in Karlovac. There he was tried and then died after abuse and violence in the prison. He died on 28 August 1945.

[75] Giovanni Host-Venturi (1892–1980), a native of Fiume in Istria, an Italian historian and politician, who went by the diminiutive "Nino," was a captain in the Arditi (an elite assault unit) and an irredentist. His name was tied to the undertaking by Gabriele D'Annunzio's legionnaires to occupy his city. A man with anticlerical leanings and one of the most diehard members of the Fascist Party, he did his best to spread Fascism throughout the northeast of Italy, making those who opposed him pay a high price, sometimes with their lives. He adopted this policy especially with the Slovenian minority and with the militants who were against the regime. When the government led by Mussolini fell in 1943, he was its minister of communications. He committed suicide in Buenos Aires.

The Italian government does nothing but create new ministries in order to satisfy the parties and to have a way of rotating appointments.

In the meantime, unfortunately, the chaos caused by that scoundrel continues, that scoundrel who at times has transformed the black shirt into a red one. We are under the impression that the Christian Democrats do not know how to assert the undeniable strength that they represent. We have hope in tomorrow.

THE TRIP FROM ROME TO THE VENETO REGION
AND TO FRIULI   27 JULY 1945

After incredible long and extenuating difficulties, on the evening of Saturday, 21 July, everything was ready for our departure from Rome. Cavaliere Pozzani's car was in Propaganda's courtyard. But a phone call from the secretary of state forced my brother to stay in Rome for a meeting with the commission to rebuild Montecassino Abbey.

We left on 22 July at 4 PM, with our cousin Lena Bottos and our housekeeper, who being from San Vito al Tagliamento, decided to go there to see her elderly father. Lena held a little three-year-old boy in her arms.

It was a long trip at a moderate speed, even though we had a powerful and fast American car. Because of an accident in Livorno, the car's oil pipe broke, and we lost some time since we had to make temporary repairs. We crossed the Porretana,[76] stopping at a high spot so that the motor could cool off. We encountered lines of trucks full of Allied soldiers, without shirts, happy and noisy. The soldiers acted as if they were in charge; their behaviour seemed insolent to us in the middle of the ruins of all those crumbled houses.

We descended toward Bologna; the ruin, the desolation, the horror of war appeared before us in all of its tragic form. Villages and several suburbs that once had seemed happy and populated, with the backdrop of a beautiful natural hilly landscape, now appear like tragic ruins: gutted houses that show the intimate family nest, where at one time life was blooming with pure joy, with the most varied of activities, with its inevitable pain; smashed bridges, shops torn open, paths ravaged by craters that were dug by bombs, a whole world destroyed. Among the remains of a house I saw a woman seated, with her elbows on her knees and her

---

[76] He is referring to a road, at the time called Via Consolare, which went from Tuscany into the Emilia region.

The Secrets of a Vatican Cardinal

head in her hands; she was the image of human sorrow, the sorrow that lies heavy like a funeral blanket covering that widespread destruction.

Groups of travellers were meeting here and there, with sad faces but with that type of passive and fatal resignation that getting used to disaster produces in human beings. Only nature, the eternal and indifferent mother, made the grass sprout among the ruins, and all the surrounding hills were enhanced by her joyous summertime layer of green.

In the warmth of the afternoon, Bologna was bustling with people. A carousel and some festival booths gave the large square a festive air, a square that is not far from buildings that had been ripped apart. But the internal sections of Bologna are in fairly good condition.

The oil pipe, which was badly repaired, was leaking. We stopped near Malalbergo in front of a fleet of Allied automobiles and asked for a litre of oil. Nothing. Typical English mannerisms – give the Italians a hard time. In Ferrara we stopped in front of another fleet of cars. I spoke with an English captain. After wobbling his head a bit, he gave us two bottles of oil, but it was like someone throwing a bone to a dog to keep him from barking.

In Battaglia Terme the car stopped, and there was no way of getting it started again. It was midnight – night had descended and we were wrapped in it. A few passers-by stopped around the car with a look of curiosity and astonishment, as if they had come upon a sick person.

We decided to spend the night there. In the town there were no hotels. All one could see were some groups of latecomers sitting at the entrance of some taverns under the glow of an electric light. The moon rose, and it filled the night with its light. The night's silence was often broken by some English military trucks or by a few motor coaches full of travellers.

Unbeknownst to me, one gentleman who was travelling with us noticed a priest whom I had met along the way, who was without shelter. But the priest didn't hear a voice offering hospitality, which is also a form of charity. I tried to sleep, but the car was an oven. A bit later, I got out and stretched out, trying to sleep, on the bank of the canal that runs through Battaglia. Nothing doing; the mosquitoes began to bite me and they made my hands ache. After an hour, I got back into the car, which had cooled off a bit. I spent the rest of the night sometimes awake, sometimes asleep.

When I heard the *Ave Maria* playing, I headed toward the village's church. After Mass, it was already daylight. The driver had found the source of the breakdown: a blocked fuel pipe.

We set off again, but the volume of trucks grew and we were forced to slow down. We found Padua full of movement; and in the neighbourhood of the demolished train station we found among the ruins the Giottesque chapel still intact. But nearby were the ruins of the Church of the Hermits showing the destruction of Mantegna's frescoes.

We finally arrived in Portogruaro. It was 11 PM on 23 July. The trip from Rome to Portogruaro had lasted 31 hours. We comfort ourselves by thinking of the journeys that our grandparents had taken in stagecoaches.

My sister Maria's house was free: some evacuees had left it a few days ago. The silo in front of the house had been ripped open by bombs. Other bombs had fallen near the house. But the house itself was free from damage. I found my sister, after more than three years, sweet and affectionate, but she had aged a bit. Left on her face were the traces of the fear she had endured for her children and herself. By the evening, I had made it to my house in Murlis.

The Dangers and the War Zones in Murlis

Murlis is a hamlet of the municipality of Zoppola, with a population of approximately 400. The village is immersed in the green of the countryside. It is surrounded by small woods and streams, and is a few kilometres from the confluence of the Cellina and Meduna streams. It is the ideal place to find easy hiding places in the small woods, hiding places that were used by the partisans. In fact, the Germans called Murlis a "partisan village." The partisans who came down from the mountains and hid in the woods would go out at night and extort money from the inhabitants, often asking for food. My relatives fed many partisans, both day and night. My nephew Augusto also gave them money and a calf.

My family told me countless tales of when the partisans appeared and about the Germans, describing the danger, fear, and plundering they were victim to. During my family's narration of events, one could still sense a sort of tension. Perhaps the nervousness that kept everyone in distressing fear was reawakened.

"It is a partisan village. We are going to burn it," said a German major one day. Later, these people were killed by the partisans, but some distance from Murlis. If the partisans had killed a few Germans in Murlis, the village would have certainly been burned down, and there would probably have been defenceless and lower-class people killed. My family never stops talking about the countless examples of the partisans' deeds. They say that the partisans from Osoppo were the best in the Garibaldi

Brigade. For the most part, the partisans were Communists. From the various stories, it seems that the partisans were real delinquents, thieves, and assassins who, under the guise of patriotism, unleashed their sinister instincts. They say that in Bannia a partisan leader was arrested, and in his house they found thousands in cash and gold. In Murlis a Yugoslav partisan named Stanko[77] reigned. He had married a girl from Murlis. A lot of money and gold had been taken away from him.

The memories left here by the partisans are anything but positive. From what I hear in this village and from other information, it is clear that the partisans played a real part in the liberation of northern Italy. But the mercenary groups were tainted by scoundrels who wanted to run to wherever they could use weapons with impunity. Under the specious banner of patriotism, these delinquents had a free hand for a time.

In truth, the good partisans laid down their arms; others held on to them and committed many crimes, and of these crimes the most horrible was what happened at Schio. Many have been brought to justice, but many still haunt the regions that have been liberated.

In almost every town there have been killings, hangings, retaliation, carried out first by the Germans and then by the partisans. There are horrifying stories about it. One of our farmers told me: "I had gone to the *Comunale* to plough. At a certain point, a dog began to bark and to run up and down scratching at the ground. I stopped the oxen and went near the dog. He had unearthed an arm. A so-called Fascist killed by the partisans had been dug up."

Our house in Murlis was subject to another grave danger. The house is made up of a large structure joined to a church.[78] If the Germans had set up a command post there, today the building would be a pile of rubble. Every day Allied airplanes flew over Murlis; perhaps they considered the building a good reference point.

[77] Lipej Kolenk (1925–2008), a Slovenian partisan born in Carinzia, who during the fight for liberation assumed the battle name of Stanko. As he was from Carinzia, he enlisted in the ranks of the Wehrmacht in 1942, and the following year he was sent to fight at Cassino. In 1944 he decided to desert and join the partisan fight.

[78] The Venetian House at Murlis, with the desecrated church (now dedicated to Saint Lucy), was bought in 1903 by Cardinal Costantini's father who, being a skilful builder, was able to make the necessary repairs and carefully renovate it after it had been downgraded to a farm dwelling by the former owners, Mr and Mrs Biglia. The huge complex, which also belonged to Celso, was his and his brother's vacation home.

WAR INDUSTRIES   MURLIS, 28 JULY 1945

The war closed northern Italy inside an impenetrable web, separating it from the rest of the country and from the rest of the world. A lot of imported products, such as soap, oil, and coffee, have run out; they either ran out or the prices of other products within the monopoly have gone up so much that they are no longer affordable.

But "poverty is the mother of invention." My nephew Augusto and others made a small press, and they press oil from different seeds: rape-seed, sunflower, peanut, etc.

Last night I helped press the sunflower oil. These seeds, shelled by machine, were heated in a *bain-marie* and then put in the press. Two men turned the press with a long crank, and the oil, pale yellow, began to trickle out. That night I dressed the salad with that oil: it does not have a lot of flavour, but it works well in a salad. And we eat it willingly.

A little while ago six geese died. My nieces took advantage of this to use the fat, along with other ingredients, to make soap. The price of silk stockings has gone up stratospherically. For this reason an old aunt of mine made a small burner to draw the thread of silk from the cocoon, and then with a small loom she will make a fabric of silk. There is no leather. My nephew bought a cowhide and, assisting himself with instructions from a book, he tanned it. And the nieces and nephews were able to make clogs that they liked and could use.

As for coffee, we easily replace it with rye and barley grain. There was no tobacco; and everyone was growing the plants, hiding them among the vegetables. They cure the tobacco and use the water from washing the leaves as a pesticide for the vegetables.

Tonight, Countess Beatrice Balbo-Zoppola asked me what people are saying about the Hon. Parri.[79] I replied, "He has enough good press and

[79] The countess' question demonstrates how Ferruccio Parri, at the time of his appointment as head of the government, was unknown by the public and even by the press. Parri (1890–1981), an Italian politician, after the First World War was editor of *Corriere della Sera* until 1922. An anti-Fascist, he was interned in Ustica and then in Lipari. He returned to Milan in 1930 and once again secretly began activities against the regime, and for this he was sent into exile for another three years. He underwent a new trial in 1942, but after 8 September 1943 he was free to devote himself to the partisan fight. One of the founders of the Action Party, he was also part of the National Liberation Committee. He was captured by the Germans in 1945 and was freed by the Allies. He became head of the government in June of the same year, a position he held until the

is making every effort to lead, as best he can, this government that isn't so much a government as a coalition of representatives from different parties. Each party thinks first and foremost of its own interests; then the ministries strive to come to an agreement regarding their different points of view. In the end, it is a government with very limited power. It is really the Allies who are in charge."

Regarding the Hon. Parri, we can note two things that diminish his character. When the abominable crime occurred in Schio, General Dunlop – one of the Allies – had scorching words to condemn the deed and to make Italy understand that it cannot accept a seat among civilized nations until it restores order in its own house. Parri, on the other hand, didn't say a word, either to denounce the deed or to investigate it, or to propose something that would put an end to these crimes once and for all. Why? Parri was a leader of the partisans. But if this government forgets moral principles, as Fascism did, it will be a castle built on sand. A second observation: Parri, the head of the government of a Catholic nation, and who has official business with the Holy See, doesn't understand that in the light of self-interest he should visit the Pope, who saved Rome and who was introduced to many important Allied figures. Parri is tied to the Action Party, in which many old masons have taken refuge. If he condones minor sectarianism, one will not be able to say that he is a statesman; he will be nothing but an ordinary man.

"Three coffins have just gone down that road," a farmer informs me. It's the authorities, who are going to dig up and bring to the cemetery the bodies of three people who were killed. They were buried in the fields of the farmer's land. One of them is Officer Bruni of the Milizia Ferroviaria [railway militia], who was head of the station at Casarsa and was brought here. The partisans gave him time so he could confess. The other two are Russians, captured near the Tagliamento River and then shot dead in Murlis, under the bank of the Cellina; one was from Stalingrad and the other from Saint Petersburg. The priest told me that there may be other

---

following December. He was a member of the Constituent Assembly. When the Action Party dissolved in 1946, he and La Malfa founded the Republican Democracy Party, which merged into the Italian Republican Party. He was elected senator in 1948 and again in 1963 on the ticket of the Italian Socialist Party. He became a lifetime senator in 1963. He founded and was editor of the magazine *Astrolabio*, which maintained a position that was critical of the central governments formed by the Christian Democrats and other minor parties.

bodies, because there was the stench of bodies in that area. They believe that there will be others dug up on the shores of the Meduna and Cellina.

MURLIS, 28 JULY 1945

With the family lives my old aunt Geltrude Altan, who is 86 years old and possesses both a youthful mind and a youthful memory. She tells me, "I was born in Austria; then in 1866 I became Italian. Then in 1918 I became German. In 1919 I once again became Italian. I was thinking about dying an Italian. Instead, in 1944 I became German. But in the end, this year I became Italian again. And I think that's enough now."

There is truly a tragic summary of national history in this *curriculum vitae*.

OVERREACTIONS   MURLIS, 29 JULY 1945

Mussolini said, "We dream of the Empire." That man, insane with arrogance and megalomania, instead of leading Italy on the road to the Empire, led Italy into an abyss. One can understand, therefore, a certain reaction against Mussolini's ill-fated dream, but one goes too far by insulting ancient Rome. C. Galassi Paluzzi[80] created the Institute of Roman Studies to celebrate the greatness of Rome, from which many lessons and auspices for the future of Italy can be learned. Galassi Paluzzi was discharged from his duties and replaced by Professor Tosatti of the Christian Democrats.

Calosso,[81] a Socialist, lashed out at Rome. The former minister Di Ruggiero ridiculed the institute's rhetoric by mentioning the Roman march, the Roman salute, the legion's emblem, the revival of ancient names, etc.

[80] Carlo Galassi Paluzzi (1893–1972), a historian and intellectual, founded the Institute of Roman Studies, whose objective was to promote and improve the historical knowledge of Rome as well as Rome's universal role. It was supported by a group that joined the Club for Roman Citizens. The city of Rome named a street after him.

[81] Umberto Calosso (1895–1959), a journalist, politician, and professor, was the host of a Radio London program during the Second World War. He joined the Italian Socialist Party, then moved to the Socialist Party of Italian Workers, and ended up in the Italian Socialist Party of Proletarian Unity. He was elected to the Constituent Assembly and to the Chamber of Deputies in the first term of the republican government.

There was, of course, some exaggeration in Fascist rhetoric. But I think they went beyond rational limits. In Aquileia, on a plaque I once read: *Genio loci Roma aeterna*.[82]

THE ATOMIC BOMB   7 AUGUST 1945

The radio broadcast a speech in which Truman revealed that an "atomic bomb" has been made; it is a tool of destruction that puts into action cosmic forces by disintegrating the atom. The atomic bomb is more powerful than 20,000 tons of explosives.

The first bomb was dropped on the port of Hiroshima in Japan. This news brings me both perplexity and pain. Where will it end? Have we found the way to destroy the world? Is it an achievement or a terrible loss for humanity?

The future is gloomy, and I cannot keep myself from feeling a sense of panic. The French scientist Jean Painlevé[83] has observed, "The atomic power of the bomb could be developed to the point where it can completely destroy animal and vegetable life on the globe, leaving perhaps intact a few small islands where savages would have to resume the process of civilization while trying to rediscover how to make fire."

But there is Providence: "*Propterea non timemus, dum subvertitur terra, et montes cadunt in medium mare*" (Ps. 45:3).[84]

They still don't know all the details about the effects of the atomic bomb dropped on Hiroshima. The Japanese city was still wrapped in an enormous blanket of smoke and dust. But they fear that there are many dead, among them women, the elderly, and children. All of this is not only anti-Christian but inhuman and brutal.

Of course, Japan made mistakes. Its attack on China was both a wicked action and a mistake. Despite this, we must not forget one fact:

---

[82] The Latin passage means "For its protective spirit, Rome is eternal."

[83] Jean Painlevé (1902–89), son of the mathematician and Prime Minister Paul Painlevé, was a complex figure. Leaning more toward surrealist ideas and connected to socialist views with anarchical principles, he studied mathematics and medicine, but he was more involved in film, as director and actor, as well as in intellectual criticism, especially "scientism," as documented in his work *La scienza è una finzione*, or *Science is a Fiction*.

[84] The passage is translated into English as "Therefore we will not fear when the earth shall be troubled and the mountains shall be removed into the heart of the sea."

Germany, Japan, and Italy all need land in which to place the surplus population increase that cannot find room in the metropolitan centres. Even Italy was in need of expansion, but it could and should have been happy with Ethiopia. One day that good fellow Ceresi said to me, "Never before have such just causes been destroyed by the ignorance and wicked deeds of those who plead them."

MURLIS, 8 AUGUST 1945

Are we moving toward a republic? I fear that we are. They confuse dynasty with monarchy. There is a lot of resentment about the King's cynicism and compliance. The King is considered just as responsible as Mussolini for the enormous national disasters – people don't distinguish between the two of them. They want to bring down the monarchy. Italy is a sad convalescent, weak, drained of its blood, and has difficulty breathing. In the midst of such disorder, may we at least not forget God!

MURLIS, 10 AUGUST 1945

I have met with many priests in different cities, with people of the aristocracy, and people of the lower classes; all of them still have horrific memories of wartime. Continual anxiety, fear of the Germans, of the searches, of the Allied raids; people escaping, hiding food, the danger represented by the partisans, the bullying by some of them, and especially by some of those in the Garibaldi Brigade, and the barbarity of the Cossacks.[85] It is a great and dreadful tragedy that has left in our hearts traces of tension, restlessness, resentment, and fear. They say that every country has incidents of barbarism to recount: executions, round-ups, looting, and arrests.

There are still remnants of the so-called partisans who refused to lay down their arms, and they are nothing but outlaws.

We still hear of sad occurrences of violence and looting – like what happened a few days or so ago in Fanna, where during the night the pharmacy was looted. People are also uneasy because of the Communist propaganda.

[85] The Cossacks are a nomadic people from Eastern Europe who are descended from a mixture of Tartarian peoples. Stalin launched a policy of "decossackization" against them. During the Second World War, groups of Cossacks served next to the Germans. A Cossack unit, trailed by its families, was deployed in Carnia and in the Alto Friuli region to fight against the partisans, and while there it committed heinous crimes.

Amidst this bleak picture shines the courageous and Christian actions of the diocesan bishop Mons. D'Alessi and of the clergy. In addition, the archbishop of Udine, Mons. Nogara, explained an admirable act of apostolic courage and civil aid. "We," the priests say, "are left astonished by the bishops' great courage, and we should state that the Germans, who looked down on the Italians as well as the important people in the Fascist hierarchy, had a respectful and fearful demeanour toward the bishops. They understood that the bishops represented an Authority that was more powerful than war, that it was the only authority left among such disaster."

ASSUMPTION OF THE VIRGIN MARY

MURLIS, 15 AUGUST 1945

This morning the radio broadcast the great news that Japan has accepted unconditional surrender. The beautiful holiday of the Assumption will remain tied to this very welcome remembrance, which represents a sigh of relief for the whole world. The war is over, but peace has still not been made. And the atomic bomb leaves in me terrifying anxiety. The bomb can still become an instrument of revenge and of destruction.

May God's will be that peace is made, a peace founded on the principles of justice and charity; otherwise, we will be right back to where we started.

ROME, 20 AUGUST 1945

My brother [Monsignor Giovanni] and I have happily returned to Rome. We got in the car yesterday at 6 PM and finally arrived at the Propaganda today at 5 PM, a 23-hour journey.

I was particularly afraid of the brigands while we were passing through the mountains in Umbria. I said the evening prayers in the car, and today I also said the morning prayers in the car.

A slow and tiring trip. But all's well that ends well.

Audience with the Christian Female Workers
I've learned that on 15 August the Italian Christian Female Workers Association was received by the Holy Father. The audience offered well-deserved recognition for the work of a great female congress.[86]

---

[86] Pius XII's formal speech for the event is transcribed in its entirety in AAS 37 (*Bollettino Ufficiale della Santa Sede*, 1945), 212–16. The observations in the diary entry can be cross-referenced to pages 214–15.

Professor Luzzati from Venice came to see me to ask about the Hon. Cini. I had a heart-to-heart talk with him while defending Cini's integrity, his dignity, and his bravery.

I gave the task of copying a manuscript by Don Antonio Cicuto to the former prefect P. A civil servant, forced to retire, he struggles with poverty. It is one of many signs of the times.

Yesterday the government gave a reception for the Allies in the Campidoglio to show their joy that peace has finally come. There was the usual rhetoric in their speeches.

While America and England held other religious events to give thanks to God, the paltry sectarianism of many small men – Parri, Togliatti,[87] Nenni[88] – has prevented us from giving a religious tone to the great

---

[87] Palmiro Togliatti (1893–1964), an Italian politician, who as a youth adhered to Socialism but left the movement in 1921 upon the establishment of the Italian Communist Party, becoming one of its founders, along with Gramsci. Having been arrested numerous times during Fascism, in 1926 he escaped abroad but continued to hold the reins of his party and later became its general secretary. He made a name for himself at the Seventh Congress of the Communist International and took on the role of leader of the Komintern [Russian abbreviation for the Communist International]. He was arrested in France when the Second World War broke out, but he managed to reach the Soviet Union and from there he went back to Italy in 1944. He was a minister without portfolio in the Badoglio and Bonomi cabinets, minister of justice in the government presided over by Parri, and in the first government led by De Gasperi. Afterwards he moved over to the opposition. In 1948 he was wounded in an attack in Genoa. From that year on, he was elected a member of parliament, putting himself at the head of the Communist parliamentary group.

[88] Pietro Nenni (1891–1980), an Italian politician and journalist, participated in the protests against the war in Libya on account of his pacifism, and for that was put in prison for a time, together with Benito Mussolini. After the First World War he initially followed the Fascist movement; he wrote for *Il Popolo d'Italia* and was the co-founder of the Fascio di Combattimento [League of Combat] in Bologna. In 1921 he moved away from Fascism and joined the Italian Socialist Party. In 1923 he became managing editor of *Avanti*, the party's newspaper. For his position against Il Duce's regime, in 1926 he went as an exile

event. Old-fashioned provincialism. It is regretful, however, that on this occasion the Christian Democrats didn't know how to or were unable to assert themselves in order to make a more impressive statement.

29 AUGUST 1945

"The news that the Italian Council of Ministers has rejected the proposal to celebrate the end of the war with a religious ceremony has left a pathetic impression and has brought about unpleasant repercussions in the United States ..."[89]

Talk, idle talk; but Italy expected the Christian Democrats to take a clear-cut and energetic position, in keeping with their "Christian" epithet. This epithet must not be a simple label to be used for publicity.

5 SEPTEMBER 1945

Today a canonical sculptor came to see me. At a certain point he exclaimed, "You know how I was always a proud anti-Fascist, but now I would become a Fascist. One cannot live this way ..."

---

to France. During the Second World War, he joined the resistance movement and became an influential member of the Garibaldi Brigade. Having returned to Italy, in 1943 – along with Sandro Pertini, Giuseppe Saragat, and Lelio Basso – he was able to unify Italian Socialists within the Italian Socialist Party of Proletarian Unity. He became its national secretary in 1944. In that capacity, he encouraged ties with the Communist Party, which resulted in the "Scissione di Palazzo Barberini" [the split in Palazzo Barbarini], led by Sagarat in 1947. In the electoral struggle with the Christian Democrats in 1948, his party saw rather disappointing results that caused them to become the opposition. In 1951 he was awarded the Stalin Peace Prize, an award he gave back in 1956 after the Soviet suppression of Hungary. This was a determining factor in his detachment from the Italian Socialist Party (PSI) – which he led – as well as from the Italian Communist Party. He went on to form a new political coalition, called the centre-left, that involved the Christian Democrats, the Italian Republican Party, and the Italian Democratic Socialist Party, which was founded by Saragat. From 1964 on, new governments were born, and Nenni served many times as a minister and was also vice-president of the Council in the first three cabinets led by Aldo Moro. He had been a member of parliament since 1948 and was appointed a lifetime senator in 1970. When he died, the PSI was in the hands of its secretary, Bettino Craxi, considered his successor.

[89] CC: *Il Popolo*, 29 August 1945.

In fact, there is in everyone a sense of uneasiness and a lack of esteem for the government presided over by Parri but controlled by Nenni and Togliatti. Brigandage is widespread. The partisans – that is, those scoundrels who disguise themselves with a new uniform (at one time, nearly all of them were Fascists) – consider themselves leaders because they have, as they say, their *compari* in the government. We hope that we will hear something from the Christian Democrats.

Let's hope that the Christian Democrats will make themselves heard. We are reminded of the Facta years.[90] At the time, the King entrusted Meda with the task of making a government. And Meda didn't accept the invitation. He ripped it up, and then we had Mussolini.

6 SEPTEMBER 1945

Today the Council of Ministers issued a sad decree: "The publishers of newspapers, magazines, and other periodicals that hire professionals and contributors who have been removed from their respective registers, or have been suspended from work due to reasons of purification, will be sentenced to three months in jail and must also pay a fine of 100,000 lire. The manager or editor responsible for the newspaper, magazine, or periodical who uses the work by the aforementioned people will, without question, incur penal action if he cooperates in the crime committed by the publisher. In addition to this, he will be suspended from professional activity for a period of no less than two months and, if he commits the same violation again, he will be cancelled from the register."

This is ultra-Fascism, and it is even more monstrous because the government would like to suggest that it is inspired only by freedom. I read,

---

[90] Luigi Facta (1861–1930), an Italian politician tied to Giolitti, was a lawyer and in 1892 was elected to parliament. He served many times as under-secretary in various ministries before becoming minister of finance (1911–14), minister of justice (1919) and again minister of finance (1921). He was appointed to form a government while the country was in a critical situation due to violent Fascist undertakings – in the face of which he proved incapable of exercising the law as well as responding to the Fascist squads' threats. In July 1922 parliament passed a motion of non-confidence in his government. Given the refusal by various political representatives – such as Filippo Meda – to take on the leadership of a new cabinet, Facta formed a second government that was weaker than the first in terms of allowing Fascist violence. He resigned on 26 October 1922, giving a clear run for the March on Rome, as well as Mussolini's ascension to power.

from a lecture given by P. Villari[91] in Florence in 1897: "A truly great nation needs more than a handful of heroes ... One cannot always have heroes close by and often one can even do without them. But it must always have millions of honourable men and honest citizens."

THE POLITICAL ITALIAN CONSTITUTIONAL COURT
26 SEPTEMBER 1945

Today the Italian Constitutional Court convened: truly empty virtuosity, a mockery of parliament with all its flaws, lacking even a legal foundation.

Gratitude

It is worth noting, however, a singular and spontaneous display that took place on Friday, 28 September 1945, at the beginning of the Council's negotiations. A statement made by Bencivenga generated an impressive ovation for the Pope:

"That great applause echoed through the courtroom of Montecitorio, and it represented the feelings of an entire nation for the Head of Catholicism, the Princes of the Church, and all the clergy who 'restored the patriotic achievements of our national revival.' However, those who lived twenty years ago in the 'real' Italy cannot be amazed if men of different and opposing ideologies found themselves united in a display of gratitude; it was the sons' gratitude to their Father ..."[92]

10 OCTOBER 1945

I went to go see the seminary building of Urban College at Castel Gandolfo which is under construction. The renovations are very state-of-the-art. The active workforce at the site comprises more than 100 people. We give them a French loaf and some soup.

The foreman fired two young men because the partisans forced him to. Those two young men were former Fascists. It is unprecedented bullying,

---

[91] Pasquale Villari (1827–1917), a historian and Italian politician, was one of the main figures in cultural life in the second half of the nineteenth century in Italy. Born in Naples, he became the "adoptive son" of Florence, the subject of much of his historical research. He published the biographies of such Florentines as Machiavelli and Savonarola. A member of parliament and then a senator, he was minister of education.

[92] CC: *Il Popolo*, 30 September 1945. The article was written by Diogene.

worse than Fascism. The good partisans laid down their arms; the others – mere riff-raff who were once Fascists and today go with the Communists – set themselves up as bosses. They commit violent acts and behave as if they control the poor Parri government, which so far hasn't found how to resolve any of the serious problems that plague Italy.

One cannot govern expecting oil and water to mix. Nitti made a noble speech. Yesterday he went to see the Pope.

Parri, a spokesman of Masonry,[93] didn't believe in going to see the Pope – who saved Rome, who helps the poor, and who can say something in favour of poor Italy. Wretched sectarianism!

Everywhere one hears how the ineptitude of the government is deplored, especially Togliatti's abuse of power. He has shown himself to be factious as well as ignorant of the basic principles of the law. But he stays at the top because, at this point, poor Italy is apathetic.

There is a sense of uneasiness in the loyal Christian Democrats because a huge error of principle has been made: the secularism of the state.

I wrote to De Gasperi to offer my congratulations for the positive outcome of the failed attempt on his life.[94] He answers me with words

[93] Masonry is an international secret society that initiates members by means of its own rites. It was inspired by Enlightenment ideals that aimed to organize the civil and political community on exclusively humanitarian and laical foundations. The association – whose name refers to its medieval origins linked to "the brotherhood of masons" – first took shape institutionally and ideologically in London in 1717, and it quickly spread throughout the United Kingdom, Europe, and America with notable effect on culture and the governments' anticlerical choices. The organization was repeatedly condemned by the Holy See. The Code of Canon Law of 1917, which remained in effect until until 1983, condemned Masonry in a generalized way with canon 684, and in a specific way with canon 2335. The latter canon provided for the punishment of excommunication sentenced *ipso facto* and was reserved for the Apostolic See to punish those who were members of "masonic sects or similar associations that plot against the Church or legitimate civil authority." Regarding this canon and the modern-day position held by the Catholic Church regarding Masonry, see B.F. Pighin, *Diritto Penale Canonico* (Venice: Marcianum Press, 2008), 362–9.

[94] Alcide De Gasperi, when he was minister of foreign affairs in the government led by Ferruccio Parri, had an attempt made on his life on 2 October 1945. He was shot at when going to Montecitorio by car, but luckily was not wounded. The shot only shattered one of his car windows.

clouded with sadness: "My warmest thanks for the comforting words from the 'mason brothers.'[95] We must keep praying because this life is painful. Yours, D.G."

A LETTER FROM VALENZA   23 OCTOBER 1945
... Although we have generally felt well here, unfortunately I cannot tell you that I will take back a favourable impression of the general condition of this region, which is usually so hardworking, honest, and upright. Banditry is widespread; people have no desire to work and seek out ventures – often dishonest – as a way to earn money without toil. This behaviour has created a situation that cannot last long, but before suffering a radical change it will lead to very ugly excesses – something everyone fears.

Extremist propaganda has subsided considerably, and now the sound part of the population, which has never stopped being sound and which is coming to its senses after a period of Socialist-Communist euphoria, is hoping for a government that does little or no politicking and instead puts into power a good administration.

Vittorio Cerruti

4 NOVEMBER 1945
The 20 October missionary message stated: "Either once again we become brothers or we will end up with the most serious of catastrophies. The atomic bomb scares us, and against it there exists no other defence but all humans living together in the Christian sense."

A scientist says that soon all nations will discover the atomic bomb and with the threat of destroying in the blink of an eye a city like New York, they will be able to launch the bomb with flying rockets.

4 NOVEMBER 1945
Nenni has proposed a new law for the purifying process. They continue to break up Italy instead of working on its reconstruction.

---

[95] CC: My brother, the archbishop Giovanni, and I began our careers as masons.

5 NOVEMBER 1945

Yesterday Arturo Marpicati's[96] wife came to see me. Her situation was normal for the times. Today they issued an arrest warrant. They are trying to hide this honest man of letters who was a Fascist like many others but did not steal and did not commit any criminal acts.

Two days ago Commissioner Pietro Campilli, an influential member of the Christian Democrats, paid me a visit. I told him firmly that when a moral principle is at stake, the Christian Democrats cannot be agnostic or servile. By taking away from professionals the option to practise their profession, the government theoretically condemns them to a life of hunger. There are innocent families and children who would be left to die of starvation. The government is doing what the Fascists did to the Jewish doctors. And they don't realize that underneath it all there is a moral issue?

13 NOVEMBER 1945

I had a meeting with the Hon. Scelba, minister of communications. I spoke to him about Cini, while leaving him the letter that Cini sent to Mussolini so that he could release himself from his appointment as minister of communications. I told him that there was widespread uneasiness among the clergy as well as among the supporters of the

[96] Arturo Marpicati (1891–1961), an Italian politician and writer, graduated with a degree in philosophy in 1917 and enlisted as a volunteer during the First World War. He had a close relationship with Gabriele D'Annunzio and other Italian literary figures. He was with the commanding officer in Fiume, where he stayed even after D'Annunzio's departure. There he married a noblewoman named Antonietta Lado, who went by the name of Ninì and taught general arts and literature at the local Dante Alighieri high school. By 1919 he had already joined the Fascist movement and became federal secretary of the Italian Regency of Carnaro. In 1929 he moved to Rome and took on the role of chancellor of the Italian Academy. In 1930 he was appointed director of the National Institute of Fascist Culture, presided over by Giovanni Gentile, and from that moment on he expanded their collaboration with numerous periodicals. As vice-secretary of the National Fascist Party, he became a member of the Grand Council of Fascism. He was appointed adviser to the state in 1938, a position he held until his death. In the *Epistolario* there are some letters from Marpicati to Costantini. Their acquaintanceship began when Mons. Celso was Fiume's apostolic administrator.

Christian Democrats because the party didn't know how to gain ground and assert itself directly with regard to:

1 the state's agnosticism and secularism regarding the celebration of peace with a religious function;
2 the new purification law; for two years, they have been mercilessly operating on the body of poor Italy.

Scelba answered by explaining the difficult situation in which the Christian Democrats find themselves, among relentless opponents, with Parri at the head of the government.

THE STATEMENT OF THE CATHOLIC BISHOPS OF THE UNITED STATES REGARDING PEACE   19 NOVEMBER 1945

The Catholic bishops of the United States made a statement in which they condemn any return "to the tragedy of a dictatorship and to the danger of pacts for the balance of power. By replacing simple expedients on the basis of justice, those nations did no more than cause one war after another ..."[97]

24 NOVEMBER 1945

A government crisis has been declared. For the most part, it has been greeted with a sigh of relief. Nenni and Togliatti have revealed themselves to be a pair of incompetent factionists. Parri, a representative of Masonry, has shown the measure of his smallness.

JEWISH REFUGEES VISIT THE HOLY FATHER   29 NOVEMBER 1945

Today the Holy Father granted an audience to about 80 Jewish refugees who came from concentration camps in Germany. They asked, according to what we read in their request, "for the supreme honour of being able to personally thank the Holy Father for the generosity he has shown those who were persecuted during the horrible period of Nazi-Fascism."

---

[97] CC: *Il Popolo*, 20 November 1945.

The group was accompanied to the audience by Father Compagnucci of the Pallottines[98] and by Commissioner Fabris, who oversees the Roman efforts of the Knights of Columbus.[99]

Upon his entrance into the hall, the august Pontiff was welcomed by a fervently expressed reverent tribute. His Holiness, after offering a friendly response to such a greeting, was delighted to make conversation with those present with words of fatherly kindness.[100]

A LETTER   5 DECEMBER 1945

"… But, how much pity and how much disgust is felt because of the pitiful tactics that impede the formation of a serious government in Italy. These petty, wretched politicians bring together nothing but hate and contempt, and they are getting ready for civil war …" G. De Martino[101]

[98] The Pallottine Fathers take their name from their founder Vincenzo Pallotti (1795–1850), a Roman presbyter who was canonized on 20 January 1963 and in 1834 had established the Society of Apostolic Life, later named the Society of Catholic Apostolate.

[99] The Knights of Columbus is a Catholic association established in the United States in 1882. However, it is also represented in other nations. The association was founded on the principles of charity, unity, fraternity, and patriotism.

[100] The audience and the Pope's speech are transcribed in *Discorsi e Radiomessaggi di Sua Santità Pio XII*, vol. 7, 291–4.

[101] Thanks to the fact that the letter quoted above is found in the *Epistolario*, it is possible to trace its sender. The sender, Giacomo De Martino (1868–1957), was appointed senator of the Kingdom in 1928. He enjoyed a long career in the diplomatic service (1891–1929), but the fullest and most productive period of his career was when he took on the role of secretary general of the Ministry of Foreign Affairs (January 1913 – December 1919). During those years he actively participated in Balkan and Mediterranean politics, thus looking ahead to make diplomatic preparations for Italy's entrance into the war in 1915. Then, as secretary of the Italian delegation at the Peace Conference in Paris, he carried out many of the difficult tasks the conference imposed on him. Following this, he served as Italy's ambassador in Berlin, London, Tokyo, and Washington. When Mussolini's regime fell, he was charged by the High Court of Justice for Sanctions against Fascism. In 1944 he was removed from office, but the order was revoked on 24 July 1946. In his letter to Costantini, De Martino asks if he can arrange a visit (through Mons. Celso) to meet the Hon. De Gasperi.

10 DECEMBER 1945

The government crisis has been resolved, but the nation's crisis is still unresolved. The Hon. De Gasperi is head of the government and has reshuffled the ministries while keeping, more or less, its previous physiognomy. He will, however, establish himself as a first-rate politician. He seems to be able to make the three following considerations:

1 It is the first time that a "Catholic" has been elected as prime minister of the government. Opinions have come a long way. Croce and the followers of liberalism, in the other crisis, didn't want to admit that a "Catholic" had been appointed as minister of education. It was due to the fact the Communists and the Socialists and Liberals lost ground. The Christian Democrats appear to be the strongest party. His own personal talents have also helped achieve his high position in the government.

2 The government, however, is still the prisoner of the six parties. They continue to govern and keep an eye on the parties. And this is not good and goes against a common goal.

3 We hoped that the Lieutenant, given everyone's weariness of the crisis, would have set up a ministry of accomplished men to run the country and set up the Constituent Assembly. Many believe that he has lost a good opportunity. But perhaps he feared an outbreak of revolutionary movements.

CHRISTMAS 1945

Yesterday the Holy Father announced the creation of 32 new cardinals for the next consistory on 8 February.[102] He gave a speech in which he talks about the universality and supernationality of the Church and therefore the need for the Sacred College of Cardinals to be viewed as a universal entity. It was a magnificent speech, marking a historical milestone and representing a sharp turn of Peter's boat that is now riding high on the open sea.

---

[102] Pius XII talks about the creation of the new cardinals, how many there will be and their countries of origin, in his speech of 25 December 1945 to the cardinals, bishops, and prelates of the Roman Curia, as can be found in AAS 38 (*Bollettino Ufficiale della Santa Sede*, 1946), 16–18. The entire speech is on pages 15–25.

I am enjoying the whole experience immensely. During the days before the conclave, after the death of Pius XI, I put together some thoughts about the Church and the Sacred College; in my heart I am championing the cause for the internationalization of the Sacred College and the Roman Curia.

The Pope had some friendly words for me when, after his noble speech, I went to kiss his hand. I am so very happy, especially about the appointment of a Chinese cardinal. That progress was made during the missions to China. When I went there, it seemed like a crazy idea to talk about having a Chinese bishop; but today the growing Church in China has a cardinal! *Deo gratias.* I had to suffer so many people telling me it would never happen, and now I have been paid back a hundredfold. May the Lord bless the Chinese Church.

Last night the Hon. De Gasperi, prime minister of Italy, came to see me. He said, "The Pope has internationalized the Sacred College. Excellent. I am familiar with your ideas on the matter."

25 DECEMBER 1945

Truman's Christmas message is being broadcast on the radio. Such beautiful words. But where are the facts?

War was waged to free Poland and that noble nation has been iniquitously sacrificed. The Italian prisoners in Algeria are treated like slaves. After two years, Italy still moans under the weight of the provisions of the armistice. They talked about freedom, about democracy, and now three men in Moscow are deciding Europe's fate. We are witnessing a colossal deception.

The Year 1946

LUX IN TENEBRIS 1 JANUARY 1946
The cold war follows the war that was fought. By now, my entries have
become less frequent. I collect only a few episodes at random that serve
to throw light on the post-war atmosphere in which we live: the tiring
efforts along the road to disarmament, the desire to rebuild, and the
coming of peace – not a peace made of retaliation but of Christian and
humane coexistence.

Among the confusion of ideas, of people and things, the peaceful and
noble work of the Pope emerges ever more clear and solemn. Political and
military figures, prelates, pilgrims, Catholic associations, representatives
of religious institutions, etc., all flock to the Pope with a renewed enthusiasm for worship as well as with great admiration for the man himself.
The Holy Father offers to everyone words of love, guidance, reconciliation, and spiritual comfort. His work is always supported and strengthened by a very large and wonderful organization of charitable work that
goes beyond Italy's borders and embraces the endless material and moral
poverty in the world. In this way his words *can* work miracles.

CAPITAL AND LABOUR   24 JANUARY 1946
Today the Holy Father spoke to a large group of employers and workers.
I will quote some of his thoughts on the pressing problem of capital and
labour:

> An erroneous theory asserts that you, representatives of the workforce, and
> you, capitalist owners – as if it were due to a law of nature – are destined to
> battle each other in a bitter and relentless fight and that industrial reconcilia-
> tion cannot be reached except by these means.

However, you realize, without needing too much subtle reasoning, that social reconciliation – if it wishes to be rational and humane – cannot be obtained with the pure and simple removal of one contrastive element. In such a case, it would extinguish active peace – a peace that gives life and strength to the public and private economy...

Today, after a terrifying war that has covered the world with massacre and ruin, in the most pensive and shrewd minds is reborn the need for a return to the spiritual traditions of this dear Italian homeland of which you are all its hard-working sons. The traditions that in every era have shown themselves to be an everlasting source of noble emotions and an irreplaceable bastion of peace between individuals and groups and the classes of the nation.[1]

THE PURIFICATION RAGES ON ...   25 JANUARY 1946

Tribunal iniquus quod vexationes creat sub specie legis [Ps. 93].[2] I have looked after, in the best way I was able, my various friends who were "purified" by the Senate and by other offices. I am happy to say that many times I found fair tolerance and understanding.

I quote two examples to illustrate this understanding better. Marcello Piacentini, the architect, writes me: "We are not dealing here with purification but with out-and-out 'persecution.' After a year of fighting, I am beginning to grow weary! The process of restarting a trial against someone who has been acquitted 'already three times'– without any new events having taken place – is an unheard-of breach of the law and clearly shows the perverted goal of persecution. I never thought I would reach this age, after a whole life filled with passion for my art, to feel so brutally humiliated."

On 6 January I sent to the Hon. Molè, whom I know personally, the following letter:

Please allow me to appeal to your noble sense of understanding with regard to the architect MARCELLO PIACENTINI who, through this my letter, is forwarding you his curriculum vitae. I know Piacentini well. He is an outstanding artist and lives for his art, as the artists of the Renaissance did.

[1] *Discorsi e Radiomessaggi di Sua Santità Pio XII*, vol. 7 (Milan: Società Editrice "Vita e Pensiero," 1946), 347–51. The quotation can be found on pages 349–50.

[2] Costantini loosely (therefore not literally) quotes the Bible passage that means: "It is an iniquitous court the one that creates oppression under the guise of application of the law."

He worked under the Fascist regime, just as Cellini and Leonardo worked for Francis I in France. He was subject to three trials regarding purification, and he was acquitted at all three.

I am his colleague at the Academy of Saint Luca, and I cannot understand how they can think of throwing out – in the name of freedom – an artist of recognized merit like Piacentini. If the voice of a person who is completely averse to politics, who desires that every effort contributes toward the reconstruction of poor and dear Italy will be welcomed kindly, it will demonstrate the *equitas* that is the pride of Roman law.

The letter brought good results. Might I allow myself to mention another document ... one that Professor Paribene wrote to me from Rome, [15 March 1946]: "Remembering always with my full gratitude your very kind attention to my situation of being exiled from teaching, please allow me to tell you that my excommunication has been revoked and I can recommence my lessons at the Catholic University in Milan. I will probably leave on Monday, and in my infinite malice (may God forgive me), I think that between Jonah and the whale, the worst was that the whale could not swallow Jonah and had to spit him back out."

THE CHURCH AND MODERN IMPERIALISM

21 FEBRUARY 1946

From the Holy Father's noble speech that was delivered for the conferment of the cardinal's biretta on the new cardinals, I transcribe a passage that illustrates a highly topical issue:

> The unity and the wholeness of the Church, highlighted by the demonstration of its autonomy, are of great importance to the foundation of social life. It seems almost that the duty of the Church is to understand and in some way to embrace, like a gigantic world empire, all of human society ...
>
> The Church – although it carries out the mandate of its divine Founder, which is to spread its message throughout the world and conquer all souls with the Gospel [N.B. Mk. 16:15] – is not an empire with imperialist precepts, as one now tends to associate this word. In its progress and expansion, the Church marks a path that goes in the opposite direction of modern imperialism.[3]

[3] The passage describing the allocution held on 20 February 1946 by Pius XII to the newly appointed cardinals can be found in AAS 38 (*Bollettino Ufficiale della Santa Sede*, 1946), 143–4. The complete speech is on pages 141–51.

THE DIPLOMATS AT THE HOLY SEE   26 FEBRUARY 1946
On the occasion of the recent historic consistory that summoned many distinguished prelates from all over the world to be participants of the Sacred College, the gratitude of all represented nations was expressed to His Holiness.

The Holy Father, recalling the impartial and charitable deeds that he fostered during the war, outlined beneficial standards to all nations in order to expedite the coming of true peace.

I would like to transcribe the Pope's speech, but it is nobler than the simple nature of these notes. However, I would like to quote this thought: "This double universality, that of the Sacred College and the Vatican Diplomatic Corps, offers a clear image of the true autonomy of the Church, which is far from casting a shadow on certain nations and expecting all to join together in sombre uniformity. Instead, it favours them and develops them by gladly harmonizing the characteristics and resources of each with respect to its autonomy and inventiveness ... During the terrible conflict, it must have seemed that this concert had been completely silenced. But this wasn't the case, and if the deafening uproar of weapons suffocated its echo, We never stopped hearing it from here."[4]

THE NEW ITALIAN AMBASSADOR AT THE HOLY SEE
10 [SIC] FEBRUARY 1946
Today the Holy Father granted an audience to Pasquale Diana for the submission of his credentials as ambassador to Italy.

"The Italian people," said the Holy Father, "have always been loved by us, singularly loved, and in these years of suffering and anguish they are held very closely in our hearts. The victims of a war that we ourselves tried in vain to avert became involved in the conflict against the feelings and will of the noble majority. They have become twice as dear to us because of this; their current distress is a new and important reason to express our paternal concern as well as our haste to come to their aid. Therefore, while offering our hand to help in a special way Italy's sons and daughters who were most hard hit by the horrible conflict, we

---

4 The speech given on this occasion by Pius XII on 25 February 1946 is reprinted in French in AAS 38 (*Bollettino Ufficiale della Santa Sede*, 1946), 152–5. The passage quoted, which was translated by Costantini, can be found on pages 152–3.

adhere to a duty of charity in the spirit of the divine Samaritan, but also to the inner voice of our soul."[5]

THE POPE TURNS SEVENTY   2 MARCH 1946
[A newspaper article]:
"Today – 2 March – the Pope celebrates his 70th birthday and seven years in the papacy. Seventy years of life and seven as a pontiff in the midst of the most perilous and intense of events – it is not an easy weight to bear on one's shoulders. Those who attended the public consistory believe they saw signs of unusual tiredness on the Pope's face: from the red of the mantel he lifted his glance, softened by the loving eagerness to search far and wide so that he could bless as many as possible. His face seemed like ivory, and his penetrating eyes did not have their usual vivacity. The long and very busy day bears heavily on his physical condition – which is renewed with energy only from his ready and eager spirit for his work.

He has liberal and generous respect for all; he is always irreproachable in his conduct, both when he converses with the most humble and unknown of his sons and with the most noted and important figures. He does not like to talk for the sake of talking. Everything he organizes within the profundity of his thoughts is always directed toward one aim: the universal care of souls. Wise and well read, he always keeps close at hand two libraries that he himself created, and every day he manages to read or pore over an enormous amount of newspapers and magazines in all languages. He neither oversleeps nor overeats, and he is impeccably clean in his grooming and dress, which is without affectedness. He is able to give what everyone sees and knows. He is to be admired.

His life is an example of fruitful busyness, of an unbending consistency that has been able to withstand all dangers. For this reason, his recent speech to the Vatican Diplomatic Corps proved very educational. When he ascended the pontifical throne we heard the rumbling of threats. He gave this warning: "Nothing is lost with peace; everything is lost with war." The conflict broke out and his teachings were constant, implacable: they were swift, well timed, and direct, just as his overwhelming universal charity was untiring. For one reason and another he became a gigantic figure; everyone looked to him, who let nothing elude him, either as a sovereign or as a father. If the first encyclical of 1939 dealt with an outline of government and the norms of everyday life, his successive speeches and encyclicals – in which the clarity and depth of thought are rendered even more precious thanks to the fact that they are written so beautifully – confirm and restate their presentation.

He was patient, tolerant, and caring even with his declared enemies; uncompromising with the doctrine, fearless in its defence, perpetually vigilant, and intelligently cautious.

If Rome owes him its escape from destruction, Europe owes him the tens of thousands of people who were saved. Without the aid that he gathered and distributed, hunger alone would have claimed a large-scale loss of victims. It is the news of yesterday and of today. He defended the rights of truth against everyone who challenged them. Today some people accuse him of being an ally of the Nazis; no one remembers Ribbentrop's ordeal that lasted for more than an hour and a half when Hitler's foreign minister had the inauspicious idea to present himself for a private audience ...

Pius XII said one day, "Salvation doesn't come to a nation by external means, just as the sword can impose the conditions of peace but does not create peace. The energy that has to renew the face of the earth has to come from within, from the spirit. The new world order, of national and international life, once the bitterness and present-day cruel battles have ceased, will not have to rest on the treacherous sands of short-lived and changeable principles, where they were left to collective and individual discretion."[6]

They are words to keep in mind continually.

PIUS XII AT THE SACRED COLLEGE
FOR SAINT EUGENE'S DAY   1 JUNE 1946
"Our thought," said the Pope, responding to everyone's good wishes, "takes us back to a year ago. Throughout the whole territory of Europe, weapons were finally put down; the turmoil of war had subsided. A sense of relief flooded all hearts which, after such long and agonizing torture, were already greeting the coming of peace. A peace that although not yet enough to fulfill all legitimate expectations, was enough to create at least bearable living conditions."

---

[6] CC: From the 22 March 1946 edition of *La libera stampa*.

"A year has passed. Today we clearly see that at the time we were quite right to let show from our words the worry we felt in our paternal heart, the trepidation that clouded our joy: 'From the arms truce (we were saying on the same occasion) to true and genuine peace, the road will be long and arduous, too long for the eager aspirations of a human race that hungers for order and calm.'"[7]

THE CHRISTIAN DEMOCRATS   7 JUNE 1946

At the elections for the Constituent Assembly the Christian Democrats [DC] asserted themselves admirably. We will be moving toward the left, but this is a fatal error. With the members of the DC there will be an element of order and social justice. Without them, we would have fallen under Bolshevik domination.

On 7 June, Guido Gonella entitled his editorial in *Il Popolo* "Niente senza di noi!" [Nothing without us!]. The assertion of Christian principles in Europe is a light of hope in the midst of so much darkness. Today the *Giornale della Sera* reports: "The victory of the Christian Democrats signifies something similar to a European event and not just an Italian event."

The Liberals

A little while ago I met with Ambassador Cerruti. Cerruti, the son of a liberal and monarchist, remains faithful to his father's ideals. As such, he is deeply pained by the fall of the monarchy.

He told me, "The Liberals are the craftsmen of the Risorgimento. We have a noble legacy to defend." I replied, "Yes, it's a pity that sometimes liberalism has been polluted by anti-religious sectarianism." He continued: "There were deviations from the primary and true concept of liberty. For this reason I told my friends from Turin to throw into the sea their old anti-clerical baggage. These days, a rift has been formed in the relationship with the Holy See. We work therefore with a truly liberal spirit to finalize the Risorgimento."

I answered him: "You Liberals are smart, but you are few in number. And today numbers count. The French Revolution transferred power from the nobles to the bourgeoisie. And today we are witnessing another revolution. Power will pass from the bourgeoisie to the masses. They are the ones who, with universal suffrage, will form the parliament and

---

[7] Pius XII's allocution to the cardinals on his name day is transcribed in its entirety in AAS 38 (*Bollettino Ufficiale della Santa Sede*, 1946), 253–60.

the government. It is for this reason that Don Sturzo rallied the Italian People's Party. We cannot turn back. Today we must make efforts to educate the masses."

THE SUNSET OF THE MONARCHY · 13 JUNE 1946

The papers announce: "Today at 4 PM the flag on the turret of the Quirinale was lowered. The former King Umberto II has left to go into exile." A cycle of Italy's history has ended in a sombre light. The government hastened the proclamation of the republic without waiting for the final verdict from the Supreme Court. Why? There was probably the unconfessed fear of foreign intervention or revolutionary movements. This has spread great bitterness against the monarchy, but it must also be based on serious reasons. However, in this epilogue of tragic events there is an observation that is worth making.

I voted for the monarchy, and now I understand the responsibility of recognizing the republic, as much as I can help in my own small way. And in this I am sustained by the thought that if the monarchy had won with just a few votes, we would now most likely be in the midst of total revolution. The extremists were armed, and unfortunately they are still armed.

I met with Giuseppe Ferrazza from Trentino, an old and fine acquaintance. He said to me, "I voted for the King, but now I am convinced that he is paying for the deeds of his father and his ancestors. The excommunications will sooner or later have a terrible effect."

These words reminded me of an unusual confluence of events in which it seems justifiable to identify the hand of Providence. The Hon. De Gasperi told me that after the assassination of the Hon. Matteotti, he had asked for an audience with King Victor Emmanuel. He pointed out to him the "moral issue," saying that the Popolari [members of the Italian People's Party] did not feel ready to collaborate with a government on which was cast the dark shadow of a murder. He said that the King could and should have made a plea to the country. The King did not appreciate nor did he value the "moral issue," and he fired De Gasperi *fin de non reçevoir*. The Popolari retreated on the Aventine and then were ousted from parliament.

After about twenty years it was in fact De Gasperi's turn, as head of the government, to go back up the stairs of the Quirinale to announce to Umberto II that the monarchy – and therefore the Savoy dynasty – had been rejected by the Italian people.

The Savoys had come to Rome and they were excommunicated. They entered into the plan already made by Providence, the plan that had decreed the end of the temporal rule of the popes. This was the *finis operis*. But the *finis operantis* – in other words, the motives of those who collaborated in that decline – were far from noble. Many wanted to strike out at the Church, and they believed they had knocked it down by taking temporal protection from it.

Victor Emmanuel III completed the Lateran Pacts when closing the historical cycle of the Risorgimento, and then he was swept away like a vase that breaks into pieces after being hurled against a wall.

Men become restless, but God leads them. It is also said in the Scripture that God is *ludens in orbe terrarum* [Prv. 8:31].[8] Excommunication does no good, as was seen in Napoleon's case. "Excommunication!" he had said, "will not make the weapons fall from the arms of my soldiers." But in Russia this did indeed happen. And Napoleon's star fell from the sky.

A GRAND AUDIENCE IN PIAZZA SAN PIETRO

22 DECEMBER 1946

The people of Rome poured into St Peter's Square to show their devotion and gratitude to the Pope. He delivered a passionate speech to the multitude of believers, a speech to which we can give a title to contradict a wicked press campaign: *The Face of Catholic Rome*:

What memories your immense gathering recalls to our hearts! First of all, that day of 12 March during the war year 1944 when the multitudes of refugees and wanderers mixed with the crowd of Roman citizens who were worried for their nation, their hearths, and their families. They came in search of security and comfort in the word and blessing of their Father and Bishop, who himself was worried about and active in the safety of the city and its people.

Then, after less than three months, the shining day of 6 June! Rome, having wonderfully escaped unscathed from terrible dangers, wanted to celebrate here the first hours of its liberation with overflowing joy.

Finally, the memorable Palm Sunday of 1945. While from far away the guns were still ominously sounding, you begged for the merciful protection of God, and We urged you not to forget your Christian responsibilities of mercy,

---

[8] "Playing in the world." The passage in Proverbs reads: "Playing in the world: and my delights were to be with the children of men."

virtue, honesty, and brotherly love, and to keep honourable the holy legacy left to you by your fathers.

With pain and indignation, you see the holy face of Rome (this holy place, the seat of the divine direction of the Vicar of Christ) exposed by the hand of wicked deniers of God – desecrators of divine things, worshippers of sensation – and stained with shame, covered with mud. But listen to this: It shows itself here today, in front of you in all of its splendour, in all its intact and inviolate beauty.

Never before has Rome's mission been more noble, more beneficial, more indispensable than now ... Make sure that your lives and behaviour, your judgment and deeds are deeply imbued and guided by the watchful and clairvoyant conscience of that unique mission, no less honorary than heavy with responsibility and duty.

The countless groups of your martyrs and saints watch over you. Show yourselves to be worthy of them. From the Roman land the first Peter, surrounded by the threats of depraved imperial power, gave a proud warning cry: "Resist ye, strong in faith" [1 Pet. 5:9].[9]

PIUS XII'S SPEECH TO THE SACRED COLLEGE
24 DECEMBER 1946

I quote here some thoughts from the speech that the Holy Father gave today to the Sacred College while responding to its holiday wishes:[10]

Humanity, having just emerged from the horrors of a cruel war whose consequences still provoke anxiety, contemplates with amazement the open abyss between the hopes of yesterday and the weaknesses of today. An abyss that, even with the most tenacious of efforts, it is difficult to get round because man, who is capable of destruction, is not always qualified enough to rebuild on his own.

Here, now almost two years have passed since the silencing of the roar of the cannons. The military events on the battlefield led to an indisputable victory of one of the warring sides and an unprecedented defeat of the other.

One thing remains, without any doubt: The fruits of victory and its repercussions have until now not only been a source of unspeakable bitterness for

---

[9] Pius XII's speech on 22 December 1946 to the faithful of Rome is quoted in AAS 39 (*Bollettino Ufficiale della Santa Sede*, 1947), 5–7.

[10] Pius XII's speech to the cardinals on Christmas Eve is quoted in AAS 39 (*Bollettino Ufficiale della Santa Sede*, 1947), 7–17.

those who surrendered, but they have proved to be a source of unending anxiety and of dangerous party divisions for the victors ...

It is not our intention to criticize but to stimulate. Not to accuse but to give aid. We know well that our words and intentions risk being misinterpreted or twisted for reasons of political propaganda. But the possibility of such erroneous or evil comments could not make us close our mouths ...

When the Atlantic Charter was first introduced, all nations were listening; finally people were able to breathe. What is left now of that message and of its provisions?

Also, in some of those states – either by their own election or under the aegis of other and greater powers – they love to show themselves to today's human race as the forerunners of new and real progress. The "four freedoms," first greeted by the enthusiasm of many, no longer seem more than a shadow or a forgery of what was in the thoughts and intentions of the most faithful of their promoters ...

In the last little while, a new factor has emerged to stimulate the desire for peace and the will to promote it with the greatest efficacy. The power of new devices of destruction that modern technology has strengthened and will continue to strengthen will create infernal-type spectres for a horrified human race to see ...

We cannot end Our Christmas message without recalling the pain and need that arise from the serious food shortages as well as the poor sanitary conditions of nations involved in the war. On 5 April of this year We issued a cry of help to the governments and people of those countries that, with their reserves, could come to the aid of the hungry. And in truth much has been done ...

If only it was God's will that those treasures of energy and means – charitably distributed to help and rescue from absolute ruin the very poorest – were enough for what is needed! Unfortunately this is not the case! So We find ourselves forced to renew the call for aid first given last spring. Throughout the vast territories of Europe and the Far East loom the ghosts of the most terrifying famine and black starvation.

Bread – in the literal sense of the word – is not available to entire nations, which therefore go on languishing, haggard, exhausted, the prey of illnesses and poverty, while becoming dangerously agitated by the hidden stimuli of hopeless resentment and deep social subversion.

The danger is so great that it blocks the dawn of a new year. It is a far more serious danger because from some of its symptoms, which reveal uncertainty and exhaustion, it seems less likely that the magnanimous work of human solidarity will be carried out before it is again used as a remedy for the ills that it once cured.

The Year 1947

PIUS XII, THE HOLY FATHER'S APPEAL FOR CHARITY
6 APRIL 1947
Today, the August Pontiff granted an audience to executives and other officers of several delegations of UNRRA[1] in Europe. The visit was led by Major General C.R.S. Stein, vice-head of the Finance and Administration Division. They came from different nations and participated in a conference held in Rome. After the individual speakers presented their respectful tributes to the Holy Father, he gave them his noble speech in English.[2] I will translate some of his thoughts: "The book of life of your organization will now close, but the spirit that wrote its most beautiful pages does not have to dwindle. There are still nations in great distress, and they still must be helped. There are still people who are upset and are

---

[1] The acronym UNRRA stands for United Nations Relief and Rehabilitation Administration; founded by the United Nations and based in Washington, it was established in 1943 to give financial and other assistance to countries that were badly damaged by the Second World War. In a second phase, its efforts were extended to defeated countries, such as Italy, which became eligible to receive its benefits in 1946. The organization received funds for post-war reconstruction from the contributions of nations that were not devastated by the war. In Italy, following the agreements in Rome on 8 March 1945 and 19 January 1946, a mission was set up to carry out UNRRA's duties with the help of provincial commissions that were presided over by a prefect and by municipal committees whose responsibility it was to distribute the aid. The foundation was dissolved on 3 December 1947.

[2] The Pope's speech can be found in English in *Discorsi e Radiomessaggi di Sua Santità Pio XII*, vol. 9 (Rome: Tipografia Poliglotta Vaticana, 1948), 11–12.

suffering in the fight to survive. They would have been destined to succumb to their physical and spiritual agony in these long, endless postwar years if the granaries of their most successful brothers had not continued – yet again and without rest – to provide sustenance ... We are certain that the needy will not be abandoned."

The Iniquitous Diktat

The *Civiltà Cattolica* of 1 May 1947 writes:

> The Marquis Luigi Meli of Soragna, appointed by and in the name of the Italian government, signed on 10 February in Paris the so-called peace treaty imposed on Italy by the Allied powers[3] ... In fact, this instrument, which has euphemistically been referred to as a peace treaty, was not drawn up in such a way that it could soothe and somehow help heal the wounds of war, thus freeing from defeat the dignity of a responsible nation in international society. Instead, it was put together in such a way as to humiliate that nation, not only with its excessive clauses, but once again with the same actions adopted

---

[3] The treaty signed in Paris on 10 February 1947 by the victorious Allies of the Second World War (USA, USSR, United Kingdom, France, Poland, Yugoslavia, Czechoslovakia and Greece) and the defeated Axis (Germany, Italy, Romania, Hungary, Bulgaria, and Finland) is made up of 6 parts and 90 articles. With regard to Italy, the treaty ordered the surrender of territories that had previously belonged to France and Yugoslavia, as well as the loss of the Italian colonies in Africa and in Europe the Dodecanese Islands and Albania. Article 16 gave a period of immunity, from 10 June 1940 until the treaty came into force, to Italians who had collaborated with the Allies. Article 51 of the treaty prohibited Italy from possessing, building, and experimenting with atomic weapons, as well as self-propelled missles. Also prohibited, under Article 49, were the military installations on the islands of Pantelleria, Pianosa, and on the Pelagian Islands. These islands were to remain demilitarized. Other restrictions in Article 49 concerned the navy, in particular a ban to build, acquire, and replace battleships and to use or test aircraft carriers, motor torpedo boats, submarines, and any type of assault vehicle. A severe limitation was imposed on navy vessels, both regarding the total amount of tons carried and how many crew were actually employed, which was not to exceed 25,000 units. Finally, it required that Italy, by way of compensation, had to make available to the victorious nations a number of specific marine vehicles: 3 battleships, 4 cruisers, 7 destroyers, 6 torpedo boats, 8 submarines, and the training ship *Cristoforo Colombo*.

by the victors ... The peace treaty signed in Paris is not a bilateral contract requiring the approval of both parties in order to come into effect; rather, it is a unilateral order whose contents were not set by communal accord; in essence and in form, it is in fact a *diktat*, an expression of the despotic will of four of the largest victorious powers. As such, the treaty would be considered valid even without the Italian government signing it, since the application of the provisions set by the stronger parties – which cannot be opposed with efficacious resistance – does not need the acceptance of the weaker party ...

Time is the best teacher, and it will certainly not miss the opportunity to make clear to those involved that in the theatre of international life, a nation of 45 million souls cannot in any way be written off with the arbitrary orders of a treaty. These are the same ones who granted to Italy – as a prize for its cobelligerency and for the help given to them with the declaration of war against Germany – the privilege of being the first and biggest victim of their selfish compromises.[4]

A Talk with Ambassador Cerruti

When nations, like human beings, reach the age of adulthood, their growth stops. What then takes over is the care of preserving the nation. England is at this age of adulthood; that is, it no longer is concerned with expanding its territories but with maintaining their condition. England is aiming to liberate the Mediterranean. To get the all-clear, it has to resolve a dilemma: either it becomes Italy's friend, using its position and friendship in a show of defence, or it counteracts Italy's influence – *ne noceat*.

Unfortunately, England has chosen the second solution. Its responsibility in the structuring of the *diktat* is obvious. England's friendship with the Italians is not at stake – the English don't hate the Italians – it is simply that the interests of a powerful nation are at stake.

But England is fooling itself. Italy, with its population of 45 million and its geographical position, will not be counteracted. The British may be able to suppress it for a while, but then it will raise its head ... and it is sad that with regard to any future collaboration, they have created in Italy an adverse feeling towards themselves. We haven't forgotten Churchill's *boutade*: to treat Italy like a donkey, with a carrot in front and a stick behind to beat it.

[4] CC: Messineo, SJ, "Pace senza giustizia," in *La Civiltà Cattolica* 98, no. 1 (1947), 353–8.

There is another consideration that has to be made regarding the *diktat*. We have made big mistakes and it is only right that we should be punished for them. However, punishment should not go beyond the limits of human possibility. One must respect a nation's right to life, a nation that was itself a victim of its leaders' bad politics and has the right and need to live. Brennus threw his sword onto the scales while saying, "*vae victis!*" But we think that the blood had been cleaned from the sword. Although we punish, we need to know how to forgive.

There is yet another consideration to be made here. The Allies are against Communism. However, they didn't consider that by reducing a country almost to the brink of desperation, they were broadcasting the seeds of psychological revolt, making the ground most favourable for the rise of Communism. America promised us a large amount of aid, and we receive it with gratitude, but we cannot forget that she, too, placed her signature on the *diktat*.

DE GASPERI'S MESSAGE FOR THE RATIFICATION OF PEACE
16 SEPTEMBER 1947

At this hour [stated De Gasperi], night will fall on one of the saddest days in our history. At this point everything has been said about the fatal, brief period of time that has led us to a painful epilogue. But at this time I do not urge you to curse the past. Instead, let us all unite in a sense of pride, dignity, and faith in the assured rebirth of our country.

My brothers, you who have been unfairly forced out of your homeland, may you have in your hearts the certainty – and nurture that certainty every day – that Italy will not abandon you, because there are no borders that can break ties of blood and civilization, the ties that unite you to the populous and growing Italian family. If the Italy of today, which is exhausted and still shaking violently from post-war conflict, still helps you as it can, tomorrow – when it will be stronger, thanks to its incomparable strength of labour and genius, and to the growth of its spirit of peace and democratic fraternity – it will be able to offer you safer moral protection.

Night may also fall on new evidence of separation, but tomorrow's sun will return to shine on the ever-present and unfailing unity of hearts, the tradition of a shared history. My separated brothers, you are not the only ones suffering tonight. All of Italian territory suffers, and those suffering most are the ones who fought for freedom and justice, and it seems almost that the scars of their wounds are reopening, and the moans around us are from the spirits of those who gave their lives on the battlefield, on the sea, in the air, in the prisons, and in the fields of torture.

We all suffer, but we all keep in our hearts the same resolution, the same faith in a better world, the same certainty that Italy will play a brilliant role in world peace. We all hear that the responsibility of the moment is not to rebel against a destiny that is stronger than we are with actions that would attack and harm our homeland more than the injustice of others. However, we must suppress our deepest feelings, in our pride, transforming them into energy for disciplined and reconstructive work. Those who also feel this great responsibility are the members of our brave navy, the combatants of a fleet that deserved compensation instead of sanctions, because they served the cause of freedom with glory. But we, a people of workers and navigators, will show the world the noble meaning of respect for the flag of the new, free Italy – democratic and peaceful over all lands and seas.

May this voice of mine, sad but resolute, be of consolation also to those in the refugee camps in Africa and among the Italians left in the old colonies which, through the hard work and the adaptable intelligence of our colonists, were economically renewed and raised to a civilized way of life.

The treaty opens for us the road to a government made on behalf of all, in order to prepare native citizens for self-government. From this day forward, we will have to double our efforts so that this road, on which are marked the honours and trials of the past, remains fairly open.

In these last days, they have lowered some of the flags that belong to the occupation forces. The work of occupiers is always thankless, and it is not easy for them to be recognized for their efforts. Nevertheless, it would be wrong to forget that those efforts were accompanied by admirable acts of aid and social brotherhood, which after the fall and defeat, saved us from hunger and epidemic – the deadly associates of other wars – and allowed us to set forth again on the path to social and economic life.

Even though mistakes were inevitably made here and there, I sense that the Italian people will allow me to express our heartfelt thanks and to reaffirm our faith that the soldiers of the United Nations – who fought the war for freedom and independence in Italy and experienced firsthand the work that our regular and volunteer troops carried out for our liberation – will be the first to support, before the court of public opinion in their own countries as well as in the international forum of the United Nations, the correction of the clauses in the treaty. The faith that these clauses – recognized as unsuitable and excessive by the United States government itself (tonight there is the echo of a telegram from Minister Bevin[5] to my colleague in Foreign Affairs [Carlo Sforza]), – that these clauses, as I was saying, may be revised, corrected, and mitigated so that Italy, this Italy tremulous with its people's energy, can soon dedicate its work and its centuries-old culture to the construction of a world without war and without dictatorship, governed by freedom and in accordance with justice.[6]

An admirable document, full of dignity, honesty, and pride. It is clear, balanced, complete, and it removes Italy from the dark pit of its own misfortunes and shines consoling rays of light on its future journey. Alcide De Gasperi has shown himself to be a leading statesman. His lucid and agile intelligence, his wealth of culture, the difficult experiences he endured, his integrity, and the interior light of his faith have created in his spirit that solid moral architecture that makes him an exemplary symbol and a wise commander.

God has obviously come to his aid and we hope that He will bless him once again.

[5] Ernest Bevin (1881–1951), a British politician, member of the Labour Party, and a staunch interventionist with relation to the Second World War, was minister of labour (1940–45) in the government led by Churchill and then was minister of foreign affairs (1945–51) in the cabinet presided over by Clement Attlee.

[6] CC: *Il Popolo*, 16 September 1947.

Conclusion

The sad events of these painful years are not recorded here for the purpose of controversy but by way of experience, an experience from which we must draw our future lessons. Let us look at certain events as a loss and as a period of confusion, and as we do so let us nurture thoughts not of recrimination but of peace, cooperation, reconstruction, and forgiveness.

The force of hate has passed over Europe like a destructive hurricane. But at this point there is nothing left for us to do but sweep away the debris and prepare the ground for a new sowing season – one that sows love, sympathy, and forgiveness, looking not so much at the past but above all towards the future and planting in the earth fertile sprouts for the rebirth of a nation. If they had listened to the Holy Father Pius XII, the world would not have fallen into the abyss in which it now finds itself. But there is still time to mend one's ways.

It is useful to remember a huge lesson taught to us by history: Until March 1867, in the first session of the Reichstag, the parliament of the new German confederation, the great founder of the Centre Party, Mallinckrodt,[1] proclaimed with a dreadful eloquence – which moved even his most staunch adversaries – the old motto of politics and true Christian wisdom: *Iustitia fundamentum regnorum*. To this he added, "I do not see this justice, gentlemen, at the rise of the new confederation.

---

[1] Hermann (von) Mallinckrodt (1821-74), a German politician, was elected to the Prussian government and took part in the founding of the "Catholic Faction"; he represented the conservative and confessional wing of the Centre Party, of which he was a founder and leader.

Prussia has started an unjust war. The triumph of its weapons has been able to turn public opinion in its favour, but the norms of justice and law are unchangeable, no less for diplomats and statesmen than for ordinary individuals." And just as courageous, five years later was the undefeated member of parliament Windhorst[2] who, when defending the Pope's words of truth and justice [in his speech of 23 December 1872] against the abuses of the German government which at the time was persecuting the Church, exclaimed: "I myself, if I didn't have the deepest veneration for the head of the Catholic Church, even if I were not a member of this Church, would be delighted if there was a place from which the whole truth was told to both the young and the old. Yes, the Pope lives; he lives and the Papacy will live on, and it will announce the truth to the world even when all that we now admire will be reduced to dust and even when we ourselves will be dust."[3]

---

[2] Ludwig Windhorst, a German politician, was the leader of the Catholic Centre Party in Prussia in 1875, which was in particular the antithesis of the heavily anti-Catholic politic put into action by Bismarck, 1872–75, with his so-called *Kulturkampf*. Nevertheless, in 1878 Bismarck joined Windhorst's party, and this brought about a positive change of direction toward the Catholic Church.

[3] *La Civiltà Cattolica*, 3, (1919). Costantini's quotation is incomplete in form and meaning, in that it is not verifiable in *La Civiltà Cattolica* of the year 1919.

Index

The date in parentheses refers to the year of the diary entry. CC refers to Celso Costantini and GC to Giovanni Costantini.

Fides agency, 17n4. *See also* Propaganda

Finland: Pius XII on war (1939), 27; Soviet aggression (1940, 1944), 38, 273, 361

First World War. *See* World War I

Fiume (now Rijeka, Croatia): CC's establishment of diocese, xxiv, 21; CC's memories of (1940), 63; fears for future of (1941), 78–9; occupation by d'Annunzio, xxi, 290; political corruption (1943), 227; Soviet occupation (1945), 387, 396, 400

Florence: demonstrations after removal of Mussolini (1943), 186; murder of Gentile (1944), 302

food. *See* economy

forgiveness: and enemies in war, 112; and the future, 439; and punishment, 436; and revenge, 330–2

Fornari, Gaetano, 280n27; bombing of Montecassino Abbey, 280–1

Foschini, Arnaldo, 16n2; as architect (1939, 1942, 1944), 16, 127, 278; on Hitler and Mussolini's self-deception (1943), 162

Fosse Ardeatine: massacre (1944), 295–6, 349; remembrance service (1945), 378

Foundation for the Assistance of Churches Damaged by the War: GC's role, 17n6

Four-Power Pact, 9n10; failure of (1938), 9–11

France (1939): alliance with England, 25; CC's visit in 1937, xxvi; Four-Power Pact (1938), 9–11; shared Catholic roots with Italy, 25; and

Treaty of Versailles, 24, 25. *See also* Allies; de Gaulle, Charles

France (1940): armistice, 53–4; Caviglia on war against, 55n41; declaration of war by Italy, 47–8; German occupation, 44, 51–2; hope for a separate peace, 51–2; Pétain's government, 52–3; Reynaud's resignation, 51; support for Pius XII, 31–2; war ministry, 51

France (1941): Atlantic Charter, 101; massacre in Nantes, 108; Pius XII's charity, 117, 122; Polish refugees, 122–3

France (1943, 1944, 1947): D-day (1944), 327; German occupation (1943), 198; Paris peace treaties (1947), 434–6

Free Church Federal Council, 38n19; Chamberlain's speech to (1940), 38–9

freedom: Atlantic Charter freedoms, 100–1, 379, 389; Churchill on (1945), 389; FDR's four freedoms (1941), 100–1; and human dignity (1940, 1941, 1943), 49, 69, 161; Pius XII on five principles of order (1942), 150–1; Pius XII on five principles of respect (1941), 114–15; Pope as defender of (1940), 56–7; as precious gift (1944), 321

freedom of speech: censorship of (1940), 43, 48, 49; FDR's four freedoms (1941), 100–1; and imprisonment (1940, 1941, 1943), 34, 49, 79, 186; loss by public (1941), 71, 76, 79, 82; need to listen to opposition (1943), 339. *See also* purification

(1941), 68; Moscow Conference (1943), 228–9, 239; natural law and leadership errors (1942), 132; as preferable to Germany (1939, 1941), 103, 105

Great Britain (1944, 1945, 1947): British response to bombing of Montecassino Abbey (1944), 298–9; Hore-Belisha's address on Poland (1944), 282; Paris peace treaties (1947), 434–6; recognition of Polish government (1945), 360; relations with Italy (1945), 362, 380–1

Greece: Atlantic Charter (1941), 101; charity for Greek POWs (1941), 118; civil war (1945), 366; food exports to (1941), 104, 105; Italian military operations (1940, 1941, 1943), 55, 58–9, 66, 88, 154; Italian POWs (1941), 84, 87; Moscow Conference (1943), 228–9, 239; Pius XII's war relief (1942), 129; posters with caricatures (1941), 83; surrender to Germany (1941), 82–4; war and decline of Italy (1941), 70

Gregory I, Pope, 68, 265

Gronchi, Giovanni, 373n32; Christian Democrat (1945), 371–5

Guariglia, Raffaele, 155n3; after removal of Mussolini (1943), 189–90; approval of Ciano (1943), 157n7

Guarnieri, Felice, 368n14; on devaluation of lira (1945), 368

Haver, Luigi, 83

Herriot, Edouard, 31n3; support for Pius XII (1940), 31–2

Hess, Rudolph, 94n25; on sexual relations (1941), 94

High Court of Justice for Sanctions against Fascism. See purification

Himmler, Heinrich, 144n26; in Rome (1942), 144. See also Gestapo

Hinsley, Arthur, 108n41; protest of massacre in Nantes (1941), 108

Hitler, Adolf (1938, 1939): as dangerous dictator (1939), 24; hope for conference (1939), 25–6; Mein Kampf, 327n78; Mussolini's aversion to (1938), 13–14. See also Germany; Nazism

Hitler, Adolf (1940): his birthday, 40–1; on invasion of Greece, 55, 58; on Nazi neopaganism, 36; Pugliese on, 37; on racial myth of bloodline, 35; on religion, 35–6; as religious persecutor, 39; Thyssen on, 38

Hitler, Adolf (1941): his birthday, 81; on Bolshevik threat, 103–4; on historical dominance of British, 70; on Jews, 68; meeting with Mussolini, 101–2; on religion, 68, 70, 95–7; speech at Sportpalast, 70–1; Von Galen's speech against, 90–3

Hitler, Adolf (1942, 1943, 1944): influence of Nietzsche on (1944), 263; meeting with Mussolini (1943), 177; military strategy (1943), 222; (1944), 310–11; Mussolini's response to his message (1942), 137; order to seize Pius XII (1943), 245; on religion (1942), 107; revenge against Ciano (1944), 255; Soviet front (1943), 222; Verona trial and execution of Fascists (1944), 255–6

speech (1943), 168; and racial laws (1940), 35

Kaas, Ludovico, 322n73; with CC at St Peter's, 322–3
Kassala, Sudan: British forces (1941), 68
Katyn, Poland: massacre (1943), 162
Keller, Adolfo, 41
Kellogg Pact, 10n15; as failure (1938), 10–11
Kesselring, Albert, 232n69; Allied military operations (1943), 232; on German views of Fascists (1944), 252; Hitler's order to seize Pius XII (1943), 245; Mussolini's call to (1944), 320
Kietel, Wilhelm, 53n35; Franco-German armistice (1940), 53
King Umberto II. See Umberto II, Prince of Piedmont, King of Italy
King Victor Emmanuel. See Victor Emmanuel III, King of Italy
Knights of Columbus, 419n99; visit by Jewish refugees with Pius XII (1945), 419
Kolenk, Lipej, 404n77; partisan criminal in Murlis (1945), 404

Labour Democratic Party: La Democrazia del Lavoro as periodical (1944), 288–90; and National Liberation Committee (1944), 288–90
labour force: deportation for forced labour (1942), 137–8; (1943), 204, 205, 211, 217; (1944), 307, 308, 311, 314, 347; Pius XII's speech on capital and labour (1946), 422–3;

Pius XII's visit with workers, 168; SS deportation role (1942), 137–8. See also economy
La Civiltà Cattolica: articles, 9, 55, 118, 120, 121, 122, 123, 435, 440; editors and collaborators, 9n7, 364n8; on Pius XII's charity, 117–23
La Democrazia del Lavoro: periodical of Labour Democratic Party (1944), 289
La Fontaine, Pietro, xxiv, xxvi, 17n6
Lancellotti, Arturo, 351n116; hunger (1944), 351
La Punta: periodical of democratic youth group (1944), 289
La Ricostruzione, 338n91; article on Moroccan soldiers (1944), 337–8
Lartisien, Father (Munich), 120
La Spezia: GC as bishop (1939, 1942, 1943), 17, 18n6, 126, 197, 199; GC's letter on his life in (1943), 201–2; German occupation (1943, 1944), 199, 310
Lateran Pacts, 365n9; benefits to Church (1939), 29; Buffarini Guidi's speech on (1941), 80–1; extraterritoriality of Holy See, 80–1, 220–1; honouring of Concordat (1941), 80–1; Mussolini's role, 205, 364–5, 365n9; Mussolini's view (1945), 377; Pius XI's role, 13n20, 365, 365n9
Latvia: religious service for deportees (1941), 89n21
Laurenzi, Laurenzio, 237n77; trade of art for food (1943), 237
Laval, Pierre, 155
L'Avanti: periodical of Socialist Party (1944), 289

restoration of Germany's colonies
(1939), 26; as revenge (1940), 39;
Wilson plan (1939), 23–4
Treia: Pius XII's charity for POWs
(1941), 118
Treviso: bombing, 309
Tribune, 246n82; censorship (1944),
296; on execution of members of
Grand Council (1943), 246–7; failure to publish after arrival of Allies
(1944), 327
Trieste: occupation by Yugoslavia
(1945), 385
Tripartite Pact, 111n44
Tripoli, Libya: British invasion
(1943), 154–5; Facchinetti in
(1942), 148
Triveneto: letter from bishops (1944),
303–4
Truman, Harry S., 379n43; atomic
bomb (1945), 408; Christmas message (1945), 421; Potsdam Conference (1945), 399–400; as
Roosevelt's successor, 379–80
Tucci, Giuseppe, 106n37; missionary
conference planning (1941), 106;
purification (1945), 369–70; on
young war dead (1941), 106
Tullio, Francesco, 393n62; purification (1945), 393–4
Tullio, Giovanni Battista, 46n28;
bombings of San Vito (1945), 388;
despair over war (1940), 45–6;
publication of CC's diary, xvii–
xviii; on war and Fascism, 108
Tuminelli, Calogero, 151
Tunisia: fall of Tunis (1943), 162,
163, 165; French attacks (1942),
139

Tupini, Umberto, 374n38; Christian
Democrat (1945), 371–5
Turin: bombing (1942), 146

Udine: noble families (1941), 107
Ultime Foglie (Costantini), 11, 17n4,
334n86
Umberto II, Prince of Piedmont, King
of Italy, 330n82; his Queen Maria
José, 161n11; title Prince of Piedmont, 192n39; CC's visit with
(1944), 352–4; his character and
faith (1944), 354; concern for his
sisters (1944), 352–4; on decorum
of sacred art and worship (1943),
192–3; king in exile (1946), 429; as
lieutenant in government (1944),
330, 352–4, 420; political trends
(1944, 1946), 289, 429–30; public
demonstration against (1945), 378
Umbria: fear of crime (1945), 410
Union of Soviet Socialist Republics.
See Soviet Union
United Nations: De Gasperi's faith in
(1947), 437–8; foundation at San
Francisco Conference, 382n48,
396
United Nations Relief and Rehabilitation Administration, 433n1; Pius
XII's speech on charity (1947),
433–4
United States: Cairo Conference
(1943), 235; Episcopate's support
for war (1942), 126; immigration
prohibition (1941), 70–1; (1942),
128; mediation with Japan (1939),
21; Moscow Conference (1943),
228–9, 239; Mussolini's declaration of war (1941), 111–12;

Yolanda Margaret of Savoy, 353n121;
Umberto's concern for (1944),
353–4
Youth Movement for Italian Reconstruction: manifesto (1943),
233
Yugoslavia: Christian Democrat Party
policy on border (1945), 375;
Hitler's military strategy (1944),
351; Holy See's recognition of governments during war (1943), 155;
invasion by Italian and German
forces (1941), 78, 79, 80, 85, 112;
Maček's internment (1941), 112;
Moscow Conference (1943), 228–9,
239; occupation of northern Italy
(1945), 385, 389; Paris peace

treaties (1947), 434n3; Pope XII's
reception of Duke of Spoleto
(1943), 155; resistance (1942),
149; San Francisco Conference
(1945), 382; Tito as dictator
(1945), 389–90, 395

Zaniboni, Tito, 266n14; president of
reconstruction conference (1944),
266; purification (1944, 1945),
283, 312–13, 370
Zara, Count, 268
Zoppola. See Castions di Zoppola;
Murlis di Zoppola
Zuani, Lieutenant (with Luciano
Costantini): death (1941), 84,
133–4